ANDEAN ENTREPRENEURS

D0707056

*Joe R. and Teresa Lozano Long Series
in Latin American and Latino Art and Culture*

Andean Entrepreneurs

*Otavalo Merchants and Musicians
in the Global Arena*

BY LYNN A. MEISCH

UNIVERSITY OF TEXAS PRESS, AUSTIN

A portion of this material is reprinted from *Annals of Tourism Research*, vol. 22, no. 2, Lynn Meisch, "Gringas and Otavaleños: Changing Tourist Relations," pp. 441–462, Copyright 1995, with permission from Elsevier Science.

Material in Chapters 3, 4, and 7 is reprinted from *Research in Economic Anthropology*, vol. 19, Lynn Meisch, "The Reconquest of Otavalo, Ecuador: Indigenous Economic Gains and New Power Relations," Copyright 1998, pp. 11–30, with permission from Elsevier Science.

Printed in the United States of America

First edition, 2002

Requests for permission to reproduce material from this work should be sent to Permissions, University of Texas Press, P.O. Box 7819, Austin, TX 78713-7819.

⊛ The paper used in this book meets the minimum requirements of ANSI/NISO Z39.48-1992 (R1997) (Permanence of Paper).

LIBRARY OF CONGRESS CATALOGING-IN-PUBLICATION DATA
Meisch, Lynn, 1945–
    Andean entrepreneurs : Otavalo merchants and musicians in the global arena / by Lynn Meisch.
        p.   cm. — (Joe R. and Teresa Lozano Long series in Latin American and Latino art and culture)
    Includes bibliographical references and index.
        ISBN 0-292-75258-x (hard : alk. paper) — ISBN 0-292-75259-8 (pbk. : alk. paper)
        1. Otavalo Indians—Industries.   2. Otavalo business enterprises—Ecuador—Otavalo.   3. Otavalo Indians—Economic conditions.   4. International business enterprises—Ecuador—Otavalo.   5. Otavalo (Ecuador)—Economic conditions.   6. Otavalo (Ecuador)—Social conditions.   I. Title.   II. Series.
    F3722.1.O8 M43   2002
    382'.089'98323086612—dc21

                                                            2001008549

This book is dedicated to my parents,
Elaine and Francis Meisch,
and
to all my Ecuadorian compadres,
godchildren, and friends.

Contents

Illustrations and Tables

TABLES

Acknowledgments

Long-term fieldwork is impossible without extensive support. My early research in southern Ecuador and in Otavalo in 1977–1979 was funded by a Fulbright Fellowship and a grant from the Institute for Intercultural Studies. Earthwatch helped support my returns in the summers of 1988–1989. In the summer of 1990, Andrew W. Mellon Foundation and Josephine Knott Knowles Fellowships through the Center for Latin American Studies at Stanford University allowed me to pursue predissertation research. My fieldwork between September 1992 and February 1995 was funded by the Institute for International Studies at Stanford, the Wenner-Gren Foundation for Anthropological Research (Predoctoral Grant No. 5483), and the National Science Foundation (Doctoral Dissertation Grant No. NSF DBS-9216489). Follow-up visits in the summers of 1996 through 1998 were supported by a Group Projects Fulbright, a grant from the Stanford Center on Conflict and Negotiation, and a Saint Mary's College of California Alumni Faculty Fellowship.

This book is an extension and revision of my Stanford anthropology Ph.D. dissertation (1997). My time at Stanford was exceptionally stimulating and challenging, a gift for which I am most grateful. I would like to thank people in many departments, especially Anthropology, among them members of my dissertation committee: my advisor Jane F. Collier, George Collier, and Ben S. Orlove of the University of California, Davis. Suzana Sawyer and Don Moore made invaluable suggestions on early drafts, Frank Salomon offered advice on several chapters and served as a reader for the University of Texas Press, and Cheryl Musch did a voluntary copyediting job that spared me many mistakes and inconsistencies.

Judith Saldamando, Karen O. Bruhns, Lauren Kunkel, Mariana Chuquín, Marti Spiegelman, Alison Brysk, Susan Anderson, Elizabeth Young, and my family, especially my parents, Elaine and Francis Meisch, helped in many capacities in the United States, not the least of which was general encouragement. Gerda Brettel, Margaret Karalis, Zak

Braiterman, and Paul Boland graciously took care of my cats. I am indebted to my housemates Susan Paskowski and Sara Kiehn, who cared for my cats and supervised subletters; and to my car-sitters Peter Fofana, Ron Williams, and Bob Gardner. Bob offered help and support on many levels through the final preparation of the manuscript; students in my Saint Mary's College of California spring 2001 Visual Anthropology and Sociology course participated in the selection of photographs; and students in my Theory course commented on parts of the manuscript.

A number of people provided me with UFO (Unidentified Flying Otavalos) sightings, informing me of the many places around the world where they encountered itinerant Otavalo merchants and musicians: Elizabeth Kaibel, Walt Bachman, Charlie Eitzen, Richard Wigen, Fritz Lichty, Tom Abercrombie, Kathy Seibold, Aleksander Posern-Zielinski, Mary Parish, Mark Freeman, Nicholas Millhouse, Ann P. Rowe, Lois Meisch, Laura Miller, Anna Gast, David and Kathy Childs, Adi Willnauer, Marie Timberlake, Peter Low, Melanie Ebertz, Blenda Femenias, Elayne Zorn, Gail Felzein, Lisa Keller, Carol Wood, Margaret Loftin Williams, and Bill Durham, among others, including some of those mentioned previously and below.

In Ecuador I would like to thank Claudio Malo Gonzáles of the Centro Interamericano de Artesanías y Artes Populares (CIDAP) in Cuenca; Edwin Narváez R., director general, Hernán Jaramillo, and Carlos Coba Andrade of the Instituto Otavaleño de Antropología (IOA); and Helena Saona, Jenny de Castillo, Gonzalo Cartagenova, and Suzana Cabeza de Vaca of the Fulbright Commission in Quito for facilitating my work. Many others were generous with their friendship, including Ernesto Salazar and Myriam de Salazar; Lynn Hirschkind; Jill and John Ortman of La Bodega, Central Artesanal, and CDX Gallery in Quito; and Nicholas Millhouse, owner of the Hacienda Cusín.

In Otavalo town I would like to acknowledge Frank Kiefer and Margaret Goodhart, owners of the Hotel Ali Shungu, for finding me a place to live and for countless kindnesses, courtesies, and cognacs. *Agradacimientos* go to Consuelo Rodríguez; Marco Proaño; Julio Chicaiza; Eva Rodríguez; Miguel Sánchez; Eva Mariana Sánchez; Germán Sánchez; Christina Alarcón; Olga, Rosa, Anita, and Isabel Otavalo; Lola, Teresa, Susi, and Anita Ramírez; Margarita Ramírez; Rosario Perugachi; José Ponce; José Yacelga; Mercedes Otavalo; Humberto and Gladys Cabascango; Luis Enrique Cabascango; José Lema; Washo Maldonado of SISA; Segundo Lema of Los Chaskis; Clemencia Paredes; the late Mercedes Buitrón Vaca; Zulay Saravino of Zulay, Diceny Viajes; Núria Rengiro de Vaca of Inti Express; Rodrigo Mora of Zulaytur; Francisco Champutiz Ramírez of Panatlantic; Fanny Arandi of Runa Marka; Pablo Baquero of Transchryver; Teresa Román of Román Cargo; Sandra Pavón of SADECOM; Pablo Flores of MS Exportación; Edwin Brito Carvajal of Mundo Export; Marco Lema of Nativa T-Shirt; Haydée Garzón of the Shanandoa Pie Shop; Hector Lema of Inca Marka; Eduardo Gonzáles of Antara; Nicolás Chiluiza Rhea of Almacén Musical Fantasia; Janet Dexter, director of the Escuela Raúl Pavón; and many others.

A heartfelt *diusilpagui* to people from San Luis de Agualongo, Pinsaquí, Peguche, Guanansi, and Ilumán, including Rafael de la Torre; Rosa de la Torre; Leonidas de la Torre; Maruja Maldonado; Carmen de la Torre; Remigio de la Torre; Pedro Bautista; Estela, Lourdes, María, and Laura Bautista; the late Fabián Bautista; Remigio de la Torre; Lucita Fichamba; José María Cotacachi; Rodrigo Pichamba; Luz Córdova; Humberto Fichamba; Olimpia Maldonado; Luis Enrique Farinango; César, Orlando, and Oscar Farinango; Vilma Maldonado; Luz Conejo; Alonso Fichamba; Cecilia Lema; Patricio Fichamba; Antonio Quinotoa; Rosa Maldonado; Narcizo Conejo; Zoila Arrayán; Daniel de la Torre; Juana Arrayán; Jairo, Julián, and Blanca Yolanda Castañeda; Luis Alberto Arrayán; Humberto and Jaime Arrayán; Michi Picuasi; Rosa Elena Cacuango Lema; Segundo Santillán; Humberto Santillán; Luz de la Torre; Carlos Conterón; Rosa Elena de la Torre; Rosa, Laura, Breenan, Marta, and Rocio Conterón; Humberto Terán; Luis Humberto Cabascango; Lucita Cotacachi; Antonio Santa Cruz; and Jaime Cotacachi.

People from Agato, Quinchuquí, Gualsaquí, La Joya, Cotama, San Roque, Imbabuela Bajo, and Ciudadela Imbaya also deserve my gratitude, including Miguel Andrango, Josefina Potosí Chiza, Luz María Andrango, Rafael Maldonado, Victor Túquerres, Cornelio Cabascango, Olga Cabascango, Carlos Iguago, Juana Anguaya, Graciela Iguago, Luis Alberto Yamberla, Rosa Elena Morales, Luzmila and Hilaria Cachimuel, Luz Farinango, Alfonso de la Torre, Mercedes Saravino, Segundo Muenala Maldonado, María Males Lema, and Humberto Muenala Maldonado.

Various transnational Otavalos generously gave me their time, including Sayri Cotacachi of Punyaro, Otavalo, and Barcelona, Spain; Bolivio Fichamba of Peguche and Barcelona; Germánico Maldonado of Agato and Bogotá, Colombia; María Olimpia Arrayán of Ilumán and Bogotá; María Lucila Arrayán of Ilumán, Ibarra, and Washington, D.C.; Lola Potosí of Ibarra and San Francisco, California; Amado Ruiz of Quito and Seattle, Washington; and Juana, Rosa, and Daniel Andrango of Otavalo, Oakland, California, and Portland, Oregon.

My work in Otavalo was facilitated by friends who offered advice and good company, including many of the above as well as Sibby and Norman E. Whitten, Jr., Linda and Jim Belote, Frank Salomon, Stephen Athens, Regina Harrison, Lauren Kunkel, Jerome Windmeyer, and members of the Demented Researchers' Potluck, including Laura M. Miller, David Kyle, Christina Siracusa, Mary Katherine Crabb, Sally Hamilton, Liz and Mark Rogers, and Rudi and Cheska Colloredo-Mansfeld. Many of them kept me supplied with my addiction, good chocolate, as did Kevin Sheehy and Bob Gardner. Jonathan Loftin answered questions about Quichua; and Lynn Hirschkind read the manuscript for the University of Texas Press, where editors Theresa May, Leslie Tingle, and Kathy Burford Lewis were extremely gracious and helpful. I appreciate the advice and suggestions I received from numerous people even if I did not always follow them.

I would like to thank the late Lawrence K. Carpenter, who lured me to Otavalo in 1978 for concerted research, provided me with invaluable background information, helped me appreciate the beauty of *runa shimi*, and introduced me to many people who became my compadres. Finally, thanks are due to Saint Mary's College of California for a course release in spring 1999 that allowed me to work on revisions.

To all of the above, to anyone I may have forgotten, and to those who asked to remain anonymous, my heartfelt thanks. I hope the results are a tribute to the information, time, laughter, energy, and financial support you have contributed to this project.

CHAPTER I

Introduction

GLOBALIZATION AND OTAVALO LIFE

On October 8, 1992, a family of indígenas from Ilumán, Ecuador, came into the town of Otavalo in tears, upset by the crash of an El Al Boeing 747 cargo jet the previous day near Schipol airport in Amsterdam, Holland. Radio and television broadcasts brought the news to Ilumán, and it spread like a flash fire through the town and neighboring communities. The crash also made the front page of newspapers published in Quito and Guayaquil which were sold in Otavalo on October 8. The death toll among the crew and residents of the Amsterdam neighborhood, most of them immigrants, totaled fifty-nine.

The reason Otavalo indígenas (the self-referential term for indigenous people) were affected so deeply by an event that took place halfway around the world is at the heart of this book, which examines how the Otavalos, an ethnic group located in a high, verdant Andean valley, cope with globalization, including extensive tourism to Otavalo and transnational migration by Otavalos to countries around the world.

By 1992, Amsterdam had become *un pequeño Otavalo* (a little Otavalo) with at least 700 Otavalos living there, selling textiles and playing Andean music. The family mentioned above had a son in Amsterdam and had reason to be worried. Otavalos were among the occupants of an apartment building that was destroyed in the plane crash and resulting fire; we later learned that they had escaped without injury. Thousands of additional Otavalos are permanent or temporary residents of every continent except Antarctica.

The Otavalos (their preferred name, although some use Otavaleños) have interested researchers because of their ability to participate in the market economy and selectively adopt features from outsiders that they deem useful, especially technology, while retaining a unique dress and other practices that are distinctly Otavalo. In Frank Salomon's words, "Otavalo contradicts the steamroller image of modernization, the as-

Lard vendors and their customers at the Otavalo Saturday market, June 1978.

sumption that traditional societies are critically vulnerable to the slightest touch of outside influence and wholly passive under its impact . . ." (1981 [1973]: 421). Recent decades have seen the arrival not of steamrollers but of commercial jets to international airports in Quito and Guayaquil, bringing more than 145,000 visitors annually to Otavalo and flying thousands of Otavalos abroad. In addition, telephones, FAXes, the Internet, radios, and televisions facilitate communication between Otavalo and distant locales, further connecting Otavalos to the world beyond the valley. Some Otavalos have their own web sites (for example, www.otavalo.com); and there is a general Otavalo web site, Otavalos Online (www.otavalosonline.com), which bills itself as "the virtual community of the Otavalos." Otavalo indígenas exemplify the paradoxes of indigenous people enmeshed in global economic systems and expanding transnational networks, and the community is engaged in debate about what this means for "our traditional indígena culture."

The title *Andean Entrepreneurs* attempts to tie together the many strands of my argument. An entrepreneur is a person engaged in a commercial undertaking, especially one that involves risk. Unlike many indigenous people, for Otavalos entrepreneurialism is part of their "traditional indígena culture." Nearly two decades ago Leo Chavez defined a deeply embedded Otavalo "entrepreneurial ethic" among commercial

weavers (1985: 159) that included an eagerness for economic independence and an emphasis on rationality, frugality, honesty, self-reliance,
and innovation in business endeavors (ibid.: 166–167). Indeed, it is difficult to find a publication on Otavalo that does not mention the Otavalos'
commercial savvy.

Since Chavez wrote, the entrepreneurial ethic or spirit (among other
values, some complementary, some competing) has helped Otavalos of
both sexes cope with globalization as knitters, sewers, weavers, merchants, musicians, and small business owners (hotels, bus lines, restaurants, etc.) launch commercial ventures in Otavalo and around the world.

The Otavalo experience must be seen against a background of pre-
Inca traveling merchants, forced labor in Spanish colonial obrajes (Sp.
textile sweatshops), and later wasipungu (Q.), debt serfdom involving extensive work for an hacienda (Sp. large farm or ranch) in exchange for the
right to farm a small plot. The mass production of textiles in the colonial era involved brutal exploitation, debt servitude, and land loss but
provided the Otavalos with the technology and experience that under-
lie their current prosperity. Foreign visitors to Otavalo and people interested in textiles often ask me if the Otavalos are becoming "corrupted"
by making and marketing nontraditional textiles, yet these two major
traditions—the production of textiles for outsiders and travel outside the
valley as merchants—are of considerable antiquity.

In Chapter 2 I summarize local developments within pre-Hispanic,
colonial, national, and international histories, emphasizing the Otavalos' agency within the constraints imposed by larger forces. I develop
several interrelated themes that characterize the Otavalo ethnic group,
including their long involvement in textile production and marketing.

Given the historical importance of cloth in the Andes, the extent to
which material culture has been immaterial to recent anthropological
concerns is surprising. This neglect is a mote in our eye distorting our
view of the Andes, which is one of the most textile-oriented areas of the
world. Researching Andean societies and ignoring cloth is like researching North America and ignoring the automobile. The textile economy
not only forms the basis for the current prosperity of the Otavalo region
but is an important identifying characteristic of the Otavalos as a group;
they see themselves and are seen by others as weavers and merchants
(and more recently as musicians).

Throughout the Andes textiles have conveyed political and cultural
messages for centuries. In pre-Hispanic societies cloth and costume
represented ethnic identity, wealth, social status, age, and gender. In

the Inca empire weavings of the highest quality were burned, buried, or thrown in rivers as offerings, exchanged at important junctures in the life cycle, bestowed by the Incas as an honor, and supplied to the state as a source of revenue (Murra 1989 [1962]; J. Rowe 1963 [1946]). Recent works have focused on the historical and contemporary importance of cloth and costume in Latin America, including the Andes (Femenias 1987; Meisch 1987, 1997; Penley 1988; A. Rowe 1977, 1986, 1998; Schevill 1986; Schevill, Berlo, and Dwyer 1996 [1991]). In Chapters 2 and 3 I document the evolution of the twentieth-century farming and textile economies, including the beginning of international tourism in Otavalo, travel by Otavalos outside the valley, and the rise in textile exports.

Another theme is the formation of the Otavalos as an ethnic and cultural group: how the indígenas of the Otavalo region came to see themselves and to be seen by others as Otavalos, as well as such legal strictures as the *mita* (Q., Sp. obligatory labor service to the state), *concertaje* (whereby indígenas became indebted to the owner of an hacienda and then worked on the hacienda to pay off the debt), and wasipungu, which affected Otavalo identity:

> The invocation of a specific ethnic identity is usually triggered by political, economic, or cultural factors in relation to other social groups. Because ethnic identity is flexible and changes through time according to the cultural material available to a particular group of people, there is no such thing as "real" or "genuine" ethnic content. (Stephen 1993: 27–28)

Ethnicity is significant in discussions of the Otavalos in relation to other groups in Ecuador, including their indigenous neighbors in northern Pichincha and eastern Imbabura provinces (Cayambes), Asian Ecuadorians and Afro-Ecuadorians, whites-mestizos (*blanco-mestizos* in Spanish, the term used in Ecuador to refer to the historically dominant nonindigenous population), and foreigners.

I also use the term "cultural identity" (following Allen 1988; Hall 1990) because the Otavalos use the word "culture" (*cultura*) to refer to beliefs and practices which distinguish them from other people: "*nuestra cultura indígena*" (our indigenous culture). The Spanish term for "ethnic group" or "ethnic identity" (*grupo étnico, identidad étnica*) is rarely used by Otavalos. In my understanding of Otavalo identity, I agree that ethnic and cultural identities are not fixed essences but historically contingent and mutable: "Hence, there is always a politics of identity, a politics of position, which has no absolute guarantee in an unproblematic, transcendental 'law of origin'" (Hall 1990: 226).

Otavalos may choose to identify as indígena at some points in their lives and as white-mestizo at others. Furthermore, Otavalos, like most of us, have multiple roles and identities which are contextual. For example, some Otavalos identify as South Americans when traveling in Europe but as Ecuadorians vis-à-vis Peruvians or Colombians; as indigenous people or as Otavalos vis-à-vis white-mestizo Ecuadorians; as merchants, weavers, musicians, students, wives, husbands, mothers, daughters, fathers, and sons; or as being from Peguche as opposed to being from La Joya or Agato, depending on the situation.

What it means to be an Otavalo indígena, and how that identity has been defined by both Otavalos and outsiders, continues to change, whether we speak of ethnic or cultural identity. Identification as an Otavalo indígena or even as "Inca" can be an advantage when Otavalos are selling textiles or playing music abroad or a disadvantage when Otavalos are faced with racism and discrimination in Ecuador or when they are abroad selling on the street illegally and want to melt into the crowd if the police arrive.

Various anthropologists (Appadurai 1991; Gupta and Ferguson 1992; Varese 1991) have posed a central challenge to contemporary anthropology: the analysis of dominant and subordinate groups and their cultures in a global context. The recognition of international interconnectedness, especially in the economic arena, is not new. Immanuel Wallerstein (1974) and Eric Wolf (1982) insisted that social and economic analyses be grounded in a global perspective. Today even models of multiple cores and peripheries are outmoded because some nations, regions, and communities serve as cores for certain flows (Organization of Petroleum Exporting Countries [OPEC] nations for petroleum, Japan for investment capital, automobiles, and consumer electronics, to use two nation-states outside the West) but as peripheries for other flows (computer technology, films, music, and fashion trends). Ecuador is a core for oil production but a periphery for technology; and within Ecuador the Otavalos export textiles and music around the globe but also receive transnational flows of tourists, ideas, goods, and capital.

Identity constructions and ethnic relations in Ecuador now occur within social, political, cultural, and economic matrices that extend far beyond local communities. Twenty-first-century ethnographers must confront new facts, including "the changing social, territorial and cultural reproduction of group identity. . . . Groups are no longer tightly territorialized, spatially bounded, historically unselfconscious, or culturally homogenous" (Appadurai 1991: 191). This statement introduces another major theme of this book, transnational contacts (tourism and travel in and out of the Otavalo region) and transnational migration. The growth of the Otavalos' transnational linkages is explored in Chapters 3 through 7.

The word "transnational" is frequently used in a loose, undefined sense. John Stack, Jr., considers it to mean "[t]he transfer of tangible or intangible items across state boundaries when at least one actor is not an agent of government or an intergovernmental organization. The idea of transnationalism freed us from the dogmatic assertion that states are the exclusive actors in world politics" (1981: 6). FAXes, e-mail, telephone calls, capital, manufactured goods, compact disks (CDs), television and radio signals, books, magazines, movies, technology, diseases, travelers, tourists, refugees, legal and illegal immigrants cross international boundaries in all directions, a torrent that is increasingly (but not entirely) outside the purview of the nation-state.

Attempts to stem the tide of transnational contacts are the proverbial finger in the dike, as evidenced by the fruitless efforts of the United States to control illegal immigration or equally unsuccessful attempts by various nations to control the Internet or keep phone "phreaks" and computer hackers from tapping into international telephone lines and computer networks (Kantrowitz and Ramo 1993). The nation-state is not obsolete and remains a major organizing principle in the global system. National borders, although porous, still exist; and nations attempt to control flows across their frontiers with police and military might. Neither the community nor the nation-state suffices as a unit of analysis, however; the world is too interconnected. How can we define borders for Otavalos when they are now living around the world?

Certain kinds of transnational interactions are frequently seen as pernicious or damaging to cultural minorities, particularly tourism from wealthier nations or locales to poorer ones (Enloe 1989; Johnston 1990; Rossel 1988; Seiler-Baldinger 1988; Silver 1993). Theorists such as Emmanuel de Kadt have viewed the "cultural impact of mainstream development on Less Developed countries through the lens of dependency theory" (1992: 55). He cites H. M. Erisman's work on the West Indies as exemplifying this argument:

> Cultural dependency results in the "incorporation of exogenous norms and values into a nation's socialization process, which can then be said to be penetrated," so that eventually the main stimuli

for cultural development come from the outside and people lose their desire to maintain a cultural identity separate from that of the dominant nation. (ibid.: citing Erisman 1983: 342)

This stance considers tourism to be a vehicle of cultural imperialism. Sylvia Yanagisako and Carol Delaney (1995) have pointed out the gendered nature of such language as "penetrated," with its implication of the rape of a virgin society that is passive and helpless against the assault of outsiders. I will refrain from using "capitalist penetration" or "cultural penetration" for this reason. There is also the problem of dating such events. When did this cultural or capitalist penetration occur? For the Otavalo valley, was it the Inca conquest, the Spanish conquest, or some particular date in the colonial era? The historical record is more complex and indicates the Otavalos' impressive ability to adapt to, resist, absorb, and reconstruct outside stimuli. Tourism and travel to Otavalo and its multiple effects are the subject of Chapter 4, while tourism and travel by Otavalos abroad is the focus of Chapters 5 and 6.

Tourism raises an important issue: the tension between cultural homogenization and heterogenization resulting from today's global interactions (Appadurai 1990: 297). Among theorists concerned with the politics of global culture the major debate is between those who see increasing homogenization of the world's peoples and cultural, if not political-economic, domination by Euro-American countries (Mattelart 1993; Schiller 1976; Wallerstein 1974; Wolf 1982) and those who see globalization as enhancing difference (Appadurai 1990; Featherstone 1990, 1995; Hannerz 1990; Robertson 1990, 1995; Worsley 1990).

Some theorists note, paradoxically, that the present era also involves a revival of the "traditional, the native, the authentic" (Edward Said quoted in di Leonardo 1991: 26). My experience in Otavalo is that those fearing homogeneity may not recognize fully the tenacity of local practices and beliefs and the ability of people to infuse global images and products (Nintendo games, Mickey Mouse, Power Rangers, Coca-Cola, Rambo, the Road Runner) with their own local, particular meanings. Recent research on international marketing reveals that cost-effectiveness in global promotion depends on the positioning of products in specific cultural contexts. "National differences in taste, style and social relations (for example the traditions of gift-giving in Japan, British class attitudes, or American family values) seem to be an aspect of consumer choice which cannot be overlooked" (Kline 1995: 121–122). Local cultural values are salient in Otavalo, as elsewhere.

Richard Wilk frames the debate in a manner that is useful to my argument, asserting that the postmodern critique of the global commoditization of local cultures, which sees these cultures as inauthentic and incoherent, as "images distanced from experience," is misleading. Wilk sees "a world where very real and 'authentic' differences in experience and culture continue to exist, but are being expressed and communicated in a limited and narrow range of images, channels and contests." He asserts that "[t]he new global cultural system *promotes difference* instead of suppressing it, but difference of a particular kind. Its hegemony is not of content, but of form . . . Another way to say this is that while different cultures continue to be quite distinct and varied, they are becoming different in very uniform ways" (Wilk 1995: 118; emphasis in original). Wilk wrote this about beauty pageants, arguing that such contests, especially internationally televised pageants, place limits on the way difference is expressed. Tourism literature and Andean music are two such channels in the Otavalo valley for the expression and communication of cultural differences in standardized ways. They are examined in detail in Chapters 5 through 7.

This book also engages the debates about the nature of postmodern societies. The postmodern era has been characterized as having new mass marketing techniques, new mass media, and new postindustrial technologies and systems of fast transport and communication, resulting in a radically internationalized culture (Milner 1991: 108) which often involves bricolage and pastiche. David Harvey argues that postmodernism's concern for difference—and its recognition of the difficulties of communication and the complexity and nuances of interests, cultures, and places—is positive (1989: 113).

Other aspects of postmodernity, such as Jean-François Lyotard's insistence on the loss of belief in metanarratives as its defining feature (1984) and the incoherence and fragmentation of identity, would strike the Otavalos (and many others) as downright silly, a Euro-American rather than local concern. Otavalos believe in progress (a metanarrative), in the possibility of an improved standard of living, especially now that their own is rising. They do not claim that religion (a major metanarrative) has no meaning; nor do most Otavalos see their identities as incoherent despite the debates about changes in "our traditional indígena culture." The manner in which Otavalos frame the discussion indicates that they believe they *do* possess a unique identity, whatever its composition.

The outmigration of Otavalos during the past two decades has brought concerns about what constitutes Otavalo identity to the forefront of local discourse. Many Otavalos now call several countries home. They are transmigrants, meaning "immigrants who develop and maintain multiple relationships—familial, economic, social, organizational, religious, and political—that span borders. . . . An essential element of transnationalism is the multiplicity of involvements that transmigrants sustain in both home and host societies" (Basch, Glick Schiller, and Szanton Blanc 1994: 7).

Such transnational contacts, especially travel outside Ecuador, were not common before the twentieth century, but they certainly occurred (especially with Colombia). By the 1970s, Otavalos in Colombia and Spain were true transmigrants. Transnational contacts, particularly the tourist boom in the Otavalo region since the 1980s and the waves of travel to and from the United States and Europe, seem to have enhanced rather than suffocated or destroyed indigenous cultural identity or at least allowed many Otavalos to see their identity with new eyes, to critique it, and to play with it. This topic is treated in detail in Chapter 8.

I have included the word "traditional" in my discussions because of many Otavalos' concern with this topic. By "traditional" I do not mean static and unchanging lifeways but practices and beliefs which have considerable time depth and which Otavalos recognize and value even as they argue about, revise, and reinvent them. Although it is current anthropological practice to insist that traditions are not static, many Otavalos see them that way or wish that they would remain so. Not all indígenas are enthusiastic about change. The issues of custom and tradition are increasingly a part of Otavalo written and oral discourse precisely because the changes in the valley are bringing these matters to the fore as the given nature of these customs or doxa (Bourdieu 1977) is challenged.

Andean cosmologies cannot be seen as pristine and untouched by European ideas after nearly 500 years of contact. Nonetheless, certain structural principles have strong continuities, including "domestic or stable centricity versus wild or restless outside world, idealized complementarity, dyadic and triadic institutional patterns, symmetry and hierarchy" (Browman 1994: 247). The idealized complementarity includes gender complementarity (Harris 1978, 1986; Harrison 1989; Silverblatt 1987) and an emphasis on harmony, balance, and reciprocity among humans and between humans and the supernatural or the forces of nature. Reciprocity has long been identified as a core value of indigenous Andean societies. It is one of the "classic Andean topics" (Starn 1992: 167).

Arjun Appadurai calls such topics "gatekeeping concepts" because they frame anthropological theorizing about a region (1986: 357); yet these gatekeeping concepts appear in Otavalos' (not just anthropologists') oral and written debates. Most Otavalos (many of whom are illiterate) have not been reading the current literature, much of which is available only in English, which suggests that these concepts are important to anthropologists working in Imbabura province because they are important to the people whose societies we study. There are other issues important to Otavalos, including a spiritual relationship to the land, the use of the Quichua language, and traditional dress. My final chapter focuses on the local debates about the changes in the valley, about which Otavalos are ambivalent. This book ends with an analysis of the fiesta of San Juan (Inti Raymi) on June 24, the most important celebration of the year, which embodies the paradoxes of Otavalo life in the postmodern era.

My basic argument is that Otavalos are coping with globalization by relying on a combination of traditional values and practices and modern technology to preserve as well as market their ethnic identity, including others' (mis)perceptions of them as Incas or noble savages. The result has been paradoxical: unprecedented prosperity amid increasing disparities in wealth; political and economic power in the region that was unimaginable fifteen years ago; geographical dispersion that threatens social cohesion; and controversy about what constitutes Otavalo identity. Yet overall most Otavalos would admit that they are better off than they were thirty years ago and that they do have a group identity, whatever its features may be.

This is neither an apologia for globalization nor an obituary, but an examination of how one society has managed to resist or harness the forces that so often seem destructive to indigenous cultures. In an era when there are international organizations named Cultural Survival and Survival International dedicated to assisting native peoples, and when ethnocide has joined genocide in our lexicon, the Otavalo case is worth analysis. I have aimed for accuracy and fairness, but the Otavalo you will read about was filtered through my eyes.

The Setting

The town of San Luis de Otavalo (population approximately 26,000 in 2001) is located at an elevation of 9,203 feet in a narrow valley between two cordilleras of the Andes in Imbabura province. The town is well situated for commerce because it is on the paved Pan-American highway just 66 miles (110 km) north of Quito, a two-hour drive, and 90 miles (150 km) south of the Colombian border. This proximity to both Quito and the Colombian frontier is a major asset, and Otavalo has long been a crossroads and commercial center. The approximately 60,000 Otavalo indígenas live in seventy-five small communities throughout the valley, as well as in Otavalo, Cotacachi, Ibarra, Quito, and other Ecuadorian and South American cities and towns. The Otavalo diaspora is now world-wide, with permanent expatriate communities in Europe, the Caribbean, and the Americas and temporary or permanent transmigrants on six continents.

Anthropologists too seldom explain why they choose a location in which to conduct their research. Among other reasons for doing research in this region (including compelling theoretical controversies), I find the physical beauty of Otavalo magnetic—Imbabura is one of the most beautiful places I know. The town is nestled among the mountains just 25 miles north of the equator. The altitude moderates the equatorial heat, so that the climate is invariably described as "spring-like." The greatest temperature variations are diurnal rather than seasonal, and the length of the days and nights varies by only about fifteen minutes annually, allowing people without watches to determine the time accurately year round and giving a certain dependable rhythm to the days.

The Andes are at their narrowest in Ecuador, and the Otavalo valley is only about 15 miles wide. Two volcanoes, one in each cordillera, loom above the town and figure prominently in local folklore. To the east broods Taita (Father) Imbabura, the male mountain, an enormous squared-off hulk 14,952 feet high (4,557 m) whose upper reaches are composed of crumbling black andesite. After a storm has raged around the peak, Imbabura is sometimes topped with snow. The lower skirts of Imbabura are a patchwork of eucalyptus groves, scrub forest, and cultivated fields in shades of gold and green, with a number of indigenous communities below and among the fields. Otavalo indígenas occupy the land around the southwestern, western, and northwestern sides of Imbabura, while the Cayambes occupy the land on the southeastern, eastern, and northeastern sides. The predominantly white-mestizo city of Ibarra dominates the north, while Lago San Pablo (Saint Paul Lake), originally called Chicapán then Imbacocha, and the Mojanda mountain chain anchor the south.

Mama Cotacachi, the mother mountain, is also known as Warmi Rasu (Snow Lady in Quichua). Cotacachi is Taita Imbabura's consort and rises 16,195 feet above sea level (4,936 m), almost a mile and a half above the

Funeral of five-month-old Lesley Dayana de la Torre. Ilumán, June 2000.

valley floor. The slopes of Cotacachi and the rolling hills at her feet are also intensively farmed. Mama Cotacachi's peak is almost always snow-capped, and people say that this is proof that Taita Imbabura visited her during the night. The result of all this activity is a child, Urcu (Mountain) Mojanda, the highest peak in a chain of low mountains south of Otavalo, whose slopes conceal several lakes. Others say that the baby is Yanahurcu or Wawa Imbabura, a small peak north of Cotacachi, but everyone agrees there are offspring. The soil is volcanic and so fertile that fence posts sprout roots and leaves and become permanent hedges. Because northern Ecuador receives year-round rainfall, the Otavalo valley is always astonishingly lush and green.

Most tourists and travelers journey to Otavalo from Quito, and there are several breathtaking vistas along the Pan-American highway, especially the pass above Lago San Pablo with Taita Imbabura and piles of white and gray cumulus clouds reflected in the lake. Mama Cotacachi hunkers in the distance with her head in the clouds, and a low hill called Rey Loma dominates the near horizon, topped by a lechero tree and the ruins of a pre-Inca fort. Tidy adobe or concrete houses with red tile roofs are set among trees and fields; their occupants are mostly out of sight but sometimes visible from the road. The quality of light alone would have been enough to make Paul Cézanne abandon Provence.

The cracks in this idyllic picture appear only on closer examination. Lago San Pablo, for example, is polluted; its waters are unsafe for human consumption, resulting in deaths during recent cholera outbreaks. Many of the homes are missing adults, who have left the valley for distant parts to market textiles, play music, or work as wage laborers; and some homes are mourning the loss of infants to diarrhea or pneumonia.

I have thirteen living indígena godchildren and five white-mestizo godchildren in the Otavalo area and others in Quito, Salasaca, Chordeleg, and Saraguro. I have returned to Ecuador to see them almost every year since 1978. The observations and adventures of my Otavalo godchildren and *compadres* (Sp. ritual kin) surface frequently in this book. During my visits I listen to their concerns, observe the growth of tourism, the textile industry, and the Saturday market, and take notes. These families range across ethnic and class categories from wealthy merchants to poor agriculturists and from schoolteachers and weavers to market vendors and shoe shiners, offering me varying perspectives on life in the valley.

Compadrazgo (Sp. ritual kinship) is often described as utilitarian, extending the social network of the family, and this is true. The obligations between compadres and between godparents and godchildren are theoretically reciprocal, even if the godparent is a foreigner. When I am in Otavalo hardly a day goes by without godchildren or compadres arriving for a visit with gifts: a woven bag, an embroidered placemat, a belt or tapestry, produce such as tree tomatoes, eggs, corn, beans, fresh milk, Chilean grapes, or even a live hen or freshly slaughtered *cuy* (Q. guinea pig), cleaned, seasoned, and ready to pop in my oven. When I need help moving, gardening, or cutting the grass in my yard I can count on my compadres and godchildren, and each year when I leave for the United States they give me a rousing *despedida* (Sp. farewell party). My godchildren frequently ask if they can help me. Sometimes the answer is yes, and we wash clothes together, weed the garden, or cut the grass. My godchildren ask for help with invitations to the United States or come to look at my Spanish books on human health and reproduction, a subject which fascinates young people everywhere, and talk to me about their boyfriends, girlfriends, spouses, dreams, and desires.

Compadres often activate the advice component of the relationship. They pull me aside and say, "*Déme hablando, comadre,* your godson (or goddaughter) [fill in the blank]: (a) talks back, (b) is lazy, (c) drinks too much, (d) doesn't want to go to school, (e) wants to run off to Europe and play music, (f) wants to get his ear pierced. *Por Dios, comadre, hay que*

Juana Arrayán with *cuy* (Q. guinea
pig) for her comadre Lynn. Ilumán,
September 1984.

jalar la oreja" (the Spanish translates roughly as, Speak to your godchild
for me, comadre. . . . For God's sake, comadre, you've got to pull on her
or his ear). I find a private moment with the godchild in question and
pull on her or his ear, literally but gently, and then dispense advice.

Compadres and comadres visit to use my computer, cry on my shoulder after a family fight, invite me to meals and fiestas, ask for advice on
new products ("Do you think *gringos* would buy this?"), borrow money,
return the borrowed money, borrow more money, gossip, and just plain
visit. In return, I know that I can ask compadres for help when I have
questions about research matters because compadrazgo enormously increases my pestering quotient. Indeed, their patience is astonishing.

Calling these relationships utilitarian does not do them justice,
however. Anthropologists, whose specialty is the comparative study of
human cultures, seem reluctant to use the words "love," "affection,"
or even "hate" with respect to the people we work with, yet these are
powerful human emotions and we feel them. The attitude that emotion
has no place in anthropological fieldwork is a holdover from the positiv-
ist position that the scientific observer must be neutral, a stance so thoroughly critiqued that I need not repeat the criticisms. I did not undertake

compadrazgo relationships because I planned to do research in Otavalo. Instead, I ended up doing research in the valley because I wanted to be near these families for whom I feel a deep affection and love (combined with occasional irritation and a strong desire to pull really hard on someone's ear). The outpouring of grief by Otavalos after the 1990 death of Lawrence Carpenter (compadre to many families) was undeniably an expression of love, and my godchildren and compadres know that my love and concern for them goes far beyond research interests.

This book has roots in my earlier work in Otavalo. In the early 1980s Enrique Grosse-Lümern, late owner of Libri Mundi publications and bookstore in Quito, suggested that I do an update of John Collier, Jr., and Aníbal Buitrón's classic monograph *The Awakening Valley* (1949). This project (Meisch 1987) forced me to look at the textile economy in a systematic manner and led me down avenues of research I had never thought to venture. Meanwhile, the members of an Otavalo weavers' association asked me if I could return to teach textile techniques. They made a formal request to the United States Embassy in Quito, which

My comadre Marta Conterón and her son (my godson) Alex Hernán Díaz in the Otavalo market. July 2001.

hired me in 1985 as a textile consultant through the United States Agency for International Development (USAID). Teaching greatly enlarged my circle of Otavalo friends and increased my understanding of the complexities of textile production and marketing, even as I questioned the implications and politics of development projects.

The field research on which this book is based began in 1973–1974, when I was a 28-year-old hippie adventurer, and involved several prolonged stays in Otavalo over the past three decades, including eight and a half months in 1978–1979, ten months in 1985–1986, and almost yearly summer visits since the 1970s. My fieldwork specifically on globalization was conducted during thirty months between October 1992 and September 1995 and the subsequent summers, with a short visit in January 1999.

Now, however, the field comes to me. In the spring of 1995, I interviewed Otavalo musicians performing in front of Stanford University's bookstore, who were selling CDs by Wayanay (1993). In June 1995 and 1996 at the Haight Street Fair in San Francisco, I interviewed sisters in the Andrango family as they sold *artesanías* (Sp. crafts; for Otavalos meaning anything that involves handwork, including items made from factory-made cloth). In 1995 and 2000, I encountered itinerant Otavalo merchants and musicians in Taos and Santa Fe, New Mexico. In 1999, one of my Peguche godsons came to live with me in California for five months while he attended high school, and his father visited for two weeks. In November 2000, his parents visited me for eighteen days. That same fall I interviewed an Otavaleña who was selling artesanías at my local Walnut Creek farmers' market. Throughout the writing of this book I also spoke with Otavalo transmigrants in Chicago and San Francisco, who kept me up to date on news of the valley through their own Otavalo diasporic networks.

A Note on Terminology and Spelling

Foreign words or phrases except proper nouns are italicized and defined the first time they are used. They are also italicized and defined in later chapters when the reader may not remember their meaning. Sp. = Spanish, Q. = Quechua or Quichua (as the language is called in Ecuador), E. = English, C. = Caribe. Because Quichua, also called *runa shimi* (Q. the people's language), was not written when the Spanish arrived there is considerable controversy about its spelling. Spanish orthography has changed over the centuries but has become standardized, while attempts

1.1. Ecuador

to standardize Quichua spelling have foundered. Because of the complex linguistic history of these languages, the reader will note inconsistencies in the spelling of both Spanish and Quichua words. When quoting or citing other authors I use their spelling. Otherwise for Quichua I use a phonemic alphabet devised by linguist Lawrence Carpenter, except for some proper names where a generally accepted conventional spelling

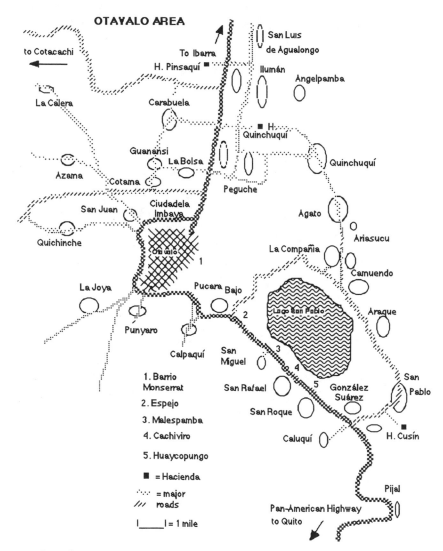

1.2. Otavalo Area

exists (for example, Incas rather than Inkas). This solution will not please everyone; indeed no Quichua orthography will.

The term "Otavalos" refers to the ethnic group as a whole; "Otavaleños" refers to male Otavalo indígenas, and "Otavaleñas" to female Otavalo indígenas. Nonindigenous residents of Otavalo can also claim to be "Otavalos," but they are much more likely to say they are "from Otavalo" to distinguish themselves from indígenas. Although I conducted my conversations and interviews in Spanish, often with Quichua thrown in, I have translated all direct quotes into English, occasionally enclosing significant Spanish or Quichua words or phrases in brackets.

$ = U.S. dollars; S/ = *sucres*, Ecuador's legal currency until 2001, when it was replaced by the dollar.

CHAPTER 2

How the Otavalos
Became Otavalos

This chapter emphasizes historical developments that I consider crucial to an understanding of contemporary Otavalo (for a more complete account, see Meisch 1997). For example, foreign visitors to Otavalo often question whether the Otavalos have been corrupted or "lost their culture" by making and marketing nontraditional textiles, yet the production of textiles for outsiders and travel outside the valley as merchants are ancient traditions. Even before the Incas arrived in northern Ecuador in the late fifteenth century, the indígenas of the Otavalo region were weavers and *mindalá*, traveling merchants (Salomon 1981 [1973]: 434, 1986: 102–106).

Otavalo was the name of the principal Caranqui *ayllu* (Q. descent group), whose territory was located on the south shore of Lago San Pablo (Espinoza Soriano 1999: 333–340). Although travel writers, tourists, and Ecuadorians including Otavalos frequently represent the group as "Incas," Otavalos are descendants of many ethnic groups, including aboriginal Cochasquís and Caranquis, populations transferred by the Incas (Q. *mitmakuna*), and migrants in colonial and recent times (Espinosa Soriano 1988: vol. 1, 62–63, 286–294). Don Alonso Maldonado (ca. 1549–1609), a colonial *cacique* (C. chief) and governor general of Otavalo, for example, was descended from the Ango leaders of the Caranquis and the Puento leaders of the Cayambes and related by marriage to a son of the Inca Atahualpa, but there is no evidence of Inca blood in his line (Caillavet 1982: 38–42). The Otavalos eventually formed a group, with residence, language, and dress as their main identifiers.

The Incas mandated that conquered peoples maintain their headdress and hairstyle (Cobo 1979 [1653]: 190), but Otavalos adopted other features of Inca dress (Ponce de León 1992 [1582]: 364). In the Otavalo region clothing was handspun from cotton and woven on the backstrap loom. These wrap skirts, mantles, tunics, and cloaks figured heavily in the textile tribute lists after the Spanish conquest. Today Otavaleña dress is one of the closest to Inca women's costume worn anywhere in the Andes. The other major lasting Inca influence in Imbabura was the Quichua language, which was introduced following the Inca conquest of the region (Salomon 1986: 189; Stark 1985a: 458) and spread by the Spanish as a lingua franca.

Colonial Otavalo and Inca Resurgence

The Incas occupied the north for fewer than fifty years before the Spanish arrived in the Andes in 1532. By 1533–1534, *encomiendas* (Sp. trusteeship over an indigenous population of a region) were parceled out to conquistadors in northern Ecuador. A large encomienda encompassing much of the Otavalo region fell into the hands of Rodrigo de Salazar. In 1551, quantities of traditional textiles including hundreds of men's and women's mantles, men's tunics, and women's body wraps were owed as tribute to Salazar every six months. Other textile tribute was European-derived: three tablecloths and three medium-sized awnings (Espinosa Soriano 1988, vol. 2, 130, vol. 3, 12–16; my translation). At this early date, Otavalos were producing not only traditional textiles but nontraditional textiles for outsiders, a pattern which still obtains. For 450 years it has been traditional for Otavalos to make nontraditional cloth.

Because Ecuador lacked the mineral wealth of Peru and Bolivia, and the existing mines played out in the early colonial era, the Spanish established textile sweatshops (Sp. *obrajes*) which ruthlessly exploited indigenous labor (Phelan 1967). The Spanish introduced sheep, European treadle looms, spinning wheels, and hand carders to increase production; these tools form the technological basis of the modern industry. Spaniards also introduced the concept of production weaving, the rapid fabrication of large quantities of cloth for commercial purposes.

The colonial era was brutal for indígenas. The labor quota or tax (Q. *mita*) was introduced in the 1570s, based on the Inca custom of a rotating labor obligation. The Incas, however, provided food from state storehouses for workers and also fed their families in their absence.

In the 1570s, many indígenas were forcibly resettled in nucleated communities (Sp. *reducciones*). The original pre-Hispanic center of the Otavalos was located in what is now the parish of San Rafael on the shores of Lago San Pablo. As part of the colonial resettlement policy the old center was destroyed under protest, and its inhabitants were relocated to the new town of San Pablo in 1578 or 1579 (Caillavet 1981: 120,

1982: 45). The colonial town of Otavalo was established on its current site, which was the territory of the Sarance ayllu.

Under the Ecuadorian mita, a *repartimiento* (Sp. population of an encomienda) sent up to one-fifth of its tributary population (able-bodied local males between the ages of eighteen and fifty) for two months to a year of forced labor in mines, ranches, agriculture, construction, households, or textile sweatshops (Alchon 1991: 77). The labor demanded was impossible for a worker to meet without the help of his family. Wages were insufficient to sustain a mita worker and his family, so the majority of laborers ended up in debt or with no net pay (Stern 1982: 76–89). The mita was in full operation by 1592, resulting in a pattern of forced labor in the current economic mainstays of northern Ecuador: agriculture and textile production.

The indigenous population of Ecuador dropped by half during the sixteenth century, mainly due to epidemics of European-introduced diseases (Alchon 1991: 57). In northern Ecuador the destruction and robbery of indigenous lands and products; excessive labor obligations, tribute, and other personal service; and the use of Otavalo-area indígenas as auxiliaries during incursions into southern Colombia, the Oriente, and Esmeraldas caused further loss of life (Larraín Barros 1980: 94; Newson 1995: 159), adding to the burden of those remaining.

Salazar opened an obraje in Otavalo in 1563, which was built and run by indigenous tributaries. By the seventeenth century, there were at least three illegal obrajes for every legal one in the Audiencia de Quito and a minimum of 28,800 indígenas working in textile sweatshops. Not only were many indígenas forced to work in obrajes to pay off debts, but the conditions were atrocious. Although a nine-hour day had been established by law, many indígenas worked from dawn to dusk chained to the loom. In John Leddy Phelan's phrase, the Audiencia became "the sweatshop of South America" (1967: 66–71).

Two legal textile obrajes in Ecuador, those of Otavalo and Peguche, were unique. They were owned by the Spanish Crown, which made the indígenas royal tributaries (Phelan 1967: 69–70). Salazar's obraje had reverted to the Crown after his death. The Peguche obraje was created in 1621, specializing in woolen cloth of varying quality. *Paño azul* (Sp. indigo-dyed wool fabric), often used for clothing, was considered the best. The Peguche obraje also produced plain-weave, coarse-weave, and undyed twill-weave wool cloth for grain sacks, blankets, and horse blankets as well as cotton cloth (Rueda Novoa 1988: 93).

Otavalo cloth was exported to Peru, Chile, Bolivia, Argentina, and

Colombia by the 1640s (ibid.: 94–95), and some was consumed in Ecuador (Tyrer 1976: 107). By this date, there were fourteen obrajes in the Otavalo valley whose income was used by indigenous communities to pay tribute, plus the two Crown obrajes (ibid.: 115). The remains of the Peguche obraje are still visible at the southern edge of town on the road to Peguche Falls.

The Otavalo obraje was located on the main square; Calle Sucre in town was once called Calle Obraje. In the early seventeenth century, indigenous textile workers from the environs of Otavalo, San Pablo, Atuntaqui, and Cotacachi were ordered to settle in Otavalo to increase the labor pool and allow the workers in the Otavalo obraje to return home at night (Newson 1995: 162, 417n42). This is significant in light of current white-mestizo insistence that Otavalo has always been a non-indigenous town and is now being "invaded" by indígenas.

The Peguche obraje relied on labor drawn from a radius of eight miles, which meant that indígenas had to walk for hours in addition to their long working days. The labor force included boys between the ages of twelve and seventeen, a practice permitted by the Crown in 1609 (Phelan 1967: 79). Throughout the seventeenth century, the Crown legislated ineffectively against abuses in the obrajes; but the laws were opposed by sheep ranchers and obraje owners, who realized that cheap labor was the key to their profits (ibid.: 77–80).

At its height in 1684, the Otavalo obraje employed 605 indigenous workers (Tyrer 1976: 119). In fact, for more than a hundred years the Otavalo obraje employed over 500 Indians, making it one of the larger factories in the colonial world. It produced an average of 20,000 varas (Sp. vara = 33 inches) of cloth a year between 1666 and 1672, and the labor force included at least 100 children (ibid.: 117–120).

In the last third of the seventeenth century, there was a resurgence of Inca nationalism in Imbabura in response to the difficult conditions of the colonial era. By that time the massacres and horrors of the Inca conquest had faded from memory and been replaced by nostalgia for a time when indígenas ruled the land. In 1666, don Alonso Inca, a great-grandson of the Inca Wayna Capac and a grandson of the conquistador Martín de Florencia, who accompanied Francisco Pizarro, was appointed governor (Sp. corregidor) of Ibarra. On the last day of 1666, on his way to Ibarra to take office, don Alonso passed through San Pablo, where he was greeted by indígenas who performed a dance pantomiming the Inca with his headdress and his consort. Don Alonso was met by the cacique of Otavalo, Sebastián de Maldonado, and led to a feast in the house of the governor of San Pablo; he was also accompanied by dancers and great pomp when he finally arrived in Ibarra (Espinosa Fernández de Córdoba 1989: 10).

Don Alonso caused considerable apprehension among the Spanish in Ibarra by giving indigenous caciques precedence over the Spanish in ceremonies, hanging a painting in his residence emphasizing his Inca rather than Spanish ancestry, wearing an Inca shoulder wrap (Q. *yacolla*) and tunic (Sp. *camiseta*) made of fine vicuña cloth, and "declaring himself the king of the Indians." Ultimately, don Alonso was denounced for conducting "ancient rites and ceremonies" during his entrance festivities, an accusation of idolatry (Espinosa Fernández de Córdoba 1989: 11–12; my translation). The Spanish were also alarmed because don Alonso's reception was more sumptuous than those for judges of the Audiencia and bishops (ibid.: 15–17). This Inca messianism probably came more from the leaders and masses than from don Alonso: they saw him as a symbol of the Inca past and projected onto him their hopes for a return to the old social order (Klumpp 1974: 128–129).

In June 1667, don Alonso was arrested and incarcerated in Quito then remanded to the court in Lima for sentencing; his ultimate fate is unknown (Espinosa Fernández de Córdoba 1989: 33). Although Ibarra was the site of the infamous massacre of Caranqui and Cayambe warriors at Yaguarcocha (Blood Lake) by the Incas during their conquest of the region, for local indígenas less than 175 years later a revival of Inca authority was decidedly preferable to Spanish rule.

The apotheosis of the Incas still prevails in the Otavalo valley and is evident in the rhetoric of indigenous organizations; the titles, songs, and album notes of contemporary music groups; the name of the political party Pachakutik; and the fiestas of San Juan/San Pedro in June, Carnival in February or March, and Yamor in September. These celebrations are often called by the names of the Inca festivals of the same month— Inti Raymi, Paucar Raymi, and Colla Raymi, respectively.

In the seventeenth century, more than half the Ecuadorian indigenous population relocated, some to seek employment on haciendas and in obrajes or to avoid the mita. Given the migration in the Inca and colonial eras, the assertion that the contemporary Otavalos are descendants of the original inhabitants of the valley or of the Incas is an "invented tradition" (Hobsbawm 1983). Some of the original inhabitants stayed in the region; but what is significant is the extent to which outsiders have been absorbed into the aboriginal Otavalo population and have participated in creating Otavalo ethnic and cultural identity.

Two Spaniards, Jorge Juan and Antonio de Ulloa, accompanied the

Charles-Marie de La Condamine French scientific expedition to South America between 1735 and 1744. They wrote that in the Audiencia of Quito "[t]he order to go to the obrajes causes more fear among the Indios than any other punishment which has been invented. The married Indias and the elderly mothers begin to mourn the death of their husbands or children the minute they are condemned to this punishment" (Juan and Ulloa 1982 [1826]: 278). It was no wonder that "[y]ou sometimes encounter on the roads Indios with their hair tied to the tail of a horse, on which is mounted a mestizo taking them to the obrajes . . ." Juan and Ulloa criticized the original encomenderos, corregidores, owners of obrajes, haciendas, and ranches, and "most scandalously" the clergy: "All of these, including the Curas, treat the defenseless Indians with greater inhumanity than they treat Negro slaves" (ibid.: 279; my translation).

November 1777 saw a major indigenous uprising in the Otavalo region over a population census ordered by Carlos III as part of the Bourbon reforms in the Spanish colonies. The revolt was a northern manifestation of indigenous unrest that erupted throughout the Andes and reached major proportions in highland Peru and Bolivia. The Ecuadorian census was essential to the reforms and represented a shift of the tax burden from communities to households and individuals.

Indigenous women led the rebellion in Cotacachi, starting in the church, where they prevented the priest from announcing the census. Indígenas misinterpreted the census as an increase in tribute which would result in the branding and enslavement of their sons (Stark 1985b: 3–12). Meanwhile, rebels throughout the region threatened to kill their own leaders (who represented Spanish interests more than local ones) and attacked clergy and church property (Moreno Yánez 1985: 181–185).

In San Pablo the rebels destroyed or redistributed the belongings of Antonio Ortiz, clerk for the corregidor of Otavalo. His wife's clothing was also given away, because she "gave Indian women wet cotton to spin and received dry thread so that the women lost the pay for their work" (ibid.: 186; my translation). Señora de Ortiz apparently forced indigenous women to spin and weighed out damp cotton. When the women spun yarn, the water evaporated and the weight was short, so de Ortiz could accuse them of theft and refuse to pay them. Weighing fleece or yarn when it is given to a worker and then weighing spun yarn or the finished garment is common in the contemporary sweater industry because the sweater producers who supply the yarn are worried about theft; but in 1777 the shoe was on the other foot.

Indígenas sacked haciendas and obrajes around Cayambe and burned written records, wool, cotton, and a suitcase of clothes belonging to a statue of the Virgin. They attacked whites and mestizos in the Cayambe church and killed several, including clerics. By November 13, troops were marching from Quito to quell the revolt, but when they arrived in Otavalo the area had been pacified. The majority of rebellious indígenas who gave an occupation in court worked in obrajes or on haciendas, and they directed their anger against the institutions that exploited them (Moreno Yánez 1985: 189–201).

A noteworthy feature of this uprising was the leadership and participation of indigenous women. Of the 103 indígenas who appeared before the Spanish tribunal after the revolt was quashed, forty-four were women. The enormous labor obligations owed by males during the colonial era imposed additional burdens on women because they had to farm in their husbands' absence (Stark 1985b: 4–10).

When I recounted the revolt of 1777 to Otavalos in Peguche, noting that some ringleaders had the same surname (Farinango) as those present, one man asked, "Why don't they teach this to the students?" I answered, "Because they don't want you to know"; teaching the history of indigenous revolts shatters the image of the docile, contented serfs of wasipungu days. CONAIE (Confederación de Nacionalidades Indígenas del Ecuador), the national indigenous federation, has documented almost 150 major indigenous uprisings in Ecuador between 1534 and 1972 (CONAIE 1989: 285–303), and the number of undocumented or little-known revolts must number in the thousands.

Abolition of the Mita and Independence

By 1808, the town of Otavalo had apparently recovered from the rebellion of 1777. There were 215 houses, and two churches which still exist today (although they were rebuilt following the nineteenth-century earthquakes): San Luis on the Parque Bolívar and Jordán to the northeast. San Luis was "only for the indios *originarios,* or those from the land called *Llactayos* [Q. *llacta,* district or region]." Jordán's parishioners were "whites, *negros* [Sp. blacks], and *indios forasteros* [Sp. indígenas who fled their natal communities]" (Santiestevan 1994 [1808]: 740; my translation). Otavalo has always had indigenous inhabitants, but until the 1980s they "knew their place." The current insistence that the presence of indígenas is new testifies to how threatened whites-mestizos feel by increasing indigenous economic and political power.

An Englishman, William Bennett Stevenson, visited the Count of

Casa Xijón's Peguche hacienda and obraje in 1806. Stevenson can be credited with the myth of the Otavalos as special, the model minority: "I never saw a race of finer looking people than an assembly of Otavalenos on a Sunday, when they meet at church or at a feast" (Stevenson 1825: 347). Another writer, however, insisted Otavalos were "inclined to laziness and drunkenness" (Santiestevan 1994 [1808]: 742; my translation).

The mita was abolished in 1812, but as one kind of indentured or debt labor disappeared another took its place. The Inca term *yanacona*, denoting an indígena in personal service, had disappeared by the early 1600s, replaced by *concierto* (Sp.), which originally meant a contracted laborer then an indígena who had become indebted to an hacienda owner and lived and worked on the hacienda to pay off the debt. Although technically conciertos were not slaves, they were bought and sold with the property.

Concertaje became illegal in 1918 but persisted for at least another ten years. The debts of parents were inherited by their children; although this was outlawed from time to time, for example in 1833, the practice continued into the twentieth century (Oberem 1981: 315). *Wasipungu* (Q. house door, the right of a male to farm a plot of land on an hacienda in return for heavy labor obligations) can be traced to the early colonial mita, although the term did not appear until the early nineteenth century (ibid.: 301). This practice resulted in a loss of status and land for women. According to pre-Hispanic custom, a woman inherited land and other property from her parents in her own right. Because of Spanish land-use practices, wasipungu plots were given to males; a widow had no right to remain on the land if her husband died unless her son became a *wasipungero*.

Independence from Spain in 1822 and from the Republic of Gran Colombia (Colombia, Ecuador, and Venezuela) in 1830 did not mean improvements for indígenas. In fact, their situation worsened because they lost the recourse of appeals to the Crown, and landowners and government officials formed a powerful oligarchy (Oberem 1981: 320). Indigenous tribute was abolished in the highlands in 1857, black slavery was abolished in 1855, and the tithe (Sp. *diezmos*, a tax on agricultural production) was legally prohibited in 1889 but continued well into the twentieth century. The burdens of tribute were graphically illustrated in a painting by Juan Agustín Guerrero (ca. 1852) entitled "Indian from Cotacachi whose parents put out his eyes when he was a child so that he would not have to pay tribute" (Hallo 1981: Plate 97; my translation).

In June 1863, Friedrich Hassaurek, Abraham Lincoln's ambassador to

Ecuador, visited Otavalo. He observed that in the Peguche obraje "coarse woolen goods are made, such as bayetas for ponchos, jergas for the Indians, and shawls for their women (these shawls are dyed red, yellow, blue or brown, but the red color is most in demand); cloth for coats, vests, pantaloons, carpets, etc." The cloth was primarily exported to Pasto, Popayán, and Barbacoas, Colombia. The workers "are almost all Indians. They are concertados or peones" (Hassaurek 1967 [1867]: 150–151). The cloth was basically the same as that produced in the 1600s. Clothing styles and home furnishings changed over the centuries, so the cloth was dyed and tailored differently; the heavy dependence on unpaid or underpaid indigenous labor remained.

Hassaurek noted that "[t]he whites and cholos of Otavalo all speak the Quechua, or Indian language. . . . To the owners of haciendas . . . a knowledge of Quechua is indispensable, for there are hundreds of Indian farm laborers who cannot speak a word of Spanish" (ibid.: 173). The pattern of indigenous Quichua monolingualism, with only a few bilingual individuals, continued into the 1950s.

Hassaurek's description of the Sunday Otavalo fair could have been written today, except that many additional products are now sold: "Here they sell macañas (a sort of narrow cotton shawl), ponchos, wool, cotton, beads, rosaries, leaden crosses, strings of glass pearls, collars and bracelets of false corals, and other cheap ornaments; meat, fruit, vegetables, salt, ají, barley meal, and such popular dishes ready made, as cariucho, locro, choclos, mashca, toasted corn, etc." (ibid.: 175).

Ethnic relations continued to be highly unequal: "[W]hile horses and mules are called bagajes mayores, asses and Indians are called bagajes menores; that is to say, as a beast of burden, the Indian is considered below the horse and mule, and on a level with the donkey." Hassaurek added that "[k]icks and brutal words are the only encouragement he receives from his betters, before whom he crouches in abject servility and cowardice" (ibid.: 105).

Hassaurek admitted that indígenas did "more work than all the other races together. . . . But his position in the social scale is in an inverse proportion to his usefulness. He is far below the North American Negro" (ibid.: 107). He added: "Filthy, servile, superstitious, drunken, indolent, as they are, they claim our sympathy and commiseration. These poor and degraded beings were once the owners and masters of the country . . ." (ibid.: 107). This "animal, vegetable, or mineral" identification of indígenas surfaced during the 1992 Columbus quincentennial protests when some whites-mestizos again described indígenas in such terms (Meisch 1992).

In 1873, the weekly fair was changed from Sunday to Saturday (Porto-carrero n.d. [1976]: 7). José Luis Portocarrero attributes this to religious guilt following the earthquake of 1869, which devastated the region and destroyed Ibarra. The fair was originally held in the Parque Bolívar, but at an unknown date it was moved to the contemporary 24 de Mayo food market two blocks west (ibid.).

Model Indians

By the time of Hassaurek's visit, the Otavalos were seen as the " 'mold image' of highland Indians," representing the nineteenth-century idea of progress as a civilizing force and the effectiveness of laissez-faire eco-nomics and liberal ideology (Muratorio 1993: 29–30). Hassaurek observed that people in Quito considered the Otavalos, especially the women, to be cleaner and better looking than other highland Indians, although he disagreed (1967 [1867]: 157–158). The view of Otavalos as model indígenas was especially evident during the world's fairs in Paris in 1889 and Chi-cago in 1893 and during the 1892 Columbus quadricentennial exposition in Madrid, Spain. The organizer of the 1892 Ecuadorian exhibition ex-plicitly contrasted the savage "Jíbaro" and "Záparo" of the Amazon with the Otavalos, whom he described as "pure" with "correct features" and "above-average height" as well as "intelligent, hard working, sober, of good manners and accustomed to neatness, order and cleanliness" (Mu-ratorio 1993: 24–25).

It seems the Otavalos underwent a remarkable transformation from the lazy, drunken brutes described by Gaspar Santiestevan in 1808 and by Hassaurek in 1863; but what had changed was the representation of Otavalos by Ecuadorian elites (especially compared to Amazonian groups) in a nationalist discourse intended for Euro-American audiences. Otavalos in the late nineteenth century were considered "proud, clean, industrious, intelligent, and so on—[which] is in effect to commend them for having qualities that one is surprised to find among Indians and at the same time to damn other Indian groups with the implication that these are precisely the qualities *they* don't have" (Casagrande 1981: 260–261). Jane Collier (personal communication, 1996) heard similar com-ments about Otavalos being clean and industrious when she lived in Quito in the 1950s.

As the nineteenth century ended, patterns emerged in the Otavalo re-gion: the formation of Otavalos as a distinct group identified primarily by residence, dress, and to a lesser extent language; wasipungu and other forms of exploitative farming relations; production spinning and weaving, usually in the context of forced labor or debt servitude; the export of Otavalo textiles throughout the northern Andes; a greatly increased workload for women and ruptures in traditional land inheritance patterns; conflation of class with social and legal constructions of race, with indígenas and African-Ecuadorians at the bottom; and the simultaneous depiction of Otavalos as the best of a bad lot.

Hard Times and Agrarian Reform

By 1900, control of prime valley land by large haciendas and demographic pressure on land available for small farming resulted in temporary and permanent outmigration by Otavalos (Males 1985; Salomon 1981 [1973]), although individuals and communities resisted the privatization of communal landholdings (Elizabeth M. Rogers 1998). Families from Quinchuquí involved in the meat and cattle trade who moved to Ibarra were among the first to leave the valley. By the 1930s, some were living permanently in Ibarra, and others had moved to Tulcán on the Ecuadorian-Colombian border (Males 1985: 7–8, 45, 79). Rather than assimilate, these families retained their Otavalo identity and maintained ties with their natal community. Indígenas from Quinchuquí also migrated to Quito and its environs (ibid.: 91). Quinchuquí indígenas living in Tulcán were animal traders, "but much later came those from Peguche to market textiles only on weekends—Saturday and Sunday—and they returned home on Tuesday" (ibid.: 45; my translation). By 1961, some Quinchuquí butchers were itinerant, but others migrated permanently. Otavalos lived in every town along the Pan-American highway north of Quito. There were also Otavalo butchers in the markets of Cayambe, Ibarra, Mira, Bolívar, San Gabriel, and Tulcán, and permanent Otavalo butchers in Pimampiro and the Chota valley (Preston 1963: 148).

Two books written in the 1940s are invaluable sources of information about Otavalo life during that decade. Elsie Clews Parsons' *Peguche* was published posthumously in 1945, based on her fieldwork in 1940–1941. In 1949, John Collier, Jr., and Aníbal Buitrón published *The Awakening Valley*, with research and photographs from the summer of 1946.

Parsons gives one account of the inception of the modern textile industry. In 1917, the owner of the Hacienda Cusín, located at the eastern end of Lago San Pablo, gave her Quito son-in-law a beautifully woven poncho as a wedding gift. The recipient was so impressed by its quality that he approached the weaver, José Cajas of Quinchuquí, and suggested that Cajas use the European-introduced treadle loom to weave imitation Scottish tweed, locally called *casimir* (Sp. cashmere, but made from sheep's wool), and market it in Quito (Parsons 1945: 25–26). A similar version is repeated by Collier and Buitrón, who credit a "white landlord" with asking an Indian "to weave him a length of woolen cloth for a suit" (1949: 160). Independent weavers had always existed, and Cajas was apparently one of them.

Presumably the casimir trade took off from there. Since twill weaves (Sp. *jergas*) had been made since the colonial era, the Cajas story raises several questions. How did the casimir differ from the usual twills? Did the landlord introduce something special? Or is the story an example of whites-mestizos claiming credit for something Otavalos were already doing? On the other hand, two extremely successful contemporary products, tapestries and sweaters, were introduced by outsiders; the Otavalos then applied their textile and marketing skills to turn them into major sources of income.

Peguche indígenas have another version of the introduction of casimir:

> The owner [of Hacienda Peguche] brought samples of English cashmere from Colombia. He locked up two weavers from Peguche on his property in Tabacundo to copy the samples. He said, if you make it you will leave safe and sound and if not you will disappear. The weavers began to copy the samples, but they did not leave safe and sound as the owner said. Enclosed in the basement . . . they had to teach other weavers how to make casimir. (Korovkin et al. 1994: 28; my translation)

It is possible that casimir was introduced in several ways, both benign and oppressive, but the indigenous side has not been heard previously. Another possibility is that Otavalos in Tulcán or elsewhere obtained English cashmere from Colombia and copied it. The date 1917 is significant because World War I had been underway for three years in Europe. German U-boats had made serious inroads on Allied shipping, resulting in a scarcity of English products in Ecuador. The casimir produced in Otavalo was intended for the Ecuadorian white-mestizo market in the absence of the British product.

Former workers on the Hacienda Pinsaquí testified to the importance of the Colombian market, "from whence came many muleteers to haul textiles" (Males 1985: 30; my translation). By the 1940s, Otavalos selling meat or cloth in Tulcán had begun to cross the border into Colombia to sell textiles. Still, travel was not common in that era: "The most enterprising person in all Peguche, Rosita Lema, had never been across the valley to Cotacachi" (Parsons 1945: 13).

As a result of the Parsons book, Rosa Lema, her daughter, and her nephew were invited to the United States in 1949. In his review of the official Ecuadorian publication on the visit, Buitrón took the government to task for mendacious publicity. Rosa Lema was not a "Princess," because "no such titles exist among Ecuadorian indígenas." The government painted a "completely false" picture of indigenous life, mentioning rural schools for the arts with indígena teachers and insisting that all three indígenas were instructors in their communities (Buitrón 1951: 271; my translation).

The government had affirmed that "[w]e have transformed the indígena into a useful member of society who produces and consumes." I can imagine the steam rising from Buitrón's head when he responded: "The truth is that they haven't taught Indians anything up to now and it is also true that the indígena has always been a productive member of society . . . We have always asked, what would Ecuador be if the Indians disappeared for even a month." Buitrón argued: "The agricultural work in the entire country, but especially in the sierra, is performed almost exclusively by Indians. The cleanliness and hygiene in the cities and towns is the work of Indians. Just to retrieve a dead dog from the street it is necessary to find an Indian because no one else will perform this task" (ibid.: 271–272).

Buitrón also took exception to the description of the Otavalos as special: "It is nice to say that these Indians belong to a tribe that has never been conquered, but it is very sad to know the reality: they were conquered and dominated by the Incas, later by the Spanish, and now by priests, hacienda owners, lawyers and clerks, city officials and political officers, tavern owners, etc." (ibid.: 272).

Olga Fisch, a European immigrant to Ecuador with a long career as an artist and artesanías seller, visited New York a year after Rosa Lema and appeared on U.S. television. The publicity surrounding Lema's visit led Fisch's makeup artist to comment: "You know, that other Indian, Rosa, was much more picturesque than you, but she was an Inca Princess and you are not." Lema's nephew "had practically stopped traffic at Rockefeller Center by sitting on a curb and his playing the rondador [Sp. panpipes]" (Fisch 1985: 188–189). Lema's nephew might have been the first Otavalo musician to play on the streets of New York. Fisch, however, contributed to the Otavalos-are-Incas myth, describing them as "handsome people, so shining, so elegant. If there is anything left of the Inca aristocracy, I think that it must live in the Otavalans" (ibid.: 198).

Lema's son, Amado Ruiz, tells a different version: "My mother, Rosa Lema, began the business in 1948, when she was sent by President Plaza to the United States to thank them for the help after the earthquake in Ambato. She took the first Ecuadorian artesanías and did the best promotion" (*El Comercio,* October 31, 1994: B-1; my translation).

Certain patterns in artesanías production were evident by the 1940s, including community specialization. Punyaro and Santiaguillo were known for baskets, hats, and winnowers made of *"zuro"* (bamboo); San Juan for cotton cloth and *fachalinas* (Q. females' headcloths and mantles); La Bolsa for ponchos and shawls; Peguche for ponchos, shawls, and casimires; Quinchuquí for blankets, shawls, and casimires; Agato for casimires, *bayeta* (Sp. plain-weave woolens), ponchos, and shawls; La Compañía for bayeta, ponchos, belts, and *esteras* (Sp. totora reed mats); Pucará for belts and mats; San Roque Bajo for mats; Ilumán Alto for casimires and hand-felted hats worn by indígenas; Ilumán Bajo for casimires, ponchos, and felt hats; Carabuela for ponchos; and Araque for hats woven from *paja toquilla* (Sp. straw, a relative of the palm).

Indigenous merchants also had specialties: those from Monserrate wool, Peguche cattle and casimires, Casco cattle, and Pucará ponchos and shawls (Buitrón 1947: 47–52). Other crafts included mats and winnowers in Malespampa and Pucará; casimir, ponchos, blankets, and other wool and cotton textiles in Romerillos, Carabuela, and Quinchuquí Alto; and felt hats in Angelpamba (Buitrón and Buitrón 1945: 200–201). Indígenas in communities close to Otavalo such as Peguche, Quinchuquí, Agato, Ilumán, La Compañía, and La Bolsa produced a number of items (especially wool textiles) that had many consumers and engaged in commerce as well as production.

Between 1935 and 1940, the weekly fair moved to the unpaved Plaza Centenario (the Poncho Plaza) in north Otavalo (Portocarrero n.d. [1976]: 7). This was a local, not tourist, event with primarily indigenous participants and rows of ponchos, casimir, shawls, *anakus* (Q. females' wrap skirts), fachalinas, cotton cloth, belts, esteras, and pottery on the ground, with food off to the side (Collier and Buitrón 1949: 15, 25). Food and household goods were also sold in the "general market," now the 24 de Mayo food market, and several animal markets were scattered around town (Parsons 1945: 30–31).

Following World War II, casimir became less competitive with European and American-made woolens; but the decline of this market coincided with the arrival of Andean Mission, International Labor Organization (Salinas 1954), and Peace Corps development programs and the growth of mass tourism in the 1960s, which moved textile production in new directions to meet the demands of outsiders.

Tapestry weaving was introduced to both Otavalos and Salasacas (Indian Textiles from Ecuador 1958–1959) through a project directed by Jan Schreuder, a Dutch artist and designer, sponsored by the Ecuadorian Institute of Anthropology and Geography in Quito and the Andean Mission (Salinas 1954: 318). Schreuder recognized "that there is no future in 'casimires' but that there is an enormous potential export market (which is what must be built up if the artisans are to survive) for a certain type of weaving which is of good quality and incorporates autochthonous designs stylised to fit into modern interiors" (ibid.: 319). The result was tapestries woven with an interlocking weft incorporating pre-Hispanic and contemporary indigenous motifs (ibid.: 312). Products from Schreuder's workshops were exhibited at the Casa de la Cultura in Quito in August 1954 and at the United Nations headquarters in New York in 1958 (Indian Textiles from Ecuador 1958–1959: 19).

In the 1940s, agriculture was still a common denominator of indigenous life. "All indios are agriculturists and the majority work their own land" (Buitrón 1947: 56; my translation). In 1962, there were twenty-seven white- or mestizo-owned haciendas in the valley, which owned most of the level farmland (Cooper 1965: 16). Various combinations of landholding and indentured servitude existed within the same indigenous community, and land shortages were acute.

Many Otavalos recount horrendous stories of life during wasipungu days. One comadre from San Luis de Agualongo, less than five feet tall and weighing ninety pounds, told me how the wife of the hacienda owner beat her when, eight months pregnant, she did not move fast enough with a load of firewood. Carlos Conterón recounted that his grandfather, José Manuel Córdova, was a wasipungero on the Hacienda Pinsaquí. Sometimes Córdova received "orders" at any hour from the hacienda owner to leave immediately *on foot* for Quito, hauling lead bullets, with a 24-hour deadline for his return. This was a 100-mile round trip over mountainous terrain. The bullets were carried in a wooden box which was extremely heavy, leaving permanent scars on José's back.

Carlos' great-grandfather, José Yamberla, was not a wasipungero but a spinner in the obraje on the Hacienda Pinsaquí, receiving ten centavos a day for his work (as opposed to the five centavos ostensibly paid to wasipungeros). He, too, got "orders" to take letters to Quito on foot

Rosa Elena de la Torre in her garden in Ilumán with two sprites: her grand-sons Alex Hernán Díaz and Curi Davíd Cabascango. July 2001.

and return within twenty-four hours. "He took a bit of toasted barley, corn, and salt and left." Yamberla was required to spin a kilo (2.2 pounds) of wool a day, when spinning half that amount was considered a full day's work. Frequently he could not finish, so he spun at home at night. When it came time to dye wool, the patrón organized a *minga* (Q. collective labor), which the spinners were forced to attend beyond their ordinary work, with no extra pay: "There was much forced labor." Both Josés brought their children to the hacienda to help them. Other compadres told me of being whipped when they worked on the Hacienda Quinchuquí. What emerges in these accounts, besides the insanely heavy labor obligations, is Otavalos' deeply felt sense that they were regarded not as human but as chattel.

Although land scarcity reached a critical point in Quinchuquí at the turn of the century, shortages developed at different rates in other parts of the valley. By 1954, it was evident that the agricultural problem "sooner or later will have to be faced realistically," but "the phrase 'agrarian reform' is regarded by many members of the land-owning classes as little more than the password to hell" (Salinas 1954: 315–316). Development programs that helped individuals while ignoring structural inequalities were not enough. By 1960, the people of Peguche averaged 0.26 *hectare* (Sp. 2.5 acres) per family and had long sought livelihood outside agriculture. Many of them worked in the nearby San Miguel textile factory, "but for the most part, domestic textile manufacture was the most important of their resources" (Pearse 1975: 194).

The impetus for the 1964 Law of Agrarian Reform was pressure from the United States and the fear of a Cuban-style Communist revolution, combined with the desire to modernize agriculture. The 1964 law was followed by a decree in 1970 and a new agrarian reform law in 1973. The 1964 law abolished wasipungu. Article 68 mandated that if a wasipungero had worked for the hacienda for ten years his service was considered equivalent to the value of the plot, which became legally his. Those with more than ten years' service were to receive an additional payment equal to the minimum wage. Other arrangements were ordered, depending on the length of service.

Agrarian reform was responsible for the redistribution of 180,000 hectares of land in Ecuador by 1979. Only 2,000 hectares were redistributed in Imbabura; but many large landholdings were broken up and distributed among the landowners' families or sold to avoid expropriation (Meier 1981: 113), and many buyers were indígenas (Korovkin et al. 1994; Lema 1995: 146–149; Meier 1981: 281). Very few indígenas received land as their private property, and even fewer were allocated plots which were large enough to sustain a family (Meier 1981: 147), but indígenas could work for themselves and divide land among all their children. The energy unleashed by the abolition of wasipungu resembled the unwinding of a tightly coiled spring; the future now held possibilities.

Meanwhile, temporary and permanent emigration continued. In the 1950s, according to Carlos Conterón, indigenous merchants traveled to Colombia, Venezuela, Peru, Chile, and Argentina. During Andrew Pearse's 1960 visit, he noted that Quinchuquí families were land poor, averaging 0.77 hectare of mainly hilly land. "Perceiving the existence of a high class market for handwoven woolen goods, they began buying textiles from the Peguche people, for sale in the capital, and later in foreign countries, reaching Rio de Janeiro, Santiago, and New York, where their striking peasant dress and pigtails gave a distinctive brand to their wares" (Pearse 1975: 194–195). Young indígenas from Peguche and other communities also became textile merchants, establishing a new trade that remained "firmly in the hands of indios (new style)" (ibid.: 195).

The 1960s saw merchants from Otavalo venture to Venezuela, Puerto Rico, and even the United States to sell their cloth. There was a sizable colony of Otavaleños in Bogotá, where they both wove and sold their goods. Otavalo merchants could be found at all Ecuadorian weekly markets and in larger cities including Guayaquil—anywhere there were tourists (Casagrande 1981: 263).

Peguche indígenas were "the richest and most industrious and have the greatest identification with national life and culture. The majority speak Spanish and know how to read and write. Some continually travel within and outside the country." The indígenas of Quinchuquí were similar to their neighbors in Peguche (Buitrón 1947: 48; my translation).

According to Pearse's 1960 census, indígenas constituted 8% of the population of Otavalo town, many drawn by the possibilities of commercial weaving. Indígenas, however, were socially invisible. José María Cotacachi, who was born in 1955 in Carabuela, told me that when he was a child "indígenas had to get off the sidewalks for the people with neckties."

The Transportes Otavalo bus line (Otavalo-Ibarra-Quito) was founded in 1950, and Transportes Los Lagos (Otavalo-Quito-Esmeraldas) was founded ten years later. Initially the buses had segregated seating: cushioned leather seats in the front for whites-mestizos and rows of wooden benches behind them for indígenas. If whites-mestizos lacked seats, indígenas were yanked out of theirs. Smaller bus lines serving the nearby communities commenced service in the early 1970s.

Only two or three foreigners visited the market each Saturday in the 1960s, many of them Peace Corps volunteers. There was virtually no tourism infrastructure, so visitors spent the night in Ibarra and took the bus to Otavalo early in the morning (Stephen Athens, personal communication, 1994).

One additional fact deserves mention: the arrival of non-Catholic missionaries. Since the colonial period most Otavalos have been nominally Roman Catholic; but missionaries, including Evangelical Christians, Bahá'is, and Mormons, have made converts and built churches in Otavalo and the surrounding communities. Evangelicals have proselytized in the valley for decades; a 1928 map of the Ilumán area shows the Evangelist Chapel in Agato. Otavalos cite various reasons for converting, including the Evangelical prohibition of alcoholic beverages and, to a lesser extent, the prohibition of traditional fiestas, which were not only an opportunity for prodigious alcohol abuse but an enormous expense. Additionally, even with the advent of liberation theology in 1968, the Catholic church was associated with the ruling oligarchy, although this has changed.

Conversions sometimes cause intrafamilial and intracommunity problems. During one indígena wedding in the late 1970s, latent hostilities surfaced among brothers who were Catholic, Evangelical, and Mormon, including conflicts over alcohol use (Chavez 1982: 78–79). Miguel Andrango of Agato attributes the decline of such fiestas as Coraza and Pendoneros to Protestant denominations that prohibit the use of alcohol and the celebration of these fiestas.

Problems arose between World Vision and indígenas in La Compañía and Ilumán in 1982 and 1983 over the distribution of development resources (Stoll 1990: 289–290). In 1982, FICI (Sp. Federation of Indígenas and Farmers of Imbabura) initiated a national and international campaign against World Vision (CONAIE 1989: 137). In 1997, indígenas in Peguche, after filing formal protests against the construction of a Mormon temple there, burned the foundations to the ground and forced the Mormons to reconsider their plans.

As the 1960s ended, for many families commercial weaving became a central feature of life at the expense of agriculture (Chavez 1982: 184). The stage was set for the economic boom of the next three decades and for increased disparities in wealth among indígenas as the income of indigenous merchants outstripped that of artisans and farmers. Otavalos were well situated to take advantage of the coming tourist boom, and networks were in place for more wide-ranging and longer migrations abroad.

CHAPTER 3

Textiles and Tourism
Move to the Fore

This chapter examines the growth of the textile economy since 1970 in the context of the Ecuadorian petroleum boom in that decade and a litany of woes in subsequent years. These include recession, hyperinflation averaging 40% annually between 1984 and 1998, over 60% in 1999, and 103% in 2000 (the highest in Latin America), electrical shortages and rationing in the mid-1990s, natural disasters including El Ñino floods and volcanic eruptions, bank failures in 1999, neoliberal restructuring, and political mismanagement, corruption, and instability over the past two decades, with four presidents in the past three years.

The OPEC oil crisis of 1973 jolted the global economy, altering agrarian landscapes and nonagrarian production in many parts of the world. The cycles of global oil production and sales reshaped the Ecuadorian economy, which resulted in the government's acceptance of neoliberal reforms and growing disparities in wealth. Because the country depends on oil for approximately 50% of its income, its economy is extremely vulnerable to fluctuations in world commodity markets; when oil prices dropped 40% between mid-1997 and the end of 1998 (*Newsweek*, January 25, 1999: 24), Ecuador felt the pinch.

Overall, the Otavalos' prosperity has increased, because they have relied on textiles and tourism rather than agriculture; but prosperity has a price. Families are working harder and longer and also mechanizing to maintain the economic status quo or get ahead. The cost also includes the relentless search for new products and markets; transnational migration, which means that the Otavalos export their own people; and the sharp rise in income differentials between wealthy merchant families and poorer agriculturists, with weavers and textile producers, who may also be farmers, in the middle. Otavalos are debating the social costs of these economic gains (a topic touched on throughout this book).

National and local events following the abolition of wasipungu set the stage for the growth of the textile and tourism economies. First, the paving of the Pan-American highway between Quito and Colombia and the construction of new bridges as part of oil-financed state spending on infrastructure greatly improved access to Otavalo. These projects were completed in 1973 and reduced travel time between Quito and Otavalo to two hours.

The second event also occurred in 1973: the paving of the Plaza Centenario and the construction of concrete kiosks for the vendors, sponsored by the Dutch government. Vendors who formerly sold their products in the Plaza Centenario were guaranteed kiosks, and other families soon vied for space. An attractive marketplace and improved transportation proved essential for textile exports and tourism.

Indígenas are now cultural, social and political, and economic participants in national society, as evidenced by the rise of indigenous federations, the increase in education, and the presence of indigenous professionals and politicians. Indígenas not only are doing the work but are reaping the rewards. They are no longer refused service in most restaurants and hotels, relegated to the back of the bus, or jerked out of their seats to make room for whites-mestizos, which was the case when I first visited in Ecuador in 1973. Indígenas now own local restaurants, hotels, and bus companies, and in May 2000 an Otavaleño, Mario Conejo, was elected mayor of Otavalo.

There are several reasons for these hard-won gains. Once such impediments as wasipungu were removed, indigenous economic advances created a tide that has lifted many indigenous and white-mestizo boats. Indígenas also organized. In 1972, to push for the completion of land reform, indígenas in the sierra formed ECUARUNARI (Q. Ecuador Indígenas Awaken). ECUARUNARI limited its membership to indígenas, stated its nonviolent intentions to avoid charges of communism, and identified with the Catholic church, which—influenced by liberation theology—supported land reform and other social justice programs. In 1974, INRUJTA-FICI (Q. Imbabura Indígenas' Great Union–Sp. Federation of Indígenas and Farmers of Imbabura) was organized to defend local political and cultural rights.

CONAIE (Sp. Confederation of Indigenous Nationalities of Ecuador), the national organization encompassing the federations of the Oriente, highlands, and coast, was founded in 1986. The May–June 1990 indigenous uprising, the April 1992 march from Puyo in the Oriente to Quito, the October 1992 opposition to the Columbus Quincentennial (Meisch 1992), and a series of uprisings between 1994 and 2001 also brought indigenous concerns to national and international attention. Ecuador now has one of the most effective indigenous organizations in Latin America, which often carries out strikes in concert with white-mestizo trade unions.

In early 1996, indígenas formed a social movement, Movimiento Unidad Plurinacional Pachakutik (Sp. Plurinational Unity Movement Pachakutik [a Quichua term meaning a world or time-space reversal]). CONAIE also announced its support of a television producer and announcer, Freddy Ehlers, for president. Ehlers, backed by Movimiento Nuevo País (Sp. Movement for a New Nation) and a coalition of groups, ran on an anticorruption, pro-environment platform in opposition to the center and right-wing parties and then president Sixto Durán Ballén's economic measures (*Latin American Weekly Report*, February 1, 1996: 38; February 15, 1996: 63). CONAIE's ability to develop a functional division of labor (insider-outsider, local-global, secular-spiritual) through alliances such as that with Pachakutik–Nuevo País makes it one of the most successful Latin American indigenous movements (Brysk 2000: 298). In the 1996 elections, Saraguro indígena and president of CONAIE Luis Macas was elected to Congress as a national representative on the Pachakutik–Nuevo País ticket, a historic first, and six other indígenas were elected to Congress as local representatives. An Otavaleño, Auki Tituaña, was elected mayor of Cotacachi, and Mario Conejo narrowly lost the contest for mayor of Otavalo.

Increased education and economic prosperity among Otavalos have resulted in political clout previously unimagined as economic power translates into political power. Indígenas are successfully lobbying for infrastructural improvements and running for important local and national political offices. While no indígenas from the valley have been elected to the provincial assembly, in the May 1998 elections an Otavaleña, Nina Pacari, was elected a national congresswoman and selected as a second vice-president of Congress, the first indigenous woman so chosen. She was also a representative to the 1997–1998 national assembly that rewrote Ecuador's constitution. Although women are at a disadvantage in competing for power and prestige, they are least handicapped in political systems where leadership rests on ability and where there is little separation between public and domestic spheres (Collier 1974: 91). Otavalos do not think in terms of this dichotomy, and women's ownership of land, resources for textile production, artesanías stores, and market kiosks gives them the economic ability to act independently.

Article I of Ecuador's August 10, 1998, constitution declares the country a democratic, pluricultural, and multiethnic state, with "castellano" (Spanish) as its official language and "quichua, shuar," and other "ancestral languages" official for use by indigenous communities, a recognition that indígenas define themselves as distinct in a number of ways, including language, dress, healing, and other customs. This is not Balkanization; indígenas see themselves as indigenous Ecuadorians or Ecuadorian indígenas, with emphasis on both words. During the 1995 border war with Peru, "Yo [drawing of a heart, meaning 'love'] Ecuador" signs were chalked on walls and doors, including ones inside indígenas' houses in the Otavalo valley.

In 1998, Transparency International in Berlin ranked Ecuador among the most corrupt countries in the world in terms of bribery of government officials. By 2000, Ecuador had the dubious distinction of being named the most corrupt nation in Latin America, ranking seventy-fourth among ninety countries worldwide (a first-place ranking being least corrupt) (www.transparency.org). Half of the 200 highest-earning Ecuadorian corporations paid no income taxes in 1997 (Yahoo! News, Wednesday, August 26, 1998). The same year saw $2.6 billion in damages from El Niño floods and a precipitous drop in the price of oil.

In 1999, Ecuador experienced its worst economic crisis in seventy years, facing a $1.2 billion budget deficit, austerity measures imposed by the International Monetary Fund (IMF) and World Bank as a condition for more loans, a plummeting sucre, bank failures and the freezing of accounts, more hyperinflation, localized strikes, and national uprisings in March and July involving all sectors of the population. Finally, Ecuador defaulted on its $13.6 billion foreign debt.

The social indicators show a discouraging decline in the population's well-being. According to the United Nations Development Program, the number of poor in Ecuador doubled from nearly 4 million in 1995 to 8 million in 2000 (out of a population of 12.4 million). Per capita income dropped from $1,600 in 1998 to just over $1,000 in 1999. The Index of Human Development, which includes such factors as life expectancy, education levels, and real adjusted income, saw Ecuador fall from 72nd to 91st place among 174 countries, the worst drop in the region (El Comercio, July 5, 2000: C-6).

In early January 2000, Ecuador's president Jamil Mahuad proposed to control runaway inflation by making the dollar Ecuador's national currency at a fixed exchange rate of S/25,000 to the dollar. The result was another national uprising and a bloodless coup in which CONAIE and members of the armed forces united to overthrow Mahuad. His successor, former vice-president Gustavo Noboa, ignored opposition and continued dollarization. He extended the deadline to exchange sucres for dollars until June 9, 2001, and slowly the country has made the switch. Signs showing prices in both sucres and dollars and newspaper articles in Spanish and Quichua explaining the value of the new currency appeared throughout the country by the summer of 2000.

Dollarization cut inflation in 2001 but also reduced Ecuador's attractiveness as a country where people could gain on the exchange rate. This caused a serious drop in sales to Colombia, because Ecuadorian artesanías and other goods were no longer inexpensive, and also reduced the income from dollars remitted from abroad.

In addition, the United States recently established a base at Manta on Ecuador's coast to interdict Colombian drug flights and in 2000 proposed Plan Colombia, an ill-conceived initiative that will spend $1.3 billion to support counterinsurgency efforts in Colombia's intractable 37-year-old civil war. The plan also proposes to cut cocaine and heroin production through the support of military operations and the spraying of herbicides in the Colombian Amazon (rather than by reducing demand through drug treatment programs in the United States). Plan Colombia raises the specter of another Vietnam, including U.S. complicity in horrendous human rights violations.

Ecuadorians are concerned about their country being dragged into the conflict, which has already spilled over into the Oriente, forcing Ecuadorian indígenas living along the border to take refuge near Lago Agrio. Otavalos worry about the loss of Colombian markets as that country becomes increasingly unsafe, the flood of Colombian refugees into Ecuador, and the possibility of guerrilla retaliatory violence or kidnappings in the sierra. Many Otavalos' solution to these political and economic problems was another round of emigration abroad, discussed in detail in Chapter 6.

Otavalo Agriculture since 1970

The farming-weaving household has long been the basic unit of social organization in the valley, and ownership of land or access to it formed the basis for full participation in indigenous life (Buitrón 1947; Butler 1981; Chavez 1982; Collier and Buitrón 1949; Colloredo-Mansfeld 1994; Meier 1981; Meisch 1980, 1987; Parsons 1945; Salomon 1981 [1973]). But it is no longer possible to say, as it was in the 1940s, that "[t]he Otavalo Indian . . . is above all a farmer" (Collier and Buitrón 1949: 49). Today

Otavalo indígenas are above all textile producers and merchants, entrepreneurs in every sense of the word.

The 1970s saw the blossoming of full-time commercial weaving or merchandising as alternatives to farming (Chavez 1982). The 1990s witnessed significant permanent and temporary emigration to every continent except Antarctica. Increasingly, people are arranging their lives not around the agricultural cycle but around the vacation and commercial cycles in the United States, Europe, and Japan and the arrival of the exporters and tourists. The centuries-old rhythm of life in the valley now has a syncopated beat.

Many Otavalos still farm as their sole occupation or in combination with textile production, music gigs, and marketing, although their number is decreasing along with the size of their holdings. Some Otavalos use the term "agriculturists," while others use *campesinos* (Sp. peasants); but they are more likely to call themselves "indígenas," "Otavalos," or "agriculturists and artisans," as does Germán Patricio Lema (1995: 14).

Some agricultural plots are so small that it is accurate to describe many Otavalos as artisans and gardeners rather than farmers. Overall, indígenas have maintained community residence and the forms of production associated with it (Korovkin 1997: 106), but in northern Ecuador they have found ways to augment or replace income from agriculture, including artesanías and music production and sales, jobs as butchers, meat vendors, and day laborers, permanent and temporary migration to Quito to work in construction, and, recently, employment in the local flower export industry.

In 1993, 95% of Peguche families owned less than 2.5 acres of land around Peguche, although 35% had other land outside the community. Virtually all families interviewed wanted to cultivate more land but cited lack of capital and lack of land for sale as the principal obstacles (Kyle n.d. [1993]). The situation is similar in other communities. In 1995, an Ilumán compadre estimated that the most land owned by any family in town was 3 hectares (7.5 acres), divided into small, scattered parcels. He and his wife, both in their early fifties, own 1.5 hectares (3.75 acres), which they will divide among their five daughters, who will in turn divide it among their nine children. By that time, my compadre said, "the parcels will be so small they will disappear." In Guanansi, where the land is sufficient for the community now, a substantial percentage of the residents would like more land (Kyle 2000: 175), and one more generational division will reduce mini-parcels to micro-parcels. The majority of Otavalo families still want enough land to grow their own food or to

Marta Conterón threshing wheat. Ilumán, August 1990.

bequeath plots for their children's houses and cornfields and admit that
what they own is insufficient.

There are also generational differences in attitudes toward land. The
wasipungu generation has an insatiable land hunger and has worked tremendously hard to buy back land in the valley. But partible inheritance,
large families, and the finite size of the valley have reduced the amount
of land available and priced it out of the reach of most families. For
younger Otavalos the question becomes: is it better to invest money in a
truck to haul merchandise, which does provide a living, or to buy a piece
of land, which is too small for subsistence in any event? Increasingly,
families are choosing the truck.

The agricultural cycle is still a major organizing principle in the lives
of most people with land, but the operant term is "with land," and even
for those who have it there are compelling diversions. Is it better to stay
for fall planting or to trust family members to handle that task and leave
to sell textiles in Venezuela, work in agriculture in Spain, or play music
on the street in Helsinki?

Because corn historically had ritual significance and was made into
the *chicha* (Sp. corn beer, Q. *aswa*) considered essential at fiestas, most
families plant corn, which seems to be taking on symbolic rather than
subsistence importance. If the rains come on time and are not too heavy,
people are harvesting *choclo* (Q. corn on the cob) by March, and every
visit from my compadres or godchildren increases the pile of sweet corn
in my kitchen. June through August see the main corn harvest; then

the dry stalks are cut and gathered in giant ricks which are used to feed livestock. Some corn is husked except for two leaves which are used to tie two cobs together. These cobs (Q. *wayunkakuna*) are slung over the house rafters and used for toasted corn kernels. Corn on the cob is sometimes cooked in the husks, tied together, and hung on the rafters to dry (Q. *chuchuka*). But even as the corn from the previous year hangs above the CD player and the posters of Bob Marley and Madonna, hundreds of younger Otavalos are thinking of June not as the corn harvest but as the time to emigrate to sell textiles and play music. The household's energy is increasingly focused on textile production and sales, and to a lesser extent on music, rather than on agriculture.

The decline of agriculture in the valley as a source of income has resulted in problems of focus for such organizations as FICI and FICAPI (Sp. Imbabura Provincial Federation of Indígenas and Peasants). The "I" and the "C," the indígenas and campesinos in these organizations, have diverged; ethnicity vies with occupation as the organizations' main rallying point. Many Otavalos no longer consider themselves campesinos, and many campesinos are not indígenas. An apartment building in Otavalo or a new Chevy Blazer confers as much status in indigenous eyes as the ownership of a few acres in the countryside, not to mention that it is often easier to purchase vehicles or buildings than rural land.

Household-Based Textile Production and the Search for Market Niches

Although the nuclear family is the ideal, many households contain extended families at some point, and these arrangements change over time. A young married couple often live with either spouse's family for three or four years while they save money to build, buy, or rent their own house or apartment. The parents' house is often inherited by their youngest child or youngest son, but this varies.

Residence depends on various factors, including access to economic resources. In one instance a young orphaned woman moved in with her husband and his parents in San Luis de Agualongo until the newlyweds established their own household. In other cases the husbands moved in with their wives' families in Ilumán and Peguche because these families had more space or owned established commercial ventures. This pattern has held for at least fifty years (see Parsons 1945: 33).

The household is still the basic unit for textile production; and the Otavalo emphasis on family, including the extension of the family through fictive kinship, *compadrazgo* (Sp. co-parenthood), is evident to anyone who spends time in the valley. An understanding of compadrazgo is essential to comprehending the social organization of textile production and marketing and the networks that Otavalos activate for help with everything from serving food at fiestas to finding a place to stay abroad.

Having religious sponsors (godparents, Sp. *padrino* and *madrina*) for children at their baptism, first communion, confirmation, and marriage has been extended by Otavalos to contexts far beyond the custom's original spiritual purpose. During wasipungu times and probably before, indígenas established compadrazgo ties with whites who could serve as intermediaries with local authorities (Buitrón 1947: 61). In the 1940s, white compadres were an asset for anyone who had business in Otavalo or Quito (Parsons 1945: 45).

Baptism and marriage are especially important. The godparents for a wedding are customarily, but not invariably, asked to be the godparents of the couple's first child. One indígena noted that godparents "intervene in the solution of problems that their godchildren create or help to solve other problems that arise" (Kowii 1992: 216; my translation).

Besides attending to the spiritual welfare of their godchildren, compadres extend the social, economic, and political networks of the family: "One of the compadre system's chief functions is to increase an individual's social assets, or those upon whom he can rely for help. For example, compadres are often asked for small favors and small loans" (Chavez 1982: 113). Godparents give their godchildren advice, gifts, preferment in employment, and sometimes economic aid. As a social insurance policy, godchildren often give goods, eggs, a chicken or a cuy, and labor to their godparents without expecting an immediate return. Later a young person might ask her indígena godparents for a job or go to her white-mestizo godparents for help with a land title problem, although using whites-mestizos as intermediaries is more rare now that Otavalos are better educated and less intimidated by government officials. Many Otavalos now have no white-mestizo compadres.

Compadres of all ethnicities owe their compadres help with the "small favors" and financial aid mentioned above, but the relationship between indígena compadres can also involve heavier labor and financial obligations. When one of my Peguche godsons was married in 1993, the indígena compadres of his parents brought substantial gifts of food. This will be reciprocated when someone in their compadres' family gets married. Having non-indígena compadres limits obligations because non-indígenas are unlikely to call upon their indígena compadres for aid of this kind. In Saraguro, Loja, people sometimes ask close relatives to be compadres in order to limit obligations on both sides (Belote and Belote 1977: 114–116), which is also true in Otavalo. There is prestige attached to foreign compadres. In fact, foreigners are replacing local whites-mestizos as desirable compadres because they can help with legal and bureaucratic problems, which are now international instead of local. More than anything, my compadres and godchildren want help with visas to the United States.

Kin and compadrazgo ties are important in recruiting labor and securing money for textile production. The treadle loom belt weavers in the community of Ariasucu depend more on kin and compadrazgo networks than on wages (Colloredo-Mansfeld 1994: 853, 1999: 146–147). Relatives and compadres are also important to Otavalos traveling and living abroad, functioning as essential links in transnational trade networks.

Peter Meier identified trends in Otavalo textile production based on fieldwork in the late 1970s. He argued that, as market participation increased, "peasant-craftsmen" would be forced to increase their productivity. Meier correctly insisted that this was possible without abandoning the household as the basic production unit, and he predicted that individual households, rather than communities, would develop textile specializations (1981: 162). This was occurring when I first visited Otavalo in 1973. Households do specialize, and many textiles are produced throughout the valley rather than in one particular town. I would add two modifications to Meier's argument, however. A family's specialty often changes in keeping with market trends, and many families have several specialties: belts and tapestry bags or fish-fabric cloth and tapestry bags, to name two.

Vestiges of the old community-based specializations remain. A few baskets are made in Punyaro. San Juan is still known for sheeting and head and shoulder wraps, Quinchuquí for blankets, Ilumán for felt hats, Agato and La Compañía for belts, and San Roque Bajo, Pucará, and La Compañía for totora reed mats. In Carabuela families who made ponchos on the backstrap loom turned to spinning yarn for sale and later to sweater knitting (Meier 1981: 195–206). All three occupations are still practiced there today, with backstrap-loom weaving the least remunerative and the least popular.

Although many households specialize, families are quick to switch production in response to demand. In the 1980s, one Peguche family wove wool ponchos for the white-mestizo and tourist trade. They also

José Manuel Bautista weaving a belt on the indigenous backstrap loom. This is the most time-consuming, least-remunerative weaving. Agato, July 1986.

bought factory-made fabric and used industrial sewing machines to tailor white pants and jackets for indígenas. In 1991, when loom-woven sweaters became popular, they switched production to these estera sweaters (named after the totora reed mats which they resemble). These quick changes are possible because the cost of retooling is minimal or nonexistent. The level of technology (treadle or electric looms and sewing machines) is relatively low, so that a number of products can be made on them without investing in new equipment.

Furthermore, the divisions between those who make goods and those who sell them are not clear cut; many families do both, and some also buy from other producers to fill gaps in their inventories. For example, many Otavalos weave tapestries and buy them from one another and from Salasaca indígenas who regularly visit the Otavalo market.

The parents of one of my Ilumán godsons have engaged in a variety of occupations and specialties since 1975, while raising five children and caring for orphaned cousins. The father, Daniel, began working at age twelve in 1967, winding bobbins in an indígena-owned factory in Otavalo. He later wove for the same factory then worked on an hacienda in

Santo Domingo and a sugarcane plantation in the Chota Valley. After his marriage in the mid-1970s, he wove for the factory again. He and his wife, Zoila, worked in the owner's artesanías store in Otavalo, sold textiles in the Poncho Plaza in Zoila's quarter-kiosk, then opened their own store on Calle Bolívar. Zoila also knitted hats and mittens.

Around 1981, Daniel and Zoila closed their store in Otavalo and bought a small house in Ilumán, turning the front room into a grocery store. Zoila ran the store while Daniel bicycled into Otavalo to weave for another indígena; later he wove at home. In the late 1980s, they closed the grocery store "because the children ate up the inventory." Daniel did construction work in Quito; Zoila spun and sold wool yarn and ran the Otavalo kiosk, while their two older sons wove hair wraps at home.

In 1990, Daniel sold artesanías in Quito, while his oldest son wove cloth for diapers at home and his second son braided hatbands for a neighbor. Throughout this decade the family members have woven tapestries that they sew into purses (with five looms in production at one period), woven estera sweaters, reverted to tapestry purses and daypacks, then made warp-faced bags. Zoila crochets or knits hats in her spare moments. Everyone helps with textile production in some way, and the entire family takes time off at planting and harvest to work the small plots of land it has access to.

As these examples indicate, families may specialize, but they do not necessarily keep the same specialty. Some people alternate between self-employment and wage labor. All the weaving-merchant families I know also plant and harvest on family land, but in no case is the food produced sufficient for subsistence.

Meier also predicted that household members themselves would specialize, resulting in commodity relationships among relatives (1981: 163). This, too, has occurred within the past fifteen years, but mainly among unmarried young people. Traditionally children wove for their parents as part of their contribution to the household. Now some young people want wages for this and will work for relatives or neighbors if their parents do not pay them.

Earnings "theoretically" belong to the earner (Parsons 1945: 33), and this is true in practice, which affords children and women (as well as men) a high degree of independence. One Peguche teenager, Juan Carlos, weaves not for his parents but as a paid worker for his sister and brother-in-law. His mother told me, "He wants clothes." Although Juan Carlos is not working for his parents, he is contributing to his support by buying his own clothes.

Adults have long been paid for textile work, especially if they work for another household. In this same extended Peguche family a great aunt and her mentally retarded son specialize in carding wool and spinning yarn, which they sell to relatives, Lucita Fichamba and José Cotacachi. They live in adjoining houses, so it is easy for the families to cooperate. Lucita's brother and his wife are paid to hem tapestries for them. This, too, is facilitated by propinquity, as the brother and his wife live about fifty feet away. Note the importance of kin networks in textile production.

Other trends are discernible, some of which are amplifications of those noted earlier. Otavalo textile production remains a cottage industry. Three local factories, Pintex and San Miguel (cotton jersey) and San Pedro (blankets), employ perhaps 300 or 400 indígenas, extrapolating from the statistics of Fredy Rivera Vélez (1988: 74–75). Otavalos do not constitute an industrial proletariat; nor are they on the road to becoming one.

Households vary in the ways in which they are involved in the textile and tourism economies. Some families process raw materials, buying wool at the Saturday market. During the week they clean, wash, card, and spin it in addition to engaging in semisubsistence agricultural work. A pound of yarn per day is typical, so they have five or six pounds of yarn a week to sell to other indígenas or to white-mestizo sweater knitters in Mira or elsewhere. Spinning is traditional in Carabuela, but there are families in virtually every community who spin.

If we tracked yarn the way we track endangered animal species, we would find surprising migratory patterns. Some yarn ends up in a sweater handknit in Mira that is sold to a Canadian importer, who sells the sweater to a store in Winnipeg, where it is bought by a visitor from Montreal. Some yarn goes into a tapestry woven in Ilumán that is sold to an indígena family living in Otavalo that sells it in the Poncho Plaza to a tourist from Italy. Other yarn is sold to a white-mestizo woman in Carabuela who sells it to indígena relatives in Peguche. They weave the yarn into estera sweaters which they sell directly to an exporter from France. Or the yarn is sold to an indígena in Carabuela who weaves it on the backstrap loom into a poncho which he sells to an Otavalo at the Saturday market.

The yarn-spinning family may be monolingual Quichua speakers who have never spoken to a *gringo* (Sp. foreigner), but their livelihood is dependent on market conditions in distant countries. They are integrated into the global economy whether they realize it or not. These fami-

Yarn and fleece vendors in the Poncho Plaza along Calle Jaramillo. Otavalo
Saturday market, October 1981.

lies are at the bottom of the textile food chain and make the smallest
profit of anyone involved in the production and marketing of the goods
made from their yarn. The spinners (often widows, single mothers, or
the elderly) still have a place in the industry because there is such a high
demand for wool yarn; but their share of the market is decreasing, and
people who are able to perform more lucrative work do so.

Another trend is that many Otavalos are abandoning the low-end,
most time-consuming, least-remunerative textile processes, beginning
with distaff and hand-spindle spinning. By the 1970s, virtually no Otavalos were spinning this way. Only once in twenty-five years have I seen
an Otavaleña using the hand spindle, in 1993 near Lago San Pablo. Spinning with the distaff or tripod to hold the fiber and hand spindle co-
existed with the European-introduced walking wheel from shortly after
the Spanish conquest through the 1960s, with an increasing share of the
spinning for production weaving done on the wheel. The Spanish quickly
recognized that spinning with the hand spindle accounted for approximately 70% of the human labor-hours involved in textile production, so
they introduced European technology and altered the gender division of
labor by making males spin in obrajes with walking wheels.

In the early 1960s, there were very few indígena workshops in Otavalo; but between 1967 and 1972 they proliferated, with the majority functioning in rented space. By 1972, there were 235 workshops in town; 200 of these were "small and traditional" with two or three treadle looms, a spinning wheel, hand carders, and three to five indígena workers, including the owner (Villavicencio 1973: 90–91).

In 1972, there were nearly thirty medium-sized textile enterprises in Otavalo, with treadle looms and two or three electric looms or knitting machines and seven to ten indígena employees. These workshops diversified production, making sweaters as well as fabric, anakus, and ponchos, shawls, and scarves with new designs. There were five indígena-owned large enterprises, "small factories" with a capitalization of S/200,000 ($8,000 in 1970), belonging to the Muenala, Cotacachi, and Lema families. The larger factories had "mestiza" workers, who sewed garments on overlock sewing machines. Some employees took work home and were paid by the piece (Villavicencio 1973: 90–91). Today the number of workshops in Otavalo has decreased considerably, replaced by artesanías stores, and fewer people do their own spinning.

By the mid-1970s, demand was outstripping the wool supply. Otavalos began buying wool and cotton yarn as well as factory-made synthetic acrylic yarn from factories in Ambato and Quito. Using synthetic yarn avoids the labor of washing, carding, dyeing, and spinning, although some families handspin acrylic leavings or brushings, called "wool from the factory." In the early 1980s, this was imported from Japan. The demand for wool yarn is now so high that the Ambato factories are importing sheep's wool from Peru, Bolivia, and Uruguay. Because Ecuador's alpacas were hunted to extinction in the colonial era, there is virtually no alpaca fleece or yarn available except from a few small herds reintroduced into southern Ecuador in the 1980s.

Besides the movement away from handspinning there has been a shift from backstrap looms to treadle looms to sewing machines. Hand weaving—a low-end, time-consuming activity—is yielding to more efficient production. The logical progression would seem to be from the backstrap to the treadle to the electric loom, but many electric looms are expensive and require a large capital outlay, often $3,000 for a used Jacquard. Furthermore, electric looms need a reliable electricity supply. Infrastructure varies among and within communities. Guanansi, located just across the highway from Peguche, still has no electricity. In Ilumán some families have electricity and others do not. Moreover, Ecuador has experienced annual periods of severe electricity shortages and rationing in recent years.

Rodrigo Cabascango with fish-motif fabric on the family's electric Jacquard loom. Ilumán, September 1995.

Warping the loom, weaving, finishing, and tailoring cloth takes time. Otavalos are increasingly skipping the spinning and weaving phases, buying factory-made cloth and sewing it. Not everyone does this; some families specialize in weaving cotton or acrylic cloth or fish-motif fabric, which they and other families cut and sew into clothes or bags, and some families specialize in making wallets, fanny packs, vests, and small bags from Gualaceo-area ikat textiles. But the shift toward using factory-made fabric is unmistakable. In the early to mid-1980s, families were already sewing cotton clothing for the local, tourist, and export market from fabric made by the Deltex, Textil Ecuador, and La Internacional factories in Quito.

Capitalism demands the constant introduction of new products and fast adaptation to changing consumer tastes: "Improved systems of communication and information flow, coupled with rationalizations in techniques of distribution (packaging, inventory control, containerization, market feed-back, etc.), made it possible to circulate commodities through the market system with greater speed" (Harvey 1989: 285). This process is observable in Otavalo in the emphasis on more efficient production, rapid introduction of new products, extension of telephone service to rural communities, and improved international communication, including FAXes and the Internet.

Around 1990, the Hilana factory in Quito began marketing wool or alpaca blankets with "Exclusive Ethnic Designs in Natural Colors or Cochineal Dye" (Q. Magazine, December 1994: 8). Other factories including Deltex make similar thick acrylic cloth. In 1991, this fabric was tailored into boxy unisex jackets in pullover or cardigan styles, with collar or hood, and patch or hand-warmer pockets. They became popular with tourists and exporters—the J. Peterman Company featured them in its catalog. The first jackets had gray or brown on cream motifs including llamas, but by 1994 the Hilana factory had added more colors. In 1998, Hilana opened an outlet in Otavalo where it sells yarn, fabrics, and finished textiles, including scarves, ponchos, capes, blankets, and bedroom slippers.

In the early 1990s, another new fabric and subsequent line of products appeared. The cloth is made from synthetic yarn with brocade motifs, often taken from pre-Hispanic Peruvian textiles. It has the weight and texture of upholstery fabric and is sold in two-meter-wide rolls in stores and in the Otavalo market. Otavalos would not tell me where they obtained this cloth except that it came from a factory in Quito, probably for fear that I was an exporter trying to get a monopoly on production. I later learned that it is produced by the Quito Deltex and Hilana factories. Some may come from Textiles Nacionales, Ecuador's largest textile factory. The cloth has an ethnic Andean look, and Otavalos began sewing it into clothing and bags.

Another trend is the blurring of gender divisions of labor. Historically, spinning with the hand spindle was considered a female occupation, while weaving on the backstrap loom was a male one. In the early 1970s, there was "a clear division of tasks between the man and woman" in textile production: "The first is charged with dyeing and weaving, and the second task especially is designated exclusively for him; the woman washes, cards, and spins the wool. On occasion, the man may also perform these activities, except for spinning" (Villavicencio 1973: 93; my translation). By the mid-1980s, Otavalos paid lip service to these divisions but increasingly ignored them in practice (Meisch 1987: 80).

By the 1990s, even lip service had been abandoned. The pendulum has swung so far that an Ecuadorian newspaper published an article about an Otavalo weaver titled "Weaving Is a Part of Me," but the weaver was a young woman, María Lucila de la Torre of Ilumán, a high school graduate. The interviewer wrote: "She is very amiable, very open. She is not inhibited by the tape recorder or the camera, posing naturally, elegantly, serenely, perhaps because the fact of being so pretty allows her to act with such security" (Miranda 1994: 8-B; my translation). The assumption that María's confidence and serenity comes from being pretty is a white-mestizo concept. Indígenas place a far greater emphasis on competence and hard work than they do on physical beauty, which is recognized but comparatively less important.

María wove one and a half or two tapestries per day, but the reporter did not say how much she was paid. The tapestries were exported because, as María explained, "It's better to export because you profit from the volume—the individual price is lower than in the fair, but in the plaza in Otavalo you don't sell as well as before because there is so much competition."

When the reporter asked if she liked to weave, María answered, "Yes, I like it very much, although in reality I want to enter the university and study English." María said her arms and legs ached at the end of the day, but she was content for now. She added: "I like the idea that my work is hung on the walls of houses so far away. It's like a little piece of me goes outside in each tapestry. That is a sensation that is very pleasant, very rare" (ibid.). Times have changed: a young woman weaver with plans to attend the university and learn English is no longer a rarity.

Otavalos are pragmatic rather than dogmatic about the division of labor. The idea is to get the job done: if a family has only daughters, they learn to weave; if the females are busy, a male may card and spin wool. Both boys and girls are educated, often as much as the family's finances permit; and many tasks, including farming, storekeeping, market sales, and textile chores, are done by both sexes. Childcare, hauling water, laundry, and cooking are considered female work, but it is not unusual to see males serving plates to guests at fiestas or, less frequently, boys helping with cooking, dishwashing, and laundry, sometimes with a baby brother or sister tied on their backs.

Another reason for the changing gender roles is the increased temporary or long-term absence of males. One woman in Ilumán who has two sons drew the line at more children. She told her husband, "Two are enough," explaining to me that he regularly travels to Guayaquil for two weeks at a time on business. She cares for the boys and the house, does agricultural work, supervises the weavers who work for them, and sells in the Otavalo market. While I do not know what type of contraception she uses, common forms among Otavaleñas include tubal ligation, the pill, IUDs, and, in desperate circumstances, illegal abortion.

To remain competitive, Otavalos are also working longer and harder. In 1994, an Otavaleño store owner told me, "For us there are no Sundays." Formerly Sunday was a day of rest, and Monday was called "little

Handknit sweaters arriving at a family's store in Otavalo. November 1994.

Sunday" because indígenas, particularly wage laborers, sometimes took the day off. That same year, I visited compadres in Ilumán on Sunday and was surprised to find them cutting and sewing vests. It was the first time I had encountered indígenas producing textiles on Sunday. A co-madre said, "Saturdays we wake up without sleeping," meaning they stayed up all night Friday to get textiles ready for the Saturday market. Evidently the family sometimes works on Sunday as well. Otavaleño sociologist (and mayor as of August 10, 2000) Mario Conejo noted the Otavalos' "self-exploitation" (personal communication, 1995). An alternative or addition to intensified production is to sell textiles and play music abroad, and many families combine these strategies. Some families are working harder and prospering, but others are working harder and longer just to stay in place.

Otavalos attempt to carve local, national, and international market niches, some of which overlap. For example, the majority of the blankets woven in Quinchuquí are sold to other Ecuadorians, but tourists sometimes buy them. This is true for many products; sweaters are sold mainly to tourists and exporters, but also to Ecuadorians.

Indígenas of all ethnic groups constitute one market for Otavalo goods. The *alpargata* (Sp. sandal) makers of communities near Cotacachi, fachalina weavers in San Juan, belt weavers in La Compañía and Agato, and mat weavers in communities around Lago San Pablo produce for the indigenous market. Ariasucu treadle-loom belt weavers also "specialize in products for indigenous women in other parts of the Ecuadorian highlands" (Colloredo-Mansfeld 1994: 846).

The few remaining backstrap-loom poncho weavers in such communities as San Roque, Carabuela, and San Luis de Agualongo weave for indígenas, as do those who mass produce ponchos on treadle or electric looms for sale in Cotopaxi, Tungurahua, Chimborazo, and Loja provinces. The weavers of hair wraps and mother and baby belts, and families who sew white pants or embroider and sew Otavaleña blouses also produce for indígenas. Otavalos are happy to sell anything to anyone, but many have a target clientele.

Whites-mestizos constitute another market. In the late 1970s, Otavalos sold more textiles to other Ecuadorians than to tourists, but this has changed. Still, white-mestizo Ecuadorians and other South Americans are important customers. In 1986, an indígena family living in Otavalo exported 800 to 1,000 embroidered acrylic dresses a month to Chile. Another indígena family in Quinchuquí received orders for several hundred acrylic ponchos each month, which an Otavalo merchant took to Venezuela (Meisch 1987: 89).

The fish-motif daypacks, an invention of Huaco Lema of Peguche, are sold throughout the Americas and the Caribbean. Many are shipped to Costa Rica, where they are sold by Otavalos in stores or on the street. In fact, Huaco said he invented the fish-motif fabric after visiting Curaçao. He noticed that there were no traditional crafts, so he invented one. In a 1995 interview, Huaco said: "In the Caribbean islands the tourists are millionaires, but there aren't any artesanías. So we export our textiles to the Caribbean, adding the label Curaçao, and the tourists buy them as if they were a product of the island" (Frank 1995: B-7; my translation). This was a lucrative business until everyone started copying him. "I built this house with the profits," he told me, indicating a new two-story house in Peguche.

The copying of successful products is a concern to many Otavalos. Some families sell textiles only from their homes or to certain exclusive stores in Quito but not in the Poncho Plaza, because they fear imitators (Meisch 1987: 91). On several occasions families asked me not to wear around Otavalo something I bought from them because they did not want others to see it. Inevitably, commercially successful items are copied because sooner or later other producers find out about them.

Foreigners, both visitors to Ecuador and customers abroad, are another market and have constituted the largest and most lucrative outlet for valley artesanías since the late 1980s. An Otavaleño with stores in Quito, who makes silk-screened and batiked T-shirts, estimated that 90% of his business was for export. There are three subcategories in the foreign market. The first is "cheap," because for some buyers price is their main criterion. They do not care if the textile was handmade by a descendant of Atahualpa in Otavalo or by prison labor in China as long as it is inexpensive. Some Otavalos think that competing on the basis of price alone is a bad long-term strategy. Mario Conejo, who founded a small artisans' organization, Fundación Tukapu, said: "The person who buys a [cheap] sweater, to give an example, will not buy another because the colors run, the knitting is bad, and the style is uncomfortable. There-fore, if we want to secure the market in the long run, we have to make an effort. We have to compete on the basis of quality" (Craps 1992: 14; my translation).

A second niche is handmade crafts resulting from cottage industry production, regardless of how many components are industrially fabri-cated or handmade elsewhere. At the least, these products are assembled in the home. Otavalos are not averse to playing up the handmade, ethnic quality of these goods. Some buyers will pay more if they believe that crafts are homemade, if not entirely handmade, and many visitors will pay a good price or not bargain hard out of a desire to support the artisans.

Because the first two niches constitute the largest segment of Ota-valo sales, it is worth examining one product in detail: handmade sweat-ers are sold as cheap goods or as handmade crafts. Sweaters also illus-trate many of the themes discussed above: household-based production, the utilization of kin and compadrazgo networks, increasing mechani-zation, and growing reliance on global sales.

Handknit or woven wool or cotton sweaters (Sp. *chompas*) count for millions of dollars in sales in the valley. By 1985, approximately 30,000 sweaters were shipped abroad annually, and Otavalo merchants were selling perhaps 3,000 more in the market (Meisch 1987: 81–82). A 1993 study by CENAPIA (Sp. National Center for Small Industry) estimated that 100,000 sweaters were handknitted in Ecuador each month by some 15,000 primarily female knitters (de Sarte 1993: B-4). A major Otavalo sweater exporter independently told me he estimated that at least a mil-lion sweaters are produced each year. The CENAPIA report focused on handknit wool sweaters, not the newly introduced woven (estera) sweat-ers, which are unique to Otavalo. Estera sweaters, produced in the thou-sands, are made from loom-woven fabric which is cut and sewn together; crocheted or handknit cuffs and collars are then added.

In 1998, handknit sweaters were sold in Ecuador for an average of $13, which means that sweaters brought in at least $15,600,000 gross annually, not counting income generated by such supporting industries as trucking, label and box production, and air freight. Top-quality sweaters sold for $16 or $17, and many exporters deal only in these; others, usually small-scale hippie exporters, buy the cheaper ones. Sweaters are sold directly to customers in Otavalo, in kiosks and stores in Quito, in border towns like Tulcán and Huaquillas, and directly from the knitters' homes. Sweaters are also shipped or carried abroad by traveling Otavalos and other Ecuadorians. Only those sweaters exported by sea or air freight are counted in Banco Central's statistics, which makes the total exported difficult to compute.

The industry is concentrated around Gualaceo and Nabón in Azuay province in the south and in parts of Imbabura and Carchi provinces in the north. Sweater knitting for cash in northern Ecuador was introduced as a Peace Corps project in 1964 by Emily Gladhart in Mira and has been phenomenally successful. Problems with the wool yarn supply in Mira were solved in 1972, when indígenas from Carabuela visited Mira with yarn for sale (Gladhart and Gladhart 1981: 13; Korovkin et al. 1994: 22). By 1979, Otavalos, including women, were involved in the sweater trade, buying directly from Mira knitters (Gladhart and Gladhart 1981: 8).

There is a frenzy of activity as fall approaches in the northern hemisphere, when sweater sales peak. Several Otavalos and foreigners have become large-scale sweater producers. Foreigners place orders through them, and they oversee a string of dyers and knitters. The producers advance the dyed wool or cotton yarn, patterns, buttons, and labels and see that the sweaters are produced and shipped on time in the correct sizes and styles. Exporters carry, mail, or FAX drawings of the desired styles to Otavalo. One producer showed me a sample sweater that looked perfect, but a careful comparison with the exporter's drawing showed that the stars in one row were knit with their points off the central axis. Producers also label, package, and ship the sweaters, charging between $1 and $2 per sweater for their services.

The knitters are primarily white-mestiza housewives who work at home, although some are indígenas of either sex. In the system described above, all costs are borne by the producer and exporter; the knitters invest only their labor. Most can knit one or two high-quality sweaters per week, for which they are paid $4–$5 each. The producers weigh the amount of yarn they give a knitter and expect the same weight back in finished goods, but there is some yarn theft. Approximately one sweater out of seven is made from "appropriated" yarn (Gladhart and Gladhart

1981: 15). When the knitters appropriate enough yarn, they make sweat-ers which they sell to Otavalo merchants (some of whom visit the knit-ting communities) or to a store or kiosk vendor in Otavalo. Independent knitters or sweater weavers can sell to exporters or producers for what-ever the market will bear.

Producing sweaters involves a large capital outlay. One producer told me he had $90,000 worth of yarn out. The value of the producers to the exporters is that, although they realize less profit, they do not have to stay in Ecuador and oversee these operations and are guaranteed delivery of the correct order on time. Large sums of money are advanced on trust, and sometimes things go wrong. Exporters usually wire half the cost of their order in advance so that the producer has working capital; the sec-ond half is paid on delivery. One U.S. producer was owed $180,000 when a Canadian exporter from Calgary went bankrupt. This same exporter owed one Otavaleño $7,000 and another $6,000, money which they may never recover.

One Otavaleño sweater producer decided to expand into tourism and invested sweater money advanced to him in his new hotel, intending to recover the money in time to meet his sweater orders. In 1995, however, the producer's hotel did not bring in profits as planned, and he missed shipments to his clients. In addition, he was owed $7,000 by the bank-rupt Canadian. Several exporters, after frantic phone calls and FAXes to Otavalo, flew to Ecuador to confront him. The day before one exporter arrived, I saw the producer's son in the Otavalo market loading a large truck with inferior-quality sweaters. The producer told his clients to take them or leave them. The clients insisted they would never work with this producer again, but other producers were not accepting more clients because they simply could not handle more business.

Around 1990, Otavalos began weaving, as well as knitting, fabric for sweaters on treadle looms in a loose houndstooth or basket weave (estera sweaters), the invention of a Peguche weaver, Segundo "Piki" (Q. Flea) Gramal. Weaving sweaters is an indígena occupation, although whites-mestizos are sometimes employed to sew the sweaters together or to knit and attach the collars and cuffs.

The sweater business is deeply embedded in the global political econ-omy. A stock market crash or plant closing abroad means that retail sales drop and exporters go bankrupt or place smaller orders in Otavalo. The 1995 border war with Peru interrupted trade, causing wool shortages in Ecuador as well as substantial losses to Otavalo merchants who sold arte-sanías to Peruvians in the border town of Huaquillas; but with a ceasefire

Lucita Cotacachi finishing the cuff on a woven estera sweater, which resembles mats (Sp. *esteras*) made around Lago San Pablo. Peguche, July 1996.

and later peace treaty, this structural barrier was removed. The 1997–1998 El Niño, which flooded the coasts of Peru and Ecuador, resulted in an abnormally warm winter in the northern hemisphere, and sweater sales dropped.

As living costs for Otavalos rise, sweater-making families have several options. They can accept lower profits, which is difficult or impossible for families operating on a low profit margin. They can also work harder or raise prices. If a $15 sweater goes to $16, the wholesaler must market it at $64; a 400% markup is standard for exporters, which Otavalos understand.

Most exporters buy sweaters for less than $15 or $16, and some take low markups. A $10 sweater will wholesale for $36 or $40 rather than the $64 charged for top-quality sweaters. Retailers usually add another 100%; hence many exporters also retail sweaters. Soon Ecuadorian sweaters will be as expensive as those made in Scotland and Ireland, but they are not as fine. The wool in cheap Ecuadorian sweaters is often coarsely spun with tiny sticks and burrs, and the dyes run; but high-priced Ecuadorian sweaters cannot easily compete with sweaters from Ireland, Scotland, Peru, Bolivia, and Uruguay that are made of cashmere, alpaca, or better-quality wool.

Ethnic art is a third, specialized market niche with few occupants. The idea is to increase the value of textiles by raising their classification from crafts (Sp. *artesanías*) to art (Sp. *arte*), a distinction which is Euro-American, not indigenous. The Sna Jolobil cooperative in San Cristóbal de las Casas, Chiapas, does this: the price people are willing to pay "will depend on whether the textiles are seen as ethnographic curios, peasant costumes, fine weavings or works of art." If textiles "appear in museums and art books, the perception is quite different than in postcards. Chiapas textiles had to be 'legitimated' through the proper institutions" (Morris 1991: 422).

Several Otavalos have successfully gone the ethnic art route. Miguel Andrango and members of the Tahuantinsuyu Weaving Workshop in Agato specialize in fine backstrap loom-woven textiles, including blankets, wall hangings, scarves, belts, shoulder bags, and small rugs. The blankets sell for $100 as a traditional Otavalo art form—art, not craft. Andrango and his family also demonstrate backstrap-loom weaving to visitors to their house and at weavers' conferences in the United States and Europe. They sell to the Jackalope Shop in Santa Fe, New Mexico, which printed a postcard of Miguel by his loom. Luz María Andrango appeared on the cover of the Lonely Planet guide to Ecuador, and this cover is framed and displayed in the family's Agato house. The publicity from the guidebook brought additional visitors to their house, which is on the itinerary of many guided tours.

Tapestries are an Otavalo standby that some indígenas have attempted to raise from craft to art. They can be sold as either, depending on their quality and the marketing concepts employed. Tapestries are usually sold as wall hangings, which helps when they are marketed as fine art because of the medieval and Renaissance European tradition of hanging tapestries on walls and the association of hanging art with the Euro-American fine arts of painting, etching, and photography.

New tapestry designs are added regularly from a variety of sources, including M. C. Escher drawings which Peace Corps volunteer John Ortman saw on T-shirts my boyfriend and I were wearing in 1973. He thought the interlocking designs would make good tapestries and asked us to bring him a catalog from an Escher exhibition in Berkeley. Later the Ortmans commissioned fish-motif tapestries (originally Mexican) to sell in the Caribbean; these have been widely copied. Ecuadorian designer Olga Fisch introduced new tapestry designs and sold tapestries as ethnic art in her Quito stores, relying on high-quality work by Otavalos and Salasacas. Other sources for tapestry designs range from Navajo rugs

Mid-level technology: José Cotacachi weaving tapestries on the European-introduced treadle loom. Peguche, July 1996.

and tapestries from San Pedro de Cajas, Peru, to the cover of Charijayac's *Cielo Rosa* album and motifs invented by the weavers.

In the 1970s, someone began joining two small, square tapestries with a handwoven band to make purses, resulting in a new market for small tapestries. The better bags are lined and have a zipper closing. Next came daypacks inspired by those used by foreigners. Some daypacks have a tapestry body, cloth lining, and a leather bottom, top, and straps. New in 1994 were tapestries with an American Southwest flavor cut and sewn into vests. Tourists short on wall space often buy something useful made from tapestries. Most of these items are marketed as crafts, with an emphasis on the amount of hand weaving involved.

José María Cotacachi and Lucita Fichamba of Peguche specialize in tapestries as art. The family members, with hired help, make well-dyed and well-designed, high-quality wool tapestries. José María often invents his own designs and surprised me one afternoon by stopping at my Otavalo house with his camera to photograph one of his tapestries hanging on my wall. He explained that he keeps a photographic record of his designs so that he can show them to exporters or repeat them as needed and had forgotten to photograph that model.

The Cotacachi-Fichamba family realized that many foreigners have more money than time, so rather than sell their tapestries unfinished with the ends left to unravel (as everyone else does) they hem them. They add a row of loops at the top for a hanging rod and tassels or fringe at the bottom that are color coordinated with the body of the tapestry. To date they are the only Otavalos to finish tapestries this way, and they charge more for them. Their next idea was to make tapestries three-dimensional by adding tiny brass charms or figures from Cotacachi or by attaching a tiny protruding yarn braid to the back of the head of a woven figure.

José and Lucita have made several trips to the United States, and perhaps their travels inspired José to sign his tapestries in the lower left-hand corner with an embroidered "José C." This, too, is an innovation and an attempt to move from anonymous crafts to signed art. It is amazing what the signature does for sales, because foreign tourists understand and appreciate the concept of a signed piece. So far José María is the only Otavalo to sign textiles.

Carlos Conterón, Rosa Elena de la Torre, and some of their family in Ilumán specialize in fine backstrap loom-woven belts and wall hangings. Family members demonstrate weaving to visitors to their store, Artesanías Inti Chumbi, which increases the visitors' appreciation of the labor involved. Rosa Elena makes dolls wearing exact replicas of Otavalo or Cayambe costume and embroiders aprons. The Andrangos and Conteróns sometimes incorporate weaving techniques from Peru, Bolivia, and Guatemala.

The fine-art niche for backstrap loom-woven textiles is small, because most visitors do not understand the amount of time invested in these pieces and are unwilling to pay what the labor demands. In terms of economic strategy, tapestries woven on the treadle loom and marketed as ethnic art are more lucrative because they can be woven more quickly and give a greater return on time invested.

The Indigenous Reconquest of Otavalo

Indigenous migration to Otavalo from rural communities because of land shortages and the desire to participate in textile merchandising has accelerated each decade since 1970. In 1974, the town of Otavalo had 2,849 indígenas, who constituted 20.5% of the approximately 13,900 inhabitants (Chavez 1982: 7). In the 1970s and 1980s, indígenas opened restaurants, folk-music clubs, hotels, bus lines, and other businesses in Otavalo and began buying or renting property in the town, until the northern half of Otavalo became 65% to 75% indigenous. In 1977–1978, the block in which Chavez lived in the northeastern sector was 71% indígena (ibid.: 61).

According to a 1995 survey, Otavalo was 70% indígena (17,500 persons), and a writer noted that "Otavalo was reconquered by the Indians" (Frank 1995: B-7; my translation). If only the northern *half* of Otavalo were 70% indígena in 1995, this meant an indigenous population of roughly 8,750. Zulay Saravino, owner of a local tourist agency, estimated that more than half the population of Otavalo as a whole was indígena, meaning 12,500 indigenous residents. Zulay called it "a complete change" and said, "The Otavaleños are the owners of Otavalo." This change includes indigenous ownership of new multistory, concrete-block apartment buildings and artesanías stores, renovated older homes, and such businesses as air freight companies, yarn stores, hotels, and restaurants. Extrapolating from the 1990 census, I estimate the 2001 population of Otavalo to be 26,000 and 70% indigenous, counting such barrios as Monserrat and La Joya.

In the early 1960s, there were "several" stores in Otavalo selling artesanías (Cooper 1965). By 1978, there 75 such stores, most of them indígena-owned and -operated (Schultz et al. n.d. [1978]: 306). In the summer of 1981, I mapped the indígena-owned stores in the north-central part of Otavalo. There were at least 78 artesanías stores, with more outside my map. In 1994, I mapped all the artesanías stores, and by November there were 135. There were 147 stores when I repeated my mapping in January 1995 and around 155 in 1999. About 90% of these were indígena-owned and -operated.

My maps show that the commercial center of gravity has shifted northwest toward the Poncho Plaza. In 1981, there were 11 artesanías stores on Calle Sucre and 24 on Calle Bolívar. By 1995, there were 44 stores on Sucre and 28 on Bolívar. In 1981, there were 5 stores on Calle Jaramillo; in 1995 there were 20. The greatest concentration of stores had moved one block north, and there were 37 stores in the row of blocks bordering the Poncho Plaza between Calles Salinas and Morales.

More than the number of stores has changed. Through the late 1980s, the artesanías stores in town were identical: dark and dusty, often lit by one bare, 40-watt light bulb. To be competitive, the owners felt they needed a little of everything. Items were stacked on shelves or hung helter-skelter around the store and in the doorway. The shops looked cluttered and junky. With such mixed but limited selections, if a store had the right size it often did not have the right color. In 1979, Lawrence Carpenter and I suggested to several shop owners that they specialize in one product, but no one thought it was a good idea.

By 1988 or 1989, however, there were four or five stores that specialized in one or two items, especially sweaters and jackets. These were
often the store fronts of producers who stockpiled for their export customers, but they attracted people off the street. Later stores specializing in T-shirts and batiked or tie-dyed clothing opened. Display styles
also changed, beginning around 1991. Suddenly light, airy stores opened,
some in new buildings with large display windows and horizontal hanging poles for sweaters or T-shirts. The electric lighting in these stores
was better, and the merchandise was displayed to greater effect. These
stores are far more visually appealing, which has probably resulted in improved sales. Some of these store owners have traveled and lived abroad
—one Otavaleño spent twelve years in Europe—and have learned about
merchandising during their travels.

In 1994, I interviewed the owners or managers of Otavalo yarn stores,
obtaining data from about three-fourths of them on yarn types, origin,
use, and annual sales to get an idea of the quantities of raw materials
used in the textile industry. Several stores were run by ten-year-olds who
had no idea of sales figures or were not about to tell a stranger in any
event, and I never encountered their parents or an adult in the shop no
matter how many times I returned.

These stores carried only cotton, rayon, or synthetic fibers. Perhaps
because there is such intense competition for wool yarn, I could not obtain wool yarn sales figures from any store that carried it. A large proportion of the above yarn is manufactured in Ecuador, but some is imported.

Textiles Río Blanco in Quito is a major producer of cotton yarn, one
of ten Ecuadorian factories that produce yarn exclusively. Río Blanco's
cotton yarn may be used in handknit cotton sweaters which are made in
the same communities that produce wool ones. Because of a scarcity of
Ecuadorian cotton, Río Blanco imports cotton from the United States.
Cotton is listed on the New York and London stock exchanges; when the
price of cotton rises internationally, the cost of cotton yarn increases in
Ecuador. Between November 1994 and July 1995, the price of cotton rose
40%. In addition, because the dollar had been rising constantly against
the sucre, in July 1995 Río Blanco increased prices 12 to 13% (*Hoy, Econo-
mía*, July 3–10, 1995: 8), another example of how the Otavalo region is
globally connected.

Exporters of Ecuadorian artesanías, who sometimes combine relax-
ation with work, make substantial contributions to the economy. In
1986, I interviewed all the foreign exporters I encountered in Otavalo
and estimated that they poured more than $2 million annually into the
economy of northern Ecuador (Meisch 1987: 88). At that time, there were

TABLE 3.1. *Yarn Sales in Otavalo, 1994*

Store	Yarn Type	Origin	Use	Annual Sales (in tons)
(A)	acrylic	"a secret"	weaving, knitting	13.2
(B)	acrylic	Delltex Factory, Quito	weaving, knitting, including Atuntaqui sweater factory	720.0
(C)	cotton	China	weaving, knitting, embroidery, bracelets	
	polyester thread	USA	sewing	
	rayon (*seda*)	Brazil, China	embroidery on Otavaleña blouses	5.28
(D)	acrylic	various, including Lanafit factory, Quito	weaving, knitting	18.0
(E)	cotton, polyester thread	USA	sewing	
	cotton	China	embroidery, "any artesanías"	1.98
(F)	acrylic	Lanafit factory, Quito	weaving, knitting	528.0
(G)	acrylic	Lanafit factory, Quito	weaving, knitting	184.8
(H)	acrylic	Quito	weaving, knitting	66.0

Total annual tonnage of yarn sold in these stores: 1,537.26.

no air cargo or shipping agencies in town; exporters hired a cab or truck to haul their merchandise to Quito. In 1994, I again interviewed all the exporters I could find, who probably constituted no more than half those who passed through town, and estimated that they invested about $12 million annually in merchandise in northern Ecuador, a figure which many exporters challenged as too low, suggesting that $50 million was more accurate.

The first air cargo company in Otavalo, Panatlantic, opened its doors in 1988. In 1993, there were seven air cargo agencies in Otavalo. By 1995, there were ten; by the summer of 1996, fourteen, and by 1998, sixteen, including Pacha Kutik, which is primarily indígena-owned. These companies are located in the north-central part of town near the Poncho Plaza. They provide boxes, pack goods, haul the merchandise to the Quito airport, and handle the paperwork, including the shipping papers and export taxes payable to Banco Central.

At the end of 1994, I interviewed all nine Otavalo air cargo companies about the kinds and amount of artesanías they handled that year. In all they shipped at least 1,500 tons of artesanías abroad. The owners or employees of some companies asked for anonymity, as they did not want their competition to know how much they shipped. Some companies had exact statistics; others estimated their tonnage.

The figure of 1,500 tons for 1994 is low, even for artesanías shipped only from Otavalo. After my census I visited a sweater producer in Otavalo who asked me what tonnage I had for the company he used. He said my figures were impossible. His shipping records were computerized; between April 1 and December 31, 1994, he shipped 138 tons of sweaters. This was higher than the figure his air freight company gave for the entire year, and it had many clients besides him. I added his tonnage to the

Artesanías boxed for export along Calle Quiroga. Otavalo, August 1996.

TABLE 3.2. *Air Cargo Shipped from Otavalo, 1994*

Air Freight Company	Destinations and Goods	Artesanías Shipped (in tons)
(A)	Mainly sweaters to New York, Canada, Germany, Italy, Portugal; woodcarvings to Spain; misc. to Venezuela	60
(B)	Wool items (sweaters, etc.) in summer and fall, cotton clothing in winter and spring. 50% shipped to the USA and Canada, 49% to Europe, especially England, Belgium, France, and Spain; 1% to Brazil, Argentina, and Chile	112.2
(C)	Wool jackets and sweaters for winter sales; also vests, bags, cotton shirts, light sweaters, ceramic cars and trucks to Spain; Holland; Switzerland; Germany; Austria; Portugal; Italy; Japan; Sidney, Australia; New York, Los Angeles, Washington, D.C., Denver, Spokane, Seattle, USA; Toronto, Montreal, Winnipeg, Vancouver, Canada; Costa Rica; Puerto Rico; Dominican Republic; Curaçao	264
(D)	Everything, especially sweaters, mainly to USA and Canada, but also to everywhere in Europe and to Japan	243.6
(E)	Everything (sweaters, jackets, bags, shirts, tapestries, etc.): the most tonnage shipped to USA; majority of clients in Europe, but they ship "all over the world"	594
(F)	A little of everything to Frankfurt, Germany; Chile; New York, USA; Amsterdam, Holland; Spain; Belgium; Switzerland; Lisbon, Portugal; Italy; and "a very little" to Singapore	66
(G)	No information on exactly what or where	26.4
(H)	All kinds of artesanías, mainly to Europe, followed by Canada and USA	66
(I)	All kinds of artesanías, mainly to Europe, especially Germany	66

Total tonnage of artesanías shipped abroad from Otavalo in 1994: 1,498.2.

company's total and included it in the above chart. In this case, the secretary made a rough calculation and obviously underestimated her company's tonnage. Additional tons of artesanías are shipped out by Michael Harrington's air cargo concern in Ibarra.

Each year the air cargo companies tell me that their business is up. This is a feedback loop, for more and better shipping facilities encourage exporters, and their business in turn encourages the establishment of more air cargo enterprises. During my strolls around Otavalo, I routinely note the destination written on boxes stacked outside the cargo offices. In the summer of 2000, these included Redding, California; Albuquerque and Santa Fe, New Mexico; Grand Rapids, Michigan; Newark, New Jersey; Atlanta, Georgia; New York City, New York; Minneapolis, Minnesota; Philadelphia, Pennsylvania; San Juan, Puerto Rico; Ottawa, Canada; Montevideo, Uruguay; São Palo, Brazil; Caracas, Venezuela; Copenhagen, Denmark; Hertogenbosch and Amsterdam, Holland; Luxembourg City, Luxembourg; Montpellier and Colmar, France; Bilbao, Spain; and Irish Craft Centre, Cork, Ireland (perhaps it is just my suspicious mind, but this suggests that Irish knitters cannot meet the demand for sweaters, so Otavalo-made ones are being sold as handmade Irish crafts).

Exact statistics on the value of goods exported are impossible to come by, especially since people underreport the cost of their goods to lower the taxes owed Banco Central. The $50 million estimate does not account for sales to visitors to the Otavalo market, Otavalo artesanías sold elsewhere in Ecuador, or goods shipped abroad from Quito and Guayaquil.

Other services opened in Otavalo in the 1990s, aimed primarily at indígenas involved in the export trade. In January 1994, a DHL package express office opened near the Parque Bolívar. For around $25 DHL delivers a small package to the United States in twenty-four hours. DHL offers Western Union money-wiring service—"money in minutes" to and from seventy-two countries from A (Alemania [Germany]) to V (Venezuela). The manager told me this was "because the Otavalos travel all over the world." United Parcel Service (UPS) also opened an office nearby.

The tourist and travel agencies in town, the first of which opened in 1985, offer money-changing and FAX services and (by 1998) e-mail. For many years the only money exchange was in the Hotel Otavalo. In the early 1990s, one opened on the northeast corner of Sucre and Colón; and in February 1995, VAZ Cambios opened on the Poncho Plaza. This money exchange advertises with a quadrilingual sign in Spanish, Quichua, English, and German and also has Western Union service. By 1998, money exchanges were sprouting like mushrooms, although with dollarization they have lost business.

Until recently, telephone service in most communities was limited to one phone in the civil registry or post office. It required months of waiting and large bribes to acquire a telephone in town. In September 1994, I passed long lines of indígenas and whites-mestizos outside the IETEL (telephone company) office in Otavalo, because they were finally expanding service. Telephones are a business necessity and a way to communicate with far-flung family members. Because so many older indígenas are illiterate, telephones are an extension of the customary oral communication. The initial cost for a line was $250. After that, basic service was only $0.14 a month plus a charge for each local or long-distance call. By 1999, several businesses in town were offering international Internet phone calls for S/3,000 ($0.27) per minute, about a third less than regular long-distance calls. A long-distance call from Barcelona, Spain, to Otavalo via the Internet was one-fifth the cost of regular long distance, as an expatriate comadre explained when she called us on the day of her daughter's confirmation in Otavalo.

Literate Otavalos with phone service and the money to invest are installing FAX machines, buying computers, getting e-mail accounts, and designing web pages. An Ecuadorian newspaper article reported that some textile stores in town had FAXes, computers, and cellular telephones (El Comercio, October 31, 1994: B-1), and a cellular phone company opened in Otavalo in early 1996. The new telephone service and the growth of air freight directly from Otavalo represent the kind of improved and accelerated information flows and rationalized distribution mentioned by Harvey (1989). In 1998, Cyber cafes appeared around town; and some of my godchildren acquired e-mail accounts through which we communicate when I am in the United States. Far from being isolated from international fashion and consumption trends, many Otavalos are a phone call, FAX, or web site away from the latest information.

Foreign Travel: "They Treated Us Like Princes"

Foreign travel by Otavalos began a slow, steady increase after the abolition of wasipungu, as did emigration to Ecuadorian destinations outside cantón Otavalo. My first encounter with Otavaleños was not in Ecuador but in Popayán, Colombia, in 1973, when I bought a scarf from an Otavaleño street vendor. I have no idea if he was a Colombian resident or on a temporary trip, but the Otavalo expatriate communities in Colombia (especially those in Popayán and Bogotá) are among the oldest Otavalo communities outside Ecuador.

By 1973, there were indígenas living in Quito, Guayaquil, San Gabriel in Carchi province, and Cayambe in Pichincha province (Villavicencio 1973: 248), but this author does not mention textile traders traveling or living abroad. She also wrote that "[l]ittle by little there is an increase in the number of Otavaleño indígenas who attend *colegio* [Sp. junior and senior high school] and even the university, and who have gone to study abroad (in Chile and the United States), without changing their dress or marrying members of other groups" (ibid.: 251; my translation).

In the 1970s, unsponsored travel to the United States, meaning travel as a tourist or merchant, was not an option, although apparently some Otavalos had the opportunity to study there. Among the earliest Otavalos to visit the United States were José Yacelga and his wife, Mercedes Otavalo. In January 1971, they were brought to Provo, Utah, by professors at Brigham Young University to help compile a Quichua-Spanish grammar and dictionary for Mormon missionary work. Their son Ricardo was born during the couple's ten-month stay in Provo. I first met José and Mercedes in Otavalo in the summer of 1989, when they stopped me on the street, asked me if I spoke English, and requested help filling out application papers for Ricardo's U.S. passport.

In 1994, I interviewed José in the family's booth on Calle Jaramillo near the Poncho Plaza, where they sell wrap skirts, headcloths, shoulder wraps, shawls, embroidered blouses, and cloth. I spoke mainly with José because Mercedes was busy with customers. José recalled: "I didn't meet any other Ecuadorians except a grandson of [Ecuadorian president] Eloy Alfaro, who was studying at Brigham Young University." Before José left Otavalo, he told his indígena friends about his trip. One of them said: " 'I wouldn't fly in an airplane for a room full of gold. You could die.' Now everyone is traveling abroad."

In the summer of 1995, José told me that Ricardo was based in Madison, Wisconsin, but traveled around the Midwest and East Coast (New York, Chicago, Miami) playing music with the Otavalo group Americamanta and selling textiles that the family shipped him, a typical pattern for young men of his generation.

Colombia has been a frequent Otavalo destination since the 1970s, but Peru was not popular before 1985, partly because of Peruvian protectionism: Otavalos were not allowed to sell textiles there. Another reason was the antagonism between the two countries dating back to the sixteenth-century war of succession between Huascar in Cuzco and Atahualpa in Quito as well as more recent border hostilities over oil-rich land in the Amazon Basin.

When Peace Corps volunteer Dennis Penley took his weaving teacher Miguel Andrango of Agato to Peru in 1973, they were harassed by Ecuadorian and Peruvian police and border guards, who were outraged that a gringo and an "indio" were traveling together. Dennis and Miguel were hauled off buses for passport checks and questioning and subjected to considerable verbal abuse. The Peru trip was still positive for Miguel. Indígenas in Chinchero, Peru, taught him their weaving techniques, which Miguel taught to other weavers in Agato and incorporated into his textiles. Miguel also visited the weaving workshop of Francesca Mayer in Huancayo (Meisch 1987: 162, 167). I know of no one who traveled to Peru besides Miguel Andrango until recently.

Foreign travel by Otavalos from 1970 through the mid-1980s was usually sponsored by development agencies and non-government organizations (NGOs), which paid expenses and helped Otavalos obtain passports and visas. A Peguche indígena, Germán Patricio Lema A., published an ethnography of Otavalo in 1995 with accounts of such trips. In 1983, Lema, representing the Cooperativa "Los Shyris de Peguche," was invited to visit Israel by NGOs. He participated in a conference on community development and toured the country (Lema 1995: 167).

On that same trip Lema visited Egypt, and the next year he participated in an international course on economic development for farmers in Europe. In 1986, he attended an international peace conference in Tripoli, Libya (ibid.: 168–169). Lema's account illustrates the extent to which he became part of an international development network that afforded him the opportunity to travel abroad.

I first visited Otavalo in 1973, but my interest was rekindled during my sojourn as a Fulbright scholar in 1977–1979. Although the focus of my research was textiles in southern Ecuador, I spent time in Otavalo. In 1979, I became the godmother by baptism to a baby from Ilumán, Blanca Yolanda Castañeda. Yolanda's aunt on her mother's side, María Olimpia, was in Bogotá, where she had been living since 1977. In a daring move for a young, unmarried indigenous woman, María Olimpia left Otavalo by herself to join the already established Otavalo community in Bogotá. She earned her living by sewing woven purses during the day and attended high school at night.

When María Olimpia returned to Otavalo for a visit in August 1979, she precipitated a family drama. The Arrayán parents were dead, and the husband of one of María's sisters decided to act *in loco parentis*. He forbade her to return to Bogotá and locked up her possessions. María appeared acquiescent but slowly retrieved her identification card and some of her belongings, which she stashed in our Otavalo apartment. María begged us not to tell her relatives, and we nodded in agreement when her brother-in-law said it looked like she was taking his advice and staying in Otavalo. In early September, we also nodded in agreement when María's relatives shook their heads in consternation and announced that she had sneaked back to Bogotá without saying good-bye.

María's main reason for returning to Bogotá was an Agato Otavaleño textile vendor with whom she had fallen in love, Germán, who sold his products in front of the Hotel Tequendama. The couple married in Otavalo in 1980 then went back to Bogotá, where they lived and raised their three children until 1996. During a July 1994 visit to Agato and Ilumán, Germán said he moved to Bogotá in 1977, when he was twenty. He estimated that there are about 500 Otavalos living in Bogotá, "but in different barrios." One way the Otavalos maintain their sense of community is through twenty different soccer teams, each with about ten players. The teams and their families meet for matches on Sunday afternoons.

Both María Olimpia and Germán wear traditional Otavalo dress, as do most of the expatriates of their generation. Their grade-school-aged son wears his hair long but does not wear the Otavalo white shirt and pants and blue poncho. Their two daughters in grade school and high school did not wear traditional dress in Bogotá, although they do in Ecuador. María Olimpia said they didn't want to be different from their classmates in Colombia. The parents cited economic reasons for their residence in Bogotá. Germán did a good business with textiles which he and hired weavers made in Bogotá and which he sold to clients throughout Colombia. He was the treasurer for the Padres de Familia (the South America version of the Parent-Teachers' Association) at his oldest daughter's junior high school and helped the school buy a television and VCR. The family visited Otavalo, proclaimed their Otavalo identity through the use of traditional dress, socialized with other Otavalos in Bogotá, and hosted their Ilumán nephews when the young men were traveling between Otavalo and Europe.

Colombia was no paradise, however. In 1985, the Otavalos' house in Bogotá was broken into by armed men who claimed to be members of a left-wing guerrilla group. They robbed the family of money and textiles and insisted the neighborhood pay them a monthly "tax." More recently,

Germán described how bombs were set off only blocks from their house in downtown Bogotá by cocaine kingpins. As insurance, María Olimpia and Germán bought a small piece of land in Ilumán, built a cement-block house, and by 1996 were living there permanently.

In 1979, Lawrence Carpenter and I became godparents to two-year-old Oscar Farinango Maldonado of Peguche at his confirmation. Until the mid-1980s, children of any age were confirmed, not just older ones. This was a boon for those who wanted foreign compadres because the ceremony was performed monthly, and they did not have to wait until after the child's first communion. Conspicuously absent from the church ceremony and subsequent party was Oscar's father, Luis Enrique, who was living in Barcelona, Spain. I did not meet my compadre until 1985, when he and I were in Otavalo at the same time.

The Otavalo expatriate community in Barcelona is important not only for textiles but for music. The members of the most famous Otavalo music group, Charijayac, grew up in Barcelona and were the first Otavalos to play on the street and record and sell music in Europe (see Chapter 5). The impetus for emigration to Barcelona was economic—the search for new markets for cloth and opportunities to work in that trade. Luis Enrique said:

> I went to Barcelona with some compañeros from below [in Peguche] in 1978, to work in artesanías. Here work was scarce, but they paid more there than they paid here. Including children, we were only 50 indígenas. We worked with knitting and sewing machines to make sweaters. Other compañeros had looms. The Barcelona community started in the 1970s. Now there are more people [Otavalos] there—they have stores, their own houses—some are already residents.

One founder of the Barcelona community was an indígena from Punyaro, José Luis Cotacachi, who became famous as the sponsor, brother, and father of members of Charijayac. His son Sayri told me: "My father was one of the first indígenas to arrive in Europe twenty-five years ago [in 1969]. We went first to the Canary Islands during the Franco era. We lived four years under that regime—I was thirteen years old. After five years in the islands—they are very small and life was somewhat boring— we arrived in Barcelona."

In separate conversations both Luis Enrique and Sayri Cotacachi commented on how well they were treated in Spain. Luis said, "The people in Spain were very amiable, really good people." Sayri was even more emphatic: "They treated us like princes." In fact, a leitmotif of Otavalos' travel stories is how much better they are treated outside Ecuador.

The senior Cotacachi brought indígenas from Punyaro to Barcelona and founded a successful weaving and sweater-knitting concern. Eventually José Luis Cotacachi employed thirty Otavalos, including Luis Enrique, who worked for him for two years and confirmed that he treated his workers well. José Luis Cotacachi became a Spanish citizen but continued to wear Otavalo traditional dress, bought apartment buildings and other real estate in Barcelona, Punyaro, and Otavalo, and in his later years flew back and forth between Ecuador and Spain several times a year.

Luis Enrique, like many Otavalos, has a photo album filled with family pictures and mementos of his sojourns abroad: "Here I am in France. I was in France to deliver merchandise and in Italy—nowhere else. First I was in Barcelona two years, then I returned here [Peguche], then I went back to Barcelona for two years. Now there is more work here. In 1978 an airplane ticket cost S/15,000 [$556.00]. Now, who knows?"

By the late 1970s, Otavalos were becoming transnational migrants, building and maintaining familial, economic, social, cultural, religious, and political relationships that span geographic and political frontiers. Such transmigrants also have public identities that are based on relationships with more than one country (Glick Schiller et al. 1992: ix, 1995: 48).

Many Otavalos become incorporated into the life of their new communities, and they maintain multiple links with their natal communities. Otavalos serve as conduits in the flow of international fads and fashions, not so much because they invariably adopt the fads or fashions themselves (although they sometimes do), but because they are willing to switch production and make them to sell. In addition, Otavalos are the kinds of transmigrants who must be analyzed with regard to "the many different racial, ethnic or national identities which shape people's action and consciousness" (Basch et al. 1994: 12): in this case the Otavalos' indigenous ethnicity, which they use to their advantage in textile marketing and musical performances.

The Rich Get Richer

There are now definite class divisions among Otavalos, from the extreme wealth of some weaving and merchant families to the poverty of those who remain primarily farmers, a process that accelerated in the 1970s

(Chavez 1982) and subsequent years. In 1978, very few indígena families owned motor vehicles. The first Otavalos I knew who owned vehicles lived in Otavalo proper and in Quinchuquí. At that time, even indígenas riding bicycles were rare, although many indígenas had acquired watches and pocket calculators. Electronic consumer goods appeared in the 1970s. Radios, blenders, and record players were the first to debut in indigenous homes, followed by refrigerators and televisions. Many families acquired propane-run cooking stoves, some of which had ovens. These supplemented but did not supplant the cooking shed which is used for fiestas and for roasting guinea pigs.

Many Otavalos consider themselves middle class by Ecuadorian standards, as evidenced by their income and purchasing power. For example, in 1994, the legal monthly minimum wage including various benefits for factory workers, day laborers in agriculture, construction, etc., was 210,667 sucres per month ($100 per month or $1,200 per year). Women working as household domestics earned half that. At the same time the government estimated that a family needed S/618,000 ($294) per month to survive (*Hoy*, January 4, 1994: 2-A), an income which many Otavalos could claim.

Artesanías can be lucrative. A sweater wholesaler generally makes a profit of $1 per sweater, and some make twice that, selling 5,000 to 250,000 sweaters annually. This is impressive in a country where the average annual per capita income has hovered around $1,100 since the end of the 1980s according to World Bank statistics. In comparative terms, in 1990 the Gross National Product (GNP) per capita for Ecuador was $1,117; for the United States $19,789 (MacGlobe 1991).

The disparities in wealth are evident not only among indígenas but between indígenas and whites-mestizos. Indígenas are among the wealthiest individuals in the Otavalo valley. For example, Luis Alfonso Morales, originally of Agato, now lives in Otavalo. "Morales had only one year of schooling, . . . Yet at 50, he is one of the two or three wealthiest men in Otavalo. Using a score of electric looms to produce 25,000 sweaters and ponchos a year, he nets the equivalent of a six-figure dollar income, mostly from sales abroad" (Kandell 1993: 32). New indigenous wealth and the disparities in wealth within and among local ethnic groups have made inter- and intraethnic relations in the valley so complex that they merit a discussion of their own in Chapter 7.

Otavalo economic gains since the abolition of wasipungu are beyond the wildest dreams and predictions of even the most prescient Otavalos or outsiders. They are a result of adaptability and hard work, including

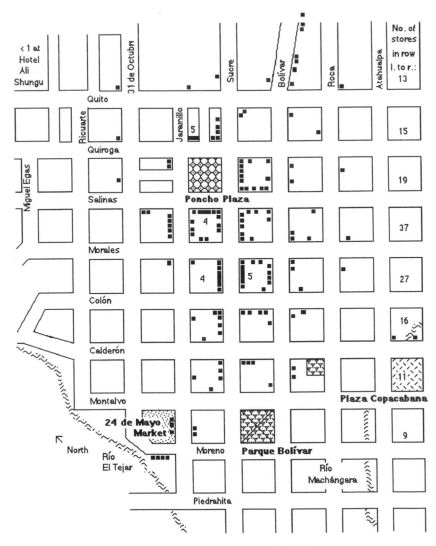

Artesanías stores in Otavalo, January 1995

Total: 147

Stores on Calle Sucre: 44   Stores on Calle Bolívar: 28

3.1. Artesanías Stores in Otavalo, 1995

the willingness to invest in textile cottage industry instead of agriculture and the ability to change production and go with global fashion trends. Yet Mario Conejo's description of the situation as "self-exploitation" suggests that success has a price. The necessity for large numbers of Otavalos to migrate to look for markets or simply to work as domestic and agricultural laborers is causing stresses within families and communities when those left at home take over tasks previously performed by absent family members or when migrants establish romantic or sexual liaisons with foreigners. The increasing reliance on export markets for textiles also makes the community vulnerable to global economic upheavals and changes in consumption patterns.

CHAPTER 4

In Search of the Noble Savage
TOURISM AND TRAVEL TO OTAVALO

International tourism is the world's largest industry, earning $4.4 trillion annually (Dogar 1998: 41) and employing 212 million people worldwide (Pandya 1995: 42). More than 600 million people traveled abroad in 1997, with travelers from the United States, Germany, and Japan in the lead (Dogar 1998); yet tourism has been neglected by anthropologists, perhaps because "tourists appear, in some respects, to be our own distant relatives" (Crick 1989: 311). In 1994, anthropologists in Otavalo debated whether it was worse to be mistaken for tourists or for missionaries. The other anthropologists were insulted to be taken for tourists, but I like the anonymity this provides.

Tourists are our embarrassing country cousins because researchers, like tourists, are outsiders visiting the area temporarily and make the same mistakes when we first arrive. Anthropologists may also neglect tourism for fear that the study of leisure will be seen as frivolous. Yet, to borrow a phrase, "consumption is as much a part of economic activity as production and exchange" (Orlove and Rutz 1989: 2). To study textile production and ignore tourists' and exporters' consumption is to miss half the picture.

The growth of tourism since World War II is a result of higher discretionary income, changing demographics including smaller family sizes, innovations in transportation and lower costs, improvements in public health, development of infrastructure, and the availability of hospitable environments (Eadington and Smith 1992: 1). These authors date the advent of modern mass tourism to the first passenger jet service in 1958, which increased accessibility on a global scale (ibid.: 5). Today travel and tourism bring $125 billion to Latin America, with an increase of 60% expected by the year 2005 (Pandya 1995: 42).

Travel means a journey for any reason including (but not limited to) business, study, religious pilgrimage, recreation, or combinations thereof. Travel is not always voluntary: refugees or military transcripts may be reluctant travelers. Tourism, for my purposes, means a voluntary, temporary journey away from home for recreation, renewal, or change (following Smith 1989: 1). Tourism, travel, and other transnational contacts form a hierarchy, with transnational contacts the most encompassing. When I refer to both tourists and travelers, I use the term "visitors"; indeed the two categories frequently overlap.

Some theorists see tourism as detrimental to the visited: "Tourism exposes cultural minorities to discontinuity, disturbance, divergence, even disintegration, and usually to dangerous dependency. These people are not even recognized as having a rich and vital identity of their own" (Rossel 1988: 13). This theory holds that tourism from wealthier to poorer countries or regions is a form of cultural and economic imperialism or neo-colonialism and that the power relations are one-sided: "It has become quite normal for privileged people to spend their holidays in areas inhabited by those who themselves do not have the means to travel" (ibid.: 2).

Pierre van den Berghe acknowledges that tourism can be beneficial or catastrophic. For ethnic tourism, the "tourist-native interaction is between haves and have-nots, with all the inequalities of wealth, status, and power that these asymmetrical relationships imply" (1992: 235). This assumes that Euro-American civilization is, if not better, at least stronger and more compelling than others, that the identity of the people visited is fragile, and that everyone wants to be like Europeans or Americans.

People travel abroad for various reasons, with different expectations, and with positive and negative effects (sometimes unintended) on the people and countries they visit. To say that all Westerners or wealthier tourists and travelers exploit local people or to objectify them as exotic is false and unfair. Blanket condemnations of tourism, nationalities, the West, the North, or a gender, such as the statement that "the very structure of international tourism needs patriarchy to survive. Men's capacity to control women's sense of their security and self-worth has been central to the evolution of tourism politics" (Enloe 1989: 133), do not do justice to the complexity of the situation. Van den Berghe concluded that in San Cristóbal, Chiapas, tourists' behavior varied: "The sensitive and discreet express concern for poverty, disease, and invasion of privacy, while the callous treat locals as providers of services and amusements" (1994: 118–119).

The two main models of international tourism are also problematical. Liberal economics sees tourism as a natural business phenomenon with generally positive consequences. An opposing model based on dependency theory views tourism as a means of reinforcing the dependency of poor nations on rich ones. The liberal model overstates the direct benefits of tourism and ignores the extent to which the income from tourism is exported in payments to foreign-owned hotel chains, to airlines and travel agencies, and for imported food. The dependency model presumes a static view of visitor-visited relations, which denies the agency of both sides (Leheny 1995: 370–371). David Leheny suggests combining the two approaches because "the financing of tourism is of critical importance to states, and . . . financial decisions are made within, and often reconfigure, political constraints" (ibid.: 371–372).

Some writing on tourism is attentive to local circumstances in determining its effects (Crick 1989; Healy and Zorn 1983; Lanfant et al. 1995; Smith 1989; Smith and Eadington 1992). Another body of literature focuses on the effects of tourism on local arts and crafts (Graburn 1976; Swain 1993; Tice 1995). In short, detailed ethnographic analysis is necessary in order for us to compare data on different types of cultures, numbers of tourists, tourist niches, and local responses to tourism (Crick 1989: 338).

I am making several arguments with respect to transnational contacts between foreigners and Otavalos. Such contacts have definite effects on identity construction, but in ways that challenge common assumptions. The first is that foreign visitors invariably have power relations weighted on their side; the second is that tourism is detrimental to the visited; and the third is that indigenous people do not have the opportunity to travel themselves.

Another argument concerns the power of images to create romanticized portraits of indigenous people which are responsible for cultural misunderstandings and for the belief that indigenous cultures are exceptionally fragile. Tourists frequently come to Otavalo with unrealistic expectations gleaned from the media and tourism literature. Many conventions of travel literature were associated with and legitimated European expansionism, including European values and white supremacy (Pratt 1992: 5–10). Euro-American travel writers have emphasized the timeless, unchanging indígena with the unspoken corollary that Euro-Americans have a lock on progress. Not surprisingly, this construction plays a role in the Ecuadorian debates about national identity and citizenship; for if indígenas are unchanging, they are unfit for the modern or postmodern world, anachronisms who are ultimately doomed. Indigenous ethnicity becomes an evolutionary stage rather than a viable, changing identity.

Marketing Ecuador

Smith identified five main types of tourism: ethnic, involving visits to indigenous people; cultural, including "'picturesque' or 'local color'"; historical, emphasizing the art and monuments of the past; recreational, which is "often sun, sea and sex"; and environmental, which is primarily geographic. These categories sometimes overlap; for example, people might combine ethnic and environmental touring (Smith 1989: 4–5). I include what are commonly called eco-tourism and adventure travel under environmental tourism.

The Organization of American States (OAS) declared 1972 "Tourism Year of the Americas." As a result of OAS promotions, Royal Dutch Airlines (KLM) inaugurated flights to Quito, making the European tourist market available to Ecuador. Both Cuenca "and Otavalo, famous for its colorful Indian fair, are worth visiting" (Organization of American States 1973: 17). In 1985, approximately 250,000 tourists visited Ecuador and spent over 200 million dollars. Colombians accounted for 36% of the visitors, followed by the United States with 21% and Western Europe with 18%, with the Galápagos Islands the most popular destination (Hanratty 1991: 139).

In Ecuador throughout the 1990s, income from tourism ranked fourth in revenue behind the export of petroleum, bananas, and shrimp (*El Comercio*, August 20, 1999: A-8). Foreign visitors reached 471,000 in 1993 (*Hoy*, July 25, 1995: 6-A). In the first half of 1994, tourism to Ecuador dropped 10%, probably because of improved conditions in Peru following the 1992 capture of the leader of the Shining Path guerrilla group. (Peru is usually the first choice of travelers to the Andes because of its rich Inca and pre-Inca heritage, including Machu Picchu.)

Still, Ecuador ended 1994 with 482,000 foreign tourists (*Hoy*, July 25, 1995: 6-A), up 2.34% from the previous year. The border war between Ecuador and Peru in the winter of 1995, however, caused a drop, and hotel and travel agency owners in Otavalo estimated that tourism was down by half. Although tourism increased during the summer, the number overall fell to 455,000 visitors, who spent $260 million (*El Comercio*, August 27, 1996: 6). Visitors increased to 493,700 in 1996 and 529,500 in 1997 then dropped to 510,600 in 1998 (*El Comercio*, July 7, 1999: B-1). The number dipped again to 508,713 in 1999, but tourism still brought in $343 million (*El Comercio*, June 16, 2000: B-4). The decrease in tourism was probably due to bad publicity resulting from national strikes and political instability, the eruptions of two major volcanoes, Tungurahua and Pichincha, and the kidnapping for ransom of foreign oil workers in the Oriente.

There is an annual rhythm to the arrivals, which peak in December and January (people escaping nasty winters in the northern hemisphere) and mid-June to mid-September (vacations from school and work). The majority of visitors enter Ecuador through Quito (37%) or Tulcán (34%) at the Colombian border (*El Comercio*, August 12, 1994: B-1); this is fortunate for Otavalo, which is situated on the Pan-American highway between the two cities. In 1997, Colombia supplied 31% of the visitors to Ecuador, the USA 20%, Europe 18%, and other countries 31% (*El Comercio*, July 17, 1998: B-7), approximately the same percentages as in 1972.

Since at least 1985, a revolving contingent of South American hippies has lived in Otavalo. They fund their stays in various ways, including the manufacture and sales of artesanías, especially jewelry, and possibly drug sales (or so they are accused by Otavalo town gossips). Except for Colombians, I have not encountered many middle or upper-class South American tourists in Ecuador; they seem to prefer Europe and the United States. The majority of visitors cluster in the 20–39 age range, with almost as many in the 40–49 range (*El Comercio*, August 12, 1994: B-1). Some are long-term budget travelers, meaning people who travel for at least a year on a tight budget (Riley 1988: 317). Within the 20–59 age group more males than females visit by about one-third. Reasons for the preponderance of males include their greater earning power, the fact that travel alone or accompanied is safer for males than for females, and the predominance of males as oil workers and businesspeople.

Ecuador experiences all types of tourism mentioned by Valene Smith (1989), with recreational tourism the least important (if someone is looking only for sun and fun, many beach resorts are closer to Europe and North America). Once in Ecuador, however, many visitors spend time on the Pacific beaches. Trips to the Galápagos Islands include lots of sun, sea, and beaches, but the primary attraction is the ecology. Visitors to the Oriente are usually interested in both ecology and indigenous people.

The following examples of advertising from a Quito tourist brochure are typical of the ads placed in the country's locally published and distributed tourist magazines:

Visit Ecuador with Turismundial • Galápagos Cruises • City tours • Indian markets • Photographic safaris • Andean trekking • Railroad trips • Special programs to most famous beaches • . . . (Vallejo Pérez 1993: 3)

Samoa turismo c.a. The Best of Ecuador • We can show it to you at
the most economic prices. Jungle. Aucas/Cofanes • Galápagos
islands • Mountain climbing • Trekking—Birding and tribes •
Beautiful beaches • Colonial city tours. (ibid.: 16)

Distinct themes unfold in these ads: Indian markets and tribes fall
under the rubric of ethnic tourism; railroad trips under cultural tourism; colonial city tours under historical tourism; Galápagos trips, jungle
safaris, mountain climbing, trekking, birding and "tribes" (the birds
and people listed together) under environmental tourism; and sports
and beaches under recreational tourism. Photographic safaris fall into a
variety of categories depending on the interests of the participants. Most
organized tours have a main theme but involve side trips. For example,
rainforest tours spend most of their time in the Oriente but usually include a tour of colonial Quito and a trip to an "Indian market." My intent
is not to create a rigid typology of tourism but to point out the many
reasons for visiting Ecuador.

Travel is part of transnational systems involving airlines, cruise ships,
railroads, travel agencies, and tour companies offering packaged trips.
The tourism information network includes promotions by governments,
word of mouth, the public relations industries, and the writers and producers of travel magazines, guidebooks, and documentary films. Print
media, especially travel guides, are an important source of travel inspiration. People do not make their vacation plans in a vacuum: they usually
get their information (or misinformation) from these sources.

For me, the major issue in tourism literature is describing difference
without implying inferiority or superiority. This is difficult because such
basic underpinnings of Western thought as the idea of progress have bur-
dened us with a vocabulary that automatically denotes hierarchy. The
belief in progress is one of the six major stories of our time, in the sense
of explanations about the world and what is likely to happen (W. Anderson 1990: 243). "Progress" as a noun connotes forward movement, an
advance or development. An entire vocabulary has evolved around this
notion, which is mainly construed in economic terms: GNP, Gross Domestic Product (GDP), and the constant improvement in the material
conditions of life. The progress and development brew has a hefty sea-
soning of evolutionism and social Darwinism. Human societies are arranged along a scale: "From being a savage, man rose to be a Scotchman,"
as one nineteenth-century writer put it (Walter Bagehot quoted in Stocking 1982 [1968]: 114). The Ecuadorian equivalent is "from being an indio
man rose to be a white" (and never mind the women).

The idea of progress has given rise to a series of binary opposi-tions. We have First World/Third (and Fourth) World, industrialized/less-industrialized, developed/underdeveloped, and progressive/backward, to list a few. For people we have such comparisons as civilized/uncivi-lized, modern/primitive, European/native, and foreigner/local. Some terms applied to countries, such as progressive/backward, can also be applied to people and vice versa, giving us a set of potent tropes. Since tourism traffics heavily in images, these tropes become a useful, if mis-leading, shorthand.

These dichotomies are obsolete, failing to reflect the breakup of the former Soviet Union and concealing such political and economic reali-ties as the tremendous gaps between rich and poor in almost every coun-try and the ability of the middle-class and rich within poor countries to travel for business and leisure (while the poor travel to look for work). It is impossible to speak of benefits or exploitation in simple binary oppositions.

The reverse side of progress and development is nostalgia and re-gret. Many inhabitants of the industrialized world (and some people in less-industrialized countries) have a profound nostalgia for vanished ways of life. Renato Rosaldo calls this "imperialist nostalgia" and notes the paradox involved in changing something and then mourning the change (1989: 68–70). Many Europeans and Americans believe we can find what we have lost in Otavalo: prosperous settlements in a pristine setting where traditional customs, community, and family are intact. One U.S. exporter called Otavalo "paradise." The notion of authenticity, meaning the quality of being true or known to be genuine, pervades Euro-American conceptualizations of indigenous people. "For moderns, reality and authenticity are thought to be elsewhere in other histori-cal periods and other cultures, in purer, simpler lifestyles" (MacCannell 1976: 3).

When fissures appear in this unrealistic picture (filthy streets, cholera, family problems, wife beating, indígenas who are dishonest or throw gar-bage in the streams—so much for natural ecologists—in short, the usual human failings plus several particular to tropical climates and countries with inadequate infrastructures), foreigners often react with outrage, especially when indígenas do not meet their ideals (whites-mestizos are deemed already corrupted).

For believers in progress and development, this loss of authenticity in the Euro-American world is regrettable but inevitable. For believers in the Green or environmental narrative of restoring a preindustrial part-nership with nature (W. Anderson 1990: 243, 246–248), this loss is reversible: we can return to a golden age, abroad if not at home. Travel writing invokes an ancient literary genre, the pastoral, which is "the form that depicts the paradise we have lost, the rustic simplicity of a good life in a golden age. . . . For the travel writer, the idyll is teasingly remote in space, but can be reached by consulting the airline schedules" (Conrad 1993: 11).

The pastoral sometimes implies the superiority rather than inferiority of the visited—the locals are assumed to possess wisdom we have lost. This romanticism is the latest version of the noble savage trope, whose variations include the savage as wise, frequently Asian; the savage as noble, usually Native American; and the savage as barbarian, often African or African-American (Trouillot 1991: 43).

Either way—backward or noble savage—nostalgia places an impossible burden on local people to live up to their visitors' expectations. American Express sells a ten-day vacation package called the "Highlands of Ecuador." The brochure says, "As we travel throughout this country of magnificent landscaped valleys, small Indian villages, towering volcanoes, colorful Indian markets, and Spanish colonial cities, you'll see the past and present unfold before you" (American Express 1991: 26). Note the insistence on "small Indian villages" as well as the phrase "see the past and present unfold before you," which suggests these places are frozen in the past, its inhabitants resembling revived woolly mammoths.

The noble savage trope is fostered by most tourism literature as well as by the New Age fascination with shamanism and the ecology movement's apotheosis of indigenous people as natural ecologists. One travel writer advised tourists to take plenty of Ecuadorian sucres to the Saturday fair, "unless you bring piglets or llamas to barter" (Morgan 1996: T-11), suggesting a precapitalist society.

Ira Silver calls the travel industry's strategy "marketing authenticity" (1993). An ad for Overseas Adventure Travel reads: "Exotic lands! Overseas Adventure Travel has 15 years experience taking travelers to remote destinations. From Borneo to Bolivia, Tanzania to Turkey, Ecuador to Egypt, Peru to Pakistan . . ." (in *Mother Jones* 1992: 68). Exotic, according to the *Oxford American Dictionary*, means "striking and attractive for being colorful and unusual" and is travel shorthand for exciting, romantic, primitive, remote, wondrous, and strange. Exotic lands by definition are not inhabited by modern or postmodern citizens but by savages, noble or otherwise.

In 1993, the *Philadelphia Inquirer* published an article on Otavalo headlined: "Under the spell of Otavalo. The Ecuadorian village nestled in the Andes is known for its impressive weekend market. But better than the haggling is the nighttime, when the Otavalenos bring out their mandolins to accompany the dances of their Inca heritage" (Enda 1993: R-1). One error is the imputed Inca ancestry of the Otavalos. The other is the "dances of their Inca heritage," an unusual classification of disco, cumbia, salsa, and hip hop, to say the least. The article implies timelessness and performance: indígenas presenting dances unchanged in 500 years before an audience of enthralled foreigners, rather than a modern music club.

Such descriptions mean that frequently the residents of tourist destinations, especially indigenous people, are not seen as they see themselves: as part of the contemporary world with their own problems and plans for the future. One of the best (or worst) examples of nostalgia as condescension is the 1976 edition of *Myra Waldo's Travel Guide to South America*, a collector's item that sets new standards for bad writing. The Ecuador chapter begins: "Once upon a time, as they say in fairy tales, there was a wonderful land, with a marvelous climate, inhabited by two happy primitive Indian civilizations, the Quitu and the Cara [i.e., the Otavalos]. They were primarily agricultural tribes, living quiet, almost uneventful lives" (Waldo 1976: 229). "Quiet, almost uneventful lives" is a strange description of local warfare and the Inca and Spanish conquests of northern Ecuador. Waldo continues: "Ecuador is a demented country. This is not said in any unkindly spirit, but rather as one would lovingly speak with reference to a dear but slightly dotty old aunt" (ibid.: 232). Ecuador with Alzheimer's: from happy and primitive to old and demented, such is the march of progress.

There is an amazing similarity in the rhetoric of tourism publicity worldwide, as if a few people were hidden in a room writing all the travel blurbs and sending them to clients over the Internet. This literature is an example of Wilk's contention that cultural differences are increasingly expressed in a limited and narrow range of images (1995: 118).

The reluctance of anthropologists, travel writers, and promoters, including Ecuadorians of all ethnicities who depend on tourism, to present a negative picture results in striking omissions. But who wants to promote tourism with photos of malnourished babies, angry strikers, beggars, litter, or the funeral of someone who died of cholera? A writer might say a particular hotel is terrible or a small town "has nothing to offer," but the overall picture must be positive or the book or article will not be published. In Ecuador, travel writing ignores human rights abuses by the police and military and neglects the country's strong indigenous rights movement. While I consider this movement a positive development, it connotes "trouble in paradise," which travel writers consider a deterrent to tourism.

Tourism literature is not the only culprit in the romantic construction of indigenous people. Movies like *Dances with Wolves* (1990) and novels do their part. In the late nineteenth century, German author Karl May wrote novels about a German hero, Old Shatterhand, who lived in the American West and his noble friend the Apache chief Winnetou. May had never been in the United States (Berkhofer 1979: 101), but his novels have sold tens of millions of copies in more than thirty languages, and he is still widely read in Europe (Kinzer 1996: A-4). Germany and the Czech Republic have full-fledged cults of the American Indian, the Euro-Indians. In Germany thousands of people in approximately 100 clubs gather for powwows and devote large amounts of time and money to buying or making Native American regalia. "The chief of one band, Old Bull, also known as Gerhard Fischer, wore a lavishly embroidered buckskin outfit, beaded moccasins and a long eagle-feather headdress" (ibid.).

In the Czech Republic, Canadian anthropologist David Scheffel studied several thousand Czech Euro-Indians. In 1992, he brought two Canadian Crees and one Ojibway to the Czech Republic to meet "the new Indians," several hundred of whom were encamped in teepees in the countryside. They greeted their visitors in versions of Native American dress which they had meticulously researched and made. One of the Canadian women commented, "Everything was backwards. We're natives and we're dressed like Europeans. I feel like, what's wrong with this picture?" This encounter is the subject of a wonderful documentary, *If Only I Were an Indian* (1995).

"The stalwart tribespeople of the Plains" have become the quintessential American Indians in the eyes of Euro-Americans and even many Native Americans themselves (Berkhofer 1979: 89). One of the Czech Euro-Indians traveled to South Dakota to speak Lakota with the elders after studying the language from Lakota-English grammars and dictionaries for seven years. Visitors bring this cultural baggage with them to Ecuador; their vision of indígenas is based on Crazy Horse. Even Otavalos masquerade as native North Americans during San Juan or in photos on CD covers.

Otavalos are actually appearing in American movies as Native American noble savages. Lorenzo Alarcón of Peguche married an American woman, and the couple lived in Santa Fe, New Mexico, for several years.

When the movie *Young Guns II* (1990; a western about Billy the Kid starring Emilio Estevez, Kiefer Sutherland, Lou Diamond Phillips, and Christian Slater) was filmed in New Mexico, Lorenzo answered a casting call for extras. The casting director phoned his wife and said, "He's the perfect Indian—can you get me some more?" She said, "There's a lot of them but they're 3,000 miles away." Lorenzo appears in the movie in a close-up, his long hair worn in two braids Native North American style, shooting at the cowboys (Christina Alarcón, personal communication, 1994).

Healers as Tourist Attractions

Local healing traditions in the Otavalo valley are part of Otavalo spirituality and, like Euro-American biomedical beliefs, are deeply held; but even the healers of the valley are tourist attractions. Local healing is a variation of a pan-Andean complex with pre-Hispanic roots. Within Ecuador the Otavalo valley merits a literature unto itself (Carpenter 1981; Collier and Buitrón 1949; Goldman 1979; Korovkin et al. 1994; Lema 1995; Parsons 1945; M. Rogers 1995; Villavicencio 1973).

By now, nearly 500 years after the Spanish conquest, the various medical systems have influenced one another, including the incorporation of Spanish colonial humoral medicine into local Otavalo beliefs. Anyone who has experienced the conflict between such Euro-American biomedical concepts as the germ theory of disease and local beliefs and practices recognizes the importance of an underlying Andean system based on the balance of forces, including those of hot and cold. For example, water of whatever temperature is considered cold and should be used for treating illnesses that are considered hot. Diarrhea is diagnosed as a cold illness, so the standard biomedical treatment for infant diarrhea, rehydration therapy, is considered inappropriate (one solution is to find a liquid that can be made from a "hot" plant).

This emphasis on the balance or harmony of opposing forces underpins the healing system, as does the concept of curing the inside and outside of a person's body. One Otavaleño who returned from Europe with infected sores on his arm applied antibiotic ointment but also refrained from eating such food as chili peppers, "because you have to cure both inside and outside."

Otavalos themselves are now writing about this tradition. According to Taita Pacho Lema of Peguche: "The belief in curanderos is great among our people. We believe in bad and good spirits; these spirits do good or harm to people, and in everything there is a spirit, in the mountains, in the rivers, in the woods, in uninhabited houses, even in the rocks. Therefore we advise respect for nature, people, plants, animals and things . . ." (Lema 1995: 24–25; my translation).

Taita Pacho described local healers' use of different kinds of supernaturals: Christian saints, the trinity, and nature spirits. He also mentioned the healers' ability to work both good and evil: "There are various healers; some who do what we say is calling the spirits through prayers; on the other hand, other healers believe in the force of the rocks, the rivers, and the mountains. These forces protect and help to cure illnesses." He said, "These same [healers] can do good or they can do harm; everything depends on how they work. Because of envy someone went to San Bernardo, the saint who carries off the souls of the dead, so that my mother would die and disappear" (ibid.: 25).

Healers, who can be female or male, have various Spanish designations including *curandero(a)*, which has a positive connotation of healer; and *brujo(a)* or *hechizero(a)*, glossed as witch, a negative word. The Quichua terms are also positive: *yachac mama* or *yachac taita* (knowing or knowledgeable mother or father) or *jatun yachac* (great healer). Healers range from what we would call general practitioners to such specialists as *frigador* (Sp. *fregar*, to rub), the equivalent of a chiropractor; *partira* (Sp. *partera*, midwife); and *hierbatero* (Sp. herbalist).

Historically, only traditional healers were available in indigenous communities; "and to them come patients with whatever physical or spiritual disease and they cure them" (Lema 1995: 25; my translation). More recently biomedical care has become available in Otavalo, and there are sporadically staffed government-sponsored health centers in smaller communities. Some indígenas use the health centers, but for most Otavalos local healers are their first resort, followed by biomedical practitioners. A FICI and United Nations–sponsored health center in Otavalo, Jambi Huasi (Q. Medicine House), has indigenous biomedical doctors and local healers working together.

Healers combine practices—Catholic and non-Christian, biomedical and traditional—in a practical way, but one that violates foreigners' preconceptions of indigenous healing. In 1993, Margaret Goodhart of the Hotel Ali Shungu asked me to help her take an elderly Otavaleña with hip problems to a curandero in Otavalo (the woman's physician of choice). The healer began his treatment with the sign of the cross then massaged and manipulated the woman's right leg, while she howled. To my surprise, the healer whipped out an X-ray of a pelvis and explained that this was what a normal hip looked like but that the *mamita*'s was probably displaced. This was followed by more manipulations and a cleaning with an egg, tobacco, and cologne.

There is room for self-help within traditional healing. Many households have backyard gardens containing medicinal plants, and many people know where to find wild plants. Parsons described a number of home remedies (1945: 62–64). People can also clean themselves or others by gently rubbing a raw egg over their body to absorb the effects of an ill wind (Q. *wayrashka*, Sp. *mal viento*), a curse, envy, or the evil eye. Many indígenas believe in these curses and express fear that business success or a dispute with their neighbors will result in illness or death. Such curses result in symptoms ranging from general malaise to serious illness. The remedy is usually effective; most people feel better after a cleaning. The egg is never cooked and eaten or used for another purpose but hidden in a field away from the house.

Healers are consulted when people feel that a self-cleaning will not do, when someone is seriously ill or is suffering from illness called *susto* or *espanto* (Sp. fright), in which case a yachac is needed to "call the soul [or shadow] back." Healers charge for their services, often a set fee of $8–$10, plus the cost of cigarettes, an egg, and prescribed remedies, which can cost more than biomedical care. People use local healers because they have confidence in them, not because they are cheaper than biomedicine. Despite centuries of attempts to "extirpate idolatry," indígenas do not see contradictions between Christianity and local curing practices, in the same way that Euro-Americans do not see contradictions between Christianity, Judaism, or Islam and acupuncture or psychiatry.

Otavalo valley healers attract indígenas and whites-mestizos from throughout Ecuador. Some people believe that the healers of the western slopes of the Andes or the Oriente are more powerful, and Otavalo healers sometimes visit distant healers to learn from them. The existence of a national clientele and highland-lowland linkages are not recent phenomena; Collier and Buitrón commented on these topics (1949: 145, 148). In the mid-1970s, some Quichua healers from the Bobonaza River in the Oriente were reputed to travel to Otavalo to renew their powers (Descola 1996: 342). I have seen indígenas from San Juan, Chimborazo, as well as Cayambes, in Ilumán. Whites-mestizos also frequent Ilumán healers, sometimes timing their visit with a trip to the Otavalo market. When my godson (grandson of an Ilumán yachac, Mama Rosa) visited from Quito in 1995, he was accompanied by two whites-mestizos

Sign advertising traditional healing. Ilumán, August 1999.

who shopped at the Otavalo fair before going to Ilumán for a healing session with Mama Rosa.

For a while, in the late 1980s, some Ilumán healers advertised openly. In July 1989, in Barrio Santo Domingo on the north side of Ilumán, a white-mestizo family hung out a large, double-faced neon sign in front of their house on the old Pan-American highway. The sign read "CURANDEROS." The husband's name was listed below in smaller script, with the wife's name beneath his. By mid-August, the sign was down. An indígena neighbor said that she had curanderos on three sides of her and that the other healers probably thought such bold advertising was objectionable because traditional healing was illegal. By the mid-1990s, healing was legalized; and in 1997, Imbabura healers formed ASHIM, the Association of Shamans of Imbabura. "Shaman" is a foreign word but was adopted because of its positive connotations. Signs advertising healers and proclaiming membership in the Asociación de Yachacs de Ilumán are now posted throughout the town.

The healers of the valley are an international tourist attraction, as one travel article illustrates: "Otavalo proclaims itself to be one of the friendliest towns in Ecuador . . . Outside the town you can plunge deeper into the mysteries of this most mysterious continent—within a day's journey you can find jungles, shamans, exotic wildlife, glacier-draped volcanoes" (Silk 1994: T2). Some healers are part of the New Age travel circuit. An article called "The Dream Changer of Otavala [sic]" in Shaman's Drum exemplifies the New Age stance. According to the editor, "High in the Andes of Ecuador, native shamans still teach the technique of dream changing, an age-old tradition that has kept Otavalan and Sala-sacan cultures alive, despite centuries of conquest" (Perkins 1994: 55). Certain names and places were changed, "to protect the fragile cultures and environments, as well as to ensure anonymity" (ibid.). The Salasacas are a poorer, more beleaguered population than the Otavalos (Meisch and Miller 1988), but neither culture is "fragile."

The Otavalo area "dream changer," called "Manco," was an old yachac taita, Marcos Guerrero, who was famous in northern Ecuador through word of mouth and because an article about him appeared in *El Comercio*. John Perkins credits "Manco" with a long discourse on dreams unlike anything I have ever heard in the valley and more like something out of a New Age book about the Malaysian Senoi. While indígenas pay close attention to their dreams and often discuss them in the morning, the idea of changing or manipulating their dreams is not characteristic. Perkins leads healing tours to Ecuador (which were advertised in the same issue of *Shaman's Drum* as his article), and the more exotic he can make the culture, the more clients he is likely to attract.

The emphasis on the "fragility" of the culture has a commercial payoff because it implies that tourists should see healing now before it disappears. The Otavalo tourist agencies, one of which is owned by an Otavaleña, Zulay Saravino, also arrange visits to healers. Such events will probably become more common because interest in shamanism is growing: "Eric Utne, founder of the hipster digest *The Utne Reader*, excitedly predicts 'shamanic journeys will be for people in their 30s and 40s what rock concerts are for people in their teens'" (Marin 1996: 44).

Although outsiders have long visited valley healers, most come because they share a belief system with the healers. They believe they can be helped, and they come to be cured. Turning healers into tourist attractions is a qualitative change. Some foreigners are searching for a cure for cancer or other illnesses, but many tourists do not come to be healed; nor would they choose a healer over a biomedical practitioner in an emergency. Some are looking for an exotic experience; others are merely curious and often exhibit a complete misunderstanding of Imbabura healing. The effect, however, is to turn healing into a paid performance rather than a collaborative event in which both healer and patient participate and share responsibility for the outcome. The Cofán of the northern Oriente refuse to stage performances for tourists, saying that healers only practice when there is a medical reason.

In a coincidence which *Shaman's Drum* neglected to point out, Taita Marcos was featured in an article in the preceding issue: "Ecstasy in

Ecuador: Experiences with Curanderos and Plant Teachers." When the author visited Taita Marcos, "[t]he son accompanied us into the room and asked for a sizable sum of money—about forty dollars—for the session. . . . As Marcos awoke and got up, it was obvious that he was drunk, and he proceeded to become even more inebriated during the ceremony" (Rymland 1994: 50). This sounds more like the Taita Marcos of local fame. Although being drunk while curing is not considered by Otavalos to be detrimental to the outcome, an inebriated healer does not meet New Age preconceptions. Two points are salient. The first is the extent to which this tradition has local and national adherents who visit curanderos instead of or in addition to biomedical practitioners. The second is local healing's growing status as a tourist performance and tourists' concern with authenticity.

Authenticity in art, artesanías, music, and ritual, presumably located in indigenous societies and invariably in the past, is predominantly a foreign preoccupation rather than an Otavalo one. "This feeling of lost authenticity, of 'modernity' ruining some essence or source, is not a new one" (Clifford 1988: 4). James Clifford proposes a new vision that "does not see the world as populated by endangered authenticities . . . Rather, it makes space for specific paths through modernity . . ." (ibid.: 5).

Wilk criticizes the postmodern critique of the global commoditization of culture, which argues that local cultures are becoming incoherent and inauthentic. He insists that "people still infuse commodities, goods and their own refashioned bodies with meaning grounded in local practice, to their own ends, and the result cannot be pushed to extremes of global hegemony and/or arbitrary artificiality" (ibid.: 118–119).

Some visitors and white-mestizo Ecuadorians express irritation when Otavalos do not meet their expectations of authenticity. Otavalos' long hair and dignified bearing conform to images of the stalwart tribespeople of the American plains, but where are their feathers and why are they riding around in Mitsubishis and selling things? Sitting Bull was not a weaver and merchant. We need to distinguish between outsiders' preoccupation with authenticity and the Otavalos' concern about what constitutes their culture, whether change is positive or negative, and how to control it.

The Euro-American notion of authenticity involves several dubious assumptions. The first is that we have the right to make judgments about other people's lifeways (whether or not they are authentic). The second is that other people have an obligation to meet our expectations about how they should live, which implies the third assumption: that other people exist for our benefit. These attitudes "reflect the West's nostalgia for reliving its own vanished past through proxies in the developing world" (Kleymeyer 1992: 28). This is a far cry from the Otavalos' discussions and decisions about the direction they want their lives to take.

One of the first comments I heard about the Otavalos' authenticity was in 1978. A U.S. anthropologist who had done fieldwork in highland Peru said, "How can they be rich and still be Indians?" Peruvian indígenas attain upward mobility by migrating to an urban center, identifying with the values of and dressing like the dominant white or mestizo groups (Orlove 1977; Turino 1993; van den Berghe 1974). To be Indian in Peru is to be poor; ethnicity and class are isomorphic. Otavalos confound this equation by being both indigenous and prosperous.

Foreigners' insistence on authenticity also extends to textile production and results in the irritation of some visitors when they learn that the Otavalos use chemical aniline dyes (invented in England in 1856) instead of natural dyes (made from plants, minerals, or insects) in their tapestries. This attitude is strange, because tapestry weaving was introduced in the 1950s; it is not an ancient local art form with a continuous tradition. Tapestry weaving is relatively new and has always involved the use of aniline dyes as well as natural-colored wool, which means that colored tapestries are traditional.

Some visitors complain that "the Otavalos are losing their culture," as if change is automatically negative and a culture could be lost like car keys. The assumption is that foreigners can take advantage of technological advances, but indígenas, our proxies, should not. A related complaint surrounds the use of synthetic fibers. They were first considered high-status miracle fibers then disparaged as déclassé: "The word polyester conjures up the image of a lower middle class tour group filing off a bus at Disneyland in pastel leisure suits" (Schneider 1994: 2). Otavalos' use of polyester or acrylic yarn is offensive to many visitors because "synthetic fibers come close to being taboo for some people" (ibid.). Natural people should use natural fibers, and never mind the local wool shortage or the many advantages of synthetics.

A travel agency owner in Otavalo also takes the Otavalos to task for inauthenticity. In an article titled "Crafts or Commerce," as if there were an inherent contradiction, she writes: "Sadly, we must recognize that the majority of the artesanías that are dispatched in our great market . . . are brought from other cities in the country, other countries on the continent and even other continents, converting the Otavalo fair into a commercial display of the products and designs of other cultures" (de Vaca 1995: 3; my translation).

The majority of artesanías sold in the market are made in the Otavalo area, but why does it matter if they are made elsewhere? De Vaca also decries "the great problem of the lack of creativity of our artisans in offering their own products, which they should renew periodically." Her solution: "If we decide to maintain production that is typically artisanal, creative and alive, the work is hard, requiring effort, . . . especially the urgent creation of a *School of Artisanal Design in Otavalo*, which prepares the artisan to stop being a mere copier and converts him into a creator of his own designs, rescuing valuable techniques of the ancestral culture of which he is the owner and ambassador" (ibid.; emphasis in the original).

Actually, Otavalos regularly create new products. Since 1990, these have included the fish-motif daypacks and the basket-weave (estera) sweaters, which were invented by Peguche indígenas, not to mention new tapestry motifs and such other new products as tapestry-fabric vests, clothing made from Cuenca-area ikat textiles, daypacks and purses which combine leather and wool tapestries, hammocks, and wool or acrylic jackets. The obvious question is: what is wrong with producing what sells? The Otavalos' ability to adapt to market trends is one of the secrets of their success. There is more than a hint of paternalism in such statements as "our artisans." Authenticity is located in the past: "valuable techniques of the ancestral culture"—bring back the obrajes.

The article is accompanied by a snide cartoon of a foreigner with a camera around his neck wearing glasses, sandals, shorts, shirt, and vest. He says in bad Spanish, "Me want to make maquila in Otavalo, understand?" He is speaking to an Otavaleño who is standing beside boxes marked "export." The Otavalo has a long braid but is wearing shoes, long pants, a shirt, a coat, and a tie. Behind him are two other Otavalos, one of whom is knitting something from a catalog. The first Otavalo explains: "Here we maintain indígena identity, making Otavalo artesanía typical of our own culture . . . while copying a gringo catalog" (de Vaca 1995: 3; my translation). Why should this be considered inauthentic, since the Otavalos have been producing for trade for millennia?

The travel industry is not the only one to market authenticity. When it comes to Otavalo artesanías, authenticity sells. During the 1990s, the J. Peterman Company marketed expensive clothing through clever sales pitches. Consider the copy for an Otavalo-made sweater, which sells for U.S. $75, the "5-button manifesto." The copy reads in part:

Hand-carved wooden buttons. Each slightly different from the next. In this age of thermoplastics, a radical concept.

Consider the colors: blue, brown, cream and six kinds of green.
A couple named Rosa and Segunda [*sic*] in a village named Peguche
   picked these shades because they happen to like them. (Not one
   single consumer panel or color "scientist" preferred them over
   367 alternative schemes.)
Examine the weave closely. Loomed by hand high in the Andes, one
   at a time. (Assembly lines may be ideal for brake linings. Not for
   something you wear all weekend.) (J. Peterman Company
   1994: 69)

One-of-a-kind sweaters are contrasted with assembly line products
(thermoplastics, brake linings). These sweaters, however, are not loomed
one at a time. The whole point of the treadle loom is that it enables the
weaver to put on a long warp and produce a number of textiles relatively
quickly without rewarping. Weavers who make cloth for such sweaters
generally warp 100 meters (109 yards) at a time.

If Rosa and Segundo had chosen the colors for the sweater they might
have used neon green or some other blinding color that does not appeal
to Euro-American tastes. Cultural differences in color preferences and
the fast-changing nature of the fashion industry are stumbling blocks for
indígenas wishing to export. Beyond a doubt, the J. Peterman designer
chose the colors, and there is nothing wrong with that, but it would
never do to say so. Another question worth raising is the misspelling of
"Segundo."

Another J. Peterman product was the "Otavalo Mountain Shirt," the
tiu camisa or Otavalo wedding shirt, which sold for $27: "It's the real
thing: the actual white cotton workshirt actually worn (and actually
made) by the actual mountain people of Otavalo, Ecuador. For about the
past four centuries . . ." (J. Peterman Company 1994: 39). The tiu camisa
is now archaic, worn only by a few old men or by music groups for performances. The shirt style is 150 years old at the most (not 400), and
the ones J. Peterman sold were made by Michael Harrington's factory
in Ibarra, where Peterman placed an order for 25,000 in 1994. The copy-
writers are marketing romance and nostalgia in the guise of shirts. What
I find strange is that the truth also sells and is (to me at least) more interesting than the fabrications.

White basket-weave (Sp. *estera*) sweaters were also available in the
fall and Christmas 1994 catalogs, titled "Not So Wild But Still Woolly."
Although the copy for these sweaters is somewhat more straightfor-
ward than the examples above, two lines are significant: "Price $60. Yet

another reason why the Scottish and Irish sweater industries are beginning to sweat a little" (ibid.: 2). The last line hints at the self-exploitation of the Otavalos: the entire extended family works long, hard hours, often on Sundays (which is relatively new). Some families are now working seven days a week to make ends meet. The $60 asked by J. Peterman conforms to the standard 400% markup that exporters need to make a profit, but Otavalos are businesspeople and do not quarrel with that.

The copy may be more offensive to me than to Otavalos, who are pragmatic in the extreme and might not care what the copy says as long as it sells vests. The counter to the "who cares?" argument, however, is that such copy perpetuates the stereotype of the timeless Andean and creates false expectations in visitors, resulting in the "it's too commercial" and "it's too touristy" complaints. When indígenas do not fit the stereotypes perpetuated by the literature, people blame indígenas rather than the purveyors of misinformation.

Although I have criticized J. Peterman, Otavalos themselves are not always paragons of truth in advertising. Some tell tourists what they think they want to hear. If a tourist asks an Otavalo vendor, "Did you weave that?" he or she will say, "Of course," even if the product is a Panamanian mola (which is not even handwoven). If a potential buyer asks what fiber an acrylic jacket is made of, most Otavalos say *lana* (Sp. wool), leaving out the qualifier "acrylic." Similarly, claims are sometimes made that dyes are natural when they are not. There are two main reasons for this. The first is self-interest; but the second reason is a desire not to disappoint people. After all, many tourists would buy a mola no matter where it was made if they liked it, but many Otavalos think that tourists want to believe the Otavalos weave or sew everything themselves.

The Growth of the Saturday Fair

It is difficult to find a foreign tourist in Ecuador who has not visited Otavalo. Lema writes: "With its handmade textiles, autochthonous music, traditional fiestas, dress, language, and food that its inhabitants produce, Otavalo has gained the respect and admiration of the foreigners who have come to visit from around the world" (1995: 116; my translation). An Ecuadorian guidebook says: "Although the whole province is full of splendors, lakes, artesanías, ethnic groups with colorful costumes, the tourist epicenter and artesanías emporium of Otavalo is outstanding . . ." (J. Chiriboga 1990: 22; my translation).

The weekly Saturday market (Sp. *la feria*) is a "must" in most guide-

Belt vendors in the Poncho Plaza along Calle Jaramillo. Otavalo Saturday market, October 1981. Note the swing set behind them, part of the old children's playground, and compare the open space with the crowding in the market in 1996.

books. My first visit to Otavalo was in 1973 as a tourist to the Saturday market, which I learned about from the traveler's bible, *The South American Handbook*. Organized tours, even those with such emphases as ecology or natural history, usually visit the fair, sometimes staying in Otavalo the entire weekend.

The Saturday fair now occupies a large part of central and northern Otavalo. Most tourists flock to the artesanías market, centered on the Poncho Plaza (as it is popularly called). In 1999, the crafts for sale included jewelry, wool, acrylic and cotton clothing, silk-screened T-shirts, tapestry wall hangings, blankets, daypacks, fanny packs, backpacks, leather goods, hammocks, fabric, ikat vests, woodcarvings from San Antonio de Ibarra, balsa wood birds (originally from the Oriente but now also carved and painted locally), dolls in traditional dress, puppets, handmade felt hats from Ilumán, antiques, baskets—the list goes on, and new products appear regularly.

The market has artesanías from other parts of Ecuador: *shigras* (Q. cabuya fiber bags) from the central sierra; paja toquilla ("Panama") hats from Guayas, Manabí, Azuay, and Cañar; ikat shawls, scarves, and belts from Cotopaxi and Azuay; baskets from the central and southern sierra; paintings from Tigua, Cotopaxi; silver jewelry from Chordeleg, Azuay; tapestries from Salasaca; and belts, bags, and handmade felt hats from Chimborazo province. Several resident Saraguros sell beadwork.

The Poncho Plaza is a strange jumble, and this is a carryover from the 1940s. The vendors of fresh and processed food along Calle Quiroga on the north end and the pottery and wool vendors on the side streets hold rights to these locales going back sixty years, and their occupants resist efforts by the crafts vendors to make them move.

In the Poncho Plaza itself a traveler suddenly stumbles on a row of indígenas sitting on the ground selling sheeting (Sp. *sábana*) and *fachalinas* (Q. shoulder and head wraps) or a row of indígenas selling handwoven belts. These are holdovers from times when the Poncho Plaza sold only textiles used by other indígenas or whites-mestizos. The plaza also has many other items of indigenous traditional dress.

Vendors in the Poncho Plaza and surrounding streets also sell imports, including Panamanian Kuna molas, Guatemalan ikats and belts, and traditional handspun, handwoven textiles from Bolivia and Peru. The market contains many artesanías from Peru: alpaca sweaters, llama and alpaca fur rugs and bedspreads, tapestries from San Pedro de Cajas and Lima, silver jewelry from Lima, jewelry made from Pisac ceramic beads, and carved gourds from Huancayo. There are ceramic necklaces and models of crowded buses and trucks from Colombia (the models are also made in Ibarra), scarves and fake coral from India, and more. According to a young man from Cayambe writing in English, who dresses like and identifies as an Otavaleño:

> Everyone buys, getting dressed with pants, jackets, vests, shirts, shirts with gold thin from Esperanza and Zuleta, money carriers and waist belts protect the money travellers have for the trajectory. It is surprising that much of what they buy is handmade. Handcrafts from other neighboring countries such as Guatemala, Peru, and Bolivia are also seen. Another tourist buys a hammock and dreams to steep a moment by Europe. Another uncle secretly finishes buying the last door grenners from "don Angelo" and in his mind closes the suitcase and off to Japan. The Indian line of jewelers–earring makers–artisans is a song-book that never ends, selling ever to the last inspiration. (Guaña 1994: 13)

Otavalos do indeed sell "ever to the last inspiration." The "door grenners" are a mystery, but there must be a market for them in Japan. And while I would not call Guatemala a "neighboring" country, there are Guatemalan goods in the market.

In addition, large portions of the town—three separate plazas and a number of streets—are devoted to nontourist items: furniture, hardware, farming implements, weaving tools, clothing, kitchen goods, plants, poultry, rabbits, guinea pigs, and raw and cooked food intended for local consumption, although the vendors are happy to sell to anyone.

The food includes produce trucked in from other parts of Ecuador: pineapples, oranges, tangerines, and fish from the coast; tomatoes, chili peppers, and avocados from the Chota Valley north of Ibarra, which are sold by African-Ecuadorian women from the Chota; onions and garlic grown and sold by the Chibuleo indígenas from west of Ambato; avocados and chirimoyas from Guayllabamba; and apples, grapes, and kiwis from Chile. The 24 de Mayo permanent food market is the center of this activity, which spreads out along the surrounding streets.

The Plaza Copacabana is potato central but also has trucks of oranges and tangerines, with the open space on the west and northwest sides lined with vendors selling wool or acrylic clothing, which is bought at the factory in Atuntaqui or homemade. The potato vendors, many of whom arrive in large trucks, were forcibly evicted from their places on Calle 31 de Octubre in 1993. An entire field in the barrio of San Juan, west of the Pan-American highway, is devoted to horses, cattle, pigs, sheep, and goats. The market contains everything but a partridge in a pear tree, which I might have missed.

Virtually all guidebooks call the market "colorful" and insist that it "is rated highly for woolen goods, though it is now rather highly organized and touristy and many of the ponchos are made of orlon (these are easily recognizable). The earlier you get there the better . . ." (Brooks 1987: 569–570). This description of Otavalo is included in almost identical form in every edition of *The South American Handbook* through 1999, the major exception being the addition of "also check that colours will not run in the rain."

Fodor's 1986 guide also calls the fair "colorful" and says in part: "The gala Saturday affair starts at an eye-opening 5:30 A.M., when the mountain Indians, brightly attired in blue, purple, and scarlet ponchos, stream into town for market. They soon fill Otavalo's steep, cobbled streets" (E. Proaño 1986: 345). The author lists the "buys" and says that "a good souvenir is one of the stiff felt hats the women wear to market" (ibid.). Nine years later, Fodor's South America guide called the fair "fabulously colorful" and insisted that "[v]illagers trudge along the road carrying huge burdens or prodding their laden burros to do the same; come Thursday or Friday, there is a good chance they're headed for Otavalo's famous Saturday market . . ." (Mauldin 1995: 374–375). Burros? Walking two or three days to reach Otavalo? What century are we in?

According to Frommer's 1987 South America guide: "The Indians are garbed quite colorfully, the women in bright skirts and shawls, and the men in equally bright colors and with braided hair" (Greenberg 1987: 310). Stephen Birnbaum calls the market "a colorful pageant" (1984: 84). In fact, the cliché "colorful" appears in almost every description of Otavalo written by non-indígenas and is applied to indígenas, the market, or both.

Myra Waldo mercifully leaves out "colorful," but her description of the Saturday fair is unreal: "Any tourist who can arrange the time to make this trip [to Otavalo] should regard himself as fortunate in having the opportunity to see a truly native, uncommercial, Indian market carried out in the same fashion as it undoubtedly has been for centuries past. . . . Now, here's the complication: the market gets under way at *dawn* . . ." (Waldo 1976: 253). A local author puts it more poetically: "Each Saturday the valley washers up with the splendor of the unfailing sun of this day. It is 5 A.M. and the fair is already" (Guaña 1994: 13).

Foreigners are not the only purveyors of Otavalo as timeless. Zulay Saravino is an Otavaleña who has traveled three times to Europe and a dozen times to the United States since 1980 and is the owner of a travel agency in Otavalo, Zulay, Diceny Viajes, Inc. She published a handbill in English that circulated in Otavalo in the early 1990s. The first line says: "Discover a Different World! Come to Otavalo and its surroundings." The circular reads in part: "Visit indigenous communities that have remained intact since the time of the Incas, where you can watch expert craftspeople at work doing some of the most extraordinary weaving in the world! Participate in folkloric festivals that will transport you hundreds of years in the past! . . . Let yourself be cured by powerful shamans of the western jungle lowlands."

Zulay knows what tourists want, which relates to Erving Goffman's insight about performances: "We know that in service occupations practitioners who may otherwise be sincere are sometimes forced to delude their customers because their customers show such a heartfelt demand for it" (1959: 18). Zulay and many other Otavalos are not just out for personal gain or being cynical but feel compelled to present their community as they think outsiders want to see it.

On the one hand, the guidebooks tout the colorful market and all the things to buy; and on the other, they lament that the market is "touristy" or "very commercial"—except for Myra Waldo, who failed to realize that the market had changed substantially by the time her book appeared. The "it's too touristy" attitude is an extension of the not-in-my-backyard syndrome: yes, we need garbage dumps (or drug rehabilitation centers), but not in my backyard. In tourism this manifests as the "no-one-besides-me" syndrome. Yes, I can visit Otavalo (or Machu Picchu or the Galápagos), but no one else should be there; too many tourists are ruining the place. Rob Rachowiecki's Lonely Planet guide, however, says of Otavalo: "Their prosperity in a changing and difficult world is only to be applauded, but a truer measure of their success is perhaps not only their prosperity but their continuing sense of tribal identity and tradition" (1992: 143).

I have discussed the representation of Ecuador in guidebooks and tourism publicity with various foreigners in Ecuador. Almost everyone said, "I never even thought about it," which is why these representations are so insidious—they operate at a subliminal level and affect visitors' perceptions and expectations of Otavalo (and of Ecuador in general).

There are no statistics on the number of foreign visitors to the fair, although Imbabura province is the third most visited locale in Ecuador (receiving 29.10% of foreign tourists) after Quito (69.51%) and Guayaquil (44.59%) (Hoy, Crucero, September 28, 1994: 6). Quito and Guayaquil lead because they have international airports. It is safe to assume that a visit to Imbabura includes Otavalo, which means that in 1999 Otavalo received 29.10% of the 508,713 visitors to Ecuador, or 148,035 persons. In 1996, the sites receiving the most visitors were Quito, Guayaquil, Otavalo, Esmeraldas, Cuenca, Baños, Galápagos, and parts of Amazonia. This confirms Otavalo's position as number three (El Comercio, Martes Económico, August 27, 1996: 6).

The 1994 article gave statistics on Ecuador's tourist attractions: 56.52% of tourists came for nature, 15.54% for culture, 5.33% for science and art, 15.54% for folklore, and 7.07% for events (unspecified). "Culture" could be colonial art and culture, but for many people it means indigenous cultures. If that percentage is added to folklore and events, then nearly 40% of the foreign tourists are attracted by Ecuador's indigenous heritage, which includes the Otavalo market.

Ecuador considers its indigenous people an embarrassment. CETUR (Corporación Ecuatoriana de Turismo) calls Imbabura "the province of the lakes" on posters and maps because of Lago San Pablo, Cuycocha, and Yaguarcocha, although these are minor attractions. It is rare to see a person swimming or boating in the lakes because they are polluted and, at

8,000 to 11,000 feet, extremely cold. The government cannot be accused of exploiting its indigenous population by turning them into tourist attractions because it ignores them completely, although many Otavalos would like to be "exploited" this way. Word of mouth, the Internet, and foreign travel literature are responsible for publicizing Otavalo.

Visitors to Otavalo include Colombians and Ecuadorians, who are often impossible to differentiate from local whites-mestizos except for visitors who have cameras or are dressed more elegantly than is the local norm. Visitors from Europe and North America are usually distinguishable by height, coloring, and distinctive traditional dress. It is therefore possible to stand at a corner of the market and count these people, ask market vendors their estimates of the number of gringos, peek into restaurants at lunch time, and ask hotels and residencias how full they are and the nationalities of their guests. The result is a semieducated guess: in 1999, the number of visitors from outside South America at the Saturday market ranged from 2,000 to 2,500 (some market vendors insist that 3,000 is more accurate) during the high season (mid-June to mid-September) and from 400 to 600 during the other months. This does not include weekday visitors, as many vendors were quick to point out. Colombian tour buses disgorge shoppers throughout the week, as do tour buses and private vehicles from Quito.

All told, the Saturday fair has seen a substantial increase in tourists. An older Otavaleño, Luis Alberto Arrayán of Ilumán, told me how the market looked before the kiosks were built in 1973, when the vendors stood in rows with piles of ponchos, blankets, belts, shawls, woolen fabrics, and handmade felt hats on the ground. He said in the 1960s only one or two foreigners came to the fair each Saturday.

The increase in visitors has resulted in an increase in the duration and size of the market. Through the 1950s, the market began at dawn (about 5:30 A.M.) and ended at 8 A.M., when local people had sold their goods and made their purchases. The clientele of the market was local; it was not a tourist market, although a few travelers and tourists came through.

This changed in the 1960s, when the market assumed the dual role it has today—traditional and tourist—and Otavalos began to make items specifically for tourists. The mushroom-shaped kiosks built in 1973 were soon insufficient, and each year spaces were painted along the sidewalks and inside the plaza for vendors to erect tables or portable stands. By 1986, counting the kiosks, there were 507 numbered spaces for vendors in the plaza (Meisch 1987: 161).

In 1979, the market started around 6:30 A.M., but it continued until noon because tour buses from Quito arrived around 10 A.M. (Meisch 1980: 26). By 1986, the market began about 7 A.M. and lasted until 4 P.M. to accommodate the late arrivals. Vendors learned it was worthwhile to stay longer, as some buyers did not arrive until after lunch and others returned for a second round of shopping. The market covered the Poncho Plaza, the 24 de Mayo food market plaza, and six blocks of Calle Jaramillo, the north-south street linking the two plazas, which was closed to vehicular traffic on Saturdays (see Map 3.1).

Frank Kiefer of the Hotel Ali Shungu observed that in 1995 a third of his guests still thought the market began at the crack of dawn and ended by noon, following the guidebooks, except for the Lonely Planet guide. Why? Partly it is sheer laziness—the writers probably have not visited the market since the early 1970s. Revisions in these books mainly include the accommodations in major cities. The second reason is the perception, often deliberately fostered, that indígenas are unchanging. Waldo's comment in a 1976 edition of her book that Otavalo has "a truly native, uncommercial, Indian market carried out in the same fashion as it undoubtedly has been for centuries past" is typical and was inaccurate when her book appeared. When books do admit change, they complain that the change is for the worse, that the market is too commercial. By 1997, however, guidebooks by Moon Travel Handbooks, Ulysses, and Footprint at least had the hours of the market correct.

The assertions beginning in 1987 in *The South American Handbook* that "very little of the traditional weaving is now to be seen" imply that the market is no longer authentic. Actually, many traditional weavings (defined here as textiles made continuously over the past several hundred years) are still sold: women's mama belts and baby belts, *sábana* (Sp. sheeting), ponchos, fachalinas, and blankets.

Statements in Fodor's 1986 guide that "a good souvenir is one of the stiff felt hats the women wear to market" and "the mountain Indians, brightly attired in blue, purple, and scarlet ponchos, stream into town for market" were anachronisms. By the mid-1970s, it was difficult to find anyone wearing the old-style handmade felt hats. Similarly, men's ponchos and women's carrying cloths (Sp. *rebozos*) underwent a color shift in the 1940s from red to navy blue and turquoise respectively. By 1980, there was not a red poncho to be seen on an Otavaleño. They are worn by some folk-music and folk-dance groups, but not by men "stream[ing] into town for market." In fact, by 1986, indígenas came streaming to the market on local buses or driving their own vehicles and wearing denim jackets, sweaters, or ponchos.

The Poncho Plaza during the Otavalo Saturday market looking south along Calle Jaramillo, with the original concrete kiosks at the left. The children's playground was removed, and the area is now occupied by artesanías vendors with plastic-covered kiosks. August 1996.

A smaller market has been held since at least the 1960s on Wednesday mornings in the Poncho Plaza. This originally functioned as a wholesale market where indigenous weavers sold to indigenous merchants, who took the goods to Colombia or to Quito and points south. Some tourists arrive on Wednesdays, but this market is still primarily a wholesale market for local merchants. The Poncho Plaza along Calle Jaramillo is lined with indígenas, mainly women and girls, selling narrow macraméd, braided, or woven bracelets (Sp. *manillas, pulseras*). These are sold by the thousands to exporters and to Otavalos traveling abroad. The only other day the manilla vendors come out in force is Saturday.

One advantage for retailers of shopping on Wednesdays is that competition is less and so is the crowding. The streets around the Poncho Plaza are open to vehicles, so a buyer can drive his or her vehicle right up to the merchandise and load. The usual support services appear on Wednesdays (and other weekdays): taxis along Calle Quiroga and trucks along Calle Jaramillo, cargadores with their ropes or pushcarts, and food vendors. Some of these vendors sell complete meals and, if I may be permitted an ethnocentric culinary observation, an alarming preparation called *sal-*

chipapas, consisting of small red sausages (Sp. *salchichas*), made from red dye #4, sodium nitrite, animal parts not normally eaten, and potatoes (Q. *papas*) fried in rancid grease.

At the same time that the Saturday market extended its hours, the market expanded in size. By June 1989, tables mainly belonging to hippie and Ecuadorian jewelry vendors lined both sides of Calle Sucre for one block south of the Poncho Plaza to Calle Morales, almost closing the street to vehicles. By March 1991, the Saturday market had expanded so much that the municipality painted numbered spaces on Calle Salinas between Sucre and Bolívar and on Calle Morales between Sucre and Jara-millo. In 1993, the market expanded in an east-west direction, with the jewelry booths on Salinas crossing Jaramillo and extending halfway to 31 de Octubre. Artesanías stands spread into Calle Sucre on both sides along the Poncho Plaza, almost displacing the pottery vendors who have occupied the space for years. The kiosks began creeping north, entirely lining the street between Calles Quiroga and Quito by 1993 and inter-mittently occupying space north a number of blocks to Calle Pasaje.

By the summer of 1994, the stands extended along Calle Sucre south to Calle Colón, and the street was blocked to vehicles at Colón, a block farther south than the previous year. By May 1998, the inevitable oc-curred: the two main plazas in town, the Parque Bolívar and the Poncho Plaza, were entirely connected by kiosks on Calle Sucre.

Then the market expanded to other days. In January 1989, indíge-nas began holding a Sunday market in the Poncho Plaza, which by Au-gust was three-fourths full. In 1991, some vendors began selling on Fri-days as well as Saturdays, Sundays, and Wednesdays. By 1992, vendors were selling in the Poncho Plaza every day of the week. As César Guaña wrote about tourists who arrived late on Saturday, "They don't know that the next day Sunday there is also a fair Monday, too and Tuesday also" (1994: 13).

Some of the vendors who occupy the Poncho Plaza during the week have space in the plaza on Saturdays; others are squatters who use un-occupied kiosks. All occupants of concrete kiosk space in the Otavalo market must register with the city of Otavalo. Occupants of space in the Poncho Plaza paid an annual fee of 16,000 sucres in 1998 (about $3.00) and a daily rental fee of 2,000 sucres (about $0.22).

Streets around the 24 de Mayo and the Plaza Copacabana food mar-kets have also filled with vendors, so the three markets may eventu-ally meet. The numbered spaces for crafts vendors in the Poncho Plaza alone rose from 507 in 1986 to 953 in 1995. There are also approximately

Lucía de la Torre and her mother, Zoila Arrayán, waiting for customers in the family's quarter-kiosk in the Poncho Plaza. Zoila is crocheting a wool hat; the family's tapestry bags hang behind them. Otavalo Saturday market, August 1998.

1,500 numbered spaces in the streets around the Poncho Plaza, although the areas farthest from the Poncho Plaza have vacancies. Competition for sales space is intense, especially in prime locations in and around the Poncho Plaza. In the spring of 1996, one indígena family bought the rights to a quarter-kiosk in the Poncho Plaza for 4 million sucres (approximately $1,500). Vendors are now selling wherever they can spread a cloth or set up a table without the police forcing them to move.

On Friday, April 2, 1993, the Otavalo municipality bulldozed earth blockades near the Poncho Plaza at the corners of Quiroga and Quito and 31 de Octubre and at the corner of Quito and Sucre in an attempt to keep the white-mestizo potato vendors' trucks from moving into this sector. The municipio had been trying for some time to move all potato sales to the Plaza Copacabana. The potato vendors said the municipio was in thrall to "rich Indians" who wanted to expand their textile sales to these streets. The municipio said the potato vendors blocked traffic and attracted vermin. (Frankly, all of downtown Otavalo is filthy on weekends, as there are insufficient public toilets and garbage cans. The mess cannot be blamed on the potato vendors, although they contribute their share.)

In the late afternoon, the police launched a tear gas attack against the vendors along Calle Quito, enlivening an otherwise boring week as the two groups engaged in a running battle up and down the street while the neighbors and I came out to watch. By Saturday, the police had succeeded in forcing the potato vendors to move to the Plaza Copacabana.

Although Otavalo indígenas constitute about 95% of the vendors in and around the Poncho Plaza (including fruit, vegetable, grain, and cooked food sellers at the north edge of the plaza), African-Ecuadorians and whites-mestizos, including people from other parts of Ecuador and South America, also sell in this section. Sales vary according to the weather, the time of year, and just plain luck. In twenty years of asking people how sales are, the answer is invariably *"más o menos"* (Sp. more or less, so-so). It is hard to know what *"super bueno"* (Sp. super good) sales would be. Even when my godson sells forty or fifty sweaters on a Saturday morning at approximately $12.50 each, he still says sales are *"más o menos."*

With all the *"más o menos"* sales and intense competition, why does the market keep growing and why do people bother to sell? First, the cost of space is minimal, roughly $0.10 per week once the yearly registration is paid, plus transportation. One sale can earn back the costs. Second, the market is a showcase, and many exporters meet the people with whom they annually place large orders in the market. Rafael Chiza, undoubtedly the largest indígena sweater and jacket producer in Otavalo, with 1993 sales of around 225,000 sweaters, started out with a small kiosk in the Poncho Plaza. Third, the Saturday fair is a social event. The people-watching is phenomenal, and Otavalos encounter friends, relatives, and compadres whom they might not otherwise see. I never miss the Saturday fair when I am in Otavalo because of the opportunity to socialize.

Shopping ranks high on the list of many tourists' and travelers' activities: "Shopping for exotic items abroad has been a favorite pastime of travelers since Marco Polo's day at least, but now the travel industry is taking notice. 'Shopping is to travelers as important as museums, as important as cuisine,' says Arthur Frommer, whose Born to Shop series is aimed directly at traveling shoppers" (Pascual 1996: 4). According to an American Express survey of 1,800 travelers around the world, 49% intended to do some serious vacation shopping during the summer of 1996. The most popular items were clothes, jewelry, souvenirs, and sporting goods (ibid.), and the first three are available at the Otavalo market. Undoubtedly, it will soon appear in Frommer's shopping guide.

Who knows how much foreign tourists spend in and around the Poncho Plaza on a Saturday during the high season? CETUR analyzed the expenses of visitors to Ecuador (including tourists, businesspeople, attendees at congresses and conventions, and people visiting relatives). In 1991, 33.40% of visitors' expenses went for lodging, 33.06% for food, 15.11% for transport, 7.79% for recreation, 6.67% for purchases, and 3.9% for other (*Hoy, Crucero,* October 19, 1994: 6). In 1999, tourism generated $343 million in Ecuador (*El Comercio,* July 3, 2000: B-4). Assuming the percentages held, tourists spent $22,878,100 on purchases, much of that on Otavalo-made goods.

If 2,500 tourists spend an average of $100 apiece on crafts per Saturday during the three months of the summer high season, they would have enriched the artisans by $3,000,000. This figure does not include purchases by tourists shopping outside Otavalo, by townspeople, by other Ecuadorian visitors to the crafts market, by Otavalo merchants for sale elsewhere in Ecuador or abroad, or by exporters; nor does it include tourist purchases made during the other nine months of the year.

Many of the disruptive effects of tourism are mitigated by the location of the market in town, rather than in a small indigenous community. Indígenas and visitors meet in the market then most depart. Very few tourists and travelers visit any of the indigenous communities, some of which post flyers and posters in Otavalo welcoming visitors to their weaving workshops. The community of Guanansi, for example, tried unsuccessfully to lure buyers to a Sunday market in that town through the use of colored posters in Otavalo in 1994.

Few visitors even leave the northern half of Otavalo to explore the rest of the town; they move in limited orbits around the Poncho Plaza and Parque Bolívar. There is not a single artesanías store, restaurant, or lodging located south of the Otavalo city hall, which backs on Calle Piedrahita. This street constitutes a white-mestizo Maginot Line, an invisible boundary between tourist Otavalo and the predominantly white-mestizo residential neighborhoods of the town proper (which also have some indígena families). Indigenous merchants, male or female, can have brief contact with several hundred foreigners on a Saturday then return home, often with a roll of bills, to live their lives in the relative privacy afforded by any small town.

The majority of visitors to Otavalo spend one or two nights and days in town, arriving on Friday and leaving on Saturday or Sunday. Hotel and restaurant owners, Otavalo merchants, and tourist agency operators all wish that tourists and travelers would stay longer and try to entice them with descriptions of horseback riding, visits to "Indian villages," local "shamans," hiking, and birdwatching in glossy color brochures. "Artesanal Fabrication hat's in Iluman where also wizards lives" suggests *Otavalo 2000*, published by NativeC@ffe.net, the Hotel Otavalo, and Jatun Pacha Productions. Fortunately, the graphics and maps are better than the English.

Otavalo is not unique in Latin America in managing to control and benefit from tourism and the sales of artesanías to outsiders: Isla Taquile, Peru (Healy and Zorn 1983), nearby Isla Amantaní, and Teotitlán del Valle, Mexico (Stephen 1991a, 1991b), are other examples, although none of these communities approach Otavalo in the quantity of visitors or of goods sold.

Boom Town: The Tourism Infrastructure

The increase in tourism brought an increase in infrastructure in Otavalo and the surrounding region: more hotels, restaurants, travel agencies, artesanías stores, bars, discos, and peñas, which in turn draw more visitors. At this point it is important to reiterate exactly who benefits from tourism to Otavalo. Van den Berghe's study of tourism in San Cristóbal documented an "ethnic division of labor" with foreign and Mexican national tourists and middlemen (ladinos and foreign expatriates), who own and run the hotels and restaurants and serve as guides, at the top and Indian "tourees," whom the tourists come to see and who benefit the least from tourism, at the bottom (1994). In Otavalo, on the other hand, indígenas are involved in every aspect of tourism, owning hotels, restaurants, tourist agencies, yarn stores, the vast majority of artesanías stores and kiosks in the market, and other businesses.

Some services arrived relatively late. The first tourist agency, Zulaytur, opened in 1986 and involved a partnership between an Otavaleña, Zulay Saravino of Quinchuquí, and a white-mestizo, Rodrigo Mora of Otavalo, which foundered amidst mutual recriminations and lawsuits. The white-mestizo retained rights to the name "Zulaytur," and Zulay opened her own travel agency directly across the street from Mora's with the name Zulay, Diceny Viajes, Inc.

Inti Express, which offers airline bookings and tickets on credit and "Indian village tours," money changing, e-mail and FAX facilities, horseback tours, postcards, and air freight, opened at the end of 1988. Inti Pungo opened right across the street in March 1990, and suddenly there were four tourist agencies clustered on Calle Sucre near Colón. As the decade advanced, agencies began sprouting like mushrooms until there

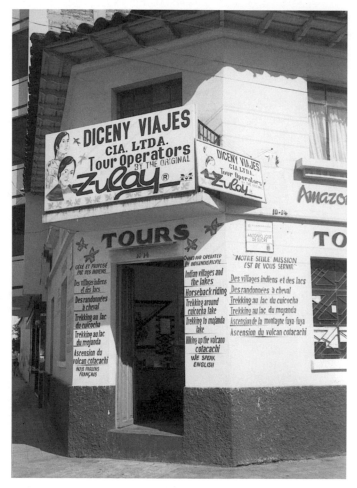

Zulay Saravino's tourist agency at the corner of Calles Sucre and Colón. Otavalo, August 1998.

were nine by late 1995. These agencies exist as much for Otavalos as they do for tourists, with their services including help with Ecuadorian documents and ticket sales on credit.

In Otavalo proper there are three kinds of overnight establishments which cater to different economic groups. The first includes cheap pensiones and residenciales, which charge the equivalent of $2 a night and cater to hippies, backpackers, Peace Corps volunteers, students, and poorer South American visitors. The Shanandoa Pie Shop, located on Calle Salinas across from the Poncho Plaza, has a notebook in which tourists and travelers can write down their adventures, comments, and critiques. The notebook includes comments on the cheaper hotels:

16/5/93 [i.e., May 16, 1993]
If you're ill or on your own in Otavalo, avoid the residencial santa marta. Despite the fact that I was puking my guts up, and freezing cold, the dueño refused to let me have another blanket and was incapable to speaking to any part of my anatomy other than my chest. Eventually I dragged myself to the Residencial Herradura (I think it's spelt?), where the dueña was far more helpful. Now I'm sitting in the pie shop stuffing my face so I guess I recovered. Catrin Jones.

Two other tourists added:

4/6/93 [i.e., June 4, 1993]
Don't worry. We paid the dueño back. We stole the blankets from unoccupied rooms to avoid frostbite and had him chasing us down the corridors with his zampoña. Mind you, we were awoken with blaring music (from the speakers in our rooms) at 7:00 A.M. Diane and Mary (Australia).

Otavalo has moderately priced establishments which charge from $4 to $10 a night and cater to visitors of all nationalities on a more liberal budget. There are a few hotels, such as the new indígena-owned Hotel El Indio, that charge around $15 a night.

The 16-room, 32-bed Hotel Ali Shungu, owned by expatriate Americans Margaret Goodhart and Frank Kiefer, opened in 1991, filling a gap in the town proper for first-class accommodations, with doubles under $45. A new, six-story hotel with 54 rooms and 108 beds, the largest such establishment in town, opened in 1995, owned by an indígena, Rafael Chiza, whose main income is from wool sweater and jacket exports.

In September 1993, there were twenty-four pensions, residenciales, hostels, and hotels, with four more under construction, in a town of approximately 24,000 inhabitants. By January 1995, there were thirty-seven. All are locally owned and operated, at least six or seven by indígenas. There are no chain hotels or multinationally owned hotels anywhere in the region. In addition, there are two indígena-owned and -operated hostels in Peguche: Aya Huma, run by Huaco Lema and his Dutch wife, Mieke de Vet, and Hostería Peguche Tío, which opened in 1996, owned by the Muenala Vega family.

Inti Raymi playing for tourists at the Hotel Ali Shungu. Otavalo, August 2000.

There are accommodations from cheap to first class near Otavalo in Mojanda, Lago San Pablo, Cotacachi, Pinsaquí, and Ibarra. The Hacienda Cusín, located outside the town of San Pablo del Lago about twenty minutes from Otavalo, was featured in articles in *Travel and Leisure, Condé Nast Traveler*, and the *New York Times Magazine* in 1992, 1993, and 1995, which undoubtedly attracted visitors to the region. Other articles about Otavalo appeared in the *Los Angeles Times Magazine, Elle*, the *San Francisco Sunday Chronicle*, and the *Philadelphia Inquirer*. The most expensive accommodations in the region are at La Mirage in Cotacachi, which charges $120 for a double, described by *Condé Nast Traveler* as "anything but Andean rustic, with its antique furniture, sauna, tennis court, solar heated pool, and stabled horses" (August 1993: 43). This kind of publicity draws even more tourists to the region, especially affluent ones.

Otavalo's prosperity is heavily dependent on tourism, which makes the region vulnerable to local, national, and global events that affect the movement of tourists and travelers. While some indígenas are critical of tourism, most would like to see more tourists arrive for the simple reason that their livelihoods depend on them.

CHAPTER 5

Otavalo Music at Home and Abroad

In 1994, Hector Lema of the Otavalo music group Quichua Marka told me: "We have two ways to earn a living in whatever locale: music and the sales of artesanías." Artesanías are still the mainstay of the Otavalo economy, but music has become increasingly important, particularly as a source of income abroad.

A musical renaissance has been underway since the mid-1980s. The signs are everywhere, from the number of young people, especially males, learning traditional music and making recordings to the dozen booths selling Andean (mainly Otavalo) music CDs and cassettes at the Saturday fair to the posters around town advertising concerts. More significantly, Otavalo music is now occupying public aural space. Every morning the UNAIMCO (Sp. Union of Indigenous Artisans of the Centenario Market) office on the Poncho Plaza broadcasts Otavalo music over its loudspeaker system, and appliance stores in the heart of downtown demonstrate their CD systems by playing Otavalo melodies.

In this chapter I make several points about the importance of music in Otavalo life. The first is the pleasure that music brings to Otavalo events, the sense of the sacred and celebration or mourning it evokes at weddings, baptisms, saints' fiestas, house warmings, and funerals. The second concerns music as an expression of correct social behavior, which involves the kinds of bands hired and music played at indigenous social events.

The third point is the salience of music as an economic activity, beginning with recordings by Otavalo groups in the early 1970s and accelerating with Charijayac, a group formed by members of the expatriate Otavalo community in Barcelona, Spain, in 1982. Charijayac was one of the first Otavalo groups to play on the streets of Europe and to record and sell cassettes and CDs abroad. Their triumphal return to Otavalo in 1987 for a concert series precipitated the exodus abroad of young musicians to earn a living through music.

My fourth argument concerns music's function in reaffirming cultural identity and its role as an integrating mechanism that creates a feeling of unity among its listeners and reaffirms social ties. Live music temporarily unites Otavalos of all generations and social classes at concerts or ritual events, and recorded music perpetuates this feeling. Along with food, music is essential in maintaining a sense of community among expatriate Otavalos. I conclude with an account of an indigenous wedding in Peguche in 1993 that exemplifies music's significance.

Mark Slobin and Jeff Titon insist that every human society has music. It is a universal phenomenon, but its meaning is culturally derived, and different cultures interpret it differently (1992: 1). Bruno Nettl argues that defining music as human sound communication outside the scope of spoken language makes it possible for us to study such "nonmusical" events as Koran reading, African drum communication, and Mexican Indian whistle speech (1983: 24). Biologists have defined music as "patterns of sound varying in pitch and time and produced for emotional, social, cultural and cognitive purposes." They expand Nettl's definition of music to include such nonhuman sounds as whales' and birds' songs and suggest that the tonal, rhythmic, and phrasing similarities between humans' and nonhumans' music have their origin in "our ancient, lizard brain" rather than "our more recent reasoning cortex" (Gray et al. 2001: 52–53). In other words, our neurobiology helps explain the universality of music making and its appeal across cultures and species (Tramo 2001), even when we may not understand all the cultural ramifications of another group's music.

In this section I examine the ethnohistorical background of Ecuadorian music, what constitutes music in Otavalo culture, the musical renaissance of the past thirty years, including how Otavalo music has become more audience- and performance-oriented in certain contexts, and the subsequent changes in musical styles and repertoires.

Music in Ecuadorian Life

In the Ecuadorian Andes music (Q. *taki*, Sp. *música*) includes instrumentals and vocals, with separate terms meaning to dance (Q. *tushuy*, Sp. *bailar*). Nettl insists that the function of music in human society is to control humanity's relationship to the supernatural, to mediate between people and other beings, and to support the integrity of social groups. "It does this by expressing the relevant central values of the culture in abstracted form" (1983: 159).

Music has been an accompaniment to Ecuadorian life for millennia. Historically, it is easier to judge its importance in religious and ritual life than to reconstruct core values of now-extinct cultures. Archaeological and ethnohistorical evidence helps us understand what instruments were played in pre-Hispanic times and later for what purposes music was made (see Coba Andrade 1981, 1989, 1992). For example, three Chorrera culture (1000–300 B.C.) whistling bottles are topped by a man playing the panpipes (Lathrap, Collier, and Chandra 1975: 36, nos. 408, 409, 410). Other Chorrera whistling bottles show men playing a flutelike instrument (ibid.: nos. 400, 401).

In Inca times, religious observances, agricultural rituals, and warfare were occasions for music and dance, although "little can be said about Inca music except that it was used for religious chants as well as for love songs" (Rowe 1963 [1946]: 290). Felipe Guaman Poma de Ayala's drawings from ca. 1613 A.D. show a male blowing the conch shell before a captured Huascar (1980 [1615]: Plate 115) and a messenger (Q. *chaski*) blowing the conch to announce his arrival (ibid.: Plate 350). In Guaman Poma's sections on pre-Hispanic life a woman is shown beating a small drum held in one hand while guarding corn from animal predators during the night in February (ibid.: Plate 135). Noblewomen are also shown playing the drum in a portrait of the sixth *colla* (Q. wife of the Inca) as well as drumming while accompanying the Inca at rituals during the fiestas of Inca Raimi and Capac Raimi (ibid.: Plates 130, 242, 258).

These practices were not limited to the Cuzco heartland. In Guaman Poma's drawings of fiestas in the four quarters of the empire, a woman is beating a drum in the Chinchaysuyu, the sector in which Ecuador was located. The accompanying text says the women sing while playing their drums (Sp. *tambor*). The men respond while blowing on an instrument made from a deer's head (ibid.: Plates 320, 294). Father Pablo Joseph de Arriaga, in his campaign to extirpate idolatry, identifies this instrument as the *succha*, made from the head of a guanaco. He wrote: "The women play little drums, which they all have, and some sing and others respond" (1968 [1621]: 50).

According to the classification of Erich von Hornbostel and Curt Sachs (1992 [1961]: 451–458), idiophones are musical instruments that yield the sounds themselves without requiring stretched membranes or strings. This category includes such ancient and modern Andean instruments as bells and rattles. Membranophones include drums, whose sound is elicited by tightly stretched membranes.

Chordophones are instruments where one or more strings are

stretched between fixed points. As far as we know, chordophones were not used in pre-Hispanic times but were introduced by Europeans in the early colonial era; they include guitars, mandolins, violins, and harps, all now part of the indigenous instrumental repertory. The *charango*, a small, guitarlike instrument with ten or twelve strings and a body traditionally made from an armadillo's shell, is typical of Bolivia and has recently been adopted in Ecuador. It is an Andean innovation from the colonial period (Turino 1993: 273). Aerophones are instruments where air itself is the vibrator. Wind instruments and whistles fall into this grouping, so that three of the four main categories of instruments were used pre-Hispanically in the Andes.

The Spanish colonial campaigns to "extirpate idolatry" in the Andes invariably mention music as an integral part of sacrifices to the indígenas' *huacas* (Q. holy sites, or sacred beings embodied in stone, wood, or the mummies of ancestors). An account from 1560 of the "persecution of the demon" in the Huamachuco region of northern Peru mentions that "[a]fter they have eaten, the male witch of the huaca serves chicha and then they engage in great drunkenness and make music [Q. *taquis*], which are songs [Sp. *cantares*] in praise of the huaca" (de San Pedro 1992 [1560]: 171; my translation). Today Otavalos make music (or hire someone to do so) and engage in ritual drinking during celebrations of major life cycle events, for Catholic religious fiestas, and for carnival.

In 1621, Father Arriaga listed the instruments used "to summon the people for the festivals and celebrations of the huacas." These included "many ancient trumpets of copper or silver, of different shape and appearance from ours, the great coiled horns which they play, called *antari* and *pututu*, and other instruments called *pincollos*, which are bone or cane flutes" (Arriaga 1968 [1621]: 69). Elsewhere he mentions "a great many well-made drums of small size, for nearly every woman brings her own for the songs and dances" (ibid.: 19).

Today in Otavalo *antara* (Q.) refers to panpipes from the Peruvian and Bolivian Andes, while *pingullu* (Q.) has several meanings. One refers to a European-style flute with a closed upper end and mouth hole on top. The other refers to a small flute with an undercut lip, small mouth hole on top, two finger holes on top, and a thumb hole on the bottom. The duct flute was introduced by Europeans (Turino 1991: 281), so Arriaga was referring to the pre-Hispanic end-notched flute now generally known as a *kena* (also spelled *quena*).

In the colonial era, when the extirpator encountered these instruments and other objects used in indigenous worship, "[e]verything that is inflammable is burned at once and the rest is broken in pieces" (Arriaga 1968 [1621]: 19). Father Arriaga even attempted to eliminate ostensibly secular musical practices. He focused on Peru; but in the mid-seventeenth century, the bishop of Quito, Alonso de la Peña Montenegro, carried out his own extirpation campaign. In his 1688 instruction manual for missionaries, Montenegro insisted that indigenous music and dance be prohibited because of their association with "idolatry and sorcery." He was adamant that drums, antaras, and deer's heads be destroyed because they were instruments of evil and vivid reminders of pre-Hispanic religious practices (quoted in Taussig 1987: 376–377). The "deer's" head trumpet, actually a guanaco's head, disappeared as these animals were hunted to extinction in Ecuador in colonial times. Pedro de Cieza de León observed guanacos and vicuñas between Cuenca and Loja in southern Ecuador in 1545, but noted that "[t]here used to be an abundance of llamas; now there are few as a result of the wanton killings by Spaniards" (1959 [1553]: 93).

The extent to which the extirpation campaigns failed "is attested by the strength of both Andean musical culture and religion presently in the rural [Peruvian] southern sierra" (Turino 1991: 263), which also holds in the Ecuadorian highlands. The introduction of European music had a more lasting effect on Andean music than religious persecution did. Throughout the Americas, missionaries found music, dance, and pageantry to be potent tools for interesting Indians in church activities (ibid.). Indeed, colonial Ecuadorian accounts in the *Relaciones histórico-geográficas* mention music mainly in the context of Christianizing indígenas. An early description of the Audiencia of Quito noted the many churches and monasteries which administered the Holy Sacraments and "teach Christian doctrine to the indígenas [Sp. *naturales*]." There were also schools "in which they teach indígenas and orphans to read and write, sing and play musical instruments [Sp. *tañer*] . . ." (Cabildo de Quito 1992 [1577]: 256; my translation).

A 1605 description of the Chimborazo area says of the "indios": "Now one can say in general that there are many in this villa and in the district of your corregimiento who know how to read and write; they are singers in the churches; they know how to read Latin and play the guitar [Sp. *tañen vihuelas*] and other instruments" ([Juan Piñan Castillo?] 1994 [1605]: 5; my translation).

Another description from the same year offers a tantalizing hint of indigenous practices in the Ambato area: "The *hijos* [Sp. sons or children] of caciques and some other Indians know how to read and write;

they know how to sing to the organ and play instruments. In their meetings and dances they repeat the memories of their histories in songs
that teach their children" (Descripción de los pueblos 1994 [1605]: 51; my
translation). This same author says of Pelileo, a town east of Ambato,
that the church has "retablos and tabernacles and other adornments for
the divine cult; very good music both plain song and organ, flutes [Sp.
flautas], wind instruments [Sp. *chirimías*], and trumpets [Sp. *trompetas*],
of which the *naturales* [indígenas] of this town are very fond" (ibid.: 55).

The chirimía and the trumpet were probably European. The former is
an oboelike wind instrument about ten inches long with a mouthpiece
made of two pieces of cane (Sp. *carrizo*) lashed together and inserted
into a conical wooden body with five to seven finger holes, counting
one underneath which is actually manipulated with the palm (Garzón
Guamán 1994: 110–113). This instrument was used by the Spanish army
in the sixteenth–seventeenth centuries and was probably introduced to
Ecuador by the Spanish (ibid.: 105). A Guaman Poma drawing of "the
singers of the holy church" show five men with lyrics on a music stand
in front of them and chirimías and perhaps trumpets (larger instruments, about three feet long) in their hands (1980 [1615]: Plate 666; my
translation).

The harp (Sp. *arpa* or *arpa criolla*) "first arrived in the New World
from Spain with the first conquistadors, then with lay colonists, then
with various missionary orders, most notably the Jesuits" (Schechter
1982: 92). Guaman Poma also illustrates this instrument (1980 [1615]: un-
numbered plate [28]). By the eighteenth century, the harp was the most
common instrument in northern Ecuador. The harp played in Imbabura
today is made of cedar, single strung, and without pedals, called diatonic
in English, with precursors that probably date to the colonial period
(Schechter 1992a: 66–71).

The author of the above 1605 document says the indígenas of Calpi
played flutes, wind instruments, and violins in church (Descripción
de los pueblos 1994 [1605]: 59). A description of Guayaquil from 1771
mentions that the "rustics" played "wind instruments [chirimías], little
flutes [Sp. *flutillas*], or panpipes [Sp. *zampoñas*]" (Requena y Herrera 1994
[1774]: 503; my translation). Post–Spanish conquest musical practices
illustrated by Guaman Poma include a woman beating a small drum
and singing in front of a Spanish "*comendero*" who is carried on a litter like the Inca. The text says the encomenderos and their women were
received by the Indians with dances and songs (1980 [1615]: Plate 554).

Warfare and rebellions in the Andes have involved music since at

A Ñanda Mañachi reunion concert at Hostería Peguche Tío, Peguche, August 1996.

least the Inca expansion. Guaman Poma illustrates an Inca warrior blowing the conch (1980 [1615]: Plate 115). Pre-Hispanic relay messengers (Q. *chaskis*) blew a conch to announce their arrival (ibid.: Plate 350); but in Guaman Poma's illustration of a postconquest chaski he is blowing a cow's horn (ibid.: Plate 811), as is an indigenous hunter (Plate 850). Music played a significant role in the 1560 millenarian movement called Taqui Onkoy (Q. dancing or music sickness), centered in Huamanga, Peru. The movement, whose adherents sang and danced, involved a rejection of all things European and a return to indigenous religion (Stern 1982: 52). What is notable is the importance of music.

The conch was blown during Tupac Amaru's rebellion against the Spanish in Peru in 1780–1781. It was so closely associated with the Incas and with warfare that its use was prohibited following the suppression of the Peruvian revolt in 1881 (Campbell 1987: 118). The conch was used in a similar fashion during the 1777 revolt in the Otavalo region. When the uprising spread, the rebel group "extended to the borders of Otavalo, with shouts and music by drums and conch shells [Q. *churus*], which were especially noisy in the barrio of Monserrate, located to the east of the town" (Moreno Yánez 1985 [1976]: 168; my translation). Churu, Hispanicized as *churo*, is Quichua for something curly, which aptly describes the spiral of the conch. The conch is also called a *quipa*. As the 1777 uprising spread, "[a]t midday on Saturday, November 15, Indians from the haciendas armed with sticks, ropes, rocks, and knives, and accompanied by the music of cow's horns [Sp. *bocinas*], conch shells [Sp. *caracoles*], and small drums, entered the plaza of Cayambe" (ibid.: 192). Conch shells were blown in the 1990s and early 2000s during the San Juan dancing in Ilumán, Otavalo town, and San Juan Capilla just west of Otavalo and undoubtedly in other places.

The Ecuadorian polymath Juan Agustín Guerrero illustrated the use of traditional instruments in a series of watercolors completed in 1852. A painting titled *Rondín* shows a night watchman blowing a panpipe or rondador with twelve tubes arranged with long and short tubes alternating, so that two tubes could be blown at once for the melody and harmony. This feature distinguishes the Ecuadorian panpipe from its southern Andean counterparts. Another painting includes a man playing a second kind of rondador, which has thirteen tubes of graduated length, with only one hole blown at a time (Hallo 1981: Plates 107 and 93, respectively). Today *rondín* (Sp.) refers to the harmonica and *rondador* (Sp.) to the panpipe.

In Guerrero's unsettling painting of a Cotacachi indígena blinded by his parents when he was a child so he would not have to pay tribute, the musician is holding a cane in his left hand and playing a small cane or bamboo flutelike instrument with his right hand. The mouth of this instrument is notched on the bottom, with a hole on top near the mouth, four finger holes farther down, and a thumb hole on the bottom. Otavalos identified it as a *pingullu* (Q.), also known as a *pifano* (Sp.). *Pingullu* means lower leg bone in Quichua, and traditionally these flutes were made from the lower leg bone of a condor (I own one such example from Cañar). By extension the word came to mean flutes of this kind made from any material.

In another Guerrero painting, a woman vendor of used clothes is carrying a violin, apparently for sale. In *Dance of the Masquerading Indians on the Day of the Kings* (Epiphany, January 6), one indígena is beating a large drum while another plays the violin. This particular wooden cylindrical drum is quite large, with two heads, probably leather, 2 or 2½ feet in diameter. It is held in front of the drummer's stomach, with the membranes perpendicular to the ground so that both ends can be struck (Hallo 1981: Plates 97, 73, 77; my translation). This kind of drum is generally called a *bombo* (Sp.) in Ecuador (Coba Andrade 1981: 88).

In contrast, there are two Guerrero paintings of a *tamborilero* (Sp.

tambor player), one indigenous, one a university student. These smaller, cylindrical double-headed drums more closely resemble those played by Otavalo musicians today. They have a wooden body and leather membranes at each end laced together across the body of the drum. Both drums painted by Guerrero have a strap that goes over the drummer's right shoulder. The drum is balanced against the drummer's left hip with the heads perpendicular to the ground. The indígena is beating the tambor with only one wooden drumstick held in his left hand. With his right hand he is playing a pingullu (or pifano) like the one described above, but with two finger holes and one thumb hole. The university student is using two wooden drumsticks. These drums are smaller than the one illustrated in Plate 70, with heads about eighteen inches in diameter (Hallo 1981: Plates 79, 113).

Guerrero was an accomplished musician with an interest in Ecuadorian folk music. In 1870 Ecuador's president, Gabriel García Moreno, decreed the establishment of a Conservatory of Music in Quito. Guerrero assumed the directorship for eighteen months in 1871–1872. Around this time, Guerrero was asked by Marcos Jiménez de Espada to compile indigenous and popular melodies for the Museum of Natural Sciences in Madrid. Jiménez de Espada later presented this music at the Congress of Americanists in 1881, without crediting Guerrero (Hallo 1981: 21, 32). Twelve of these pieces, ten with musical notation for the piano (which is not a popular folk or indigenous instrument), are included in the Hallo volume (ibid.: 163–174).

Hassaurek's account of the fiestas of San Juan and San Pedro in Otavalo and Cayambe in 1863 mentions that the flute, violin, guitar, rondador, trumpet, drum, and harp were played by indigenous musicians (1967 [1867]: 150–155). Traditionally, the harp was considered essential for a baby or child's wake (Q. wawa, Sp. velorio), usually with a golpeador (Sp. beater) marking time on the sounding box, as described by Hassaurek for San Juan (also documented by Schechter 1982, 1992a). An indígena harpist playing at a child's funeral, with a small altar visible inside a hut, is illustrated in a painting (ca. 1900) by Ecuadorian artist Joaquín Pinto titled velorio (León Mera 1983 [1892]: front and back cover). A blind mestizo harpist is illustrated in another Pinto painting of the same year (ibid.: 115–116). According to Carlos Conterón of Ilumán, in 1995 a harpist charged S/40,000 to S/50,000 ($16 to $20) per day to play at a child's funeral, which lasts 2½ to 3 days, while a violinist only charged a total of S/80,000 ($32) total. For that reason, violinists are now hired more frequently than harpists. When my godson's baby sister died in the summer of 2000, her parents hired a violinist and guitarist rather than a harpist for the funeral.

Harp music was recorded by Chopin Thermes between 1973 and 1977, played by members of the Imbabura band Ñanda Mañachi. "Huanu-pamba," a "sanjuanito," was played by legendary harpist Juan Cayambe, with Hermelinda Males Thermes beating the rhythm. The album notes say in part: "The harp is an instrument required for such ceremonies as weddings and also the funeral of children (during the wake)" (Ñanda Mañachi 1983; my translation).

The harp is not played as much today, although in 1999 there were still harpists in the communities of Carabuela, Agato, and Peguche and around Cotacachi. I had not heard the harp played live for years until August 28, 1996, when many of the original members of Ñanda Mañachi and several younger musicians united for a concert at Hostería Peguche Tío in Peguche to support Verónica Barahona Lema, the indigenous candidate for Reina de Yamor (Sp. Queen of the Fiesta of Yamor). At that concert Francisco Lema played the harp. I also heard Mariano Cachimuel (Maestro Chavo), a well-known Carabuela harpist, play for a private San Juan gathering in 1997.

Imbabura Music in the Twentieth Century

Northern Ecuador has a rich musical tradition, including the Afro-Ecuadorian music of the Chota Valley, which is beyond the scope of this discussion. Photographs and paintings from the turn of the century show indígenas in northern Ecuador playing the instruments mentioned above, including a bamboo or cane rondador (Chiriboga and Caparrini 1994: Plate 38). A large rondador with thirty-four tubes was photographed in the mid-1940s (Collier and Buitrón 1949: 189). In a photo from around 1900, a male indígena is playing a rondador with twenty-six tubes (Chiriboga and Caparrini 1994: Plate 59).

A photo titled "Day Laborers from Zámbiza" (near Quito) shows males playing small drums and flutes like the tambores described above (ibid.: Plate 36). The photo of the "Musical Band from the Hacienda La Concepción" (in Imbabura), dated 1897, is so grainy that it is difficult to distinguish the instruments. Nonetheless, brass makes an appearance in what look like simple trumpets. Other musicians appear to be playing harmonicas, and two are blowing on what look like huge gourds (ibid.: Plate 39). Finally, a 1906 photo of "A Trio from the Quito Area" shows a male indígena playing the guitar. While we do not know what kind of music was played (except for Guerrero's musical transcriptions), it is evident that certain instruments have long been used in northern Ecuador, while other instruments were absent (for example, the *siku* or double-row panpipes of southern Peru and Bolivia).

One Joaquín Pinto watercolor dated 1899, *el bocinero* (Sp. the *bocina* player), shows an indígena with the bocina, a long instrument made from cow or oxen horns fitted together or attached to a cane tube and used to call people to a *minga* (Q. communal work) or community meeting. Pinto, like Guerrero, painted a *rondín* (in 1900) playing his panpipes, which alternate longer and shorter tubes, typical of the Ecuadorian rondador (Samaniego Salazar 1977: Plates 16, 5). The Spanish names *rondín* and *rondador* came from the Ecuadorian custom of having a night watchman (Sp. *ronda*) play the pipes as he made his rounds (ibid.: commentary on Plate 5).

Two other Pinto paintings dated 1900 portray street vendors. The *cajonera* (Sp. seller of common items or notions) holds two rondadors on her lap. The *vendedor ambulante* (Sp. ambulant vendor) is carrying odds and ends including a guitar (ibid.: Plates 31, 10). Since Guerrero painted a street vendor with a violin for sale, it seems that in the nineteenth century these vendors were a common source of musical instruments.

The history of Imbabura music groups in this century is better seen as a forest than as a tree. By mid-century, many groups—white-mestizo, indígena, and mixed—sprouted at the same time. Some groups flourished, while others withered. Still others had their members grafted onto already existing groups or became the seeds of new groups.

As Hassaurek observed, indigenous Otavalo musicianship is open to anyone willing to learn, from tiny children to grandparents, and most musicians are amateurs who "enjoy the double pleasure of playing and dancing" (1967 [1867]: 156). Local custom holds that males play instruments and sing, females sing but do not play instruments except the drum or *chajchaj* (Q. rattles made from llamas' or sheep's hooves) on occasion, and both sexes dance. At some unknown date, the custom of females playing small drums at fiestas disappeared in most, if not all, of highland Ecuador.

I have no exact date for the formation of the earliest named Otavalo folk music group, that is, a group that played in restaurants and peñas and represented the community at folk music festivals, rather than playing only at local life cycle celebrations. In the early 1940s, although Imbabura was known throughout Ecuador as a music center, "no records of Indian-played music, instrumental or vocal have been made" (Parsons 1945: 116).

Parsons made casual observations about music in the 1940s: the harp was played at weddings, the violin at children's wakes; flutes, pingullos, drums, and panpipes were played by indígenas, and brass instruments were played by a band of white musicians at saints' fiestas sponsored by *priostes* (Sp., also called *capitanes* [captains], the sponsors or managers of a fiesta) (ibid.: 57, 83–84). In general, "[t]here are a few harps, more guitars, one or two violins, perhaps one or two *bandolins*, a few flutes (*flautines*), the immense flutes called *tundas* being almost obsolete, panpipes (*rondadores*), *rondín* and the *bocina* at harvesting and to take cattle to Quito" (ibid.: 116). Panpipes, then as now, were sold at the Saturday market (ibid.: 30). *The Awakening Valley* corroborates Parsons' account with both text and photographs of musicians (Collier and Buitrón 1949). Lema insists:

> Indígena music is the living sentiment of the people, which they sing in honor of the harvests, earth, gods, humans, life and death. Instrumental music is music of the soul, which expresses days of sorrow or happiness. Instruments such as the flute, rondador, pingullo, quena, conch shell, ocarina, bocina, violin, and harp accompany our songs. (1995: 109–110; my translation)

Within this schema, Lema distinguishes local genres, insisting that "festive music for weddings cannot be played at funerals or for San Juan; the warrior music for San Juan cannot be played at weddings or funerals, just as funeral music cannot be played at weddings or San Juan" (ibid.: 110). He also notes that the rondador, pingullu, and flauta are played at weddings, masses for the saints, bullfights, and carnival; the harp and violin are played at funerals; and all the instruments are played during San Juan (ibid.). Lema and older Otavalos like Carlos Conterón note that wind instruments were often played when indígenas walked along the paths on errands or took their sheep and cows to pasture, but this practice is disappearing.

Sanjuanitos and Other Musical Genres

Musical arrangements called *albazos, fandangos, yumbos, danzantes, aires típicos, pasillos* (Sp.) or *yaravis* and *huaynos* (Q.), sometimes with vocals and sometimes as instrumentals, appear on the early Imbabura records, except for *Ñanda Mañachi 1*, which has only Sanjuanes (1984 [1973–1977]). The aire típico and albazo "have been converted into displays of Ecuadorian criollismo. They have a fusion of two rhythms as a

Javier de la Torre plays the charango while his uncle Alfonso de la Torre looks on. Fiesta of San Juan/Inti Raymi, June 2001.

consequence of the evolution of Ecuadorian vocal music." The yumbo and danzante are lively dances performed in pairs or in a group, and the passacalle is a Spanish *pasodoble* (a kind of march) "with national characteristics" (Coba Andrade 1994a: 56; my translation).

The fandango and its variants the *malagueña, rondeña, granadina*, and *murciana* (Sp.) were brought to the Americas from Spain in the seventeenth century (Guerrero Gutiérrez 1993: 132). Many musicians say that some music (for example, the albazo) has disappeared from the Otavalo repertoire. Cornelio Cabascango insisted: "Indígenas don't play this music anymore." This appears to be true, as an analysis of contemporary tape cassettes and CDs suggests.

The influences on Imbabura indigenous music in the 1960s and 1970s were mainly Ecuadorian—the white-mestizo styles mentioned above—while the 1980s and 1990s saw influences from Bolivian, Peruvian, and Colombian Andean music as well as from reggae, cumbia (coastal music), rock and roll, rap, techno, hip hop, and salsa.

If records had been made before 1970, they would have included Sanjuanitos, a musical genre that is typical of Imbabura province. One of the earliest Otavalo-area indigenous music groups was Ñanda Mañachi (Quichua for "lend me the path," which people call out when they walk on a path past another person's house). All the songs on *Ñanda Mañachi 1* (1984 [1973–1977]) are Sanjuanitos (also spelled San Juanes, Sanjuanes, etc.). The name comes from San Juan Bautista (Saint John the Baptist), whose feast day is June 24, during which Sanjuanitos are played. This fiesta is often conjoined with the fiesta of San Pedro on June 29; both are now called Inti Raymi after the Inca solstice festival.

When Hassaurek visited Cayambe during San Pedro in 1863, he wrote of the indigenous music: "The orchestra consisted of a trumpet, a big drum, two flutes, and a horn. They played the same tune, consisting of only a few notes, during the whole of the mortal two hours that the dance lasted. This tune is also called 'San Juan'" (1967 [1867]: 162–163).

Sanjuanitos have been described as "monotonous, pitiable" (ibid.: 150) and "trance-inducing" (Kyle 1995: 241). I find them melodic and hypnotic. On a more technical level the Sanjuanito is characterized as having a simple 2/4 meter. "Especially in performances with the harp, amidst the regular repetition of a single, primary motive, one new break, or secondary motive, may be inserted" (Schechter 1982: 247). Sanjuanes are repetitive, with one predominant motive, usually eight-beat phrases with close or identical first-half and second-half rhythms, characteristic pitch and rhythm, and harmony that demonstrates a bimodal relationship of minor to relative major. "These features give many . . . *sanjuanes* a similar sound, and provide the grammar of the musical language of Cotacachi Quichua *sanjuan*" (Schechter 1992b: 401–402). For beginning listeners, the eight-beat phrases and the repetition are diagnostic and easy to discern.

Traditional Sanjuanitos are sung in Quichua, which makes them particularly indigenous and incomprehensible to the majority of other Ecuadorians and foreigners. Sanjuanitos have other important characteristics. They can be played on one instrument (for example, a harp, harmonica, or guitar), with feet stamping out the rhythm (or a golpeador beating on the harp), or by a group of musicians. They can be sung by one person or many, by males, females, or mixed groups.

Typically, in many Otavalo-area Sanjuan performances the musicians (male and female) call out or talk above the music, often in a falsetto, and also yip and hiss. These features are particularly characteristic of Otavalo Sanjuanes and are not typical of Peruvian and Bolivian Andean music. Otavalo female vocalists sing in a falsetto, which is pan-Andean. When a violin is part of the ensemble, there are frequently two eight-beat violin instrumentals between verses. None of these technical descriptions captures the beautiful, haunting, soulful quality of Sanjuanes, the exuberance of many performances, or the extent to which a Sanjuanito evokes images of home for Imbabura indígenas.

Sanjuanitos are intended for dancing, not for performance in front of a group of standing or seated listeners, and they do not conform to Western musical standards of alternating chorus and verse with a musical resolution. When listening to Sanjuanes in a folk-music club in Otavalo, one American friend asked me, "Where's the rest of it?"

Any music that has been played for at least several centuries (if not longer) can be called traditional. The time depth of traditional Sanjuanitos results in variants of many songs. John Schechter recorded numerous versions of such typical Sanjuanitos as "Rosa María" (1982, 1992a). Over time new Sanjuanitos are composed and old ones change or drop out of the repertoire. When I asked Otavalos who, if anyone, "owns" Sanjuanitos and other songs, Carlos Conterón answered that some musicians, such as Galo Maigua of Hualpo, a barrio of Ilumán, are recognized as composers of certain Sanjuanes, "but much more we speak of music from a certain place." This concept is expressed in the phrase *cada llacta* (Sp. each, Q. town or place), meaning "that each community is to a degree unique among area communities." For example, during San Juan "musicians descend from all the circum-Cotacachi comunas playing flute and melodies peculiar to particular comunas" (Schechter 1992a: 8).

This association of Sanjuanes with communities is evident on recordings. For example, the Ñanda Mañachi/Bolivia Manta album *Churay, Churay!* (1983) contains eleven titled Sanjuanitos, each listed with its associated community: for example, "Ñuca Llacta, Sanjuanito, [from] Punyaro, Imbabura, Ecuador." Other Sanjuanitos on the album are associated with the communities of Zuleta, Otavalo, Yacuchimba (Cayambe area), Carabuela, San Juan Capilla, and La Rinconada, and several are identified as being from Imbabura province.

According to Nettl, music supports "the integrity of individual social groups . . . by expressing the relevant central values of the culture in abstracted form" (1983: 159). How do Sanjuanitos, which Otavalos consider particularly theirs, fit this thesis? Otavalo values include an emphasis on participation and inclusion and on harmony, balance, and reciprocity among humans and between humans and the supernatural or the forces of nature. With regard to music, these values can be considered in relation to lyrics, performance practices, and album notes, especially if the notes are written by Otavalos themselves. I am much less convinced that core values are expressed in musical form and structure (or, if they are, how it would be possible to substantiate this).

In an elegant analysis of the Sanjuanes of the Cotacachi area, Schechter asks how Cotacachi lifeways are reflected in the verse structures or texts of Sanjuanes (1992b: 402). While lifeways are not isomorphic with core values, lifeways usually express these values. Schechter notes the frequency with which *purina* (Q. to walk) and its variations appear in Sanjuanes. "*Purina* may be traced through its various metaphoric courses—from walking along the *chaki ñan* (footpath), to walking for the benefit of the comuna or for one's own betterment, to wandering, going about, for love, sadness, or as an outlet for other emotions" (1992b: 405). With the increase in ownership of motor vehicles and international travel, "driving" and "flying" might well replace "walking" in future Sanjuan lyrics.

The values of inclusion and participation are expressed in Sanjuanitos in a number of ways. Sanjuanes are first and foremost dance music, with steady, rhythmic beats—and everyone dances. Adults encourage toddlers to dance by clapping their hands and calling *baile, baile!* or *tushuy, tushuy!* (Sp., Q. dance!). Some dancing is done by individuals moving in a circle in which everyone joins; some dancing is by couples, but the couples may be mixed by age. Both kinds of dancing often occur at the same time in the same space. Traditionally, the concept of a concert where musicians played while people sat around and listened was as alien as an adults-only party. Today the music played at social events is still dance music, and most people dance. After Otavalo fiestas, I find most American parties hopelessly sedentary.

Participation is also encouraged in music-making itself. Although Otavalos recognize different levels of musical talent, playing an instrument, singing, and dancing are considered abilities that everyone possesses. No one is discouraged from singing, playing, or dancing at fiestas or is criticized for not being good enough. (Professional or semiprofessional music groups have developed more stringent standards.) Women who could never compete with Joan Baez sing along with everyone else. Little boys join their father's or big brothers' San Juan group, huffing and puffing on harmonicas. They are neither corrected or criticized nor praised.

The importance of spirituality and reciprocity in and between the human and spiritual realms is expressed musically in various ways, including the occasions on which music is played and the lyrics. Music is considered essential at all religious and ritual occasions.

The entrepreneurial ethic is expressed in the mass exodus of young men to play on the streets of Europe and North America, the Otavalos' attitude toward the commercialization of music, and the current prodigious output and sales of cassettes and CDs. I have never heard Otavalos criticize the commercialization or commoditization of music, because commercial success of any kind is admired (and sometimes envied). The commercialization of music has its roots in textile merchandising and the Otavalos' emphasis on entrepreneurship and business acumen.

The First Recordings

According to Nicolás Chiluiza Rhea (who produced a series of at least six folklore records, "Alegrías del Imbabura," in the 1970s and early 1980s), the group Los Corazas, consisting of Señor Mena and his sons (mestizos from Cotacachi and Otavalo), was founded in the 1940s but did not record until twenty years later (Los Corazas n.d. [1969]). Another early group, formed around 1950, was the Grupo Típico de Luis Aníbal Granja, mestizos from Ibarra who did not record until 1970. Cotacachi's famous Orquesta Típica Rumba Habana (1983) was not a folklore group but contributed to the national reputation of the region, while La Banda de Andrade Marín (1989) played fiesta music.

Rhea's series included music by such white-mestizo groups as Inca-Taki (n.d. [1978]), Los Ulpianinos (1981), and Lucho Soto y Su Conjunto (n.d. [1979 or 1980]). Many of these musicians were full-time professionals who played at private events (weddings, funerals, baptisms, etc.); some also joined folklore groups. Indigenous groups like Ñanda Mañachi (1979, 1983, 1984 [1973–1977], 1988), Conjunto Rumiñahui, later known as Conjunto Indígena "Peguche," which included dancers and musicians (1977, 1979, 1986), Hijos de Imbabura, and Conjunto Indígena Folklórico Indoamérica (n.d. [1976]) were conceived as self-consciously traditional and folkloric (i.e., indigenous).

These groups and Inca-Taki (whose members were Otavalo whites-mestizos) came into existence between 1967 and 1977 and played at folk-music clubs (Sp. *peñas folclóricas*), civic events, and local and national music festivals. A founder of Inca-Taki, Eduardo Gonzáles, opened Antara around 1975, the first store in Otavalo to sell musical instruments. Antara is still in operation on Calle Sucre near the Poncho Plaza.

The growth of tourism and textile merchandising also contributed to an increase in the number of musical groups in the Otavalo valley. By 1977–1978, it was possible to speak of a musical renaissance:

> . . . the Otavalo area seems to be going through a cultural renaissance, at least in terms of music. Many young Indígenas have formed groups which combine local folk music with general Andean folk music. Not

surprisingly, these young people live in town or in the villages also known for commercial weaving. In addition to playing in local restaurants which cater to tourists, many of these groups have recorded albums. (Chavez 1982: 71)

Chavez mentions Ñanda Mañachi, Conjunto Peguche, Indoamérica, and Los Chaskis (ibid.).

A Peguche community oral history also treats the beginnings of the musical revival: "The music groups formed in the '70s. The first group, Rumiñahui, was organized by a mestizo family. The majority of the group were also mestizos, but they played indígena music. They received lots of publicity" (Korovkin et al. 1994: 30; my translation). The next step was the formation of indigenous groups: "Young indígenas, seeing this example, felt the need to form their own groups. Thus appeared Ñanda Mañachi, Peguche, Atahualpa, Obraje. They were part of a cultural movement. They didn't just play music, but spoke of the need to defend indigenous culture, to struggle for our own identity" (ibid.: 30).

According to Lema:

Alejandro Chahuala of Peguche, a music aficionado, formed the first music and dance group, "Atawallpa," which performed in the fiestas of Otavalo [e.g., Yamor]. From this experience numerous music and dance groups were formed: duos, trios, soloists, who have exalted our own music, succeeding in spreading it within and without our country, such as "Peguche," "Ñanda Manachi," "Charijayac," and others, conserving the cultural feeling of autochthonous music. (Lema 1995: 110; my translation)

Lema omits Rumiñahui, which was a mestizo group. When he credits Atawallpa as the first Peguche group, the word "indigenous" is implied.

Conjunto Indígena "Peguche" made three $33\frac{1}{3}$ RPM recordings over nine years, *Folklore de mi tierra* (Sp. Folklore of My Land) in 1977, *Mushuc Huaira Huacamujun* (Q. A New Wind Is Sounding) in 1979, and *Huiñai Causai* (Life Keeps Growing, meaning from generation to generation) in 1986. The conscious emphasis on music as an expression of indigenous values, and its role in cultural resurgence, is evident from the album notes of *Mushuc Huaira Huacamujun*:

We who form the Conjunto Indígena "Peguche" offer this partial sample of our cultural values. This eagerness to reencounter our roots represents years of silent dedication.

Now we can see the face of nature, not to dominate her, but to understand and to feel her as equal to humans. It is our proposal to com-
mence a new history: not to dominate humans, not to dominate
peoples, not to dominate nature. Conjunto Indígena "Peguche." (1979;
my translation)

The *Huiñai Causai* album notes include similar sentiments, ending
with the admonition that "[t]hose who do not recognize their historical origin and culture are like trees without roots" (Conjunto Indígena
"Peguche" 1986; my translation).

There was a major difference between musicians and textile merchants traveling within Ecuador and abroad from the mid-1960s through
1980. For the most part, music or music and dance groups were sponsored by governments or nonprofit organizations, while textile merchants ventured out on their own. For example, Lucita Fichamba of
Peguche told me that her father traveled to Mexico in the late 1960s
with Conjunto "Peguche" for an official performance. In 1976, when Lucita was fourteen years old, she sang for a year with the Peguche troupe
Grupo Indoamérica. Lucita said she was "the first indígena woman
singer in a group" (which, whether strictly true or not, speaks to the
fact that female singers were rare). Lucita continued: "We sang in Quichua. The group played mostly here in Peguche, but also in Quito and in
Ambato—we were invited to play for Carnival—but we didn't leave the
country." Later Indoamérica became part of Ñanda Mañachi, one of the
best-known and most enduring local groups.

Ñanda Mañachi was formed in 1969, from a combination of four different bands, including singer Enrique Males' group Los Pucara (1977).
Males is a well-known musician from an Ibarra Otavalo indigenous
family who continues to record (1994) but does not wear a braid or traditional dress. Almost immediately, the newly formed group toured France
(under what auspices I am not sure, but I suspect that a formal invitation and French financial help were involved; Enrique's sister, Hermelinda Males, who wore Otavaleña dress, married a Frenchman, Chopin
Thermes, and Enrique himself married and later divorced a French-
woman). It is no surprise that Ñanda Mañachi's first trip abroad was to
France, because the French have long been aficionados of Andean music.
As a result of this trip, a strong Ñanda Mañachi–French connection was
established.

The cobbled-together Ñanda Mañachi dissolved into separate groups
after the French tour, one of which included Enrique Males, while
another segment retained the Ñanda Mañachi name. Chopin Thermes

moved to Ecuador and became the promoter of the group, recording the music for their first record, *Ñanda Mañachi 1*, between 1973 and 1977. A sidebar credits the deceased Hermelinda Males with being the golpeador (the person who beats the rhythm on the side of the harp) for one piece with harpist Juan Cayambe. (She died in childbirth before the album was released.)

The musicians did not all belong to the group at the same time. Zoila (Zulay) Saravino, for example, was in *colegio* (Sp. seventh through twelfth grade) in Quinchuquí when Chopin approached one of her teachers and asked if he knew a female who could sing for *Ñanda Mañachi 1*. Zulay's teacher recommended her. "I wasn't a [professional] singer, but I knew some of the songs. They had all the words written out, so I sung with them for two days. I was innocent; I wasn't paid anything."

The hand of Chopin Thermes is also evident in the 1979 album *Llaquiclla* (Q. sadness) by Quinchuquimanda Imbayacuna (Q. Imbayas from Quinchuquí), which credits Chopin with the recording. Olga Fisch called Thermes a major promoter of Ñanda Mañachi (1985: 202)—and, I would add, of Imbabura indigenous music in general.

According to the album notes of Quinchuquimanda Imbayacuna, members of this extended family left Quinchuquí after the destructive earthquake of 1868, selling or bartering textiles and engaging in the animal trade in Ibarra. By the 1940s, a number of families had settled in Ibarra permanently. The album notes from their 1979 album *Llaquiclla* say: "The Villa of Ibarra, a strange and hostile world, full of discrimination and exploitation, as much physical as emotional. Now the city rather than the countryside was the center of their world. Now they did not trade or sell blankets, but did business in animals, specializing in the raising of pigs which they converted into a true art" (Quinchuquimanda Imbayacuna 1979).

As the notes emphasize, the Imbayas did not become whites-mestizos but maintained their ties with Quinchuquí, returning to plant and harvest, celebrate fiestas and weddings, visit relatives, "to be born and to die." In Ibarra they celebrated San Juan and San Pedro and spoke Quichua, struggling to maintain Otavalo traditions. "Nonetheless, the city and its inhabitants have learned much from the Imbayas, of their fiestas, of their work, of their manner of being, of their vision of the world" (ibid.).

The Imbayas of Ibarra organized the first indigenous soccer team, playing locally and nationally. According to Carlos Conterón, the music group formed when the soccer players held a mass for their victory in a match and entered the soccer field playing musical instruments. Photos of the team are included on the inside of the album, along with a list of their triumphs.

The Imbayas' album is the first example of Otavalo diaspora music. Slobin argues that music can forge coalitions or create ethnic boundaries by resisting or accommodating the sensibilities of the larger society. "It can stay hidden within local confines or move up in visibility, being noticed, or even celebrated, by the commercial and governmental powers that be. Alongside food, music can be—and usually is—the main means of identification of diasporic groups . . ." (1994: 245).

Music has become increasingly important to Otavalos as a unifying force, especially as more Otavalos live outside the valley. Throughout Andean South America, there has been a steady flow of people from the countryside to major cities, and music has often served as a reminder of ethnic and cultural roots. In Lima, Peru, in the 1970s migrants from the Peruvian altiplano formed urban panpipe ensembles that played for their own private events behind closed doors and sometimes at public folklore events (Turino 1993: Chapter 6).

According to Carlos Conterón, Quinchuquimanda Imbayacuna was one of the first folklore groups to play in Europe, traveling to Spain in the 1960s. Ñanda Mañachi was one of the first to play with other Andean musicians. During one of their European tours they hooked up with Bolivia Manta (Q. From Bolivia), a group of expatriate Peruvian and Bolivian musicians. Nicolás Rhea recalled how, around 1980, Ñanda Mañachi and Bolivia Manta walked together from Peguche to the center of Otavalo past his store on Calle Bolívar, playing music during the fiesta of Yamor. The musical influences were bi-directional, with each group learning the other's music. The album released as a result of the encounter (*Churay, Churay!* recorded in 1982 in Cologne, Germany, and released in 1983) contains sixteen selections: twelve Ecuadorian, two Peruvian, and two Bolivian.

Otavaleño sociologist (and current mayor) Mario Conejo Maldonado credits such musical groups as Ñanda Mañachi and Grupo Peguche with being significant agents in the Otavalo cultural renaissance: "They developed our dance and music, but at the same time amplified our ethnic discourse and gave more motivation and substance to our struggle for the land and culture" (1995: 169; my translation). He also emphasizes the importance of Bolivia Manta's concerts in Ecuador, which he says "convulsed urban Indians," whose situation was "complex." These urban indígenas included the generation of Otavalos growing up in Quito, Ota-

valo, Ibarra, Tulcán, and other towns and cities. Conejo, himself an
"urban Indian" who grew up in Bogotá, Colombia, describes the effects
of Bolivia Manta's concerts in Ecuador in the early 1980s:

> They [urban Indians] were subjected to a strong process of accul-
> turation which began with dress, braid [guango] included, continu-
> ing to their language, and ending with their mentality. Everyone said
> we had to change. In the middle of this Bolivia Manta arrived, and
> caramba! Indígena music was also good. You could hear it on the radio,
> with quality, and Indians could also perform on a well-lighted stage
> with good amplification, with publicity on radio and television, say-
> ing interesting things between songs. It turns out that there could be
> handsome Indians with their own clothes, braid, and hat. The Qui-
> chua language could be not only internal, but also for a larger public,
> with the capacity to transmit poetry and truth. Then, in a subliminal
> form, the urban youth were impressed. Very simply, they appropri-
> ated the image and perspective brought by these musicians. (ibid.: my
> translation)

Southern Andean music has long been more popular in Europe than
in the United States, and Andean groups played in Europe throughout the 1960s, 1970s, and 1980s. The early groups consisted primarily
of whites or mestizos; travel was not an option for Peruvian, Bolivian,
or Chilean indígenas. The Peruvian group Urubamba helped popularize
Andean music in Europe. In 1965, they were known as Los Incas and appeared on the same bill as Paul Simon and Art Garfunkel at the Théâtre
de L'Est Parisienne in Paris, France. Los Incas recorded one of the most
famous Andean melodies, "El Condor Pasa," with Simon and Garfunkel.
They collaborated with Paul Simon on his first solo album and accompanied him on a concert tour in the fall and spring of 1973. He produced
Urubamba's 1974 album.

A Chilean group, Los Calchakis, also contributed to the early popular-
ization of Andean music. They performed the music for the soundtrack
of Mikis Theodorakis' *State of Siege,* a film about the Tupamaro guer-
rillas of Uruguay. They released the soundtrack recording of the film in
1973 as well as another recording that year titled *Música indígena de
América.*

Table 5.1 illustrates important features of the early Otavalo valley
record albums. They were recorded within a sixteen-year span between
1970 and 1986, with many clustered in the late 1970s, the period iden-

tified by Chavez as witnessing a musical renaissance. This renaissance coincided with the growth of the tourism and textile industries. Except for *Churay, Churay!* all albums were recorded in Ecuador and contain only Ecuadorian music, mainly Sanjuanes.

The table does not include tape cassettes because there is insufficient information on many cassettes or their covers. There is a booming business in Ecuador in bootleg cassettes, which are sold in the markets or on the street. This makes it impossible to determine the recording date and locale and deprives musicians of their royalties. Hardly any musicians are now recording $33\frac{1}{3}$ RPM records; instead many groups have simultaneous CD and cassette releases. As with many technologies, there were overlaps in the production of records, cassettes, and CDs, with the last important Otavalo records produced around the same time as the first CDs. For example, Conjunto "Peguche"'s last record album, recorded in Quito, was released in 1986, and Runallacta's record, recorded in France, was released in 1988. Meanwhile, Ñucanchi Ñan recorded their *Ñucanchi Causay* CD in West Germany ca. 1984 and their *Kangunapag* CD in Berlin ca. 1985. The more established group of older musicians recorded with older technology in Ecuador, while the younger group recorded with newer technology in Europe.

The original Ñanda Mañachi made their last recording, appropriately called *Internacional*, consisting of twelve Sanjuanitos, in Paris in 1988 (this concert did not include Bolivia Manta). As opposed to some Otavalo music groups, Ñanda Mañachi saw their main purpose as presenting traditional Imbabura or Otavalo music. The group continues with new musicians, many of whom split into smaller groups during the summer months, including Mashicuna (1996), who travel in Europe and North America.

In early December 1994, Ñanda Mañachi played in Peguche for Luis Felipe Duchicela, national secretary for indigenous affairs and ethnic minorities, when he visited the town. On August 19, 1995, a young version of Ñanda Mañachi played in the Plaza Santo Domingo in Quito for the Month of the Arts celebration. In 1998 another Ñanda Mañachi branch released a CD, *Peguche* by Ñanda Mañachi Shikan, that includes an electric guitar as well as traditional instruments, launching their album with a concert at Hostería Peguche Tío in Peguche on January 31.

Radio Bahá'i in Otavalo began broadcasting in 1977, with programming in Spanish and Quichua. The station plays traditional music, including many of the albums listed above, and also sponsors an annual

TABLE 5.1. 33$\frac{1}{3}$ RPM Records of Imbabura Music

Group	Provenience & Ethnicity	Album Title	Date	Where Recorded or Manufactured	Percentage Ecuadorian Music
Grupo Típico de Luis Aníbal	Quito, Otavalo, Cotacachi mestizos and indígenas	Llacta-Pura	1970	Quito, Ecuador	100
Indoamérica	Peguche indígenas	Alegrías del Imbabura, Vol. 3	1976	Quito, Ecuador	100
Conjunto "Peguche"	Peguche indígenas	Folklore de mi tierra	1977	Quito, Ecuador	100
Los Pucara	Ibarra indígenas	Canción y Huayno	1977	Quito, Ecuador	100
Inca-Taki	Otavalo mestizos	Alegrías del Imbabura, Vol. 4	1978	Quito, Ecuador	100
Conjunto "Peguche"	Peguche indígenas	Mushuc Huaira Huacamujun	1979	Quito, Ecuador	100
Quinchuquimanda Imbayacuna	Quinchuquí indígenas	Llaquiclla	1979	Ibarra, Ecuador	100
Los Ulpianinos	Ibarra mestizos	Alegrías del Imbabura, Vol. 6	1981	Quito, Ecuador	100
Los Corazas	Otavalo area mestizos	Aires de mi tierra	1982	Ecuador	100
Ñanda Mañachi	Otavalo and Ibarra area indígenas; Peruvians and Bolivians (Bolivia Manta)	Churay, Churay!	1983	Cologne, Germany (in 1982)	75 (25 Peruvian and Bolivian)
Ñanda Mañachi	Otavalo, Ibarra, Cayambe indígenas	Ñanda Mañachi 1	1973–1977 (released 1984)	Ibarra, Ecuador	100
Conjunto "Peguche"	Peguche indígenas	Huiñai Causai	1986	Quito, Ecuador	100

folk-music festival. Its radio programs helped draw attention to and promote local music. Because weaving is a repetitive activity, many weavers listen to music while they work, with the clattering of the heddles and thump of the beater keeping time to the music. Long before families had record players or tape cassette players, they owned battery-powered or electricity-operated radios which were tuned to Radio Bahá'i.

The early 1980s also saw the first *peñas folclóricas* (Sp. folk-music clubs) open in Otavalo. These clubs offer drinks, snacks, and live Andean music and are open only on weekend nights. They attract a mixed crowd of foreign visitors, Otavalos, and local whites-mestizos. By 1986, there were three peñas; by 1995, there were five. One of the earliest peñas, Los Chaskis on Calle Quiroga across from the Poncho Plaza, closed; but the eponymous group still exists and tours Europe in the summer. Many Otavalo restaurants also hire local and foreign Andean musicians to play on Friday and Saturday nights.

Restaurants and peñas serve as a venue for the transmission of musical genres, not only Ecuadorian but Peruvian, Chilean, Colombian, and Bolivian, as young musicians from these countries travel throughout South America and abroad earning their living playing gigs. The Chileans have contributed a particular leftist brand of music called *nueva canción* (Sp. new song), popularized by Violeta Parra and Victor Jara. When the more famous southern Andean bands, such as Los Kjarkas of Bolivia, tour Ecuador they play larger venues (concert halls and coliseums) but have local groups open for them. After Los Kjarkas played in Ecuador in 1989, some of their tunes (such as "Llorando se fue") appeared in the repertoires of Otavalo groups.

Ecuadorian folklore groups often face a choice between adherence to local traditions and audience appeal. A Saraguro folklore troupe formed in the 1970s faced this dilemma: "In early performances the troupe sought to maintain as much 'authenticity' as possible, for the members felt it important to be genuine representatives of the indígenas of Saraguro. This was not always easy, as the long and repetitive nature of many Saraguro traditional performances diminished audience appeal" (Belote and Belote 1981: 469).

Otavalo music was never intended for performance before a crowd of passive onlookers. The repetitive nature of Sanjuanitos makes them perfect for long, extended dance numbers but much less compelling for seated listeners. In the fall of 1978, I attended a Ñanda Mañachi concert in Quito. The famous elderly harpist Juan Cayambe performed a solo. But once Cayambe began to play he would not stop; he was playing traditional harp music in the traditional manner, as if he were at a child's funeral where the music goes on all night. The master of ceremonies approached from the sidelines several times then shrugged and let the harpist play for another fifteen minutes, as the audience applauded his decision.

The change from participatory to performance music began in the mid-1970s and accelerated rapidly in the 1990s with the advent of Otavalo musical globalization. At this point it is worth recalling Wilk's argument (1995) that cultural differences are increasingly expressed in a limited range of channels and images. The average selection on a European or American pop recording runs three to four minutes, and buyers of cassettes and CDs are accustomed to a variety of selections rather than one thirty-minute Sanjuanito. Beginning with records made in the 1970s, Otavalos have recorded traditional music in two- to five-minute selections for a good reason: this format is familiar to their customers, and it sells.

Otavalo Music in Spain

Two events which profoundly affected Otavalo music transpired in Spain in the early 1980s. The first was the formation in 1982 and subsequent recordings of Charijayac, which became one of Otavalo's premier music groups even though its members live in Spain. Charijayac, which has now disbanded, consisted of Sayri (Luis H.) Cotacachi, Chasqui (Segundo) Tituaña, Mayu (Marcos) Quiñones, Quipus (César H.) Cotacachi, Raymi (Humberto) Tituaña, and Rupay (Alberto) Cachiguango. The members of the group are residents of the Otavalo expatriate community in Barcelona. By taking Quichua nicknames (or Hispano-Quichua ones—"Quipus" has the Spanish plural), the group affirmed their Otavalo ancestry. When they were young, members of Charijayac played music with older members of the Barcelona weaving and sweater-making community during their lunch-hour break.

The second event was Jesús Fichamba's 1985 triumph at the OTI, an international Spanish- and Portuguese-language song competition held annually in Spain. Fichamba is an Otavaleño from Peguche who wears traditional dress but lives in Guayaquil. When he tied for top place at the OTI, it was a victory not only for Ecuador but for indígenas. Because Charijayac did not become known in Otavalo until 1987, Jesús Fichamba's 1985 success came first in terms of having an effect on Otavalo.

The annual OTI music competition is open to citizens of Spanish-

Jesús Fichamba performing at Peguche Falls. Peguche, October 1994.

and Portuguese-speaking countries. This contest is virtually unknown among Anglos in the United States but carries tremendous prestige in Latino communities and has launched several careers, most notably that of Julio Iglesias, who won the OTI several decades ago.

Each country holds its own competition to send to Spain a soloist, duo, or trio singing an original composition by one of its citizens. In 1985, Jesús Fichamba, an Otavaleño with a beautiful tenor voice and no formal musical training, won the Ecuadorian competition with a song about Christopher Columbus' ships, the *Niña, Pinta*, and *Santa María*. Fichamba wore Otavalo dress whites (white shirt, pants, and sandals), with his hair in a braid, and a poncho when he won the Ecuadorian contest and again when he won in Spain. After his OTI victory there was a parade and reception for him in Otavalo, for which the whole town turned out. He was, in fact, a national hero because this was the first time an Ecuadorian had won. Fichamba has a number of LPs, cassettes (1991), and CDs on the market. His specialty is romantic ballads, the pasillos and albazos, rather than Sanjuanitos or other indigenous or folkloric music. For that reason his musical following is mainly white-mestizo, although Otavalos are tremendously proud of him and turn out in force whenever he performs in the area. Because much of his family lives in Peguche, Fichamba frequently performs for special Peguche events such as the mothers' day celebration in May 1996.

In October 1994, my compadre Luis Enrique Farinango sat at his loom in Peguche weaving estera sweaters while he recounted life in Barcelona, where he lived and worked from 1978 to 1980: "We made music— we played music as a diversion, not as a business like now. We had the Grupo Huayra Apamushka at that time, adults and youth." (The group's name is Quichua for Brought by the Wind, which aptly describes the feeling of many Otavalos abroad.) "The Barcelona community was so small, fifty persons including children, that we all knew each other and worked together. The people from Grupo Charijayac worked with us—they were young boys the age of my son [age sixteen]—making and sewing sweaters. We played music when we were resting at lunch or in the afternoon. The group is now famous."

A month later in Otavalo one of the founders of Charijayac, Luis (Sayri) Cotacachi, who had come from Spain for his father's funeral, picked up the story: "Charijayac was founded twelve years ago, in 1982 [in Barcelona, Spain]. It arose at a time when Ecuadorian music needed a renewal. The Sanjuanitos hadn't changed in many years." Sayri credited his late father with helping the group get off the ground: "My father was one of our promoters, which is to say, economically he helped us with instruments, etc. He provided total support until the last day of his life. He was the father of the group."

Sayri also said: "We had our first work playing on the streets in Europe in almost every country. We recorded our first cassette, *Ajchasuni* (Q. Long Hair) in 1984 [in Barcelona, copyright 1985]. It was a success because we were one of the first groups of indígenas to play on the streets of Europe and to record our music." Charijayac's second cassette, *Cita en el sol* (Sp. Meeting in the Sun), was released in Barcelona in 1986. But what really ignited Otavalo was Charijayac's third cassette, *Cielo Rosa* (Sp. Rose Heaven), recorded in Barcelona in 1987. The title was in honor of his mother, Rosa, who died in Barcelona shortly before the cassette was made. "This was a renewal of the music, and it had an impact on Otavalo," Sayri told me.

Indeed it did. Charijayac included enough familiar material to appeal to Otavalos but added new music that caught people's attention.

Sayri Cotacachi of Charijayac. Otavalo, November 1994.

The members of the group are gifted musicians who composed their own music and adapted Peruvian and Bolivian pieces. There are eleven selections on *Cielo Rosa*. Three are traditional Bolivian tunes; one is traditional Peruvian; one ("Antonio Mocho") is credited to Galo Maigua, mentioned above as a local Ilumán composer; and one is listed as "Tradicional Quichua (Ecuador)." Four pieces are credited to individual members of the group and one to Charijayac as a whole. Significantly, even though the members of the group live in Barcelona, or migrate between Barcelona and Otavalo, they credit the origin of their songs to "Otavalo, Ecuador."

Although the members of Charijayac grew up in Spain, they have thoroughly mastered Otavalo musical genres, including Sanjuanitos, and speak fluent Quichua. They included enough familiar-sounding material on their early albums to appeal to an Otavalo audience, but they also pushed the envelope of traditional music. "Agua fresca" (Sp. Fresh Water) from the *Cielo Rosa* album, for example, has verses in Spanish in a slow, ballad format, the chorus in Quichua in Sanjuanito 2/4 time with eight-beat phrases and talking above the music, and a key change between verse and chorus. The song includes sophisticated sound effects (running water) and traditional instruments such as the panpipe.

In 1987, after the Ecuadorian release of *Cielo Rosa*, Charijayac made a triumphant return to Otavalo and played a series of concerts, complete with screaming indígena and white-mestiza groupies. The cover of Charijayac's *Cielo Rosa* cassette is a photograph of the shoulders and backs of six heads, all with the old-style white shirts, dark felt fedoras, and long black hair. But instead of being braided, their hair is pulled back and tied with ribbons in a long ponytail. Charijayac started the vogue of unbraided hair among young men. The Charijayac album cover also inspired woven tapestries showing the backs of heads with hats and long hair. Charijayac's fourth album, *Otavalo y . [punto]*, recorded in Barcelona in 1989, was also successful in both their Spanish and Ecuadorian homelands.

Charijayac served notice that Andean music was popular and lucrative in Europe and in the 1990s inspired a full-fledged exodus of Otavaleños to try their luck abroad at becoming the next Charijayacs. Young Otavaleños are quickly learning a musical instrument, forming bands of six to eight musicians, and heading for the United States or Canada if they can get a visa or for Europe if they cannot. The adventures and misadventures of Otavalos abroad, the social consequences of the Otavalo diaspora, and the changes in Otavalo music are treated in the following chapters.

Oscar and Lucita's Wedding

The wedding in March 1993 of two young Otavalos, Oscar from Peguche and Lucita from Guanansi, exemplifies the importance of music in Otavalo life, the occasions on which music is played, and the kinds of music performed. I was already godmother to Oscar through his confirmation. The family asked me to be the *madrina de la boda* (Sp. godmother of the wedding) and to find a suitable *padrino* (Sp. godfather). He was sociologist David Kyle, who was in Ecuador doing research on transnational migration (Kyle 1995, 2000). David's wife, Christina Siracusa, became a second madrina, and Oscar's family to this day makes jokes about their *ishkay madrinakuna* (Q. two madrinas).

The wedding had its traumas and dramas, including two postponements. The first involved the *teniente político* (Sp. political officer), who operated the Peguche civil registry and who insisted the bride's papers were not in order because he wanted a bribe. He had to be chased into Otavalo by the bride's brother and paid off. The second postponement occurred because the bride and groom were minors and needed a dispensation from the bishop in Ibarra. After these hurdles were surmounted, things went more or less as planned. Instead of giving a detailed account of all aspects of the wedding, I focus here on those segments where music was important.

The first musical event occurred on Saturday, the night after the civil ceremony (which by law must occur before the church wedding). About a hundred friends, relatives, and compadres of Oscar's family assembled by 8 P.M. at the groom's house for the *maki mañay,* also called *el pedido* or *pidiendo la mano* (Q., S. requesting the hand of the bride). Although the arrangements for the marriage are invariably made beforehand between the families of the bride and groom, the request is the public declaration. The relatives of the bride gather at her parents' home; she remains out of sight during the proceedings.

At the groom's home in Peguche, some of the women were busy dispatching fifteen fat hens and an equal number of guinea pigs to another incarnation and dipping the little corpses in boiling water to remove the feathers or fur. Some relatives, mostly women, were busy tying ten live cuys and ten live hens upside down to two long poles, a sight guaranteed to give animal rights activists the fits. Other relatives, including a male cousin of the groom who worked as a professional chef at the Hotel Embassy in Quito, were clustered around smoky wood fires in the cooking sheds of two separate houses and outside in the yard, preparing immense quantities of food which would be served to the guests at the house and carried to bride's family.

In the dim light in front of the house, five or six young men were playing music and dancing in a circle with the musicians in the middle. These were friends and relatives of the groom and included members of Ñanda Mañachi. They were providing the music essential to the occasion by playing Sanjuanes on stringed instruments: violin, guitar, and mandolin; later someone brought out a harmonica. David Kyle was invited to join the dancing; Oscar then invited his two madrinas to dance.

As is customary at such events, copious quantities of food and drink were served to the guests. Men and women made the rounds with bottles or buckets of *trago* (Sp. 90-proof sugarcane alcohol), chicha, whiskey,

Otavalo musicians playing in front of the groom's house for the *pedido* (Sp. request, asking for the hand of the bride). Peguche, March 1993.

brandy, beer, and wine. The hapless guest is offered a cup which must be downed on the spot. This forced ritualized drinking with the intent of rapid intoxication is the bane of every anthropologist who has done research in the Andes and accounts for the foggy nature of my memories of the end of the wedding when participation overcame observation. Each guest was also given a bowl of *api* (Q. corn meal soup) containing meat and/or *muti* (Q. boiled corn kernels) and a plate piled high with potatoes and chicken.

In a typical pedido, up to a ton of food is carried to the house of the bride, depending on the resources of the groom's family. At this event we carried approximately 1,000 pounds: cases containing 12-liter bottles of beer, huge baskets of corn, bread, and cooked potatoes topped with chickens and cuy, *quintal* (Sp. 110-pound) sacks of potatoes which the men tied on their backs, huge bunches of bananas tied on backs or to poles, bottles of trago, wine, and rum, as well as the live animals on poles. I was given a basket of cooked potatoes so heavy that I staggered under its weight.

At around 9:30 P.M., led by the musicians, with both males and females carrying food, we set off in the cold, starry night down the street for the bride's house. This residence was right behind the groom's, but going through the backyard did not allow time for the music or for the public display of food. People sang along to several tunes, and the group danced in a circle several times while proceeding down the street, around the corner, and back up the next street. The musicians entered the house first, formed a circle, and played and danced in the front room while the food was laid at the feet of the bride's family. Bananas and rolls were immediately redistributed to all present, and bottles and buckets of liquor made the rounds. Someone told me that the idea was to make the bride's relatives drunk so that they would be amenable to the groom's request for the hand of the bride in the early hours of the morning. The musicians and young men continued playing music and dancing in a circle in the front room of the house throughout the proceedings and were still going strong when we left the party at 11 P.M.

The next day, Sunday, was the wedding at Otavalo's main church, San Luis. After the ceremony, hundreds of relatives, compadres, and friends of the bride, groom, and their families converged on Oscar's home in Peguche, many carrying wrapped wedding gifts, a recent adoption of white-mestizo practices. A brass band (Sp. *banda*) of white-mestizo musicians from San Roque had been hired for the reception. The band consisted of ten men playing the large and small drum, cymbals, saxophones (three), trumpets (two), and French horns (two). They charged S/200,000 (U.S. $110); one of the groom's sisters paid half and the padrino and I each paid a fourth.

The band members sat on benches in front of the house and were served food and drink along with the rest of the guests. In fact, alcoholism is an occupational hazard for musicians. These musicians did not wear a uniform of any kind, just ordinary white-mestizo workaday dress. As soon as the guests began arriving in force, the musicians stood up and played music that does not fit any genre familiar to me—a march is the best way to describe it, and it may have been a pasodoble. The musicians kept at it more or less steadily all day and into the night, and the guests danced more or less steadily (in both senses of the word) as the reception wore on. The bride and groom danced a few numbers with us, their in-laws, and each other and then disappeared.

Later in the day, when I sneaked into the house to escape yet another round of drinking, I heard merriment coming from a back room, where I found Oscar, Lucita, dozens of young, hip indígenas, and a few whites-mestizos. A cassette-CD player was turned on high and all were dancing to salsa, Latin rap, and reggae, three genres currently popular among

Friends and relatives of the groom arriving at the bride's home with 1,000 pounds of food as part of the formal request for her hand in marriage. Peguche, March 1993.

The white-mestizo band from San Roque strikes up a tune at Oscar and Lucita's wedding while relatives of the couple greet guests. Peguche, March 1993.

young Otavalos. From what I could tell, they considered the brass band in the front patio hopelessly old-fashioned. This segregation by age and music is new at Otavalo fiestas.

The next day, Monday, was the *ñawi mallay* (Q. face washing), which is performed the morning after a marriage has been consummated, usually the day after the church ceremony. Parsons calls this ceremony the *chaqui mallay* (Q. foot washing) but describes the same ritual (1945: 195). Every ñawi mallay I have attended has been slightly different, but the basic ritual consists of members of the wedding party and immediate relatives pairing off (groom and madrina, bride and padrino, etc.) and washing each other's faces, arms, and legs with water, flower petals, and stinging nettles mixed together in a large tub, while offering advice on proper behavior to the newlyweds.

This ceremony was held at the bride's relatives' home in Peguche. After the ritual, the newly married couple, several young relatives, the padrino, and I retired to one of the rooms, where the groom's cousin, Richard (originally Ricardo) Maldonado, played a tape of Andean music which his group Winiaypa had recently recorded in Europe. The theme of travel abroad surfaced frequently at the wedding in conversations among young people, in queries about absent relatives and friends, and in discussions about who had made recordings or was planning to play music and sell textiles abroad the coming summer.

Later a truck pulled up to the house bearing the instruments for the fourth kind of music played at this wedding by an amplified band called an *orquesta* (Sp. orchestra). The bride's brother (substituting for her parents, who were dead) paid for the orchestra. Orquestas have amplifiers, speakers, and a microphone and include such instruments as a portable Yamaha organ, guitars, brass, wind instruments, and maracas. Unlike bandas, which play only instrumental music, orquestas usually have vocalists, including women. The music is blasted at brain-damaging volume to alert the entire community that a fiesta is underway.

The bandas and orquestas play a variety of music, including *música costeño* (Sp. coastal music) and *cumbias* with African influences, salsa, and *música nacional* (Sp. national music), also called *verbena* or *verbenita* (Sp. festival music), which sounds like calliope music with a catchy beat. The selections range from the national verbena favorite "La rasca bonita" (Sp. The Pretty Itch) to such Andean favorites as Los Kjarkas' "Llorando se fue," also known as the "Lambada" because it was the theme song for the Brazilian movie about the lambada dance craze.

Finally, the *discomovil* (Sp. mobile disco) should be mentioned, although it did not appear at this wedding. The discomovil is a portable sound system for recorded music and can be rented in many Ecuadorian towns and cities. It is trucked to the party, complete with different musical choices and a disc jockey. The main appeal of the discomovil is cost: it is less expensive than live music. I had never seen a discomovil at a wedding until that of my Ilumán godson in June 1998, where a discomovil supplied music the first day and an orquesta played the second; the discomovil is more common at graduation ceremonies and confirmation parties.

Except for the discomovil, Oscar and Lucita's wedding included within three days every kind of music, live and recorded, vocal and instrumental, that is commonly heard in the Otavalo valley, from Sanjuanitos to verbena to reggae, played by foreigners, Otavalo indígenas, and whites-mestizos. The mere listing of what kind of music was played when, however, fails to convey several important points. The first is the sheer pleasure that music brings to Otavalo events, the way it moves our hearts and souls (and prehuman lizard brains) and creates a deep sense of the appropriate emotional tone.

The second point is the use of music as a statement of correct social behavior and social class: the wedding would not have been a proper event without live music, the discomovil being seen as somewhat dé-classé. There is an element of conspicuous consumption in hiring ban-das and orquestas, especially two. At the same time, the kinds of music played made a statement about generational differences among Ota-valos, with the adults insisting on the live music customarily played at weddings and the younger crowd insisting on a more hip, international recorded sound. If younger Otavalos were not playing music themselves, they preferred to dance to music they considered more current than mú-sica nacional.

The third point is the importance of music as an economic activity, exemplified at the wedding when Richard Maldonado played his latest recording, not to mention the conversations among young Otavalos about who was planning to travel abroad or who was joining which group.

The fourth point is music's function as an integrating mechanism, linking the local (Sanjuanitos and Peguche), national (cumbias, verbe-nas, and Ecuador), and global (reggae, rap, salsa, and the Caribbean, New York, and Europe) and temporarily uniting Otavalos of all generations and social classes. This was especially true on the days before and after the church wedding, the pedido and ñawi mallay, the most traditionally Otavalo events, when only one kind of dance music was played.

Many of the young musicians playing for the pedido or demonstrating their tapes at the ritual washing were returning not only to their fami-lies and communities on this occasion but to the source of the Otavalo music they play on the streets of Los Angeles, Montreal, and Antwerp. By playing for the maki mañay the young Otavaleños were musical par-ticipants, not just onlookers, actively renewing their sense of family and community. Such rituals as weddings help communities maintain their bonds and their sense of the past and "can be seen as batteries which charge up the emotional bonds between people and renew the sense of the sacred" (Featherstone 1995: 94). Furthermore, "a sense of home is sus-tained by collective memory . . . The important point here is that our sense of the past does not primarily depend upon written sources, but rather on enacted ritual performances and the formalism of ritual lan-guage" (ibid.). Far-flung sheep were brought back into the fold at Oscar and Lucita's wedding, and a sense of Otavalo cultural identity was re-affirmed through music.

CHAPTER 6

Otavalo Merchants and Musicians in the Global Arena

This chapter focuses on the Otavalo diaspora since 1970, with an emphasis on the 1990s boom in musical production and international travel to sell both textiles and music. Otavalo music has become globalized, part of the world music beat influencing the music made by others, with Sanjuanitos considered emblematic of Otavalo or Ecuadorian music. While Otavalos emphasize Sanjuanitos as particularly theirs, they adopt and adapt other musical genres to improve their performances and album sales.

The last three decades witnessed a change in the quantity and quality of Otavalo travel from short, temporary trips by a few traders within Ecuador or to Colombia to longer trips or the permanent emigration of thousands of Otavalos to destinations around the world. Foreign travel skyrocketed in the 1990s because of such economic pressures as land shortages, intensified competition for textile sales, and hyperinflation. Other factors include experience traveling to nearby countries to sell cloth; the coming of age of the first generation born after the abolition of wasipungu; increased transnational contacts through linkages with NGOs, exporters, researchers, tourists, and missionaries; the ability to obtain airline tickets on credit; and the influence of such groups as Charijayac, who alerted Otavalos to the financial rewards of playing and recording Andean music.

Economics is the major motivation for Otavalo transnational migration. An Otavaleña from Ilumán, whose husband makes annual trips to the United States to play music and sell textiles, said, "People are traveling abroad because there is no work here. And when we earn dollars we gain in the exchange" (this was before dollarization). A compadre wrote to me in January 1996, asking for an invitation to visit, because "here we are without work." He and his family weave estera sweaters, and when he wrote the wool sweater season was over. The most common explana-

We film in their market; they film in ours. José María Cotacachi videotaping in the Walnut Creek, California, Farmer's Market. November 2000.

tion for travel abroad is "too much competition" in Otavalo. Ironically, so many Otavalos are selling abroad that they are now complaining about "too much competition" there. In May 1996, an Ilumán godson wrote to me from Germany: "We can't work because of the rain and other things. Also, in Germany it's difficult because of legalities, and for us it has been difficult because of the competition." He, his brother, and two cousins were pursuing the Otavalo dream of selling artesanías and playing music on the street.

As the previous chapters illustrate, Otavalo long- and short-term transnational migrants maintain multiple linkages between their homes, wherever those homes might be. I define long-term transnational migration as a stay abroad of at least a year. Many long-term migrants settle permanently abroad and become residents but maintain close ties with their natal communities. Short-term transnational migration involves a stay of less than a year. Subsumed within short-term migration is seasonal transnational migration. The latter two can be one-time or frequent, with the migrant commonly based in his or her native country but maintaining permanent links with people abroad. The permanent Otavalo residents of Bogotá and Popayán; New York, Madison, Minneapolis, Chicago, San Francisco, Portland, and Seattle; Amsterdam;

and Barcelona are long-term transnational migrants. Otavalos who travel to Canada or France for eight months to a year to play music or sell textiles or to Spain and Italy to work as domestics, in hotels, or as agricultural laborers and then return to Otavalo are short-term transnational migrants, while the annual summer exodus of Otavalos abroad to play music and sell merchandise is an example of seasonal transnational migration.

World systems theorists have tended to reduce migration to labor migration, eliminating the different racial, ethnic, or national identities which affect people's action and consciousness (Basch et al. 1994: 12). This caveat is particularly apropos for Otavalos, who first left the valley as textile entrepreneurs or small-scale meat or textile merchants rather than as proletarians or agriculturists seeking wage labor, although the latter became more common following the bank failures in 1999. Most Otavalos are pursuing the capitalist dream of ever-expanding markets for their products. Those who work for wages abroad usually work temporarily for other Otavalos then start their own businesses, although this pattern changed with increased Otavalo migration to Spain to work in agriculture.

The term "Otavalo diaspora" does not strain the definition of diaspora (from the Greek word "to scatter"), as there are now permanent Otavalo expatriate communities in Europe and the Americas and individuals or families residing on six continents. The concept of an Otavalo diaspora is not just a Euro-American construction. The term is commonly applied to the Jews, who dispersed throughout the world following the destruction of the temple in Jerusalem but maintained the idea of a homeland in Israel. Washo Maldonado, an expatriate Otavalo who returned to open SISA (Q. for flower; the acronym stands for Salón de Imágenes, Sonido y Arte [Sp. Salon of Images, Sound, and Art]), a restaurant and cultural center in Otavalo, called Otavalos "the Jews of America." He noted that "necessity forces us to leave in order to live by those activities at which we are most able, artesanías and business. And music" (*Hoy,* May 25, 1993; my translation).

An article about Otavalos in Ecuador and Colombia titled "Binational Identity" says: "Ecuadorian indígenas who sell in the commercial sectors of Colombian metropolises, an Ecuadorian airline that fills with passengers in Cali, or a transmitter—Radio Calidad—that has programs dedicated to Ecuadorian music are expressions of a binational identity." One Otavaleño from Pinsaquí had lived in Cali for two years with his wife and daughters. He sold artesanías to white-mestizo Colombians and

Otavalo estera sweaters for sale along Calle Sagárnaga in La Paz, Bolivia. July 1997.

made friends with Guambiano indígenas (Bedoya 1993: A-2; my translation). This family is among the increasing number of Otavalos who have binational or trinational identities.

The decision to sell textiles abroad is not made lightly and involves mobilizing large sums of money for documents, the plane ticket, and merchandise. Kyle notes that traveling to play music involves very little start-up investment as opposed to textile merchandising (1995: 242). In addition, musicians are more mobile, as they do not have to transport heavy bundles. Adults sojourning for whatever reason must consider who will farm, weave, or sell in their absence, family needs, which countries are hospitable, where sales are good, and many other factors. If they are financing the travel of relatives, they need to decide how many family members to send and how long these members should stay.

Otavalos on the Move

Among Otavalos and foreign researchers, Peguche (or Pe-Gucci, as one researcher put it) has a reputation for being on the cutting edge of social change (Buitrón 1947; Conejo Maldonado 1995; Kyle 1995: 334–341, 2000: 169; Meisch 1987: 105), including foreign travel. Several residents of Peguche, however, insisted that indígenas from Quinchuquí and Agato began traveling earlier. Lucita Fichamba and José María Cotacachi said in 1994 that "[t]hose from Quinchuquí and Agato are traveling more. The merchants who sell in Colombia and Guayaquil go on to New York— some friends from Agato are now residents in New York." Lucita and José mentioned Segundo M., "who left for the United States around 1970, to escape debts; he also went to Barcelona. He lived there a long time, nearly fifteen years." In fact, José said, "Most of the first travelers left in a mess [*fracasando*] and returned successful."

Lucita and José mentioned themselves as among the first of their Peguche generation to travel to the United States as tourists. The Cotacachi-Fichamba home cum weaving workshop and store is a major stop for tour buses, exporters, and individual travelers, so the family has a large circle of Ecuadorian and foreign compadres and customers. Around 1984, an American woman who owns a bed and breakfast lodge in California's Napa Valley visited Peguche. She decided to furnish her inn with the family's textiles and invited Lucita and José to visit.

In 1985, few indígenas were applying for visas to the United States; the couple was known to the embassy personnel because they, too, visited the Cotacachi-Fichambas in Peguche. Lucita and José were given five-year multiple entry visas (subsequently renewed several times). Their ethnicity helped them because indígenas applying for tourist visas were rare, and the consulate saw them (correctly) as being established in their community and unlikely to stay illegally in the United States.

In the fall of 1985, José received an invitation from his American compadre Lawrence Carpenter, a professor at the University of North Florida. José stayed with his compadre for a month, giving weaving demonstrations and talks to the Spanish classes at the university. Lawrence held several open houses during which José sold enough goods to pay for the trip, have an eye exam, and buy eyeglasses and gifts.

Lucita and José made another trip to the United States in 1990. José said he did not want legal problems, so he always traveled "well organized." He arranged through a client to sell tapestries at an international artisans' fair in Ohio and to a store in Saint Augustine, Florida. He has since made several trips to Peru and Bolivia to sell Otavalo goods and buy alpaca sweaters and traditional textiles, and both José and Lucita have visited me recently in California.

A significant feature of these early trips is that Otavalos traveled on their own and paid for their tickets. Granted, many of them relied on the invitations and hospitality of foreign friends, but these were private trips. Taita Pacho Lema of Peguche had no intention of traveling; but one of his daughters, who was selling artesanías in Europe, invited him to visit. In October 1990, he flew to Germany. He emphasized that "I didn't leave like the others with the help of institutions, I left through my own effort and sacrifice. I spent money on papers to get my passport, to buy my passage, and to buy merchandise to sell, for all of this I went into debt alone and with my family . . ." (Lema 1995: 163; my translation). The ability to pay for such trips was a direct result of the growth of the textile and tourism industries.

By the 1990s, Otavalos were appearing on the social pages of the Quito papers. *El Comercio* has a daily column featuring photos of Ecuadorians traveling abroad. In 1995, a photo of an Otavaleña appeared with the title "Masters in English." The caption says: "Luz Olga Arellano, of Otavalo, traveled to the Dominican Republic to study English in the Institute of Languages of that country" (*El Comercio*, January 16, 1995: C-12; my translation). Later that year, a photo of an Otavalo family appeared in the same column. The caption reads: "Markets for artesanías in England" and says that "Lucita Tonta [a misunderstanding of the name Atunta], Antonio, Edison, and Myriam Morales, proprietors of Tumi, Cia., traveled to England in search of markets for Ecuadorian artesanías made of wood" (*El Comercio*, July 29, 1995: C-8; my translation). Rather than being ignored by the media, indígenas boarding international flights are now seen as newsworthy citizens.

The United States and to a lesser extent Canada are favorite intended destinations of Otavalos. I say "intended" because these countries require visas, which are increasingly difficult to obtain. Since 1992, half of *all* international visitors entering the United States by air overstayed their visas (Freedman 1996: A-14). In 1998, the consulate raised the application fee to $45 to cover processing costs and discourage repeat applications. Even so, in Quito hundreds of people line up outside the United States consulate daily to obtain visas.

The consulate tries to ensure that a visitor to the United States will return home by demanding proof of "sufficient ties" in Ecuador, including land, house, and automobile titles, bank accounts, business ownership or investments, and proof of employment. The consulate also uses a profile of those most likely to stay illegally (headed by young, unmarried men but followed by just about everyone else).

As early as 1985, indígenas asked my help in obtaining visas to the United States. By 1990, I could have set up shop as a immigration facilitator. Fortunately for me, the embassy prohibited Americans from accompanying Ecuadorians to the consulate to plead on their behalf. Otherwise I would have spent 90% of my time in Quito, because it is almost impossible to turn down requests for help from compadres, godchildren, and good friends. Many applicants for tourist or business visas who meet the economic requirements are still rejected; the process seems capricious.

One example illustrates the consulate's requirements as well as the economic resources of a typical merchant family. In 1993, the parents and three boys and a girl (ages six to sixteen) lived on the old, dusty Pan-American highway in Ilumán in an unprepossessing two-story painted adobe house with a tile roof. Nothing distinguishes this house from dozens of others on the same road. The inside is minimally furnished, which is typical of most indigenous homes. They do not own a motor vehicle; nor do they appear wealthy.

In September 1993, the two oldest sons, Humberto and Jaime, received an invitation to visit an Otavaleña aunt who is a United States resident. Humberto had to comply with Ecuadorian law requiring registration for military service. Young men between the ages of eighteen and twenty must serve a year in the armed forces and cannot obtain an Ecuadorian passport without their military registration booklet and discharge certificate. Most Otavaleños simply buy their documents for about $150–$200. The bribery system was out of whack, and Humberto was unable to buy his papers, which left Jaime, who was almost eighteen and not yet eligible for military service.

The family came to me for help with the application. The husband and wife possessed notarized titles for the house in Ilumán and two pieces of land there; rent receipts for their store on Calle Imbabura in old Quito where they had sold textiles since 1985; registration for two quarter-kiosks in the Otavalo market; the registration and rent receipts for two open-air kiosks in old Quito; and the passbooks for two savings accounts, one of which they had possessed for nine years, the other for two or three. The savings accounts held about $8,000. I convinced them not to open another account, which the consulate frowns on because a common scam involves borrowing money to open an account for visa purposes then immediately closing the account and (if the person is honest) returning the money. Although I had known the family for many years, I was surprised by the extent of their holdings, especially their savings. In 1994, the father opened another successful business, a shop off the Poncho Plaza that sells wool yarn from the Ramos family's factory in Ambato.

Meanwhile, Jaime returned to the consulate with the forms, letter of invitation, a round-trip airline ticket, and the pile of documents. By then he was four days past his eighteenth birthday; although nothing had changed in his living situation (he was still a dependent of his parents), the consulate refused him a visa on the grounds that he now had to provide proof of economic resources in his own name. The airlines are undoubtedly making a killing on charges for refunded tickets, and if the ticket was bought on credit the agency still demands interest.

The refusal of Jaime's visa must be seen in light of illegal immigration from Ecuador to the United States. In 1985, when I visited friends in Gualaceo, Azuay, they pointed out large houses built with money remitted by local residents who had emigrated illegally to New York and New Jersey (see Kyle 1995; Miles 1997). A trickle of illegal emigrants from Azuay became a torrent; and by 1993, according to the Immigration and Naturalization Service (INS), Ecuadorians constituted the largest number of illegal immigrants in New York State (27,100), followed by Italians, Poles, Dominicans, Colombians, Haitians, and Jamaicans (*El Comercio*, September 3, 1993: A-1). By 1996, there were an estimated 40,000 illegal Ecuadorians from Azuay in New York City, with smaller numbers in Chicago, Atlanta, Houston, and other cities (Tello Espinosa 1996a: A-7). There were so many illegal Azuayans in Brooklyn that the Catholic church in Cuenca sent a priest to the parish of Saint Bridget to help them maintain ties with their families (Tello Espinoza 1996b: C-7). By 1999, according to the New York City Planning Department, Ecuadorians represented 46% of the immigrants in the city. More than 600,000 Ecuadorians, 70% of them illegal, were living in New York, New Jersey, and Connecticut (Carrera 1999: 7).

The Central Bank of Ecuador estimated that in 1993 migrants (overwhelmingly illegal) to the United States from Azuay and Cañar remitted $187 million to Ecuador (*El Comercio*, July 26, 1995: B-1). Another article estimated the annual amount remitted to Azuay at $200 million, which was equivalent to or greater than the annual income from all industries in the province (*El Comercio*, October 10, 1994: E-1).

I know of no Otavalos who have taken the tortuous overland route to the Mexican border used by most illegals; they are more likely to enter the United States on business or tourist visas. Some observe the time limits of their visas; others overstay their allotted time but return to Ecuador eventually; some reside in the United States permanently but illegally or obtain residency papers, while others applied for citizenship under the 1986 amnesty.

Although white-mestizo Ecuadorians and some indígenas (mainly from the central and southern provinces) are immigrating illegally to the United States as proletarians and need to disguise their identity to blend into the general population, Otavalos are in a different situation. Many of those traveling on tourist visas pay for their trip by playing music and selling textiles on the street, which is technically illegal, but their ethnicity is a draw. Even those Otavalos entering the United States on commercial visas often get into trouble by not complying with legalities that are unknown or unimportant to them, such as obtaining a permit to sell or play music in public.

The U.S. embassy in Quito and customs agents at major airports, especially Miami, are aware of these activities. Increasingly, Otavalos on tourist visas with large bundles of textiles entering through Miami are questioned, made to pay duty, not allowed to import the goods, or refused entry. One musician and merchant said the Cuban-American customs agents in Miami were "racist" and hard on Otavalos: "We want to enter through Los Angeles, Houston, or New York." Once inside the country legally, Otavalo ethnicity tends to be advantageous.

The problem faced by Otavalos at ports of entry is illustrated by one of my Peguche godsons. In April 2000, he was arrested at the Houston airport upon arrival from Quito even though he had a valid student visa. Immigration refused to believe that he spoke such good English after having studied in the United States for only four months and accused him of being a "coyote" (people smuggler). He was handcuffed, jailed for several days, and returned to Ecuador with his visa canceled. He did not know that he was allowed a phone call or a lawyer and therefore had no recourse. As an American friend later pointed out to me, my godson was not "traveling as an Indian." He was wearing the latest hip-hop fashions rather than poncho, hat, and dress whites and therefore appeared generically Latino, obviously to his disadvantage. Had he looked more Otavalo, he might have been allowed in.

Back to Jaime in Ilumán, who was afflicted with travel fever. The family tried again with a trip to Amsterdam, where Jaime had an Otavaleño cousin. This fits the pattern. According to the National Police in Ecuador, the preferred European destinations of Ecuadorians are Spain and Holland (*La Hora*, July 18, 1999: B-2). Canada, Italy, and Germany are also popular (*El Comercio*, August 15, 1999: A-10). As Jaime prepared to leave in May 1994, four young Otavaleños from Peguche were refused entry to Holland because they had only $250–$300 in cash and the Dutch insisted that the Otavalos prove they were tourists by showing $1,000. Jaime despaired, but his father loaned him the money. (Otavalos quickly discovered that they could circumvent the cash restriction by borrowing money, showing it on entry, and then wiring it home.)

Jaime was traveling with one cousin and meeting another. In most cases, Otavalos activate kin and compadrazgo networks for help abroad. Otavalos, like indigenous Zinacantan and mestizo Mexican truckers who sell produce in Los Angeles, must "confront not just the risks or uncertainties that attend any business expansion, but the disadvantages, as well, of having to penetrate foreign turf where others' cultural styles dominate" (Alvarez and Collier 1994: 625). In Jaime's case, he and his cousin had kin in Amsterdam to offer a roof and help understanding Dutch culture.

Abroad, as at home, there is tension between the values of reciprocity and entrepreneurialism. Members of Otavalo diasporic communities are not thrilled to see their compatriots following hot on their heels. One Otavaleño complained to me that his relatives were cold to his brother when they met in Amsterdam. An Otavaleño in New York City said: "The only interest is in individual survival. . . . There's the fear that the other fellow is in direct competition with you. When I arrived here, I expected my *compañeros* to tell me the best places to sell, and give me some practical advice. But they never did" (Kandell 1993: 34).

This is not to say that Otavalos regularly reject their relatives or compadres; Jaime was helped by his cousins. Much depends on the degree of consanguinity and perceived competition. A sister joining her family to help with sales is much more likely to be well received than a second cousin who wants to sell his own goods. The number of arrivals in a given period and their length of stay also make a difference. One American woman who was married to an Otavaleño said that she and her husband finally had to refuse guests because the steady stream of Otavalos through their apartment created chaos. On the other hand, in a later article about Ecuadorians in New York titled "Otavaleños in the Capital of the World," José Lema Vega said that there were 250 Otavalos in the city and that they had formed an "Organization of Otavalo Indígenas Resident in New York." The author observed that "[t]heir nucleus is so solid that they all know and help one another" (Cifuentes 1994: 7-A; my translation).

Jaime and his cousin were not concerned about Dutch visas because until recently Ecuadorians did not need visas to enter most European countries for a stay of ninety days or less. In 1993, France, Spain, and the United Kingdom still required visas of Ecuadorians, and Germany required traveling Otavalos to fill out papers at the German embassy in

Quito. Many Otavalos stayed ninety days in each country and moved on; others simply stayed in one country illegally. By 1998, however, Otavalos were allowed only ninety days in the European Community, so many went to Poland after their time expired or simply stayed illegally.

Jaime's family bought a round-trip airline ticket for S/3,500,000 ($1,670) on credit from Gran Turismo in downtown Quito: "Lots of Otavalos know about this agency." Before Jaime left, his mother told him not to get involved with gringas because they might be "lazy" like a young woman his cousin became involved with. Jaime's mother told me she was worried that he might learn "bad habits" abroad.

Jaime took small artesanías (bracelets, Peruvian earrings, hats) to sell because, as his brother explained, "there's more profit in small things." When the family talked with Jaime by telephone in July 1994, he was in Portugal on his way to Italy, selling artesanías and playing music with several Bolivians, "in order to survive." Jaime repeated the Otavalo mantra "lots of competition" and said sales were "a bit down." He stayed in Europe eighteen months, and according to his family he "suffered." A photo he sent home worried his parents because he looked so thin; and when I gave the family a photo of him I had taken before his departure, his father wept.

It is difficult to comprehend the magnitude of Otavalo transnational migration because there are no statistics for them as a group. The economic crisis of 1999 hit Ecuador so hard, however, that 172,360 Ecuadorians emigrated to Europe in just the first three months of that year (La Hora, July 18: B-2). By the end of 1999, the chief of migration of Imbabura said that "twenty to thirty Imbaburans were abandoning the country each week" (La Hora, December 14, 1999: A-7; my translation). Ecuadorian newspapers are now using the term "diaspora" to describe the exodus (El Comercio, July 10, 2000: A-7). By August 2000, there were an estimated 100,000 Ecuadorians in Spain alone (El Comercio, August 11, 2000: A-7).

Out of a population of around 60,000 in 2001, I estimate that approximately 4,000 Otavalos are permanent transmigrants and that another 6,000 are abroad on a short-term basis. Diario del Norte published a cartoon showing a man in a hat and poncho standing on the tarmac with a ticket in his hand, watching people board a plane. He says: "Every day, thousands of Ecuadorians leave the country. In time, Ecuador will be empty" (July 22, 1999: 4; my translation). During northern hemisphere summers, there are hundreds of Otavalo bands in Europe and North America, not to mention merchants. An estimated 500 indígenas were in Holland in the summer of 1993 and 3,000 or 4,000 total in Europe (Van Der Spek 1993: 6-C). A 1993 survey revealed that residents of Peguche, a town of 2,128 persons, had been to 23 countries (Kyle n.d. [1993], 2000: 202). Otavalo publications (Lema 1995) and my interviews with Otavalos and foreigners bring the number of countries visited to at least 32 for Peguche alone, including Libya, Israel, Finland, and Russia.

It is virtually impossible to talk to an Otavalo who has not traveled abroad or who does not have a relative who is living or traveling outside Ecuador. Otavalos have told me about their travels to Salta, Córdova, Mar de Plata, and Buenos Aires, Argentina; Antwerp, Brussels, and Iepers, Belgium; Chipaya, La Paz, Oruro, and Tiahuanaco, Bolivia; Rio de Janeiro and São Paulo, Brazil; Montreal, Ottawa, and Toronto, Canada; Iquique, Santiago, and Viña del Mar, Chile; Beijing, China; Bogotá, Cartagena, and Santa Marta, Colombia; Curaçao; Copenhagen, Denmark; Paris, France; Hamburg, Germany; Haiti; Amsterdam, Holland; Italy; Tokyo, Japan; Luxembourg; Ayacucho, Chinchero, Cuzco, Huancayo, Lima, and Machu Picchu, Peru; Portugal; Barcelona, Madrid, and Pamplona, Spain; Sweden; Switzerland; Albuquerque, Chicago, Minneapolis, Hawaii, Jacksonville, Saint Augustine, Los Angeles, San Francisco, Oakland, New York, Salt Lake City, Portland, Seattle, and Washington, D.C., USA; Montevideo, Uruguay; and Venezuela. In addition, many North Americans or Europeans have seen Otavalos in their own country; the number of UFO (Unidentified Flying Otavalo) sightings is amazing.

In early 1994, I attended an Otavalo wedding which had a typical assortment of guests. An older Otavaleño in dress whites, hat, and poncho sat down next to me and introduced himself as Luis Enrique Cabascango, owner of the Hotel El Cacique in Otavalo. "I've traveled to twenty-five countries," he said. His journeys took him to all of South and Central America, parts of the Caribbean, the United States including Hawaii, and Asia. He described Haiti as "very dangerous" and Japan as "very expensive! A hotel costs $120 a night and I stayed eight nights. They weren't cheating me, either—the rates were posted in the airport." He traveled as a textile merchant, but in the 1990s artesanías and music converged as economic activities abroad.

Otavalos must surmount various obstacles to make a living at these enterprises. The first is an Ecuadorian passport. One Otavalo met a man in Quito who said he specialized in governmental paperwork. He gave the man $400 for his younger brother's passport, and the man disappeared with the money. They saved more money then obtained the passport themselves. I have already mentioned the bribes necessary for military documents unless Otavalos actually complete military service (which is rare). Otavalos' ability to buy their way out of the military adds more fuel to the fire of white-mestizo envy.

The second hurdle is the airline ticket. Several Quito agencies including Gran Turismo, Viajes Andinos, and Ecuamundo sell tickets on credit, as do such agencies in Otavalo as Inti Pungo and Inti Express. In March 1994, Inti Express distributed flyers that said: "Are you traveling to Europe or anywhere in the world? Don't buy your ticket before you consult our prices. We have the lowest tariffs in the market and the best conditions for credit in Otavalo." The ad continued: "We also ship your cargo to every country in the world" (my translation), and it offered other services.

That same month a Chilean woman came through the Saturday fair greeting indígenas in Quichua and handing out publicity for the Ecuadorian airline SAETA (Air Ecuador). She gave postcards to Otavalos, not foreign tourists, "in case you're traveling to New York." In July 1994, SAETA opened an office in Otavalo. The Ecuadorian flagship airline Ecuatoriana also has an Otavalo office, and the German airline Lufthansa and Spanish airline Iberia opened Otavalo offices in 2000.

In June 1994, Inti Express sold round-trip tickets to destinations in western Europe for $1,050 cash. For credit the terms were a down payment of S/690,000 ($319.14) and S/620,000 ($287.03) monthly for three months. The total for tickets bought on credit was $1,180.55, of which $130.55 was interest, a rate of 12.4%.

Obtaining tickets on credit makes travel within the reach of almost all Otavalos. Some agencies require collateral such as farm animals, land titles, looms, household electronic equipment, and vehicles. The ability to acquire tickets on credit accounts for the predominance of Otavalo bands globally. Indígenas with no travel experience beyond a trip to Quito launch themselves into the cosmos with astonishing sangfroid. One sixteen-year-old had all the documents, including parental permission and a ticket to Europe, and was on his way to the Quito airport in 1995—without a clue as to where Europe was, but he was going.

Some Otavalo musicians have parlayed their visas to play music into opportunities to sell textiles; and in many cases it is impossible to separate Otavalos into musicians or textile merchants. The music group Sisa Pacari from the Otavalo barrio of La Joya is typical. One member, Cornelio, joined the group in 1987 and played with them until 1993. Sisa Pacari made travel connections through a 1990 international indigenous meeting in Ecuador sponsored by CONAIE to plan opposition to the Columbus Quincentennial. Sisa Pacari played at the closing party and received invitations from Native North Americans to play in the United States. There, as in Colombia, Otavalos are networking with other indigenous groups; some Otavalos play music and sell artesanías at powwows.

Cornelio explained that "Sisa Pacari went abroad for the first time in 1991. We played in New York at the universities and in other places." He showed me his passport, which contained the following stamp from the United States consulate in Quito:

VISA B-1. Nonimmigrant. Cultural Exchange sponsored by OXFAM. 14 May 1991–13 November 1991

Cornelio did not know what Oxfam was, although he knew the organization had sponsored their first trip. When their American visas expired, the group went to Canada for six weeks and played in Montreal, Ottawa, and Toronto. Cornelio said: "For my second visa I went to the American embassy with my passport and nothing else and they gave me the visa. Others went and were refused, and I don't know why." Cornelio's second visa was for five years: "B-1 B-2. Multiple Entry Nonimmigrant."

Cornelio makes annual trips to the United States, primarily to New York, Chicago, and Minneapolis to sell merchandise and play music. He recounted the usual misadventures: the New York City apartment he shared with other Otavalos was robbed, and on one trip customs held his merchandise and made him pay duty. Yet the trips are sufficiently lucrative for him to repeat them. On one trip he hit the street musicians' jackpot, selling at least 300 cassettes at $8–$10 apiece at a festival in Minneapolis. Such stories lead other Otavalos to think the streets of the USA are paved with gold. However, Cornelio admitted such windfalls were rare. "In the United States, by passing the hat you can earn a maximum of $10 a day—good for a McDonald's. The sale of cassettes depends on the locale. In New York you sell 20 cassettes in a day maximum. In Minnesota you can sell 50 tapes." Street musicians have learned that people will part with their money more easily if they can walk away with something concrete.

There are so many street sweeps in New York City that Cornelio became adept at evading the police. His wife laughs and calls him "the Road Runner" after the cartoon, which is shown on Ecuadorian television. The street peddlers have not gone unnoticed. The *New York Times* ran a front-page article on illegal street vending, with a photo of two Otava-leños selling tapestry purses on Canal Street near Broadway. It said that "Luis and Marcelo Yamberlo, father and son, arrived laden with hand-woven sweaters and bracelets from Ecuador, their native land" (Sontag 1993: A1). This article confirms the United States embassy's suspicion that legal tourists frequently overstay their visas:

> Bilingual in Spanish and Quechua, Mr. Yamberlo, 40, was a high school teacher until he unexpectedly received the United States tourist visa he had long sought. Quitting his $100-a-month job, he packed a change of clothing and hundreds of sweaters, ponchos and bags from the famous marketplace in Otavalo. He had no doubt that he would be starting out as a street vendor, just like the Otavalan immigrants who had preceded him and settled in Corona, Queens. (ibid.: B2)

A photo in the second section shows an Otavaleña selling on Canal Street. The author estimated that "[a]bout 10,000 vendors work the streets illegally in New York, becoming the most visible and controversial representatives of the city's growing underground economy" (ibid.: A1–B2). Most vendors wanted to get off the streets: "Mr. Yamberlo puts his hopes for the future on his 18-year-old son, Marcelo, whom he hopes to send on to college and a more secure future" (ibid.: B2).

If foreign travelers to Otavalo differ in their appreciation of Ecuador, Otavalos, not surprisingly, differ in their perceptions of Europe and the United States. Humberto Cabascango of Otavalo told me that Italy was his favorite foreign country because the language was similar to Spanish and he liked the food. He learned to order chicken and potatoes in the language of every country he visited, and that was all he ate (he was twenty pounds heavier when he returned to Otavalo). Orlando Farinango of Peguche said he liked Switzerland "because it's pretty, like the paintings." He liked Italy least, "because it's dirty like Guayaquil." Another Otavaleño described the Germans as "racist," but said that individually Germans were kind to him. Yet another was favorably impressed by German technology.

One godson had a miserable time at the running of the bulls in Pamplona, Spain, in 1999, "because there were 200 other Otavalos there, all with the same merchandise. I didn't get a stamp at the border so the police confiscated my merchandise and wanted a $400 fine. My cousins and I lived out of the car, with two of us sleeping in the back seat, and my cousin was fat. There was no place to bathe except the river once a week, and sometimes we went hungry." These are not the usual images we have of Pamplona; where are the bulls and the happy crowds?

An unusually good or bad experience makes a lasting impression, as does a foreign girlfriend. Many Otavalos are homesick and suffer culture shock on their arrival. In May 1996, my Ilumán godson wrote from Germany that "[i]t's also difficult because here life is distinct, a total change. When I arrived I felt sad for the first days in Holland because I missed my family and because I felt so far away from everything. But later I decided to accustom myself because it was my desire to travel, and finally I am making a tremendous effort to excel and recover the cost of my ticket" (my translation).

Otavalos like Holland because of Dutch tolerance; the city is described as "very free." One Otavaleño told me he liked the Indonesians in Holland because they, too, ate rice. He learned batik from an Indonesian girlfriend then started a successful batik T-shirt business back in Otavalo. There is even a Dutch Center for Indigenous People in Amsterdam (Van Der Spek 1993: 6-C).

Survival Strategies

Once Otavalos are abroad, the next hurdle is survival, and people have various strategies. Some join relatives and compadres until they become established, are asked to leave, or decide to move on. Others buy a car and camp during the warmer months. A Peguche musician who travels in Europe said, "Cars there are cheap—a car is a resource for working." Musicians needed to move around to maximize their profits. His group slept in their car at camp grounds: "You have to minimize your expenses in order to save money for your family. I never stayed in a hotel." They ate breakfast in restaurants and used the restrooms to wash up. The group returned to Hamburg, Germany, on weekends. "A friend loaned us his house and we paid 100 marks [about $60] monthly rent among eleven persons."

Some Otavalos stay in hotels; others rent apartments or houses. More than a few sleep on park benches or in doorways. Some stay with European families or friends they made when these people visited Otavalo. Other Otavalos hook up with Euro-American women. Musicians attract groupies, and the Otavalos are no exception. Their long hair, striking looks, and dress make them exotic. One musician told me in amazement, "They take us home right off the street." Living with a *gringa* (as foreign women are called) is much more enjoyable than sleeping in cheap hotels or living out of a car, not to mention more economical since the gringa usually pays for rent, food, and other expenses. Gringas also provide invaluable aid in navigating the local culture and in helping Otavalos establish business contacts. If gringas are willing to take them home "right off the street," most Otavaleños are happy to oblige. "The majority [of Otavaleños abroad] have lovers and live with them," admitted a musician from Peguche, who has traveled in Germany, Denmark, and Sweden.

Some Otavaleños consciously or unconsciously play on Euro-American misconceptions and guilt, and some of their behavior is frankly exploitative: insincere declarations of love, failure to tell their lovers they are married, making long-distance phone calls without asking permission or offering to pay the bill, showing up for events and "forgetting" to bring money, or permanently "borrowing" money and possessions. Most Otavalos are married by age twenty-five, many by age twenty, so many Otavalos traveling abroad are married; but people are often unaware of this.

Otavalos strategically deploy their ethnicity in musical performance and album sales the same way they do in textiles merchandising, with a chameleonlike ability to meet audience expectations while still identifying as Otavalos. They are aware that their ethnicity has been beneficial in textile marketing; this carries over to music. According to Otavaleño sociologist and current mayor Mario Conejo, "Away from their communities, they [Otavalos] learned to value their dress and their language even more, including their function as economic strategies, demonstrating pride in their inheritance and cultural personality" (1995: 9; my translation). Young Otavalos who normally wear Euro-American dress wear ponchos and dress whites to perform, especially in formal concerts or in music clubs. Traditional dress is not always appropriate abroad: ponchos are too hot in the summer, and alpargatas and thin white trousers do not provide enough warmth in other seasons. Euro-American dress also helps males blend into the crowd during street sweeps, but even in Euro-American-style clothes they are still identifiable by their black braids or ponytails and fedoras. Otavaleñas usually wear traditional dress but often add overcoats or heavy jackets and sweaters in cold weather.

The emphasis on Otavalo ethnicity is evident in the album notes of Otavalo releases. The English liner notes of Sisa Pacari's 1994 CD say: "Over the years, we have maintained the customs and traditions that we inherited from our ancestors. The music of Sisa Pacari is the cultural expression of the Andean people. We are the new generation of the Quichua Nation, making our Otavaleño culture known to the whole world."

Karullacta's 1993 album says: "The authentic melodies and rhythms of the Andes are the identification of the past, present and future of our race. Although we are far away from our land, our hearts and sentiments always will be with our people." The notes are in English; several members of the group are married to American women, who are probably responsible for the insistence on the authenticity of the melodies. Following Charijayac's lead, the members of Karullacta have taken Quichua names: Amauta, Rupay, Rumi, Aspic, Sisa, Pakarina, and Inti.

Hector Lema, member of a band originally named Quichua Marka (n.d.), said they changed their name to Inca Marka (Q. Inca Land), "because it's easier for Europeans. They don't know what 'Quichua' is." Inca Marka has played on the streets of Spain, France, Switzerland, Germany, Italy, and Holland since the summer of 1988: "We went to the same countries, but not to the same places—we went where we would be a novelty or a surprise." In 1994, Hector told me that "this past year we didn't play as much music because there are many groups and people are tired, saturated. I dedicated myself more to the sales of artesanías."

Other groups use the name "Inca": Yawar Inca (Q. Blood of the Inca) and Ecuador Inkas (1993). Charijayac's *Cielo Rosa* album is subtitled *Inca-Quechua*. The inside cover notes for Runakuna's 1996 CD read: "'Runakuna' is a group of native Inca Indian musicians from the village of Otavalo, in the mountains of Ecuador, South America. . . . This music has been passed down from generation since 1400 AD and is mainly performed annually in June at the Runakuna native Inca Indian Festival in Otavalo, Ecuador." The notes advertise that "[i]n addition to selling tapes and CDs of their music, 'Runakuna' sells handmade crafts created by the Inca Indians of Otavalos." Just in case the reader has missed the point, "Inca" is repeated again on the back cover.

The notes for Quillas' *Ecuador* CD (1993) recorded in Belgium say: "We are 'Otavalos,' descendants of Inca-Quichuas. At this moment, we are passing through the world, singing during the days of sun and the nights of moonlight, we follow the way of the rainbow, which always conducts us to the region Tawantinsuyo." These notes sound a typical Otavalo marketing strategy: pragmatic eclecticism combined with an emphasis on authenticity.

The notes for Yuyari's 1995 CD also emphasize the Inca connection: "Otavalo (indigenous community) is a town of hardworking people, artisans, and agriculturists with a rich cultural heritage handed down from their Inca ancestors" (my translation). Richard and Louis subtitle their album *Inka Quechua* (1996). They appear to be the offspring of Charijayac; but rather than taking Quichua names, this new generation of Inkas changed their Spanish names to English ones: Ricardo to Richard and Luis to Louis. They wear suitcoats, list the titles of their songs in Spanish or Quichua and English, advertise their telephone, FAX, and "Cellular Phone" numbers on their CD, and include a snappy little reggae composition called "Mi Pais/My Country."

Some groups play on foreigners' insistence that authentic Indians should be above petty commercial concerns. Thus Ecuador Inkas' 1993 CD says: "There is no commercial aspect in playing our music. We wish to convey the message of the Inka-culture we want to protect and conserve." At the bottom, however, is the notice "© 1993 all rights reserved," and they charge for their CDs and concerts.

In the following analysis of the cover art and visual marketing strategies used by Otavalo musicians on their CDs I am relying on the basic principle of semiotics that the relationship between the components of a sign, the signifier, and the signified, is culturally constructed (de Saussure 1960 [1949]). In addition, I agree with the assertion that the gap between the local and the global is most effectively crossed by the visual image (Mirzoeff 1999: 255).

Otavalos consciously invoke what they believe a particular image or word (the signifier) means to their potential buyers. Some groups use photos or drawings of Peru because this country connotes South America. Many Europeans and Americans are confused about Ecuador's location or have never heard of the country, but almost everyone is familiar with Peru and the Incas, which accounts for the frequency of "Incas" on Otavalo CDs. None of the CDs mentioned below identifies the people or locales in the cover art; I am making identifications based on my knowledge of the region.

CD covers in the category of "Peru equals South America" include Peruvian indígenas in traditional dress playing music on Llaqtaymanta's 1992 album; a Peruvian girl with a baby on her back on Llaqtamasi's 1994 album; and a painting of a poncho and chullu-clad Peruvian flute player on the 1996 Runakuna CD mentioned above, consistent with their emphasis on being Incas. The *chullu* (Q. knitted hat with earflaps) is emblematic of Andean costume for most people but is worn in Peru and Bolivia, not Ecuador. To add a schizophrenic transnational twist, the back cover is a photo of five Otavaleños playing music in a concrete and brick urban setting under a semaphore with a "No Turn on Red" sign; the album was recorded by Disc Makers, Pennsauken, New Jersey, and the contact address for one of the Otavalo musicians is in Jamaica, New York.

Sometimes Bolivian images are used because foreigners cannot distinguish between Peru and Bolivia. A photo of alpacas in the Salar de Uyuni in Bolivia appears on Yawar Inca's *Sturm in den Anden* (1992); a member of a Bolivian panpipe ensemble is on the cover of Ecuador Inkas' 1993 CD; and a similar Bolivian group graces the cover of American Inkas' 1992 CD. The cover of Llaqtaymanta's 1992 CD is either Peruvian or Bolivian. The men in this stunning color photo of a procession leaving a mountain chapel are wearing chullus and ponchos, and one woman is wearing a bowler hat. This cover is less deceptive than some, however, because the musicians identify themselves as Peruvians, Bolivians, and Ecuadorians.

Some CD images convey Ecuador, if not Otavalo. Cochasqui's *Tawantinsuyo . . . Libertad* album (n.d.a) has a studio photo of two elderly musicians playing the *gaita* (Sp. a flutelike instrument). They are wearing red Chibuleo-style ponchos and the old-style white felt hats from Natabuela. The lettering of "Cochasqui" is Art Nouveau, which connotes anything but South America, although this is somewhat overridden by the striking photo of the two indígenas. The back cover shows a young, barefoot Otavaleño wearing hat, poncho, and white pants and playing the rondador. Yahuar Wauky's 1993 cover is a photo of two Otavaleñas dressed in a folklorized (and inaccurate) version of Cayambe costume. Karullacta's 1993 CD has a photo of a Salasaca tapestry on the cover, while Otavalomanta's third volume (n.d.) has a photo of an Otavaleña on the front jacket and Salasaca Corpus Christi musicians and dancers on the back. Ñucanchi Ñan's CD (n.d. [ca. 1984]) has a photo of Chimborazo, the highest peak in Ecuador, which is not remotely near Otavalo but at least is in the right country.

Some Otavalo groups do use photos or drawings of themselves or of Otavalo landscapes. The cover of the Sisa Pacari 1994 CD shows seven Otavaleños in traditional dress. Kapary-Walka's 1992 CD has a photograph of an elderly Otavaleño with braid, hat, and poncho, playing the guitar. The 1994 CD cover of *Lo mejor de Runallacta* (Sp. The Best of Runallacta) is a photograph of an Otavalo fiesta with Imbabura in the background. Otavalomanta's 1995 CD has unposed photos of Otavalo musicians and dancers celebrating the Pendoneros fiesta with a small inset of a Coraza, an important figure in this and other Otavalo fiestas

Luis Alberto Terán selling Otavalo groups' CDs in his stand
on Calle Sucre at the edge of the Poncho Plaza. Otavalo,
July 1999.

who connotes authority. Surprisingly, even the drawings on the inside
cover and on the CD itself are of an Otavaleño; this CD wins the cover
art consistency award.

Other CD covers also emphasize the Otavalo-ness of the musicians.
The front cover of Chacras' 1996b CD is a profile photo of a little Otavaleña in traditional dress. Quillas' 1993 CD has an unposed front cover
photo of elderly Otavalo musicians at a fiesta wearing traditional dress
and playing the gaita. The front photo of Chacras' fourth volume (n.d.)

shows five Otavaleños wearing dark fedoras and, at first glance, blue ponchos, but they have actually wrapped themselves in blue cloth. The point, however, is to convey Otavalo identity, and they succeed. The CD says "printed in Canada," and I imagine that the musicians did not have their ponchos with them.

Cocha Marka's 1997 CD covers shows five musicians against a backdrop of Otavalo town, and Karu Ñan's, Quichua Mashis', and Pachamama's CD covers from that same year also picture Otavalo indígenas. Quillas' n.d. CD features a silhouette of Pendoneros musicians, and Runallacta's sixth CD (1998) features a photograph of Otavalo musicians in the Coraza procession, suggesting that the late 1990s witnessed a return to an emphasis on Otavalo identity.

Several CD covers are veritable semiotic circuses, with signifiers and signifieds rampaging like elephants gone berserk. Chacras' 1996a CD has a front cover photo of a fiesta on the Bolivian altiplano with Aymara women in their bowler hats and a back photo of Otavalos dancing at a fiesta. Native's' 1995 CD is titled *Continuidad* (Sp. Continuity). A drawing of a feather floats beneath the title on the front cover, suggesting Native North Americans, a strange continuity for Otavalos, to my way of thinking. This association is reinforced by a photo of three young Otavaleños wearing jeans, shirts, and hats with high crowns; one musician is also wearing a vest. Their long hair is unbraided and flowing over their shoulders. The photo bears an uncanny resemblance to drawings and photos of Native North Americans of the Great Plains taken between 1870 and 1930, when men began mixing indigenous and white costume, wearing long hair, eagle feathers, and fringed leggings with suitcoats and brimmed hats (Maurer 1992: entries 264, 272). The *Continuidad* album was recorded in Barcelona, Spain, and appeals to Euro-American stereotypes of indigenous people, resulting in Oglala Otavalos in Barcelona with a mispunctuated English group name (Native's), a contradictory Spanish album name (Continuity), and a CD with lyrics in Spanish and Quichua.

Otavalomanta's 1994 CD cover is a photo of eight Otavalos wearing hats and black vests with pants and shirts of varying colors. A blonde young woman in Otavaleña traditional dress is seated on the ground in front of them, implying she is the wife, girlfriend, or lover of one of the young men, which is reinforced by her body language in an inside photo, where she is seated beside and leaning against one of the Otavaleños.

The back cover is a painting of a Native American mounted on horseback. He is wearing a loincloth, eagle-feather headdress, and moccasins, with his arms outstretched and face raised toward the sky. The iconography, especially the warbonnet and horse, signifies the noble Native North American. The eagle-feather headdress, for example, appeared in European art by the sixteenth century, and "this image of the Plains Indian has become synonymous with Indians of every region [of North America]" (Horse Capture 1992: 232).

The full title of Otavalomanta's 1994 album utilizes three languages (Quichua, German, and English). There are three contact addresses and phone numbers: one in Budapest, Hungary, one in Culver City, California, and one, "Irma Longworth: Public Relations Director," in San Gabriel, California. What a strange odyssey this album's art conjures up: Dakota Otavalos from the barrio Don Bosco of Ibarra living in southern California by way of Germany and Hungary, with a pseudo-Otavaleña valley girl public relations director. I suspect that Irma Longworth is the blonde in the photos on volume 4 (1994), and this is confirmed by Otavalomanta's 1995 CD.

Other CD covers are also visually disjunctive, especially for anyone who knows Ecuador. The photo on Runakuna's 1991 CD includes seven Otavaleños in a row wearing hats and dress whites. They are shown in three-quarter view so their braids are visible, standing in a wheat field that is as flat as the eye can see and totally unlike any Andean landscape. The cover makes sense when we learn that the CD was made at the Basement Tapes Studio, Amsterdam—the Otavaleños were photographed in a Dutch polder.

The second incongruous cover is Charijayac's CD *Quemando las nubes* (Sp. Burning the Clouds), released in Spain in 1992. The front cover is a photograph of Sayri Cotacachi in profile, bare shouldered, wearing a headband and face paint, with his hair loose. The back and inside photographs in the notes show all seven members of the band similarly attired. They are not painted like rainforest Quichua or Huaorani but like Native North Americans. Sayri told me they wore warpaint to show their opposition to the Columbus Quincentennial, intentionally evoking the trope of the North American warrior.

Yuyari's 1995 CD was recorded in Spain, and the cover art was obviously inspired by *Quemando las nubes*. The front cover is a photo collage of seven Otavalos also dressed like North American warriors. Judging from the cover art, I would expect the title of this CD to be *Authentic Chants of the Lakota*, but it is titled *Volveré* (Sp. I Will Return), with Sanjuanitos, a Cayambeña, cumbias, and Peruvian and Bolivian tunes. The Barcelona Otavalos, especially, seem drawn to images of Native North Americans. It may be that Europeans placed them on the wrong continent, and they finally gave up and accepted this designation; but it is equally likely that Otavalos learned that the warrior image sells. As I have argued, many people worldwide associate long hair with Native North Americans, so the Otavalos' hair facilitates this misidentification.

The covers of these albums are prime examples of postmodern pastiche, indicating cultural confusion on the part of the cover designer (who may or may not have been Otavalo), canny commercialism, a what-the-heck-we-need-a-picture attitude, or some combination of the above. The intent, however, is to convey an Otavalo, Andean, or New World indigenous identity that will convince potential customers to buy these recordings.

Finally, a word about the names of the groups and the albums. Most group names are Quichua, which makes a strong statement about ethnicity while simultaneously conveying exoticism: Pucará (Fortress), Kausay (Life), Chayag (Visitor), Tucuy Yahuar (All the Bloods), Runallacta (People's Land), Ñucanchi Ñan (Our Path), Ñuca Llacta (Our Land), Peguchemanta (From Peguche), Taki Sumaj (Beautiful Music), Sisa Pacari (Awakening Flower), Sisai (Blossoming), Chacras (Corn Fields), Quichua Mashis (Quichua Companions), Yahuar Wauky (Blood Brother), Yawar Inca (Blood of the Inca), Karullacta (Distant Land), Llaqtaymanta (From the Land), Cocha Marka (Lake Country), Karu Ñan (Distant Path), etc. The nonstandardization of Quichua orthography is apparent: Llacta vs. Llaqta, Inka vs. Inca, and Yahuar vs. Yawar.

If album titles are Quichua, they are often followed by subtitles in English, Spanish, German, Dutch, or some other European language. For example: Runakuna's *Shamuni* (Q. I Come), *Native Music from the Andes* (1996), and Kapary-Walka's *"Alpamanda"* (Q. From the Earth), *Traditional Music from the Andes, Ecuador • Perú • Bolivia* (1992). This is logical; exoticism is one thing, confounding the customer is another. Even if the group's name is foreign and unpronounceable, buyers know what kind of music they are getting, which is becoming a generic Andean ethnopop, "Inca Top Forty," as Frank Kiefer puts it (personal communication, 2000).

Other Otavalo groups, following the same logic, use Quichua band names but Spanish album titles with explanatory subtitles. Americamanta's 1994 album *Mundo Nuevo* (Sp. New World) also says on the front cover: *The Music of the Andes "Diferente" Version original*. The liner notes on many CDs are in a variety of languages. Again, if Quichua is used, a translation in Spanish, English, or some other language is usually provided.

Not surprisingly, with Otavalos dispersed around the globe, newspapers in the locales where they are found are publishing stories about the unusual visitors. These are not travel articles about tourism to Otavalo, but news or feature articles about Otavalos in foreign countries (Bedoya 1993; Cifuentes 1994; Conejo 1995; Febres Cordero 1993; Kandell 1993; Ode 1992; Sontag 1993; Straub 1994; Van Der Spek 1993; and various anonymous journalists). For example, the daily newspaper of Metropolitan State College of Denver, Colorado, ran a feature about an Otavalo selling sweaters in the student union (Straub 1994).

An article titled "Shuttle Capitalism" noted that Otavalos have become "the international sales brigades of an Andean capitalism that has elevated the Otavaleños to an affluence not attained by Latin America's indigenous peoples since the white conquest of the New World" (Kandell 1993: 30). A large photo of three young Otavaleñas and one Otavaleño selling on the streets of New York City (ibid.: 30–31) shocked Otavalos back in the valley because the gray, concrete cityscape was so unlike their idealized conception of the United States.

These articles sometimes perpetuate the same stereotypes as tourism literature. Occasionally the Otavalos themselves are responsible for this misrepresentation. In an article that appeared in Flemish in the Ieper, Belgium, newspaper in July or August 1993, the Otavaleños are quoted as saying, "To us, peace, friendship, and honesty are holy issues. Michael Jackson brings forth his message in his own enormous way; we use our own limited means to show our pride in our personal and cultural heritage. We are not in it for the money." This is pure propaganda; the musicians have families to support, and they are not playing for free.

The article also emphasizes the supposedly simple lifestyle of the group: "Only being used to oxen, they spend a whole day looking at a farmer on his tractor on the land." This surprised us back in Otavalo, since the father of two musicians regularly drives down Calle Quito on his tractor. Also: "They don't know bread or coffee. They don't sleep on a mattress, but on a thick carpet." These statements are patently false, and it is impossible to know where they came from, but the intent of the author seems to be the establishment of dichotomies between Ecuador as technologically simple and noncommercial and Europe as advanced and profit-oriented.

Occasionally something is lost in the translation. From what I can tell, the young men talked among themselves in Quichua then spoke to their hosts in Spanish, who translated into Flemish for the reporter. Back in Otavalo, two Dutch travelers translated the article from Flemish, which is similar to Dutch, into English. Thus, "[t]heir instruments are

homemade panpipes, blowing instruments, and sets of little sheeplegs."
After some thought I realized the "sheeplegs" are chajchaj, rattles made
from sheep's' hooves, or llama hooves in the southern Andes. As for cuisine, "horsemeat on the table is wrong, for the horse is a noble animal in
Ecuador. Little Spanish rats (*Spaanse ratjes*), on the other hand, are a deli-
cacy" (Claus 1993: n. pag.; translated by Rob van den Bergh and Jac Schoe-
makers). Although guinea pigs might look like rats to some travelers,
they are a separate species. The article has a photo of the group in dress
whites, hats, and ponchos, standing in a semicircle playing their instruments, although these young men normally wear Euro-American dress.

The Globalization of Otavalo Music

In analyzing the globalization of Otavalo music, I am referring to two
distinct but interlinked phenomena. The first is the presence of Otavalo
musicians on the global stage in the most literal sense. Otavalo musicians are everywhere, playing in malls, on street corners, at music festivals, and in concert halls and clubs and recording and selling their music
globally. The second is the extent to which Otavalo music has become
part of the world beat or global ethnopop music scene, adopted by musicians from other ethnicities and nationalities. Related to this is the
Otavalos' incorporation of others' musical genres, melodies, and instruments, resulting in reggae Sanjuanitos and Beatles tunes played on the
panpipes.

Otavaleños are playing at a variety of venues. Ñucanchi Ñan, a band
of seven Otavaleños from San Juan Alto, was one of the earliest groups
to leave Otavalo, play on the streets of Europe, and record cassettes and
CDs there. When asked about their most important experiences abroad,
they answered, "In August of last year [1995] we participated in the World
Festival of Music in Hamburg representing Ecuador" (Guaña 1996: 7).
In 1989, Charijayac, joined by several other Otavalo musicians, played
at a music festival in Springs, near Johannesburg, South Africa, along
with musicians from Asia, Europe, and Africa. "Our dress and our long
hair attracted the attention of the South Africans, who were fascinated
to see Indians [indios] from America" (Lema 1995: 191–192; my translation). Note that Lema identified himself as indigenous in the broadest
sense. Otavalo bands have played at the Cedarfest and Powderhorn Park
festivals in Minneapolis, Minnesota; at the July Art Fair in Ann Arbor,
Michigan; at Westlake shopping center in Seattle, Washington; at powwows throughout the United States and Canada; in front of the Stanford

University bookstore; at Sather Gate on the campus of the University of California at Berkeley; in Taos, New Mexico; at the folk-music festival in Poznan, Poland; on streets in Montreal, Paris, Seville, Córdova, Madrid, Avila, Salamanca, San Sebastián, and Valladolid—the list is endless (Tom Abercrombie, Karen Bruhns, Melanie Ebertz, Rodrigo Fichamba, Alex Johnson, Elizabeth Kaibel, Aleksander Posern-Zielinski, personal communication, 1990–2000; and my own observations).

Otavalos are so ubiquitous on streets in the United States and Europe that a book about Bolivia notes that Bolivian music recently has become well known in Europe and North America: "Station concourses, shopping arcades and pedestrian precincts from London to California echo to the distinctive sounds of the high Andes. Although street musicians usually dress in the characteristic costume of the Otavalo Indians of northern Ecuador, the music they play is authentic Bolivian" (von Lindert and Verkoren 1994: 65). The musicians are not described as being Otavalo indígenas but as wearing Otavalo dress. Are the musicians Bolivians dressed as Otavalos or Otavalos playing Bolivian music? Neither is uncommon. The authors elide the mixture of Bolivian, Chilean, Peruvian, Ecuadorian, Colombian, and sometimes Argentine music played by street musicians of whatever nationality and ethnicity.

Otavalos are seen as prototypical Andean indígenas, and many other Andean musicians now wear their hair in a ponytail or braid to meet audience expectations. If the Otavalos are identifying as Oglalas as a playful gesture or a commercial ploy, other Andean musicians are identifying as Otavalos in an endless round of ethnic musical chairs, resulting in the development of a generic, Pan-American indigenous identity. This Pan-American identity finds expression in the term "Abya Yala," a Panamanian Kuna word for the Americas. Thus, the liner notes of Americamanta's 1994 CD say: "To join the important brotherhood from our continent, we collect all that put us together, all that is common to the main reality of the big country Abya Yala . . ." The liner notes for Cochasqui's 1994 CD contain a poem in Spanish which reads, "I am the man of the Andes, I am the man of Abya Yala . . ."

The ubiquity of Otavalo musicians in the global musical landscape is illustrated by three examples. The first is Universal Studios' City Walk indoor theme park in Los Angeles. City Walk, which is housed in an enormous building on the Universal Studios lot, is a reproduction of a southern California cityscape: a simulated street two blocks long resembling Santa Monica, with more than forty famous shops and restaurants, complete with an ocean-front bar with sand and simulated ocean waves.

Why would anyone would go to City Walk instead of a beach town? The answer is security: no homeless people, drug dealing, or muggings. City Walk is an enormous success, with more than two million visitors the first year it opened (Latham 1994).

In the center of City Walk is a simulated Santa Monica plaza where an Otavalo band, Sajama (Q. Dreams), plays and sells cassettes (Marie Timberlake, personal communication, 1996). This is not exactly Jean Baudrillard's simulacrum (1983), a copy of a copy with no original, but it comes close. Indeed, one of the Otavalo musicians (Dave "Jo Jo" West) is not Otavalo at all but an Ecuadorian who was adopted by Canadians as an infant and who imagines that he might be Otavalo: imaginary Otavalos in an imaginary city plaza in Los Angeles (itself a collection of suburbs in search of a city).

The second example is from the Bolivian archaeological site Tiahuanaco, a showplace of ancient Aymara culture. When I visited in July 1997, the local restaurant was playing a cassette of Otavalo music (mainly Sanjuanitos) called "Música Tradicional Andina, Paris, France." The waiter insisted the tape "was better than Los Kjarkas" and had copies for sale.

Cable News Network (CNN) shows short commercials, called "The Sights and Sounds of [fill in the country]," to illustrate its global reach. In "The Sights and Sounds of England," the usual visuals are included: Big Ben, Parliament, and the changing of the guard at Buckingham Palace. The background music is not British ballads or Scottish bagpipes but Andean, possibly Otavalo, music, and one shot is a musician's hand beating a drum (thanks to Jim Belote, who brought this to my attention). The "sights" of England may be English, but the "sounds" of England are Andean.

Anthropologists and musicologists, like their colleagues across disciplines, are grappling with the question of global cultural trends, including musical homogeneity versus heterogeneity. Positing the choices in terms of binary oppositions, however, is not the best approach to the issues of the future of musical creativity and the survival of local musics.

New recording technologies, mass media, mass marketing, and the global traffic in music are affecting local musical traditions in unpredictable ways (see Baumann 1992; Frith 1989; Manuel 1988; Nettl 1985; Robinson et al. 1991; Slobin 1993; Stokes 1994; Taylor 1997; Titon 1992; Wallis and Malm 1984). On the one hand, "the postmodern world music commodification scene is dominated by surfaces, neon signs of musical heterogeneity that glow in the ever-present shadows of expanding musical homogeneity." On the other hand, "amplified musical diversity resists, in a rather literal way, the dramatic silencing or muting of indige-nous voices by transnational development interests" (Feld 1995: 96–97).

Vertical integration of the music industry and the consolidation of transnational music production and distribution coexist with thousands of vital local musical scenes which integrate, resist, ignore, or influ-ence Euro-American popular music. Some local music makes ripples in the larger pond, where it is called world music or world beat, a recog-nized category for Grammy awards. World beat includes reggae, Afro-beat, West African high life, klezmer, Brazilian samba, Cuban rumba and mambo, Andean, Punjabi-British bhangra, Indonesian pop, and other musical genres. Feld argues that "a world-beat blur, a more and more generic ethnopop music, can also be accompanied by marked, intensi-fied, and highly dramatic assertions of resistance-tinged local musics" (1995: 110).

The question of who is stealing from or appropriating whom does not capture the nuances of the situation and is based partly on the falla-cious assumption that until recently musical traditions and musicians did not borrow from one another. Critiques vary depending on the di-rection of the borrowing. For example, if Euro-American musicians in-corporate musical genres from less wealthy countries it is called "appro-priation" or "stealing." If the reverse occurs it is called "borrowing" or being "influenced by." This is not to deny the serious ethical and legal issues involved in world beat music, particularly when a musician or group makes millions from a hit using musicians from or the melodies of another ethnic group which does not share in the bounty. These legal and ethical dilemmas are not dependent on the success of the music, but success usually highlights them. Paul Simon's *Graceland* album (1986) raised these questions and caused considerable controversy because of his "appropriative mixing and copyrighting practices" (Feld 1995: 106).

Usually discussion focuses on Euro-American appropriation of ethnic music. Hector Lema of Quichua Marka (aka Inca Marka) observed that a similar problem occurs among Otavalos, which was also noticed by those of us buying cassettes and CDs at the Saturday fair. Certain selec-tions, sometimes entire recordings, sounded identical to those of other groups. I am not referring to musicians who were playing songs played by other groups, since traditionally Otavalo music was not considered to be owned by anyone, but to groups taking others' recordings and putting their names on them. Hector said that one Otavalo group was not ready to record because it was "of a low artistic quality," so Hector's group sold them the master of their album *Tushuy Cumari*. "The other group didn't participate. In reality it's the music of Quichua Marka." This was a legal sale. Hector said: "In the United States many resell masters. Others re-record illegally and change the cover and names. This is neither just nor legal nor correct, and it's a violation of rights. It pains me but there's nothing I can do. Many groups are interested in the money and not in the music."

Ñucanchi Ñan said: "[W]e have interpreted the themes of great musical groups such as "Let It Be" by the Beatles and "The Sounds of Silence," among others, using our own arrangements, which include mixing in the electronic. People have liked this, including the elders who have given us really positive reactions. This work is dedicated to love" (Guaña 1996: 7; my translation).

I wonder if the Beatles and Simon and Garfunkel would have "really positive reactions" if they learned of this CD, as it does not appear that Ñucanchi Ñan obtained permission or paid royalties for the use of these compositions. The band is cognizant of copyright issues, because their 1995 cassette, which includes "Sonido del silencio," has "Reproduction Prohibited" on the album jacket. (Paul Simon, as I noted above, has had his own problems in this regard.) Dedicating the work to *amor* (Sp. romantic love) is straight out of the Euro-American tradition and is probably something the band learned from Latin music in Ecuador or during their travels in Europe.

Charijayac exemplifies the paradoxes involved in the globalization of ethnic music. Sayri Cotacachi told me about the evolution of their music: "Around 1990, I went to London for nine months. I brought back all the music of Bob Marley, which is why reggae and Sanjuanitos are mixed together on 'Tamia,' which was recorded in Barcelona in 1991 [meaning *Otavalo y . (punto)*, recorded in 1989, released in 1990], and on '500 Años' [*Quemando las nubes*, released in 1992]." Sayri said that "Sanjuanitos have not changed in many years," so he composed "reggae Sanjuanitos."

The perception of reggae by indigenous peoples outside the Caribbean as oppositional ethnopop has led to its local adoption by migrants and indigenous people in places as diverse as Europe, Hawaii, North America, Australia, Papua New Guinea, South Africa, and Southeast Asia. The form also has generic connotations that are often nonpolitical (Feld 1995: 110). Reggae is highly popular among younger Otavalos. Many like its sound, but for some it represents resistance to white society by a minority ethnic group.

The members of Charijayac, although living in Spain, have adopted

Quichua nicknames and continue to wear traditional Otavalo long hair and hats. Otavalo has become an "imagined community," meaning a community too large and too dispersed for face-to-face contact (B. Anderson 1983), but as Akhil Gupta and James Ferguson have argued in another context, imagined does not mean imaginary (1992: 11). Modern technology has allowed the musicians, the music, and the musicians' community to exist simultaneously in different times and spaces. This paradox results from the nature of recorded music: it freezes a particular musical moment, allowing it to be repeated hours or years later in the same locale or in different places and for any number of audiences, a condition Murray Schafer calls "schizophonia" (1977: 90) and Walter Ong calls "secondary orality" (1991). As Steven Feld notes above (1995), recording has preserved many indigenous musical forms that might otherwise be lost and allows dispersed peoples to hear the music of home even when they are far away or separated from the musicians making that music.

The Barcelona Otavalos sing, "Otavalo, I will sing of you, Otavalo, I will return to you" (my translation) on *Otavalo y . [punto]*, Charijayac's 1990 cassette recorded in Spain. The musicians have no intention of living in Otavalo permanently, although several spend time in both countries. Nonetheless, Charijayac's music is extremely popular among Otavalos not only because of its musicality but because the group represents loyalty to an Otavalo identity and helps assuage the anxiety felt by many over the cultural consequences of the Otavalo diaspora. Schizophonia and secondary orality have their uses, and one of them is creating and maintaining links among dispersed Otavalos. Slobin calls this kind of in-group activity "diasporic interculture, which emerges from the linkages that subcultures set up across national boundaries" (1993: 64).

Charijayac split up around 1993, but they reunite occasionally for concerts, most recently in Otavalo in March 2000 for "The Concert of a Generation" (my translation). Former members play in two bands, Jailli and R.Y.CH., both of which push Andean music in new directions. R.Y.CH.'s *Runa Song* CD (1997) includes selections identified as "reggae, rumba, rock, tobas, tecno, pop, cumbia/reggae, huayno, sanjuan, lambada, and jayac. tecno." They recently flew to South Korea to perform one number on the Korean equivalent of the *Ed Sullivan Show*. This was "La Bamba," which was well received according to Frank Kiefer and Margaret Goodhart, who saw a video of the program (personal communication, 1999), although I wonder if the Koreans thought this U.S. pop hit of the 1950s sung by Ritchie Valens was a typical Andean tune.

While I have emphasized the significance of Otavalo music as an economic activity, I want to stress its importance in creating and maintaining identity and community. Paul Connerton's argument that societies collectively remember the past not through the written record but through such commemorative ceremonies and bodily practices as holidays, fiestas, family rituals, costume, and performances (1989) is especially apropos for Otavalo, where people historically were nonliterate and where illiteracy is still high, especially among the older generation. Hearing Otavalo music recorded or live, performing Otavalo music, and dancing at parties are extraordinarily effective and important in maintaining a sense of community in Ecuador and abroad. "Alongside food, music can be—and usually is—the main means of identification of diasporic groups . . ." (Slobin 1994: 245).

This note of community, continuity, and Otavalo (or indigenous) identity is sounded clearly in many of the CD album liner notes. Compared with album notes from the 1970s, the sentiments are far more positive. There is more talk of cultural pride and an awareness of Otavalo's international influence and less mention of oppression, although that surfaces, especially in connection with the Columbus quincentennial. The notes of Americamanta's 1994 CD read: "Since our origins we have dedicated a few months each year to divulge our music, first in our country and little by little spread the message to other countrys and nations of this, our world." The 1996a Chacras CD notes say: "We are descendants of an old culture of a town in resurgence just as the Sarances, Otavalos and Caranquis cultures rich in thought with a way of living through traditional music. We are the outcry of a new generation with feelings of Tahuantinsuyo and the great sillia." I am baffled by "the great sillia," but the general idea comes across.

When Charijayac played a concert in Otavalo in March 1994, they started a near riot because they departed from their usual format. The band members plus the Otavalo-identified Canadian Dave West wore red blazers, flowered shirts, blue jeans, and cowboy boots instead of Otavalo traditional dress. Worse (from the crowd's point of view), they went electric, with amplified guitars and bass. Charijayac announced that their first numbers were "an experiment" and played rock, while the crowd hollered, hissed, and booed. They played more rock and finally a "reggae Sanjuanito" (Rhonda Bekker, personal communication, 1994).

The Ibarra newspaper headlined the concert "Charijayac Defrauds." The subheadline read: "A changed folklore group (?), which initiated its career in Spain and from there projected [its music] to our country, seems to have confused its roles and begun to interpret rock in a program which invited the best Latin American groups." The author castigated Charijayac for rock, the "San Juan Reggae," and its dress, "in which you could notice the foreign influence on the mentality of our Indians" (Che-Flechas 1994; my translation). Note the possessive "our Indians" (Sp. *nuestros indios*), as if wasipungu still existed. Despite the patronizing tone, the article accurately captured the displeasure of the audience, which included Otavalos, whites-mestizos, and foreigners.

Why the fuss? Old musical favorites evoke bygone times, and the crowd wanted to hear such Charijayac hits as "Agua fresca," "Otavalo y punto," and "Carretero," which were mentioned in the article (Che-Flechas 1994). There is something comforting about the Barcelona Otavalos returning to Otavalo and affirming their identity and loyalty to the community, and Charijayac failed to meet these expectations (which is reminiscent of the opposition that Bob Dylan encountered when he went electric at the Newport Folk Festival in 1965). In times of rapid change, people frequently want their musical icons to be conservative.

Otavalo musicians abroad often sell artesanías and play paid gigs to obtain cash then invest the money to make their own recordings. In 1995, an Otavalo friend told me that his son's group in Portugal had bought 1,000 tape cassettes for recording their music. Otavalo bands have financed, recorded, and produced a plethora of cassettes and CDs which they sell during performances, on the streets abroad, or in their stores and market kiosks, completely bypassing established multinational recording and distribution monopolies. (In 1998, these were BMG Entertainment, EMI Recorded Music, Sony Music Entertainment, Universal Music Group, and Warner Music Group.) Otavalos rely instead on their own production and distribution network, their diasporic interculture, including friends in host countries. This increases their control and their profits, although it also limits their reach, but not as much as we might think, given the global networks Otavalos have created.

The most impressive example of these networks is found on the back of Americamanta's 1994 CD. The contacts include names, phone numbers, and some addresses in "Ecuador, USA, Italia, Suiza, España, Japon." The contacts are not just other Otavalos living abroad; some appear to be friends of the group: for example: "USA—Rankin Skinner" and "Japon—Chieko Sakurai." Chayana'k's 1995 cassette is a close second, with contacts in "Ecuador, España, Portugal, Noruega." It is a rare CD that does not give contacts in countries other than Ecuador.

Sanjuanes are played and recorded along with Andean tunes that are more appealing to Euro-Americans, and Ecuadorian genres generally constitute a minority of the selections on an album (see Table 6.1). One Otavalo musician who plays in the USA observed, "We sell more tapes when we play 'El Condor Pasa,'" the Peruvian tune popularized by Simon and Garfunkel. By 1997, however, some groups had come full circle. Pachamama, from the Centro Cultural Peguche, released a CD recorded and mixed in Quito and Ibarra. All nineteen selections are Ecuadorian, fourteen of them from the Otavalo valley, including many Sanjuanes.

The music played and recorded by Otavalo musicians has become much more performance-oriented and attuned to what Otavalos (usually correctly) perceive to be foreign preferences. On Yahuar Wauky's 1993 CD *Yarina 500 Years*, the notes say in English: "In order to share our message on a broader scale, we have created compositions in: Quichua, Spanish and English." The album, recorded in Connecticut, credits several U.S. musicians as songwriters and performers.

The commercial emphasis is not unique to Ecuadorian bands. During the 1984 foreign tour of Peruvian group Ayllu Sulca, their British organizer observed that "[a]fter meeting the musicians, instead of talking about their music I was immediately presented with a very long hand written list of goods the group had brought with them with prices in Peruvian soles, and I was asked to work out an equivalent price in British currency. Economic transactions were uppermost in their minds" (Fairley 1991: 273). I mention this in light of the Euro-American insistence that commercial concerns are impure and inauthentic, as if Andean musicians did not have to earn a living. But if Sitting Bull was not a weaver and merchant, neither was he a traveling musician.

Otavalos are adopting and adapting foreign music, and foreigners are doing the same with Otavalo music. Otavalo musicians play Los Kjarkas tunes, and Chilean, Bolivian, and Peruvian bands play Sanjuanitos. On a sunny Saturday afternoon in November 1996, a friend and I approached Union Square in downtown San Francisco. The sounds of Andean music became more distinct until we said, "Otavalo music! Sanjuanitos!" Two Bolivian musicians from the group Aymuray were alternating live music with selections from their albums, and they had recorded the Sanjuanito on their CD. In a restaurant in Cuzco, Peru, in 1997, I listened to a local folklore group play the usual Bolivian and Peruvian melodies; then they played a Sanjuanito ("Huambrita"). In October 1994, an 85-member Swiss chorus presented an Andean Mass at Peguche Falls in honor of Día de la Raza (Sp. Day of the Race) before a large audience of all the ethnic groups in the valley, including tourists and resident for-eigners. Many dignitaries were present: the daughter of Ecuador's presi-dent; José Quimbo, an Otavaleño who was secretary for intercultural re-lations; Felipe Duchicela, national secretary for indigenous affairs and ethnic minorities; the president of the Ecuadorian congress; Luis Mejía Montesdeoca, the prefect for Imbabura; other local and provincial offi-cials; and diplomats from the Swiss embassy and consulate in Quito. The presence of Ecuadorian dignitaries is a tribute to the growing economic and political power of Otavalos; such a turnout was unheard of fifteen years ago.

The introduction was in Quichua and Spanish. The mass was sung in Spanish to Andean melodies, including Sanjuanitos, and the chorus was accompanied by three Chilean and two Ecuadorian musicians play-ing Andean instruments. Following the mass, Otavaleño Jesús Fichamba sang romantic ballads. In a mix typical of the musical and sartorial cross-cultural influences prevalent in the valley, Swiss musicians wear-ing patchwork jackets from the Otavalo market sang Andean music in Spanish and Ecuador's OTI competition winner, wearing Otavalo tradi-tional dress, sang romantic ballads in Spanish. The performances were a smashing success.

In the early 1990s, several Italian musicians visited Otavalo, learn-ing traditional music. Back in Rome in 1992 and 1993, with Otavalo and Salasaca guest musicians, they recorded a double album. Of twenty-four selections, twenty-three were composed by the Italians based on tradi-tional Otavalo music, and one tune was taken from Ñanda Mañachi (and credited to them). The album, *Zig Zag*, was produced by Sayri Cotacachi of Charijayac and recorded at the "Digital Inca's Studio, Roma, Italia."

The Italians have completely mastered Otavalo musical genres. One selection, "Italianomasicuna" (Q. Italian Companions), is sung by Ital-ian female and male musicians in Spanish and Quichua with Otavalo-style falsettos and vocal inflections. The verses are composed in a San-juan musical framework complete with an eight-beat violin bridge. For all intents and purposes the song is a Sanjuanito. A song titled "Ecua-volley" (Sp. Ecuadorian Volleyball) also has Quichua lyrics. Another song on the album is dedicated to Juan Cayambe, the legendary harpist who played with Ñanda Mañachi.

In "¡Huambrarap!" (Q. Young Person Rap), the first verse says in Qui-chua, "I turn on the power: Wordstar appears. I sit in front of my per-sonal computer. Then I open a file. I will write a song with your name" (my translation). The chorus is "Huambrarap!" Another verse translates from Quichua as: "We are the young people of today. We must shout to the world: We are the sons of Imbabura. Long braids!" Partly because the lyrics are in Quichua with references to Imbabura, partly because groups like Charijayac have composed new songs and combined musical genres, and partly because Latin rap is heard on interprovincial buses, television, and radio, the words and music do not seem impossibly foreign to Otavalos in Ecuador or abroad. *Zig Zag* became a huge hit in Otavalo; it was played throughout the valley during the summer of 1995. Most people insist the group is Otavalo; I got into several arguments about this in Otavalo that summer.

There are now Otavalo indigenous transmigrants living and recording music in Barcelona, Spain, influenced by rock, techno, and reggae and becoming the musical voice of their dispersed indigenous community, and Italians recording tunes in the Inca's Studio in Rome and singing in Spanish and Quichua about karaoke, computers, long braids, volleyball, and Imbabura, with musical influences ranging from Sanjuanes to Gregorian chants to Western classical music to American hip hop, but who somehow sound more Otavalo than the Otavalos themselves—Otavalos refuse to believe they are Italian. The result is a pastiche of musical and cultural influences, cross-currents, and identity constructions that can only be called postmodern (or perhaps confused). In the words of W. Anderson, "reality isn't what it used to be" (1990).

Otavalo music has become more self-consciously local, with Sanjuanes seen as "our music," radically internationalized with the incorporation of outside musical genres, and part of the world music scene. The Italians are mistaken for Otavalos precisely because the Otavalos are playing and sometimes recording music on six continents, absorbing and recombining musical influences and exporting these syntheses back to Otavalo to become part of the local musical culture.

It is poignant that the Italian women in the music group Trencito de Los Andes are so prominent on the *Zig Zag* album because music-making is increasingly seen by outsiders and Otavalos as a male preserve: people now mainly see males making music, either live or pictured on cassette and CD covers. Traditionally, Otavalo males have played instruments and females have participated as vocalists and occasionally as percussionists; there is no separate female or male music. When Ñanda Mañachi toured Europe in the 1980s, the young women in the group came along, but the trip was an organized and chaperoned concert tour.

The declining participation and recognition of women vocalists is not necessarily a male conspiracy, but an outgrowth of musicians playing on the street or in peñas folklóricas. Parents will not let their young unmarried daughters tour Europe camping out of a car; and married women, especially those with children, usually stay home to mind the house, land, textile production, and store. Besides, car camping for six months or even staying in cheap hotels is hardly the ideal situation for a woman with small children.

Equally disconcerting as declining female musical participation is that when females do sing on albums they often are not credited. Female vocalists can be heard on Charijayac's *Cielo Rosa* album, but they are unnamed. *Zig Zag* credits all musicians by name. The 1997 Pachamama album also credits the female vocalists; and in 1998, Jumandy, consisting of four Otavaleñas, released their CD *Eclipse de amor*. In general, however, the rise of street bands has meant the decline of Otavaleña musical participation.

Table 6.1 illustrates several features of contemporary Otavalo music, including the quantity of CDs produced outside Ecuador. I bought or analyzed every CD of Otavalo music that was available in Otavalo or in the United States (around 100 different titles) and did not find one that was produced in Ecuador until 1997, unlike the earlier 33⅓ RPM albums. Nor are these CDs produced by major or minor recording companies; they are Otavalo productions.

The second feature is the decrease in Ecuadorian music on albums since the 1970s. Even where the exact provenience of the music is omitted, some songs have such titles as "Bolivianita," "Pueblo de Ayacucho" (Peru), or "Llorando se fue" (a composition by Los Kjarkas of Bolivia). Except for the Charijayac and Trencito de Los Andes CDs, the covers say "Traditional Music from the Andes: Ecuador • Peru • Bolivia" or "Traditional Music from Latin America" or something similar. The Ecuadorian music that *is* recorded on these CDs, however, invariably includes Sanjuanitos.

Trouble Abroad: "Europe Is Burned Out"

Otavalos encountered problems in the United States and Europe as early as 1992. Some Otavalos holding cultural exchange or tourist visas entered the United States with so much merchandise that customs agents confiscated it until the Otavalos paid import duties. In 1992, I heard of Otavalos being deported from the United States and Europe, usually for overstaying their visas or selling without a permit. Given the Otavalos' experience with the Ecuadorian legal system, these problems

TABLE 6.1. *CDs of Otavalo Music (all groups composed of Otavalo indígenas unless otherwise indicated)*

Group	Provenience & Ethnicity	Album Title	Date	Where Recorded or Manufactured	Percentage Ecuadorian Music
Ñucanchi Ñan	San Juan Alto (Otavalo)	Ñucanchi Causay	1984	West Germany	69
Ñucanchi Ñan	San Juan Alto (Otavalo)	Kangunapag	ca. 1985	Berlin, Germany	60
Ecuador Inkas	Otavalo area	Ecuador Inkas	1990	Germany	50
Runakuna	Otavalo area incl. La Compañia	Music from the Andes, Ecuador	1991	Amsterdam, Holland	$33\frac{1}{3}$
Kapary-Walka	Otavalo area	Alpamanda	1992	Bogotá, Colombia; CD mfd. in Hamburg, Germany	50
Charijayac	Otavalo area indígenas living in Barcelona, Spain	Quemando las nubes	1992	Barcelona, Spain	6 of 9 are new compositions mixing traditional & Euro-American music
Llaqtaymanta	Peruvians, Bolivians & Otavalo area indígenas	Traditionelle Musik der Inkas	1992	Hamburg, Germany	50

TABLE 6.1. Continued

Group	Provenience & Ethnicity	Album Title	Date	Where Recorded or Manufactured	Percentage Ecuadorian Music
Trencito de Los Andes	Italy (non-indigenas)	Zig Zag (2 vols.)	1992–1993	Rome, Italy	23 of 24 are new compositions based on Otavalo traditional music
Kanatan Aski "Clean Land"	2 Otavalo indigenas, 1 Otavalo & 1 white-mestizo from Quito, 1 Peruvian	Andean Colours	1993	Toronto, Canada	30
*Karullacta	Quinchuquí (Otavalo)	Quinchuquimanda	1993	USA (area code Minneapolis/St. Paul, MN)	66
Yahuar Wauky	Otavalo area	Yarina: 500 Years	1993	Union, CT USA	10 of 13 are new compositions
Quillas	Otavalo area	Ecuador	1993	Belgium	42
Llaqtamasi	Sara Urcu, San Roque (Otavalo)	Llaqtamasi	1994	Munich, Germany	38

Otavalomanta	Otavalo area	*Ñucallacta, Vol. 4*	1994	Budapest, Hungary	50
Runakuna	Otavalo area incl. La Compañia	*Sumaj Punlla*	1994	Amsterdam, Holland	50
Sisa Pacari	La Joya (Otavalo)	*Sisa Pacari*	1994	Ontario, Canada	not given (includes Peruvian and Bolivian music)
Taki Sumaj	Otavalo area	*Taki Sumaj*	1994	Bogotá, Colombia; CD mfd. in Minneapolis, MN	33
Runallacta	Otavalo area	*Lo mejor de Runa-llacta Otavalomanta*	1994	Canada	25 to 40
Yuyari	Otavalo area	*Volveré*	1995	Spain	40 to 50
Quichua Mashis	Otavalo area, incl. Peguche	*Catishun*	1996	Seattle, WA	42
Pachamama	Peguche	*Antología de la música indígena*	1997	Quito, Ibarra; CD mfd. in Pennsauken, NJ	100
Jumandy	Otavalo area	*Eclipse de amor*	1998	Ecuador	33 to 40
Quillas	Peguche	*The Best of the Quillas*	1999	New York	47

* Composed of tracks pirated from Llaqtaymanta's CD (above), plus three songs taken from another group's album.

were predictable. Lema wrote that the authorities in Otavalo could be bought and that if a "humble indígena" protested a theft he or she was often jailed. "The police existed only to abuse us; they grabbed anyone in the street, man or woman, and took them to jail saying they lacked respect" (1995: 32–33; my translation). Some Otavalo merchants and musicians have a lackadaisical attitude toward permits, contracts, and showing up on time and lost opportunities to play or wore out their welcome with Europeans and North Americans who were trying to help them.

When one of my godchildren's brothers returned from Europe earlier than expected in July 1993, I learned that he had been deported from Holland when the car he owned broke down in front of a police station in Amsterdam. When the Otavalos got out to push the car, the police asked for their papers and discovered that they were illegal. The Otavalo said there were at least 400 Otavalo music groups in Europe and that people were "tired" of Andean music. In 1994, Otavaleños returning from abroad said Europeans were "bored" with Andean music and felt "lashed" by the noise. In some cities there were several Otavalo bands playing near each other and trying to drown each other out, and Europeans were walking by with their fingers in their ears. My godson's brother said, "They say that in Holland you can encounter Otavaleños every five minutes."

In Belgium the police made a sweep of the two-week annual summer fair in Ghent and picked up and deported seventy-two illegal Otavalos. An Otavalo playing music in Belgium wrote to his compadres that "[o]ne problem I had in Belgium was that I used up my three months and stayed illegally, but God helped me find some good Belgian friends who helped me obtain three months more so that I could continue working in Belgium."

In mid-June 1993, seven members of an Otavalo music group and their Canadian friend were playing music and selling cassettes in old-town Albuquerque, New Mexico, when INS agents arrested them for vending without a license and for engaging in commercial activities in violation of their tourist visas. A merchant had complained to the police that they were playing too near his store. Earlier that day they had played in a flea market, and, unknown to them, an undercover agent bought one of their tapes. They had been in the United States only a month, and most had purchased airline tickets on credit. They needed to pay for their tickets and save money to support themselves and their families, so getting arrested and deported was a financial disaster.

The eight young men were put on a bus and driven six hours to El Paso, Texas, where they were held in a federal facility for illegal immigrants. "There were some Asians and Africans and *lots* of Hispanics," one of them told me. Their passports were confiscated, and someone drew a big "X" through their visas. The Canadian and two Peguche musicians were released on bail provided by an older American woman friend. The two Otavaleños immediately returned to Ecuador without their passports, which were never returned, although all charges were dropped. Everyone eventually was released.

Although more males than females are traveling, Jonathan Kandell notes that "[t]he presence abroad of larger numbers of Otavaleño women is a phenomenon of the past decade. They are under 25, unmarried and determined to return home with sizable savings" (1993: 34). One 21-year-old unmarried Otavaleña from Ilumán regularly makes trips by herself to Santa Marta and Cartagena, Colombia, to sell artesanías, unfazed by civil war, narcoterrorism, or thievery.

In the fall of 1993, two Otavaleñas, Zuelma from Peguche and her cousin from Quito, flew to Belgium with artesanías. They sold enough bracelets to cover their plane tickets then drove to Berlin to visit a German friend, Adi Willnauer, who had lived with Zuelma's family in Peguche. Unfortunately, all was not smooth selling. The Otavaleñas were stunned by the cold, spoke no German, and were totally dependent on Adi. She helped them sell sweaters at Christmas fairs and in the health food coop where she worked, but their asking price of 100 marks was too high for most customers.

Then Zuelma was arrested on the street for selling without a license by a plainclothes policeman who confiscated her merchandise. He gave her a ticket which said she had three days to leave Germany. When Adi went to the police station to recover Zuelma's merchandise, the police told her the fine was more than the merchandise was worth and she should forget it. The young Otavaleñas left Germany shortly thereafter (Adi Willnauer, personal communication, 1994).

I have many such stories in my field notes. In every case where I talked to Otavalos who had been arrested and deported they expressed their surprise that the police in Europe and the United States did not mistreat them. From their knowledge of the Ecuadorian penal system they automatically expected a beating or worse. No Otavalos (as far as I know) have been arrested abroad for theft, drug dealing, assault, or other violent crimes, despite rumors to the contrary. They are arrested for the types of infractions mentioned above.

American hosts comment that their Otavalo guests are impressed by Americans' observance of what seem to Otavalos to be minor and unimportant laws, especially when no police were present. Anthropologists Linda Belote and Jim Belote took the Otavalo group Inti Raymi touring in northern Minnesota. The Otavalos expressed surprise that the Belotes stopped at stop signs even when no one was there. At Lake Superior they visited a trout-breeding stream, where the Otavalos said, "Dinner!" They were amazed when the Belotes said it was illegal to catch the trout; nor did the band understand when the Belotes refused to hunt deer out of season (Linda Belote and Jim Belote, personal communication, 1993). A Salasaca told me he was impressed by how "organized" Americans were when they drove, signaling turns and stopping at traffic lights.

In the summer of 1993, twenty-six Otavalos were arrested in the Bijlmermeer neighbor of Amsterdam near the site of the 1992 El Al crash. Otavalos "from Belgium, Germany, France, etc., congregated to talk, play football, and drink beer. . . . Neither the police nor the officials knew about these people or why they had come to Holland. For them they were simply illegals and suspected of drug trafficking, robberies, and other crimes" (Van Der Spek 1993: 6-C; my translation).

Most of the Otavalos arrested "lacked a stamp in their passport that formally they had to obtain within eight days of arrival from the police of the foreign ministry. This was a regulation that nobody knew about and that no one informed them about when they entered at the airport." So many Otavalos were in jail in Amsterdam that a FICI representative, Luis Maldonado, flew to Holland. He negotiated with the Dutch government for the Otavalos' release and for time to wrap up their affairs and leave the country voluntarily: "This worked out well for the Dutch government: they saved fifty thousand dollars on airline tickets which would have been used to deport them" (ibid.).

Maldonado said that indígenas "impelled by their precarious economic situation in Ecuador try their luck in rich Europe. Nonetheless this massive migration often results in other kinds of penury." He admitted that "[t]he towns of the Ecuadorian sierra have a false image of Europe. We want to publicize the difficulties of working informally here so that our people have a better standard of judgment before they travel." Maldonado mentioned the "clash of cultures" when "Quichuas" were unaware of local laws and customs (El Comercio, August 13, 1993: D-8; my translation). Directly below the El Comercio article was one announcing that the Dutch airline KLM was improving its service from Quito to the Caribbean and Europe, a mixed message to say the least. Note that the Otavalos acted independently of the Ecuadorian government through the provincial indigenous federation to resolve their problems in Holland. Otavalos no more expect help from their government abroad than they do at home.

By the summer of 1995, the bloom was off the musical rose. One problem was the decline of interest in Andean music because of market saturation, and a second was the quality of the music. Several musicians distinguished between the older, more serious groups, mentioning Ñanda Mañachi, Los Chaskis, Yahuar Wauky, Grupo Peguche, Ñucanchi Ñan, and Charijayac, and the newer ones. Segundo Lema of Los Chaskis said: "Now there are many musicians, a massive proliferation of commercializers of music. Music signifies a mentality. The occasional musicians don't understand what music is, but they know how to play. There are very few who maintain this line [of the groups mentioned above]. We work for the culture and for the family." Segundo and others felt that unaccomplished musicians were bad representatives. Indeed, while musicians learn by practicing, hearing them practice by performing in public is painful. From time to time the hotels, peñas, and restaurants in Otavalo hire groups that are just plain awful: they play and sing off key, are not tight, substitute volume for finesse, and pitch songs too high.

I was at the Hotel Ali Shungu in Otavalo when the owners received a call from their godson in Europe, who said he was coming home because "Europe is burned out." Otavalos had ceased to be novel and were seen as nuisances—exotic nuisances, but pests nonetheless. According to Linda Belote (personal communication, 1999), the Andean bands playing in the American midwest have to travel to ever smaller and more remote communities to generate interest.

Earnings from music and the sales of artesanías have dropped. In Holland: "You can feel the competition. A daypack which used to sell for 60 Dutch florins (S/60,000) now sells for perhaps half that amount" (Van Der Spek 1993: 6-C; my translation). Humberto Arrayán of Ilumán said, "Everyone thinks you can earn a fortune in Europe, but it isn't like that." Rodrigo Pichamba of Peguche said: "On my first trip [in 1991] I had a debt of $1,500 but there weren't many people [Otavalos] and not much competition and I earned $1,500 in one month. Every year the profits have gone down. The people in Europe are tired of Andean music. It's nothing special. Now it takes an entire summer to cancel the debt for a ticket."

I asked Otavalos why they persisted in illegal street activities when this ruined things for all of them. Some blamed the Peruvians, Bolivians, and Chileans. Several Otavalos were particularly irritated by South American musicians who wore their hair long and were mistaken for Otavalos. One said in disgust that the Peruvians in Italy urinated against the side of the church (as if Otavalos did not do the same).

Others said that if they did not sell artesanías and play music on the street someone else would, an example of "the tragedy of the commons" (Hardin and Baden 1977). Gary Snyder calls this "the dilemma of common-pool resources," meaning that if I don't do it the other person will (1990: 35). In this case, Otavalos see the globe as a common-pool resource, available for the exploitation of artesanías and music sales on a first-come, first-earned basis.

The number of bands abroad has probably peaked, but as long as there is money to be made young Otavalos will head overseas. Otavalos have other motives for going abroad, although economics is foremost: "adventure," "to know [a foreign place]," and peer pressure—"all the youth are going." Travel abroad has become a rite of passage, especially for young men. If the present pattern continues, however, young men who play music will return to textile sales. Clothes wear out, and people need Christmas and birthday presents; live Andean music may be a passing fad.

Is the Valley Postmodern Yet?

For Otavalos, foreign travel has resulted in the "radical internationalization of culture" that Andrew Milner (1991) characterizes as postmodern. Many Otavalos and members of other Ecuadorian indigenous groups have leapt right into the postmodern world, skipping modernity in the process: from serfdom to Amsterdam in one generation. Some examples of the internationalization of life in the valley:

A Salasaca indígena who has lived in Otavalo for twenty-five years and visited the United States at least seven times since 1982 has two dogs. One is named "Salchipapa" (after the alarming fried sausage and potato dish) and the other "J. C. Penney."

In July 1994, I watched an Otavaleño drive a new sedan down an Otavalo street. On the windshield in the passenger side was a large plaque with the words "BROOKLYN, New York."

On Saturday nights young indígenas cruise Otavalo's Parque Bolívar in cars and trucks with stereos blaring. Some of the vehicles are outfitted with neon disco lights around the lower part of the chassis, an American fad.

An Agato weaving family has spent extensive time in Santa Fe, New Mexico, where their family keeps an apartment. In 1993, they completed a new two-story stuccoed, concrete-block home in Agato. In contrast to the traditional unadorned nature of indigenous homes, the outside of their house has planters and grinding stones in the corners, and the walls of the patio are hung with old spinning wheels, corn stalks, dolls, and a sheep's skull, Santa Fe–style decoration.

At an Otavalo indígena wedding in 1994, an Otavaleño asked me to dance. Instead of facing each other, not touching, and two-stepping back and forth as is customary, he held me in ballroom dancing position. As we danced (the only couple among hundreds of guests to dance this way) he asked, "Parlez-vous français?" I answered, "No." He said, "Pourquois pas?" I said in Spanish, feeling slightly disoriented, "Because I'm in Ecuador, and I'm trying to improve my Spanish and Quichua." He said in Spanish, "What a shame! I lived two years in Paris, and I want to practice my French."

The unsettling nature of such incidents for foreigners and Otavalos alike, and the sense that life in the Otavalo valley "isn't what it used to be," is evident in changing ethnic relations and in considerable local discussion about what is happening to "our traditional culture," the topics of the next two chapters.

CHAPTER 7

Otavalo Wealth and Changing Social Relations

The ethnic groups in the Otavalo valley have a long history of uneasy and unequal coexistence characterized by almost castelike hierarchical relationships until the years following the abolition of wasipungu. This chapter examines the profound shift in social relations and power that has occurred over the past thirty years, an ethnic earthquake that has rearranged the local social strata to the extent that the terminology has changed and some ethnic categories have disappeared. I am using "power" in the classic Weberian sense as the ability to impose one's will and realize one's goals even against the opposition and resistance of others (1947: 192).

The cause of this seismic upheaval is the increase in indigenous prosperity, which has brought social and political power that has altered social relationships among indígenas and between indígenas and other local groups. While there are no data on Otavalo income levels, since 1978 I have noted the increased acquisition of consumer goods by families I know. These range from blenders and stereos to sewing machines, refrigerators, and motor vehicles (Meisch 1987, 1997, 1998b). Rudi Colloredo-Mansfeld's thorough study of changing household consumption patterns in Ariasucu confirms this trend and documents other concrete signs of new indigenous wealth, including the construction of substantial homes in the countryside (1994, 1998b, 1999).

Foreigners are now a potent ingredient in this volatile ethnic brew. Ethnic and racial terms in Ecuador vary regionally, and I am confining my discussion to Imbabura and especially the Otavalo valley. Today Otavalos and Cayambes constitute approximately 70% to 75% of the population of Imbabura. Historically each Imbabura ethnic group has had preferred self-referential names for itself, with disparaging terms used by outsiders (Stark 1981). Some Ecuadorians considered these divisions based on heredity (race or caste) and others on culture (or ethnicity):

"No one single schema explains the social divisions of modern Ecuadorian society; both race and ethnicity exist as social facts" (Colloredo-
Mansfeld 1998a: 201). I use ethnicity rather than race as a description of
Imbabura's divisions because the emphasis on culture is more analyti-
cally appropriate, given the movement between ethnic categories.

Increased indigenous prosperity (albeit unevenly distributed) also
challenges assimilationist models of development and the Ecuadorian
government's policy of *mestizaje*. Since the late 1960s, the government
has proclaimed that "[w]e are all mestizos" and that indígenas will cease
to be a problem when they cease to be Indians. This philosophy is ex-
pounded in classroom lectures, school textbooks, and the media (Stutzman 1981). On September 15, 1972, Ecuadorian president Guillermo
Rodríguez Lara proclaimed in a speech in Puyo: "There is no more Indian
problem. We all become white when we accept the goals of national culture" (Whitten 1976: 268).

The assumption behind mestizaje is that white culture is inherently
superior and that indígena equals poverty; one way to erase poverty is
to assimilate indígenas. Mestizaje is based on Enlightenment notions of
a monocultural nation-state, rather than on the pluricultural and pluri-
ethnic realities of Ecuador, so CONAIE represents mestizaje's antithe-
sis. Indeed, a primary thrust of mestizaje is to "whiten" indígenas (Stutzman 1981). Many Ecuadorians hope indigenous culture will be subsumed
by white culture, although it is logical to ask why it should not be the
other way around. If everyone is mestizo why not become indígena?
But rather than moving toward the middle, ethnic categories have polar-
ized: "Only one ethnic boundary in Ecuador is socially and culturally
defended by both sides, that between self-identifying indígena and non-
indígena" (Butler 1981: vi–vii). Most Otavalos have no intention of becoming mestizos. Textile and music production and marketing have
strengthened rather than weakened cultural identity and increased Otavalo economic power to a degree unimagined thirty years ago. The Otavalo example confounds the indígena-equals-poverty equation and challenges the dubious assumptions of mestizaje.

How did Otavalo wealth change local social relations, from indígenas
on their knees before whites in the 1960s to indígenas owning half the
town and flying off to England or France and assuming the mayoralty
in 2000? There has always been movement between categories, generally defined as upward mobility or acculturation, but this mobility across
ethnic lines does not mean the absence of boundaries. Ethnic boundaries involve processes of exclusion and inclusion which maintain dis-

crete categories despite changing participation and membership in the course of individual lives (Barth 1969: 9). In other words, just because some individuals in the Otavalo valley changed ethnic categories, this did not mean that ethnic boundary markers were unimportant.

Since the Spanish conquest, there have been externally enforced negative consequences for those identified as indigenous, including the payment of tribute, the mita, exploitative labor relations on haciendas, denial of education, sexual abuse of females by members of dominant groups, and despoliation of land and possessions with no hope of legal redress, not to mention the thousands of insults and humiliations which indígenas still recall with pain: ethnic slurs ("dirty Indian"), being forced off the sidewalk "by the people with neckties," being sent to the back of the bus or hauled out of a bus seat to allow a white-mestizo to sit, cuffs and curses, kneeling before whites and kissing their hands, the need to treat members of superordinate groups with elaborate courtesy without that courtesy being returned, and more. The wonder is that anyone identified as indígena when it was possible not to, except that there were obvious compensations, one of which was membership in a community and the concomitant support of that group. For Otavalos, another major compensation was that their ethnicity has been a commercial asset.

Such terms as *blanco, mestizo, negro,* and *indio* or *indígena* are socially constructed, not natural or innate, although some Ecuadorians defend these categories as essentialized and God-given. Because these terms are culturally constituted, they can change and they have. *Indio* is a highly charged word. Even though some writers appear to use *indio* in a nonpejorative sense (Buitrón and Buitrón 1945; Pearse 1975), thirty years ago among Otavalos the word *indio* was "considered an insult" (Weinstock 1970: 159). Today the preferred term is *indígena.*

Throughout the Andes, dress historically has served as the main boundary marker between the ethnic groups. By the 1940s in Imbabura, *cholo* or *chola* designated an indígena who had changed his or her dress in an attempt to discard indigenous identity; hence the title of an article by Muriel Crespi, "When *Indios* Become *Cholos*" (1973).

Obviously, since these distinctions were not based on phenotype but on social, cultural, and economic criteria, the boundaries were permeable, changing, and ill-defined, as Buitrón and Buitrón's phrase "cholos o mestizos" indicates (1945). As clothing styles among cholos, mestizos, and whites became similar throughout the 1970s and 1980s the boundaries between the categories became blurred, until sometime in the 1980s the word *cholo* dropped out of use in Imbabura.

In 1966, "[f]or Indians without land or crafts, shedding at least the external symbols of their ethnic category may be a better strategy than accepting the menial, low-paying jobs reserved for Indians" (Walter 1981: 321). Barbara Butler focused on indigenous ethnicity, and she, too, noted that indígenas "change their ethnic status when they cannot be successful as indígena" (1981: 81). This enables indígenas to "escape discriminatory treatment in anonymous interaction with non-indígena" (ibid.: vii). A similar process occurred in Saraguro, Loja, where transculturation from *indígena* to *blanco* is undertaken mainly by individuals from the lowest socioeconomic levels of indígena society, a "drain from the bottom" (Belote and Belote 1984: 24).

Agrarian reform, which freed indígenas from indentured servitude on large non-indígena haciendas, eliminated a major external force for retention of indigenous identity (Butler 1981: 452). In the decade following the abolition of wasipungu, some Otavalos took advantage of the absence of this external force to try out other identities temporarily or permanently for their children, if not for themselves (Meisch 1987). Some realized, especially as artesanías' sales boomed, that there were opportunities for being successful as indígena, and indígenas were also accorded more public respect.

It is difficult to date language change; but around 1990 I noticed the mestizo and blanco categories becoming one hyphenated word in Imbabura, and the compound term *blanco-mestizo* or *mestizo-blanco* appeared in Ecuadorian print media. This change is partly because the distinct clothing styles that distinguished cholos, mestizos, and blancos disappeared, until two basic types remained: indigenous and nonindigenous dress. There is always a lag between social change and terminology, so some people of all ethnic groups still use *blanco* or *mestizo* separately.

Further confounding the old hierarchy, in which indígenas were socially, economically, and often legally subordinate to whites-mestizos and accepted it (at least in their public dealings with them), indígenas are now for the most part not subordinate, and members of all ethnicities know it. Many whites-mestizos depend on indígenas as customers, landlords, and employers and are therefore more polite to them, despite the exceptions mentioned below. The building boom in Otavalo is primarily indígena-financed and owned; whites-mestizos compete with their own group and with other indígenas for housing. Nastiness can mean losing out on a rental. Mario Conejo noted that "[a]cquiring confidence has been a long process. Today we are proud to be Otavalo Indians" (Ortiz de Rozas 1994: D10; my translation).

Rather than "indios becoming cholos," there are whites-mestizos becoming indígenas by wearing traditional dress to improve sales in the market, play in Otavalo music groups, attract foreign women, marry a prosperous spouse, or obtain the benefits of development projects. Young whites-mestizos who identify as Otavaleños usually wear the old-style dress-whites daily just to make sure everyone gets the point. A number of Otavalo bands have members who have chosen indigenous identity. Indígenas who changed their dress to white-mestizo clothing or whose parents raised them as white-mestizo are now reverting to indigenous identity.

Even Peruvians are becoming Otavalos. One member of the Otavalo music group Inti Raymi, which plays in the United States, is a Peruvian who grew his hair long and wears Otavalo dress-whites to play with the group. Sometimes he even wears a hat. In a photo shown to me by anthropologist Linda Belote, I could not distinguish him from the "real" Otavalos (Meisch 1998b).

In addition, some young Otavalos are using the term *indio*, as in Benjamín Terán's article "Opinión: Los indios plásticos" (1991). An Otavaleño from Peguche told me, "We are reclaiming this word." Self-referential terms for indígenas are changing. I have heard Otavalos call themselves *indígenas, runa, naturales,* and *indios.* Most Otavalos, however, prefer that others use the word *indígena,* because *indio* still carries disparaging connotations.

In October 1995, Margaret Goodhart of the Hotel Ali Shungu wrote me that "[m]estizo girls are actually dressing up like indigenous to get indigenous boyfriends and there are more than a few of these couples. This tells me that Indigenous are now DESIRABLE" (personal communication). In June 1996, an Ilumán comadre told me that a "mestiza from Agato" married an indígena, wears Otavaleña dress, and "speaks Quichua better than he does." She and her sisters added that many whites-mestizas want an indígena husband "because they see them driving around in their cars." Ethnic categories have become increasingly fluid, resembling two amoebas dancing the lambada rather than a stack of boxes with the one at the bottom labeled "indígena" and the one at the top labeled "white."

Indígenas are occupying positions in Otavalo formerly reserved for whites. In 1994, the Banco del Pichincha in Otavalo had three young women clerks sitting behind desks with computers. One was white-mestiza and the other two were Otavaleñas in traditional dress. The "supervisor," sitting behind a large, impressive desk, was an Otavaleño

The inauguration of Mario Conejo Maldonado as mayor of Otavalo. On the left is the Coraza, symbolizing authority and holding the staff of office which he will present to the mayor. In the middle is Mario's wife, Tania Benalcázar. Otavalo, August 2000.

wearing dress-whites. The white-mestizo-owned VAZ money exchange has white-mestizo and indígena clerks. Indígenas are holding political offices in Imbabura previously considered beyond their reach. The changes include Auki Tituaña's election in 1996 and re-election as mayor of Cotacachi in 2000, an Otavalo indígena's election as mayor of Atuntaqui in 2000, Mario Conejo's election as mayor of Otavalo, and Luis Enrique Cachiguango's election to the Otavalo city council that same year.

In 1970, there were five ethnic categories: *blanco, mestizo, cholo, moreno,* and *runa* or *indígena*. In 1990, there were three: *blanco-mestizo, indígena,* and Afro-Ecuatoriano or *negro*. The *negro* category conflates ethnic and racial identity, but people with African ancestry may self-identify and be identified by others as members of other ethnicities depending on dress and phenotype.

If the only indicator or criterion were economic, indígenas would be at the top of the hierarchy; but residual colonial prejudices rank whites-mestizos above indígenas overall, partly because they have dominated politics in Imbabura since the conquest. In 1994, Mario Conejo predicted that "[t]en years from now Indians will control political power" (Ortiz de Rozas 1994: D10; my translation), and certainly they are now sharing it.

The fluidity of ethnic identity does not mean that intergroup tensions have eased. In fact, an improvement in the power, status, and wealth of indígenas threatens some whites-mestizos. At the same time, whites-mestizos recognize that indígenas are responsible for the prosperity of the region and that indígenas are essential to tourism because "tourists come to see Indians." Some whites-mestizos are not only envious of indigenous wealth but are baffled and perturbed by foreigners' attraction to indígenas and to indigenous culture and jealous of indígenas who date or marry local whites-mestizos/mestizas. In July 1995, a graffito on the wall of the main plaza in San Pablo read: "*Aviso. Ojo. Mata un indio y reclama una chica*" (Sp. Warning. Be alert. Kill an Indian and claim a girl).

Some white-mestizo townspeople use demeaning terms of address or insults to fight this loss of power. Young sales clerks address indígena women twice their age as "*hija*" or "*hijita*" (Sp. daughter or little daughter). In April 1994, the garbage truck driver called the young Otavaleñas who work at the Hotel Ali Shungu "*indias vagas*" (Sp. idle Indians). Racist graffiti appear around town, such as the "*longos subhumanos*" (Sp. subhuman Indians) painted on a wall near the Poncho Plaza.

In Otavalo white-mestizo young men so consistently started fights with indígenas at the Disco Club Habana that the owner segregated the club, with whites-mestizos and indígenas in attendance on different nights. One of my godsons complained, "Those people are racist against indígenas." In 1992, a traveler wrote in the Pie Shop's notebook: "P.S. → These people are *very* racist! There are certain nights that they won't allow indigenous people to enter and it's usually just a bunch of meat market mestizos → go to Amauta peña around the corner from the 'Pie Shop' if you want to get a taste of Ecua. folkloric music." In August 1993, another traveler commented: "Otavalo . . . Skip the Habana Club. extremely racist people, won't even let indigenous people in certain days of the week."

One former exporter noticed a decrease in interethnic violence (Shannon Waits, personal communication, 1994). On the other hand, there were several attacks on indígenas in Otavalo between 1992 and 1999, especially late at night on weekends, when young whites-mestizos jumped indígenas on the street. Indígenas leaving the peñas folklóricas with gringas were especially targeted. After recounting one incident, my godson's brother said of town whites-mestizos, "They're envious because some indígenas are getting rich." He thought interethnic relations were "worsening." The term *envidia* (Sp. envy) recurs constantly when indígenas discuss ethnic relations. An indígena from Ilumán said: "Indígenas go to Europe to play music and they return rich. They buy new cars and drive through Otavalo playing loud music—tun, tun, tun [on their car stereos]. They can afford to buy or build large houses and the mestizos are envious." Although indígenas do not start fights with whites-mestizos, they now have fewer compunctions about fighting back. Significantly, both indígenas and whites-mestizos have commented on the decline of intra-indígena fistfights. These were common until the abolition of wasipungu and represented aggression and anger turned inward.

Some whites-mestizos have expressed their resentment to me about the ease with which they think indígenas can obtain visas when they themselves cannot. As early as 1974, an Otavalo indígena was portrayed in an Iberia Airlines billboard in Quito, saying he had just come back from Europe and asking when the reader was going to travel. This ad might have backfired, provoking irritation and envy among whites-mestizos rather than admiration (Harrison 1989: 9–13).

In 1993 and 1996, I interviewed Janet Dexter, director of Otavalo's Bahá'í primary school. She said they were having problems keeping a 50-50 mix of indigenous and white-mestizo students in the school. In 1991–1992, the school was 47% indígena; in 1992–1993, 58%; in 1994–1995 and 1995–1996, 65% to 70%, which equals the percentage of indígenas in Imbabura. Even in 1995–1996, half the parents of students at the school were illiterate, a commentary on the unavailability of education for those born in wasipungu times.

Janet gave several reasons for declining white enrollment. The school is expensive in Ecuadorian terms—$150 per year—and indígena parents are often wealthier than whites-mestizos. In addition, the Bahá'í school refuses to favor white-mestizo students. Janet said that in June 1993 an indígena won the sixth-grade medal for the best grades. At graduation, a white-mestiza parent got up and publicly criticized Janet for not awarding the medal to her son. Her son, embarrassed, tugged at his mother's sleeve and said, "But mamá, I wasn't the best student." Janet said that in most Otavalo schools the awards go to white-mestizo children regardless of merit.

When Janet attended a meeting of the Federation of Ecuadorian Non-Catholic Private Schools (FEDERPAL), the Bahá'í School was the only one that had more than two or three indigenous students. She said that most local Otavalo public and private primary schools and colegios are still segregated and some (Sarance, Inmaculada, Santa Juana de Chantal) have only a few indigenous students. During enrollment, when indígena parents walk in, administrators say, "Sorry, the class is full." When whites-mestizos arrive, their child is admitted.

Janet observed "much resentment" among whites because of the shift of wealth in Otavalo. The Bahá'i school conducts a yearly parents' survey and among their findings is that "agriculture really isn't a profession in the Otavalo region. Most people actually earn their living by other means, for example, artesanías." Janet said, "I don't think cultures should be put on a shelf like a pot in a museum. Would you like to live the way your people did two hundred years ago?"

In 1994, José Luis Cotacachi, the father and brother of Charijayac members, was killed in a mugging by whites-mestizos late at night in the Poncho Plaza. I interviewed a feisty white-mestiza who owns a restaurant fronting the Poncho Plaza about safety. She recounted how she confronted mayor Fabián Villareal and said, "Otavalo lives on tourism. Why don't you do something for our neighborhood?!" Pueblo Quichua Otavalo, an indigenous group aimed at improving safety in the town, was formed in the wake of José Cotacachi's murder.

Since money or connections can tip the scales of justice, there was a much greater likelihood of conviction in this case than is usual when whites-mestizos murder indígenas. Although Charijayac had split up, the group returned to Ecuador for four concerts in honor of José Cotacachi in mid-February 1995, with profits going to the Pueblo Quichua Otavalo project. Otavalo can ill afford ethnic strife or to lose the tourist trade, so there was some official support for this project.

When I told a leader of Pueblo Quichua that I was writing another book about Otavalo he said, "I hope you will write about our problems," referring to the Cotacachi murder. Another leader said to me: "A community develops from the foundation of its problems. We have multiple ethnic problems here. I hope with luck these problems don't continue. We want to live in peace. These lands are ours." He also observed that "we are succeeding in economic development and the mestizos don't have this possibility. They aren't accustomed to seeing Quichua people make economic gains and it's very difficult for them to accept this. The rumors of drug trafficking are economic jealousy. Our women work hard. In general, we work more than mestizos."

On the positive side, there is change for the better in ethnic relations, with the younger generation more open and less prejudiced. Members of all ethnic groups have united behind common economic and political goals. In July 1999, after indígenas joined the mainly white-mestizo taxi drivers, transport workers, and other social movements in a successful national uprising to block gasoline price increases, a taxi driver in Otavalo told me the strike was a success, "thanks to the strength of the indígenas." Indígenas working on Mario Conejo's mayoral campaign estimated that he received at least 30% of the white-mestizo vote, and some whites-mestizos actively campaigned for him and helped arrange his inaugural ceremony. (Mario is married to a white-mestiza, but it is hard to know if this helped or hurt him.)

Many non-indígenas are willing to look at a candidate's achievement and potential rather than his or her sex and ethnicity. Auki Tituaña's example in Cotacachi encouraged whites-mestizos, who noted that Cotacachi was far cleaner, prettier, and better run than Otavalo. One of my white-mestiza goddaughters, who voted for Mario Conejo, expressed this sentiment. There are whites-mestizos throughout Ecuador who support indigenous rights and work with indígenas in political parties and campesino-indigenous federations for a more just society.

Yamor: Contested Fiesta

Another arena for the contestation of power and prestige in Otavalo during the past two decades has been the September festival of Yamor. This fiesta is an invented tradition (Hobsbawm 1983), started by a group of whites and mestizos from the barrio of Monserrat in the 1950s, based on the indigenous corn harvest celebration. Yamor includes the selection of a white or mestiza queen, the sale of chicha and special food, sports events, and nightly street dances in Otavalo's barrios complete with pickpockets, heavy drinking, and fights.

Previously, indígenas were recruited to provide local color, including the selection of their own *Sara Ñusta* (Q. corn princess), and they were obliged to march in the inaugural parade through town. Miguel Andrango of Agato told me that in the 1960s political officials forced indígenas in surrounding communities to participate by fining those who did not parade. Note, too, the subordination implied by an indigenous princess but a white queen. In addition, the white queen was always chosen first, and far more money was allotted to her contest and prizes.

Arrangements for the festivities were eventually taken over by the municipality, and Yamor became the official town fiesta. In the early 1980s, indígenas objected publicly to their role in Yamor and to the commercialization of the event. In 1983 and 1984, FICI organized a boycott

New wealth: Otavalos arriving at the Coya Raymi celebration in their pickup truck. Lago San Pablo, September 1994.

of the activities (Crain 1990: 51). In 1985, I was invited to an alternative, indigenous Yamor at Lago San Pablo. Meanwhile, the municipality each year prints large colored posters for Yamor, "the happiest fiesta in the friendliest city in the country," with drawings or photos of indígenas, implying that the fiesta is an indigenous event. This is conscious, since the municipality knows why tourists come to town.

The attitude of indigenous individuals, communities, and political organizations has varied from participation to boycotts to alternative Yamors. Participation in the Sara Ñusta contest declined from several dozen candidates twenty years ago to only four in 1994. In 1995, Lauro Farinango of FICI said that "Otavalo is a city shared by two cultures, and its greatest potential is within the indigenous sector. In that sense, we think that the interests of indígenas have not been well represented within the Fiesta Committee because it has not taken into account our aspirations" (Coronel 1995: 1; my translation).

The situation came to a head in 1996, when indígenas from Peguche and Otavalo decided to abandon the Sara Ñusta event and enter an indígena as a candidate for queen of Yamor. While Sara Ñusta candidates are usually selected by their communities, the candidates for queen are sponsored by a social club, trade union, commercial establishment, or NGO. Several indigenous groups wanted to sponsor candidates but eventually agreed that one candidate would be entered as a test case. They wanted to present a young woman with stellar qualities, and they selected Verónica Barahona Lema of Peguche, a student at the Universidad San Francisco de Quito, who had been an exchange student in the United States for a year and spoke Quichua, Spanish, and English.

On July 29, 1996, the group went to the Otavalo town hall to ascertain the eligibility requirements, which were that she be an unmarried young woman at least eighteen years old and a resident of cantón Otavalo. The next day, Otavalo's mayor Fabián Villareal convoked a secret emergency meeting of the white-mestizo town council, during which they passed a resolution that only mestizas could be candidates for queen. Marcia Sánchez, owner of Papelería Sánchez in Otavalo, was the only dissenting vote. When indígenas went to register Verónica, they were informed of the new regulation, and she was rejected.

An uproar of national proportions ensued, and opinion did not divide strictly along ethnic lines. True, many white-mestizo townspeople said

The Sara Ñusta and her court during Coya Raymi. Seated third from the right is Otavalo mayor Fabián Villareal, with his wife next to him and Carmen Yamberla, president of FICI, on the end. Lago San Pablo, September 1994.

Verónica Barahona Lema and her parents at the rally in support of her candidacy for Queen of Yamor. Hostería Peguche Tío Peguche, August 1996.

that it was customary to have a white-mestiza queen and an indígena Sara Ñusta and that "the Indians are taking over everything—Yamor is all we have left." Others pointed out that the resolution not only discriminated against indígenas but against Asian-, African-, and Euro-American Ecuadorians and that the incident was an embarrassment. Many white-mestizo young men and women interviewed on national television said, "Of course, an indígena could be queen." Articles about Verónica's disqualification made the editorial and front pages of local and national newspapers, and she was received by Ecuadorian president Abdalá Bucaram, who spoke out against discrimination. Programs about the controversy also appeared nationally on Teleamazonas and on the television program *Primer impacto* (Sp. First Impact) on Gamavisión.

Municipal officials stood firm, and Verónica's sponsors decided not to formally boycott Yamor but to present a case before Ecuador's Tribunal of Constitutional Guarantees. The case could not be heard until after Yamor; but although there was no formal boycott, indígenas were not very interested in the fiesta. The Sara Ñusta competition was canceled, and there was virtually no indigenous participation in the parade or other aspects of Yamor, except the four-wheel-drive mud racing which always draws the biggest crowds of the week.

Verónica Barahona's disqualification illustrates the desperate attempt of the old Otavalo oligarchy to reassert its former dominance—an unsuccessful effort, as it turned out, because by the end of Yamor the town council had annulled the resolution barring her. Verónica's father, Marco Barahona, hit the nail on the head at a rally I attended in support of his daughter when he said: "This is more than about my daughter. We are talking about political power in Otavalo. In the year 2000 we will be the government at the local, provincial, and national levels." In 1997, 1998, and 1999, FICI held separate Sara Ñusta contests as part of Coya Raymi, celebrating the equinox on September 21.

At the fiesta planning meeting in 2000, the two directors of the fiesta committee, Patricio Guerra and mayor Mario Conejo, set September 1–10 for Yamor and September 21–23 for Coya Raymi, which would be coordinated as usual by FICI. The "few mestizos and indígena majority present" decided there would be only one queen and that there would be no Sara Ñusta because "this was not an integral part of indigenous culture and was imposed by mestizos. This left open the option that any young woman, mestiza or indígena, could run for queen with complete liberty" (*Diario del Norte*, July 22, 2000: 7; my translation). Because of the economic crisis, Yamor was subdued. No indigenous young women entered the queen contest. Having won the right to participate, they chose not to. (See M. Rogers 1998 for a discussion of the contradictions embodied by Ecuadorian beauty pageants.)

Ethnic prejudices and tensions in town, although diminishing somewhat, involve all ethnic groups. Such prejudice was not a European introduction to the Americas; most Native American groups have names for themselves which gloss as "people" or "humans" and disparaging terms for their Native American neighbors (Sollors 1995 [1986]: 220). The Quichua term *runa* (person) is an example. Rain forest Quichua call themselves *sacha runa* (Q. rain forest people) and their Huaorani neighbors *puka chaki auka* (Q. red-footed savages). In the Otavalo valley, numerous Otavalos openly express racist attitudes about their Afro-Ecuadorian neighbors. A young Otavaleña from Cotama asked me if I were afraid to live alone in Otavalo. I said, "No." She said, "But there are *negros* on that side. *Negros* are worthless. They assault people and go out at night to rob." I said, "My neighbors are good neighbors. I don't think we can say all *negros* are robbers." She was firm: "*Negros* are bad people." I said, "That's what white people say about you, that you're all thieves." She said, "But with *negros* it's true!" I dropped the subject.

Gringas and "Madison Avenue Andean Indians"

Foreigners are now significant players in the ethnic dramas of the valley not only because of tourism but because expatriates and researchers live in the region, and romances, sexual liaisons, and marriages between Otavalos and foreigners result (Otavalos also meet nonindigenous women abroad). Otavalo-foreign interactions challenge the concept that tourism is primarily a manifestation of patriarchy involving the exploitation of local women by visiting men (Enloe 1989). Margaret Swain (1993) also argues for a reevaluation of Cynthia Enloe's thesis through careful examination of gender norms in small-scale indigenous communities that are involved in crafts production and the international tourism economy.

Most tourists and travelers come to Otavalo for the weekend and leave: their interactions with local people are friendly but minimal. Others, usually young foreign women, engage in one- or two-night stands with young indigenous men or stay and have longer affairs. These affairs are sometimes based on mutual misunderstandings (or downright dishonesty) and false romantic notions about the other person. The young women are often looking for romance, an authentic experience or connection to indigenous culture, and sometimes a husband, while the young men are looking for sex, for romance, and occasionally for someone to exploit financially, especially when they are traveling abroad. In other cases, however, both the men and women seem to be interested in merely a brief sexual encounter, and both parties part amicably after a short time. The large number of gringa-Otavaleño liaisons is relatively new, beginning around 1985.

One reason for the recent plethora of gringa-Otavaleño affairs relates to the abolition of wasipungu and the increase in indigenous wealth, which has resulted in better education, nutrition, and medical and dental care. The ideal mate or boyfriend for a Euro-American woman is generally taller, wealthier, and better educated than she is. The indígenas born as wasipungeros are usually short, many under four and a half feet tall, illiterate, missing teeth, and Quichua monolinguals. Some knelt and kissed the hand of a mestizo-white or foreigner; indeed some still do so, which is highly disconcerting.

Indígenas born after 1964, who came of age in the mid-1980s, are often six inches to more than a foot taller than their parents and grandparents. Eggs which were formerly given to the patrón or compadres are eaten at home. Families have the resources to raise or buy meat and dairy products, not to mention fruits, vegetables, and iodized salt, which were formerly unavailable. The 1970s coincided not only with the beginning of an economic boom in Otavalo but with Ecuador's emergence as an OPEC nation. Oil money meant such infrastructural improvements as potable water and health centers which provide basic care, including vaccinations for babies. The result is a generation that is on the whole healthier, taller, better educated, wealthier, more traveled, more sophisticated, more self-confident, and considerably less obsequious than their elders. In short, they meet Euro-American standards of sexual attractiveness.

Moreover, Otavaleños' travel abroad is associated in Euro-American culture with high status, and the fact that a young man has been in ten different European countries and speaks German or French adds to his appeal. By 1985 and 1986, when the post-wasipungu generation came of age, the number of gringa-Otavaleño sexual liaisons had increased considerably. One woman from the United States explained the Otavaleños' attraction: "These guys are so sexy! Long hair, high cheekbones, white teeth, well-built, nicely dressed, friendly . . . Sometimes I just like to sit and look at them. They're Madison Avenue Andean Indians."

As for gringas' visions of Otavalos (and other indigenous people), their romanticism is basically the latest version of the noble savage trope. Dean MacCannell's writing on tourism, particularly his chapter on "Staged Authenticity," which draws on Goffman's discussion of front and back regions (1959), offers a related reason why affairs with Otavaleños are appealing to gringas: "The front is the meeting place of hosts and guests or customers and service persons, and the back is the place where members of the home team retire between performances to relax and prepare" (1976: 92). He notes that "[t]ourists like to visit the back region . . ." (ibid.: 98). What could be more backstage, offer a more intimate experience of a culture, than being invited into someone's bedroom and bed? Unfortunately, this behavior often backfires, for reasons I explain below.

The foreign-local romances in Otavalo are almost all between gringas and Otavaleños or whites-mestizos rather than between foreign males and Otavaleñas or white-mestizas. In 1994, Frank Kiefer of the Hotel Ali Shungu said that during the first two years the hotel was open at least thirty foreign women staying there tried to bring Otavaleños to their rooms for the night, but that no male guests had attempted to bring in Ecuadorian women of any ethnicity. The hotel's policy allows only registered guests, so the young men are turned away.

Young Ecuadorian females in general are more sheltered and protected than young males for all the usual reasons: fear of rape or consensual sex and pregnancy and damage to their reputation. Indigenous women have much more freedom than their white-mestiza counterparts, but rape is a genuine indigenous concern with antecedents in the Spanish conquest. Within recent memory, the wasipungu system made indigenous females vulnerable to mestizo-white sexual abuse, especially those who worked in the hacienda house as cooks, servants, and nursemaids (Q. *wasikamas*).

Although young Otavaleñas are traveling abroad as merchants in increasing numbers, they are often accompanied by or going to meet a relative who functions as a chaperon. Young Ecuadorian males can travel, go to the peñas, or stay out late at night with less cause for parental concern. Some young Otavaleñas do travel abroad with another woman or completely alone, although this is less common. At the Congress of the Americanists in New Orleans in 1991, I met a young indígena, Mercedes Cotacachi, from Peguche who was identifiable by her traditional dress. She was studying for an M.A. in education at the University of New Mexico and was attending the congress on her own.

Foreign women in Otavalo are often alone and away from their families, boyfriends, or husbands. For many their trip to Ecuador is a liminal period, which gives them the feeling that their behavior in Otavalo does not really count because they will never return and no one at home will know about their activities. "Because of the fleeting nature of tourist relations, a tourist does not become part of any long term reciprocity structure. While there are rules for behavior toward strangers in a culture, tourists are not of the culture at all and usually know few local rules" (Crick 1989: 331). Malcolm Crick defines tourists as "outsiders not part of the visited culture's moral fabric," who have "stepped beyond the bounds of ordinary reality, into what has sometimes been referred to as a 'ludic' or 'liminoid' realm" (ibid.).

Otavalo is a friendly community in general. Indígenas invite people to their homes with an alacrity that alarms some foreigners, who worry that indígenas might be taken advantage of. Besides the market and the artesanías shops, the cafes and restaurants around the Poncho Plaza serve as meeting places for young people. Peñas, like their Euro-American counterparts (bars, pubs, and music clubs), are places to hear music, hang out, and meet the opposite sex.

Rhonda Bekker, a Peace Corps volunteer in Otavalo in 1992–1994, said that young whites-mestizos often ask her why gringas prefer indígenas. The young men felt it was because indígenas have more money than they do and cars to boot (an interesting reversal of the usual situation), but

Rhonda tried to explain that part of the reason was the Otavaleños' approach. Foreign women are hissed at by whites-mestizos and sometimes physically harassed in public. Indígena males generally do not behave in a threatening manner, whereas encounters with whites-mestizos are more problematic. There is a greater cultural fit between the indígenas' approach and the way in which foreign women expect to be courted. The other reason is the gringas' romantic attitude toward indígenas, which is difficult for whites-mestizos to understand.

Because indígenas historically have been a disparaged and vilified population, many whites-mestizos find it impossible to believe that foreigners would prefer an indígena to themselves under any circumstances. Some gringas do have affairs with whites-mestizos, but the majority are attracted to indígenas because of their search for an unspoiled lifeway or a general attraction to indigenous culture. The Otavalos' wealth is certainly a plus, and some Otavaleños are substantially richer than their visiting gringa girlfriends (a noble savage with a credit card and a Chevy Trooper is hard to beat), but the main attraction is the gringas' interest in indigenous culture or an exotic encounter.

There is a cultural fit between Euro-American and Otavalo culture in other areas, too. Indigenous women enjoy a high degree of social and economic equality, so many Otavaleños are not surprised or put off by independent women. Otavaleñas are not shrinking violets, and indigenous women have become increasingly active in local and national political federations. Gringas find many Otavaleños far less offensively macho than most other Ecuadorian males and more likely to share tasks, including housework.

(Post)modern Romances

Many of the young women who come to Otavalo out of curiosity or in search of an indígena lover or husband first meet Otavaleños outside Ecuador. If travel in Ecuador is a liminal period for gringas, then travel in Europe is a liminal period for Otavaleños, and (as mentioned in the previous chapter) most of them have lovers abroad. Sometimes, to everyone's discomfort, these lovers decide to visit Otavalo.

Margaret Goodhart said that more than a dozen foreign women have complained to her that in their relationships with Otavaleños they always pay for everything and that they feel used. Why do Euro-American women permit this behavior? Some women are lonely, and footing the bill is worth the company. Others feel guilty for being privileged First World citizens and/or want to help indígenas, while others sooner or later put their foot down. Sometimes the relationship ends; sometimes it continues, but the exploitative behavior stops.

In the summer of 1993, one researcher talked to a German woman in Peguche who had provided room and board in Germany for an Otavaleño who lied about his marital status. When she bought tickets for the two of them to visit Otavalo, it precipitated the revelation that he was married. She went anyway since she already had her ticket, but she said, "Never trust an Otavalan" (Kyle 2000: 178). Needless to say, the wives and fiancées of Otavaleños are equally distressed when they find a love letter in their husband's pants pocket, pick up mail for him at the post office from his foreign lover, receive a phone call intended for him, or are surprised by a gringa at the door.

The behavior of foreign visitors, especially predatory gringas, baffles many Otavalos. One young woman called "Mary from Ohio" by locals met a young Otavaleño, Juan, when he was playing music on the street in Costa Rica. While Juan was still abroad, Mary arrived in Ilumán, told Juan's family she was his fiancée, and moved in with them. She caused many problems because she neither paid room and board nor helped the family with their work, and they finally asked her to leave.

When Mary returned to the United States, she sent love letters to Juan's uncle's store in Quito and sometimes to his relatives in Bogotá. The Bogotá uncle told us that while Juan was visiting them he received a certified letter. His two young cousins were with him when he opened it. "Some little hairs were taped to the top of the letter," the uncle explained. *"Pelitos?* Oh, *pelos* [Sp. hairs]," I said, touching my head. "Yes," the uncle said, "hairs, but from the other end." Mary mailed Juan some of her pubic hair (and we wonder why gringas have a bad reputation). By the summer of 1995, Mary from Ohio had disappeared from the picture, much to the relief of Juan's family.

In Ilumán, Juan's former Otavaleña girlfriend, Bianca, was upset by Juan's involvement with Mary and other gringas whom he met in his travels. They sent him postcards with gushy sentiments which the Ilumán postmistress broadcast around town. Bianca's neighbors said, "Stop crying and forget him. You're still young and single." Meanwhile, a "girl from Germany" was calling and writing to Juan at his uncle's store in Quito, and an Otavaleña in Quito is said to be in love with him. My bet is on the Otavaleña.

Students also become involved with Otavaleños. So many students have spent their time involved sexually with Otavaleños instead of involved intellectually with their research projects that expatriate Americans call this the "Jennifer Syndrome" after one particularly notorious young woman. Generally, it is the younger researchers who do not plan to have long-term connections with Otavalo who engage in affairs, as anyone familiar with the culture realizes that this can damage relations with the indigenous community.

Older Otavalos do not approve of their young men sleeping around any more than they approve of gringas or their own young women behaving this way. The young men, however, have more freedom of movement than young indigenous women for reasons mentioned above. Some of them run their own or their family's stores in Quito or Otavalo, which usually have small living quarters attached, so it is much easier for Otavaleños to keep their affairs secret, especially if they pick up gringas in Otavalo and take them to Quito. Ironically, although foreign women may think that an affair with an Otavaleño will bring them closer to the indigenous community, the effect is frequently the opposite: the young men do not want the gringas to meet their families or visit their towns.

Very few gringas who come to Otavalo looking for an indígena husband find one, usually because their behavior subjects them to censure. Those European, Canadian, and American women who marry Otavaleños usually leave the marriage eventually because there are simply too many cultural, social, and educational differences between the spouses. I know of four such dissolved unions and have heard of others.

On the other hand, several European women have married Otavaleños from Cotama and Peguche and are living there, and I know of one Otavaleña who married a Frenchman, and these marriages seem as happy as any. There are also a number of Otavaleños who have married women in Europe, Japan, and North America and who are living there. The brother of one of my godchildren met a Belgian girl in Belgium and had a baby girl with her in 1994, but he married an Otavaleña the next year.

It may be that the marriages where the Otavaleños live abroad are more successful than those in which the foreign women move to Otavalo for various reasons. Living conditions are better, and some aspects of life are much easier in the United States and Europe than in the Otavalo valley. When my Peguche compadre saw my washer and dryer in my home in California he exclaimed, "It's another person!" His wife still washes clothes in the irrigation ditch. If the couple lives in the wife's country, she usually has the protection and support of her family. Her Otavalo spouse often establishes an artesanías business and does fairly well economically, or the wife works at a well-paying job.

With all the sexual activity at home and abroad, the possibility of AIDS poses a serious threat that seems to be ignored by Otavaleños and gringas alike. Otavaleños, if they know anything about AIDS at all, consider it a homosexual's disease. So far there are no known cases of AIDS among Otavalos, but there is little or no HIV testing being done and virtually no AIDS education, although I have talked about this to some of the young men in my compadres' families. Chances are good that there are already HIV-positive Otavalos. A smarmy Ecuadorian rhyme that appears as a decal on buses expresses local attitudes toward AIDS: *Mejor una chola conocida, que una gringa con SIDA* (Sp. Better a local girl who is known than a gringa with AIDS).

Many gringas ignore the risk. One reason is the myth of timelessness that pervades so much thinking about Otavalo. If the inhabitants of the indigenous "villages" are living in a preindustrial utopia, by this reasoning they are also living in the pre-AIDS past. Another reason is the complete lack of alarm about AIDS and the lack of AIDS education in Otavalo and in Ecuador in general (Meisch 1995).

The gringa-Otavaleño romances show no sign of abating. Although a pattern of unhappy encounters between gringas and Otavaleños emerges for those of us with extended experience in Otavalo, the situation is unique for each new young woman arrival. There will always be gringas coming through town looking for a noble savage, a sexual fling, or both.

"Go to Denmark Right Now"

Not all visitors share the attitudes mentioned above; nor do all tourists and travelers behave in the same way. Many are courteous and sensitive and appreciate what is unique and interesting about the region. Human nature being what it is, not everyone likes Ecuador or Otavalo, as evidenced by entries in the Shanandoa Pie Shop's notebook. The following, dated March 20, 1993, is from two Danish young men who had obviously been on the road too long:

> Go to Denmark right now. Forget all about stupid Ecuador. Wonderful Copenhagen—no rain, no beggers, no beans, no Indians, no muddy forest (only, nice clean roads), no cockroach, no skinny dogs, no hazzling on the streets (in Denmark we don't speak to other people), no S.T.D., no mountains to stop you, only beautiful horny Danish girls who love to suck your dick. [signed] Lasse and Eric [addresses and phone numbers included].

Some tourists comment on the political situation, as in the following entries from April 1993:

The Strike of April '93
Indigenous peoples descend on the highways and prevent any kind
of transportation by • Placing entire trees across Roads • Large rocks •
Burning tires. If that doesn't work . . . Dig ditch across the roads. It's
factual, it's actual . . . so if/when it happens, chill. By 3 tall gringa
chicks from New York, where life happens.

Someone added, "I might do the same if my social security system had
just been privatized." Another entry had more to say about these complaints:

Hi!—or better Hola.
Listen—all the complaints you have already read about are child's
play. We live in New York (City) and suffer these obscenities every-
day. We can tell that few of you spent any time in the U.S. military
otherwise you wouldn't be so thin-skinned. So why don't you join up
for two years so you'll learn to want what you get instead of always
trying to get what you want. You're a bunch of cry babies, so go haunt
a house.

Anyhow—Galapagos was great. Go to the jungle—if you liked ma-
laria, you'll just love yellow fever. Pick up a parasite or two for good
luck. Hrach & Susan 7/30/93—New York City.

What do Otavaleños think of the tourists and travelers who trundle
through the town each year? One complaint on the part of indígenas
occurs when tourists are absent: "There aren't any people. The market
is dead." This view is shared by virtually everyone involved in tourism.
This is not to say that whites-mestizos or indígenas uniformly approve
of foreigners' behavior, but they certainly recognize the economic benefits of their presence. According to Lema, "Tourism has benefited the
economic development of Otavalo, which has allowed the young people
of these times to prepare themselves by studying, and to travel outside
the country carrying their message, their language, their music, their
textiles, and their costume" (1995: 117; my translation).
    Young and old Otavalo merchants of both sexes have definite ideas
about visitors' national characteristics; they are keen observers of others'
behavior. In 1979, an Otavalo compadre looked at the cover of a *Time*
magazine which Lawrence Carpenter and I had lying on our coffee table.
It showed a young Soviet soldier poking his head out of a tank follow-

ing the Soviet invasion of Afghanistan. "What kind of person is that?" he asked us. "Russian," we answered. "Hmmm," our compadre pondered. "Russians. Are they gringos or are they French?" For this Otavaleño the French were obviously a category unto themselves. While I love to repeat this anecdote, there are examples of disgraceful or peculiar behavior by members of every nationality or ethnic group that has visited Otavalo (see Crabb n.d. [1994]).

A godson who sells in Quito and in the Otavalo market told me that "Israelis speak very fast and are a little aggressive. North Americans have more patience and are very polite." My godson's brother said, "You can distinguish Americans and Europeans by their clothes. The Europeans wear bright colors like red, and the Americans wear blue jeans and a shirt." He also said there was a difference between the younger and older tourists. Up to age thirty they were likely to be students and "you have to ask less for sweaters. Older tourists can pay more." He said that when he worked in his family's store in Quito's old city he often helped younger tourists find less expensive lodgings. Sometimes he even took them to the Gran Casino Hotel (known on the tourist circuit as the "Gran Gringo").

Another young Otavalo merchant offered the following assessment of national characteristics in the summer of 1993: "The Israelis are the hardest and insist on the biggest discounts. They usually end up paying only S/500 to S/1,000 [$0.24–$0.50] more than the cost of a sweater or jacket, but a sale is a sale. And most Israelis are students and don't have much money. The Germans don't drive such hard bargains. As for Americans, I say 'S/15,000' and they say 'fine.' Americans don't bargain at all."

Laura Conterón of Ilumán also credits the tourist market with the preservation of such textiles as handmade felt hats: "Thanks to foreign tourists who have appreciated this type of hat—almost a folklore item for them, the fabrication of this hat is increasing, although the technique for making them has been modified . . ." (n.d. [1985]: 24). As Lema pointed out, tourism has provided the wealth that not only fueled economic growth but allowed indígenas to travel abroad in large numbers. In general, because foreigners treat indígenas with more respect than do locals, Otavalos are less critical of visitors than are many Ecuadorians or express this criticism in subtle ways, including the repetition of rumors.

Rumors function as social commentary, allowing people to express indirectly sentiments they might not want to be held accountable for. Under the guise of merely conveying important "news," a person can recount a rumor, especially an unfavorable one, without being held responsible for its content. James C. Scott designates gossip and rumors as the "arts of political disguise," meaning indirect political conduct (1990: 142–148). Rumors are embedded in an unspoken, culturally specific matrix of shared assumptions. The examples below, which circulated in the Otavalo area while I was there, were repeated by both indígenas and whites-mestizos. Rumors, like geological fault lines, are surface indications of deeper stresses and ruptures, illustrating the tensions within and among local ethnic groups and foreigners.

I heard several versions of the "cocaine smuggling in shirts" rumor, which was repeated by Otavalos and local whites-mestizos alike and went like this: Otavalos are getting rich in Europe (they're millionaires!) because they're smuggling cocaine sewn into the collars of Otavalo wedding shirts. After the Otavalo merchants take out the cocaine and sell it, they sell the shirts with slit collars on the street in Belgium (or Spain, etc.). The drug smugglers undercut other indígenas' prices for these shirts, so the other Otavalos report them to the police and the smugglers are arrested. In a slightly different version of this rumor, the slit collars on the shirts in the street made the police suspicious, and they uncovered the smuggling scheme.

My response was, why would anyone who is making millions smuggling cocaine need to earn an extra few hundred dollars by selling the shirts, much less shirts with slit collars in public? With all that money they could pay a seamstress to repair the collars. The content of this rumor, however, is culturally specific. Otavalos are such irrepressible merchants that no one, white-mestizo or indígena, could imagine Otavalos *not* selling the shirts. Destroying textiles rather than selling them is inconceivable. In addition, the rumor has a powerful subtext: envy. Rather than credit Otavalo success to hard work, some whites-mestizos, especially, prefer to believe that the new Otavalo wealth is illegitimate. Intra-Otavalo rivalry, envy, and competition for market share is expressed in this rumor when the Otavalos presumably report other Otavalos to the police because of their anger over the underpricing of textiles.

A related rumor charges the wealthiest indígenas in Otavalo with drug trafficking, for which there is absolutely no evidence. The hundreds of sweaters piled in the store of one major indígena sweater producer and his constant hard work make no dent in this rumor. One white-mestiza grocery store owner said to me in 1994, "Who knows where indios get their money? They say some work with the Mafia, in drugs. I've worked thirty years and look what I have. Nothing. They buy two houses in a year."

A white-mestiza restaurant owner, whose business faces the Poncho Plaza, told me that Otavalos were now *muy desapreciados* (Sp. very unappreciated, devalued) in Europe because of their bad behavior, getting drunk in public and engaging in fistfights. She repeated the rumor of an Otavaleño in Europe who played the guitar extremely well, so a European family invited him home to their large, beautiful house. They threw a party for him, and he got drunk. That night while the adults were sleeping he got up and raped their seven-year-old daughter. In this rumor, white-mestizo Ecuador's worst fears about miscegenation and racial purity bubble to the surface, not to mention their envy that Otavalos are able to travel to Europe when most of them cannot.

This businesswoman was disgusted by the behavior of foreign women who have affairs with Otavaleños. She called "indio" culture *muy desaseado* (Sp. slovenly, unclean) and said that these relationships would never work because the cultures were so different. The gringas were blonde and blue-eyed and looked pure from the outside, but they were "dirty or filthy inside and every country has its filth. Gringas and the *longos más fieros* [Sp. fiercest, wildest Indians] get together like that" (she snapped her fingers).

Neither the grocery store owner nor the restaurant owner had compunctions about using the most insulting local terms for indígenas or about expressing these opinions to me. They have many indígena customers whom they treat well, but evidently this is business courtesy. The pervasive envy of the Otavalos' wealth and their ability to travel surfaces in both rumors discussed above.

The "gringos are stealing children and selling them for their body parts" rumor swept through Otavalo several times during my recent fieldwork. A version of this rumor provoked the brutal beating of an American tourist in Guatemala in 1994. In a common Otavalo version, the teller always knows someone who knows someone whose son or daughter was found (sometimes alive, sometimes dead) by the side of the road with his or her eyes (liver, kidney, lung, etc.) removed and dollar bills pinned to her or his clothes. Gringos have stolen the body parts to sell abroad for organ transplants. A variant rumor has gringos kidnapping the entire child and taking him or her abroad to be cut up for body parts.

These rumors represent a profound ignorance of the biology of organ transplants, including the necessity for tissue matches, careful preservation of the organs, and their immediate transplant before they decay. The

The de la Torre–Arrayán family. Jaime (far left) is typical of the post-wasipungu generation, noticeably taller than his parents (standing, back right). Jaime's brother Lucho was playing music in Europe when this photo was taken. Ilumán, July 2000.

rumors represent a medically impossible situation, but logic has never squelched a rumor. I asked people if they thought gringos carried fresh hearts, lungs, and eyeballs in a bucket through customs and onto the airplane or perhaps overland on a month-long bus ride. ("Anything to declare?" "Yes, this bucket of human eyeballs.")

The subtext, however, is a folk expression of dependency theory: wealthy foreigners are able to extract resources from Latin Americans down to the organs of their children. Nancy Scheper-Hughes argues that the body parts rumors are existentially if not literally true, expressing the extreme income disparities and power imbalances between the rich and poor in many countries and the many people who have politically "disappeared" (1996). In the southern Andes, this rumor is congruent with existing folktales of an evil fat extractor, a maleficent being, the *pishtaku* or *ñaqaq* (Q.), who sucks fat (life essence) from indígenas secretly at night. In the Otavalo region there are similarities with indigenous folk tales of the *chipicha* or *chificha* (Q.), who eats children (Parsons 1945: 131–143), but whites-mestizos also love to repeat this rumor because it's a way to criticize the tourists.

The very existence of such rumors and graffiti shows just how much the status hierarchy has changed in the past thirty-five years. Who in the 1960s would have talked about indígenas getting rich in Europe by illicit means? Indígenas were not rich and were not in Europe. And who worried about local girls finding indígenas better social and economic marriage prospects than mestizos and whites? Just as an earthquake permanently changes the physical landscape of a region, indigenous wealth resulting from artesanías and music has altered the social ecology of the Otavalo valley, resulting in near equality between the groups that was previously unimaginable. Economic advances are bringing social and political power. There is a lag between the economic and political gains, but the current is unmistakable.

CHAPTER 8

Coping with Globalization

Otavalos consider certain traditions, beliefs, and lifeways important con-
stituents of *nuestra cultura* (Sp. our culture) or *nuestra propia cultura
indígena* (Sp. our own indígena culture). In the following discussion I
am not implying that all Otavalos share the characteristics mentioned
or that they agree on their importance; nor do I mean to suggest that
these are natural or essential fixed traits and categories. Change and flux
within historically and socially defined limits are salient features of Otavalo life in the 2000s. Tourists who visited the valley in 1960 would recognize where they were in 2001, but they would also be astonished by
the growth of the market and the town and by the improvement in economic conditions among many indígenas. Less obvious are the changes
in the attitudes, perceptions, and behavior of many Otavalos, especially
those who have traveled abroad.

In this chapter I analyze what these changes mean for Otavalo culture, that is, how Otavalos are coping with globalization. My central argument is that they *are* coping, if not thriving, which does not deny
stresses, dislocations, and disturbing trends (both to Otavalos and outsiders). I emphasize issues which Otavalos themselves consider important, especially land, Quichua, traditional dress, and fiestas.

The extent to which travel and transnational migration have altered
Otavalos' assessment of their life and customs is evident in Otavalos'
publications and conversations. Many see their dispersion as a challenge
to their cultural identity. These challenges are more a result of travel out
than of travel in, and many young indígenas, especially those who have
been abroad, are cognizant of this. Observing how other people live in
their own communities (not just how they behave when they visit Otavalo) can reinforce the view of Otavalo culture as natural or given, which
means constructing others as unnatural and deficient, or it can challenge
the concept of Otavalo life as natural, which calls for a reassessment

Women singing Quichua hymns at a ñawi mallay.
The younger women (top right) illustrate generational differences in dress: they are not wearing
headcloths and their beads are smaller than the
older women's. Ilumán, May 1993.

of local lifeways and more or less conscious decisions to change or to
preserve "our culture." Pierre Bourdieu calls the taken-for-granted and
unquestioned aspects of culture "doxa," as opposed to the realm of discourse and opinion. He notes that an objective crisis "brings the undis-
cussed into discussion, the unformulated into formulation" (1977: 168–
169). Germán Lema's 1983 trip to Israel led him to make comparisons
between Native Americans and other societies:

[F]rom the epoch of the Egyptians and Romans the Israelites were
persecuted and sacrificed for wanting their autonomy. Jewish immi-

grants in Europe continued to suffer persecution. In the same epoch that the Indians of America paid with their blood for the riches and predominance of Spain, the Jews were expelled from the territories of the Crown of Castile. (1995: 167)

Segundo Lema of Los Chaskis said his trips to Europe taught him how much indigenous culture was borrowed: "In Spain they have the custom of the *vacas locas* [Sp. crazy cows] to entertain the children. Here it is considered traditional, but it was brought by the Spanish. In Italy they have the custom of dancing with bells on their backs, from the Arab and Roman culture, but in San Rafael it's traditional." He also observed that "[t]he Spanish almost erased our culture. But they didn't take away our language, the color of our skin and hair. Coraza [a fiesta] is nothing more than a mixture of cultures. Speaking of music, the guitar and charango— they call it the charanga in Spain. And the Italians play panpipes."

To many Otavalos it seems that almost everything is in flux. Some of them romanticize the past or certain aspects of it, although no one romanticizes wasipungu. Carmen Yamberla, president of FICI, said: "The youth are emigrating to Europe and the United States. They have been neutralized with respect to the community. Each one is working for his own gain" (Frank 1995: B-7; my translation). Despite Yamberla's claim, we know that there has been tension for nearly a hundred years between the values of entrepreneurship and community, but I think these tensions have increased. Otavalos now have "modern traditions" (Windmeyer 1998).

Nature and Spirituality

Land, water, religion, and spirituality form a complex of practices and beliefs that have considerable historical depth. Although some researchers (Meier 1981; Pearse 1975) have focused on the economic importance of land ownership, for most Otavalos land is more than real estate; it is a core spiritual component of Otavalo life. The countryside, particularly mountains, high hills, ravines, rivers, waterfalls, and springs, is imbued with spiritual forces. For example, after each field is sown, the dregs and chaff in each person's bag or carrying cloth are thrown to the wind while the person says in Quichua: "*Frutu Mama, Frutu Mama, Frutu Mama. Tukuisha tarpushkakuna, shamupay*" (Mother of Fruits [of the Earth]. All that is sown, please come). These farming practices and a deep attachment to the natural world are part of a profound spirituality derived in part from pan-Andean, pre-Hispanic religious beliefs, including mountain worship. "Sacred geography refers to the geographical features (mountains, rivers, lakes, boulders, caves, springs) believed to possess supernatural powers or to be the embodiment of supernatural beings. In the Andes the high mountains were (and still are) considered among the most powerful of traditional deities" (Reinhard 1991: 13).

The two main mountains flanking the Otavalo valley, Taita Imbabura and Mama Cotacachi, are gendered. High mountains in Ecuador are often considered male-female pairs (for example, Taita Chimborazo and Mama Tungurahua in the central sierra), reflecting the gender complementarity and emphasis on the male-female pair that is an important aspect of indigenous social organization. Indígenas in Imbabura share certain elements of mountain worship with people of the southern and central Andes, one of which is the belief that the mountains control the weather and therefore the fertility of crops and animals. This has an ecological basis since rain, snow, hail, clouds, lightning, and thunder often originate in the mountains (ibid.: 31).

In Otavalo these beliefs co-exist with Christian (originally Roman Catholic) ones. I heard a beautiful expression of this principle at a ñawi mallay in May 1993. The couple, their families, and the *padrinos* (Sp. the wedding godparents) were members of the Grupo Corazón de Jesús in Ilumán. This Catholic lay organization has taken many of its practices from the local Evangelicals, especially prayer meetings, Bible reading, and abstention from alcohol. As one member explained, "We're Catholics but we don't drink."

Instead of ritual drinking, this ñawi mallay was preceded by prayers and speeches in Quichua, led by the padrino and the father of the bride. Some of the women and men among the several hundred guests also spoke. One man said that the ñawi mallay was a sacrament of the runa, not of the *mishus* (Q. whites). He said that the ritual existed long before the Spanish came: it was sacred, a sacrament, and something to be proud of. Another guest said: "Before the Spanish came the mountains and hills were sacred and people considered them to be gods. We were Catholics, but we didn't have the Bible. People perform the ñawi mallay to remember these gods."

Individual or communal rituals of varying antiquity are conducted in times of agricultural crisis. If the rains are slow to arrive, farmers light fires high on the slopes of Imbabura, Cotacachi, Mojanda, and Yanahurcu to send a message to God. In late August and throughout September, the sky is often hazy with smoke from these fires. (Some fires lower down are lit by farmers clearing land for crops.)

A practice that is disappearing involves indígenas' climbing Imbabura to the *páramo* (Sp. the land above the timberline), taking their children and specific offerings: a black guinea pig, a white hen, and bananas or bread. These are offered to the mountain while the children cry in Quichua, "*Achilitaitiku, yacuguta caray!*" *Achilitaitiku*, glossed as beloved or special father, refers to both the mountain and God, and the phrase means, "Beloved father, give us water!" When it finally rains people sometimes say that Taita Imbabura is pissing on the valley.

Another emergency measure during droughts is the rogation mass. In Ilumán, Catholic catechists carry the image of the Virgin of the Presentation through the streets, playing special musical instruments including a condor bone flute (Sp. *pifano*) and small drums. Following the procession there is a mass in the park. One comadre told me, "Maybe it was a miracle, but the first drops of rain fell after the mass." Too much rain can be as destructive as not enough, but droughts seem to be more of a threat.

In March, when the first corn on the cob appears, people go into the fields and pick immature corn, before it has worms. Before they take a bite they say: "*San Francisco taitalla, pukuchipangi, San Francisco taitalla, diusilupagui*" (Father San Francisco, for that which you have caused to ripen, Father San Francisco, thank you), a Christianized version of thanking mother earth (Q. *allpa mama*). In addition, many families time their planting according to the phases of the moon. The full moon is a bad time, and the second day of the new moon is considered most propitious, perhaps because of the association of the growth of the crops with the waxing of the moon. An Ilumán family who had abandoned this practice said, "We are losing our culture."

Water for irrigation and drinking is so essential that in May 1996 violence (Otavalo-style) erupted between the indígenas of Ilumán and San Luis de Agualongo. The issue ostensibly concerned public transportation, which is also essential to life in the valley. The two communities had long been served by the white-mestizo-owned 8 de Septiembre bus line, but indígenas complained that the drivers were surly and overcharged them, so they invited the indígena-owned Imbaburapac Churimi Canchic line to take over the Otavalo–Ilumán–San Luis route. Indígenas from San Luis objected, and the communities engaged in two rock-throwing confrontations in which several people were injured.

"Ostensibly" implies a hidden agenda, and there was one. The leaders of Ilumán and Araque met secretly, and those from Ilumán agreed to request Imbaburapac bus service, many of whose bus-owners were from Araque, in return for access to Araque water. The Ilumán group said 8 de

Septiembre paid indígenas from San Luis de Agualongo to oppose the change. By the time I arrived in the third week of June 1996, Imbabura-pac was serving Ilumán, 8 de Septiembre was serving San Luis, and the Araque-Ilumán water project was underway.

It is no accident that several major incidents involving violence be-tween communities in 1994–1996 were over land and water, scarce re-sources for which competition is intense. Because land historically has been the basis of indigenous life and both land and water have spiri-tual components, the movement away from the land, literally and figu-ratively, gives rise to the sentiment among some that they are losing im-portant cultural values.

Quichua and Spanish

The Quichua language is a second realm in which change is engendering discussion. There are two main Quechua language groups in the Andes, Quechua I and II (Torero 1974). Ecuador belongs to Quechua I, with three dialects (or languages—there is some debate) of Quechua spoken in the country, which are called Quichua, with an *i*. The Otavalo dialect is designated as Quichua B (Cerrón Palomino 1987). Otavalos call the lan-guage *runa shimi* (Q. the people's language), Quichua, or *yanga shimi* (Q. humble or worthless language). The last is probably an internalization of white-mestizo prejudice.

After nearly five centuries of contact, Spanish and Quichua have in-fluenced each other considerably. One linguist identified what he called "*Media Lengua*" (Middle Language), a form of Quichua with Spanish vo-cabulary and Quichua grammar that is transitional when communities are switching from Quichua to Spanish (Muysken 1985: 393). Other lin-guists argue that "Middle Language" is not found in Imbabura, although some Otavalos use the Quichua term *Chaupi Shimi* (Middle Language) to describe the Spanish-influenced Quichua spoken in other communities (Jonathan Loftin, personal communication, 2001). Undeniably, there is considerable Spanish influence on Quichua, particularly in vocabulary.

The influence also goes the other way. Many spinning and weaving terms, food and plant names, and toponyms are Quichua. Even white-mestizo Ecuadorians who insist they do not speak a word of Quichua use *wawa* (Q. baby), *cuy* (Q. guinea pig), *ñaña* (Q. female's sister), *ñaño* (brother, ñaña with a Spanish gender suffix), and say that they woke up *con chuchaki* (Q. hung-over). *Minga*, meaning collective work, has also become part of the general vocabulary. The Ibarra newspaper announced a *"Minga de limpieza en el Mercado 'Amazonas'"* (Q., S. Work party to clean the Amazonas Market), calling on the citizenry to join the effort (*Diario del Norte*, September 19, 1994: 2).

Many Spanish terms, especially nouns for which there are no Quichua equivalents, are used with their Spanish pronunciation (for example, *pantalón*, pants) or Quichuized, adapted to the Quichua three vowel system (*a, i, u*). For example, in Otavalo the old-style handmade felt hat is called a *sumbru*, from *sombrero*. This borrowing is sometimes used as an example that Quichua is impure or dying, rather than as an example of its vitality.

In 1973, there were approximately 115,000 Quichua speakers (Otavalos and Cayambes) in Imbabura province, about 60% of whom were monolinguals (Stark 1985a: 459). With population growth since 1973, the number of Quichua speakers has undoubtedly increased, even with a rise in the number of indigenous Spanish monolinguals. Although far more indígenas are now bilingual in Quichua and Spanish, some Otavalos are monolingual Spanish speakers, and some also speak English, French, German, Italian, or Portuguese in addition to Spanish (and/or Quichua).

Increasing indigenous bilingualism has resulted in increasing white-mestizo monolingualism in Spanish. Today it is rare to meet a white-mestizo in the valley who speaks Quichua. In the colonial and republican era it was common, as it was in the 1950s. Clemencia Paredes, a white-mestiza who was born in the Otavalo barrio of Copacabana, recalled that her father, the teniente político and commissioner of the market in the early 1950s, spoke fluent Quichua. "He had to, in order to communicate with the indígenas." This was true up to the early 1970s. Gladys Villavicencio wrote that most Otavalo mestizos spoke Quichua:

> It is the most effective instrument for keeping them in their position of inferiority and submission. . . . With the indígenas' own language they set prices, convince them of the value or lack of value of a product or article, take advantage of them and exploit them. This doesn't happen with those indígenas who know Spanish and knowing how to read and write are aware in general of economic mechanisms, basic prices, and the quality and variety of products. (1973: 225; my translation)

Villavicencio observed: "They prefer to do business with indigenous women, the majority monolinguals, who are not 'rebellious or knowledgeable like those who speak Spanish'" (ibid.: 226). The truth of this was brought home to me in 1980, when I sent a $50 money order to a Quichua monolingual comadre. The bank clerk at the Banco Nacional de Fomento took advantage of her illiteracy and monolingualism to tell her the check was worth $5, not $50. His accounts balanced because he pocketed $45.

Quichua has been stigmatized by white-mestizo society (Harrison 1989: 14). Indigenous attitudes toward Quichua are ambivalent and to some extent represent class and geographical differences, with poorer families and those in remote communities emphasizing the importance of learning Spanish and wealthier or more politically active indígenas consciously using Quichua in certain situations as expressions of ethnic pride (Carpenter 1983).

Around 1986, younger indígena couples began giving their children Quichua names. Previously, the local civil registrar insisted that the law only permitted certain Spanish names, particularly saints' names, and this was enforced for everyone. The parents of my white-mestiza god-daughter, Ruth Elizabeth, born in November 1985, wanted to give her another name, but the registrar refused. In 1986, the registries in Otavalo and Peguche began allowing Quichua names, but only one; either the first or middle name had to be Spanish. Little Tupacs, Sayris, Ñustas, and Sisas began appearing on the rolls.

By 1992, families were able to name their children whatever they wanted: Sayri Pachac, Curi David, Jefferson Atahualpa, Nina Ñawi, Inti João, and Curi Mallki come to mind. In the spring of 1998, a hot seller in Otavalo bookstores was a dictionary of Quichua names (Kowii 1998). Such names are powerful and explicit rejections of mestizaje and a statement of faith in indigenous identity, implying that a child will not be better off if he or she is white-mestizo. With a name like Sayri Pachac no one will think he is.

Some older indígenas also changed their names. Nina Pacari was born María Estela Vega. When she received her law degree from Quito's Central University in the 1980s, she legally changed her name to Nina Pacari, which means Awakening Fire. Dr. Pacari said that taking a Quichua name "was one of the first things because when we went to work in the communities we said, 'We must rescue Kichua, we are losing it. . . . the young people . . .'" (Bulnes 1990: 57; my translation).

The members of Charijayac took Quichua nicknames, which they list on their recordings along with their Spanish given names. In Peguche, the writers for and publishers of a local bilingual Spanish-Quichua magazine, *Shimishitachi* (Q. Spreading the Word), adopted Quichua first names. In issue number 8 (September 1991), the first names of the indígenas on the masthead were in Spanish. By issue number 11 (April 1992), the first names were Quichua: Rumiñavi, Samac, Ninacuru, Anti, and Sayana.

The use of Quichua in the media and at public events has political overtones. Every other Thursday between 1996 and 2000, *Hoy* published a bilingual Quichua-Spanish column "Imbabura Comenta" (Sp. Imbabura Comments) by Otavaleño Ariruma Kowii. Many publications by CONAIE, local organizations, and the publishing house Abya-Yala are in Quichua and Spanish (CONAIE 1988; Korovkin et al. 1994; Ulcuango et al. 1993). In 1992, an Otavaleño, Fausto Jimbo, ran for Congress. His political poster read: "*Partido Socialista Ecuatoriano. Fausto Jimbo Diputado. Runacunamanta Ñaupaman Catishunchic*" (Sp. Ecuadorian Socialist party. Fausto Jimbo Representative). The last phrase is Quichua: Indígenas Will Continue Advancing Together. This is a direct appeal to the indigenous vote and an assumption that whites-mestizos probably would not support him. (He was not elected.) A recent film by Peguche filmmaker Alberto Muenala, *Mashicuna* (Q. Companions), about two Otavaleño boys growing up together, is in Quichua without Spanish subtitles, although a version with English subtitles is available.

The oft-repeated opinion that Quichua is disappearing is represented by Galo René Pérez, director of the Royal Academy of the Ecuadorian Language, who insists that "Quichua is disappearing little by little because of the mestizaje suffered from Spanish culture" (*El Comercio*, August 24, 1994: D-3; my translation). This belief is disputed not only anecdotally in that the language is heard daily everywhere in the valley—in the markets, homes, fields, streets, buses, stores, and schoolyards and sung by folk-music groups and by worshipers in the churches—but by José Cajas, coordinator of Quichua at the Catholic University in Quito (ibid.), and by a carefully executed 1992 national survey of selected communities (Büttner 1993). The survey was conducted by Quichua-Spanish bilingual researchers, which undoubtedly increased its reliability, as indígenas could respond in Quichua and probably felt less stigmatized admitting that they spoke it. Thomas Büttner had no precise figure for the number of Ecuadorian Quichua speakers, but the *El Comercio* article suggested 1,100,000 (August 24, 1994: D-3).

In the predominantly indigenous Otavalo-area communities surveyed, Quichua was spoken as the maternal (Büttner's term) or first language by 73% to 100% of the population (Büttner 1993: 97). Among people who spoke Spanish as their maternal language there were high rates of bilingualism; they also spoke Quichua. The majority of people surveyed in these communities were born in Imbabura province, 95.5% to 100%, and even in the same *parroquia* (Sp. parish), 77.3% to 100% (ibid.: 103). The outmigration, of course, does not show up. When people were asked which language they preferred to speak at home, there was a strong preference for Quichua (ibid.: 104–106).

My Otavalo compadres and godchildren give these statistics a human face. I have twelve indigenous godchildren in the Otavalo region, ranging in age from fifteen months to twenty-five years. Quichua is the preferred language in their homes. Ten of the godchildren are bilingual and the youngest two will be. The children hear Spanish all around them in the media and in public, so they learn it too.

In the summer of 1996, I encountered the first resistance to Quichua among my godchildren when a comadre told me that her two oldest boys (one a godson), ages sixteen and seventeen, asked her to speak less Quichua and more Spanish because Quichua was *fiero* (Sp. fierce, wild, ugly). The young men were selling artesanías in Quito and may have been taunted because of their relative newness to city life. In any event, their mother told them that Quichua was "the preferred language of the people" and the family would continue to speak it at home.

Büttner's survey also found gender and generational differences in language use. More women than men found Quichua the "easier language," and fewer children than parents spoke it (1993: 106–107). In my experience the Quichua monolinguals tend to be the older people, those of all ages who live in more isolated communities, and children before they enter school. The Spanish monolinguals tend to be younger Otavalos, especially residents of communities outside the valley, although there are also some young people from valley communities, including Otavalo, whose Quichua is minimal or nonexistent. Kyle's 1993 survey of Peguche confirms Büttner's data: 67% of the Peguche inhabitants regularly speak Quichua, 21% speak Spanish and Quichua, and 11% speak only Spanish (Kyle n.d. [1993]). Many of the Spanish monolinguals are Peguche whites-mestizos, but some are indígenas.

Büttner's survey found no relationship between the level of education and bilingualism, nor between the maternal language and bilingualism (1993: 101). This makes sense from my experience. Many indígenas I know over the age of thirty have had little or no formal education, but they have had considerable exposure to Spanish. For example, the 55-year-old father of one godson is minimally literate but bilingual, having learned Spanish as a boy while traveling with his father to sell textiles in Ambato and Quero, Tungurahua, rather than in school.

Büttner's teams asked about the language used in church but did not distinguish among the denominations. All respondents mentioned that Quichua was used, although Spanish predominated in some parroquias, Quichua in others (Büttner 1993: 111–112).

The Catholic church's policy in the early colonial period was to preach to indígenas in Quichua, "the general language" (Phelan 1967); but in later centuries Spanish rather than Quichua became the language of the church, and the church became associated with oppression. (This changed in the 1970s with the advent of liberation theology supported by such clerics as Bishop Leonidas Proaño of Riobamba.) In Colta, Chimborazo, Protestant missionaries initiated Bible classes in Quichua in 1957, launched a Quichua language radio station in 1961, and published a Quichua translation of the Bible in 1973, all of which contributed to a large number of conversions (Muratorio 1981: 515). In Otavalo, Radio Bahá'i has been broadcasting in Quichua since 1977, but the Catholic church has been playing catch-up. By the mid-1980s, Quichua had appeared in the Catholic liturgy; and by 1992, it was common, including one Quichua hymn sung to the tune of the "Battle Hymn of the Republic." I have no doubt that indígenas feel more connected to their churches when Quichua is used.

Evangelical Christians continue to use Quichua as a missionizing tool. In September 1994, three members of one such church stood in the Otavalo market selling cassettes such as *Grande es el Señor* (Sp. Great Is Our Lord) by Cantores del Rey (Sp. Singers of the King). They wore patchwork vests from the Otavalo market and displayed Andean folk-music instruments. One side of the cassette has Spanish hymns—for example, "A mi Jesucristo" (To My Jesus Christ)—the other Quichua, including "Canca Ñuca Diosmi" (You Are Our God) and "Jesús Ñucata Cuyashca" (Jesus Loves Me).

Because so many Ecuadorian children enter school as monolingual speakers of indigenous languages, CONAIE fought for bilingual, bicultural education. In 1988, the government established a department for intercultural and bilingual education, DINEIB (Sp. National Board for Intercultural and Bilingual Education), which functions in 15 provinces with 3,600 teachers and 80,000 indigenous students (Paz y Miño 1994). In the sierra this means instruction in Quichua with the purpose of completing schooling in Spanish.

In his inaugural speech in August 1992, President Durán Ballén promised to institute instruction in Quichua, mandatory at all public schools through the university. Although this was a nice gesture, it will never work for a number of reasons, including an acute shortage of bilingual teachers. There are not enough whites-mestizos interested in learning Quichua and not enough bilingual indigenous teachers. Teachers are paid so abysmally that some Otavalos who worked as bilingual teachers quit after a few years because they can make more money in artesanías or music.

The bilingual program has resulted in publications in indigenous languages, which are far more sensitive to indigenous culture than are the slanders propagated in the regular textbooks (see Stutzman 1981). The 1980s also saw the rise of an ambitious publishing program of books not only about indigenous affairs but by indígenas.

The bicultural aspect of the program has not been realized, and the problems the children face with insensitive teachers are real. A FICI document calls Ecuadorian education "alienating," teaching "values and patterns that are not in accord with our culture," including "the cults of individualism and private property which go against our communitarian tradition." FICI criticized "mestizo teachers who on principle consider us incapable of learning. It is not rare to hear said to a child who has to overcome language and cultural barriers and who doesn't understand the lesson, '[Y]ou are an indio bruto' [Sp. ignorant, brutish Indian]" (CONAIE 1989: 131; my translation).

Even so, Quichua-Spanish bilingual education is not universally accepted by indígenas themselves. In 1994, Carlos Conterón, who teaches in the Quinchuquí primary school, said that indígena parents supported bilingual education, but they wanted it to be Spanish-English or -French or -German. He hopes for a "revalorization" of Quichua and of traditional male dress. Some parents who oppose Quichua-Spanish bilingual education think it is unnecessary—their children learn Quichua at home. In 1996, an Otavaleña bilingual education teacher, Estela Bautista, said some parents objected to Quichua being spoken in her preschool class because they wanted their children to learn Spanish.

The Raúl Pavón Bahá'i Spanish-English bilingual school in Otavalo is popular with indigenous parents even though it is the most expensive primary school in town because the children learn English. Indígena parents want their children to learn Spanish because it is the national language and third languages because they are important in business. In Büttner's survey, high proportions of parents wanted their children to attend a monolingual Spanish-speaking school regardless of which language they spoke at home (1993: 117).

Because three main Quichua dialects are spoken in Ecuador, linguists at the Catholic University in Quito embarked on a program in the late 1980s called "Quichua unificado" (Sp. unified Quichua) to convince everyone to speak and write the same way. Not only is this a white-mestizo, top-down imposition, but the differences among the Quichuas are such that unified Quichua is unlike that spoken by anyone, a Quichua Esperanto. There is no consensus on Quichua unificado. One young Otavaleño favored it and said it would solve the problem of bilingual textbooks because one book written in unified Quichua could serve the entire country.

As with other aspects of indigenous life, Quichua is used by whites-mestizos, foreigners, and indígenas in Otavalo in a folkloric sense, especially in the names of businesses: the Residencial Samay Huasy (Rest House) and Hotel Ali Shungu (Good Heart); Artesanías Millma Huasi (Wool House); restaurants named Inti Ñan (Sun Path), Camba Huasy (Your House), and Ali Micuy (Good Food); the Imbaburapac Churimi Canchic (You Are Sons of Imbabura) bus line; the Peña Amauta (Wise One Folk Music Club); and the Sara Ñusta (Corn Princess) of the fiesta of Yamor, to give a few examples.

Whites-mestizos and indígenas are also using Quichua to appeal to indígenas as customers or voters. The VAZ money exchange in Otavalo distributes publicity in four languages, Spanish, Quichua, English, and German, and also has signs on its building in these languages. The new Transportes Otavalo bus terminal has signs that say: "*Bienvenidos, Ali Shamushka Cay*, Welcome." An ad for cellular telephones in CONAIE's newspaper by Movilcel of Quito says in the largest type in the ad: "*May sumacta rimarina pacha ña campac maquipimi.*" The message is also printed in Spanish and glosses as: "The true power of communication now in your hands" (*Pueblos Indios*, May–June 1996: 12). Obviously, Movilcel assumes that indígenas are potential customers, and it is probably appealing to the most affluent group, the Otavalos. Some signs in the Otavalo town hall are in Quichua, another recent innovation. In 1998, the Otavalo municipality printed its first poster with slogans in both Spanish and Quichua, designed by Otavaleño Narcizo Conejo, as part of an antilitter campaign.

In June 1999, UNAIMCO broadcast appeals for donations to its Inti Raymi–San Juan programs over the Poncho Plaza's loudspeaker in Quichua, acknowledging the indigenous nature of the fiesta and assuming that whites-mestizos probably would not contribute. When Mario Conejo was inaugurated as mayor of Otavalo, a young woman announcer spoke first in Spanish then in Quichua throughout the event inside and outside city hall. Mario himself gave his inaugural address and subsequent remarks in both languages.

The situation with Quichua is paradoxical. On the one hand, some young indígenas are not learning runa shimi. On the other hand, there is a renewed valorization of and pride in the language. Indígenas are using Quichua as a statement of cultural or ethnic pride when they give their folk-music groups Quichua names and record in Quichua, even though the majority of those who buy their music do not understand it. For Otavalos, Quichua symbolizes indigenous Andean music to the extent that most of the songs on the two-volume CD of the Italian indígena-wannabes Trencito de los Andes recorded in Rome, whether traditional or newly composed, were in Quichua.

More recently, globalization in the form of international travel and the Internet have added English vocabulary to the linguistic mix. In the summer of 1999, I was surprised to hear my Peguche compadres and godchildren saying "wow!" This expression was obviously brought back to Peguche by transmigrants who had been living in the United States and picked up by the Peguche avant-garde. The web site http://www.otavalosonline.com uses "Kichwa" instead of "Quichua," the current politically correct spelling, with English "Ki" and "wa" replacing the Spanish "Qui" and "hua." It publishes its bulletins in Spanish, has a glossary of Kichwa terms, and includes such commands as *Washaman* (Q. go back), *Volver a la página principal* (Sp. return to the main page), and *Haz Click Aquí* (Sp., E. click here).

Dress as Cultural Capital

Traditional dress (or costume) is the third main topic of discussion among Otavalos concerned with social change and identity. Two decades ago, "[t]o be Indian in Ecuador . . . one must be known to be a native speaker of an indigenous New World language, or dress in a costume stereotyped as 'Indian'" (Whitten 1986 [1974]: 175). Today, although some people in the sierra do not wear traditional dress but still identify as indígena, dress is the main ethnic diacritica and is often a metonym for indígenas. For example, a 1996 newspaper headline about the national elections read: "Colta: the ponchos and anakus paint the ballot box in colors" (*El Comercio*, May 20, 1996; reproduced in *Kipu 26:* 144; my translation).

Dress continues to convey multiple messages with contextually dependent meanings. For example, within an Otavalo community subtle details of dress can identify an indígena as wealthy and of high status, while the identical dress on the national level marks the person as a member of a stigmatized ethnic group ("indio"). Abroad, where indí-genas are often exoticized and romanticized, an indígena wearing this same costume frequently receives preferential treatment. Otavaleños abroad utilize costume strategically, wearing dress whites and ponchos for musical performances but dressing in Euro-American clothes while selling illegally on the street because, as one of them told me, "It's easier to run and hide from the police if we don't stand out."

In addition, Ecuadorian indigenous groups differ among themselves in their styles of self-presentation under identical circumstances such as visits to government offices (Casagrande 1981). Otavalos have been among those groups, including Saraguros, Salasacas, and some Cañaris, whose members wear traditional dress publicly outside their communities. Otavalo, Saraguro, and Cañari males wear long hair (usually in a braid), which marks them as indigenous in any event. Groups most dominated by the hacienda system have tended to identify traditional dress with humiliation and subjugation, while those groups with a history as free communities or less dominance by haciendas have regarded traditional dress more positively (ibid.). For Otavalos, costume histori-cally identified them as weavers and merchants and thereby helped sales (Stark 1985a: 459).

Every item of female and male dress can now be bought in the Ota-valo market. Families need not weave or sew at all to wear traditional dress but can buy everything they need. By the 1970s, a pan-Otavalo cos-tume style was developing, with the gradual loss of community distinc-tions. This trend has accelerated to the extent that except for substyles in Natabuela and Cotacachi only one community marker remains: red or coral-colored bead necklaces worn by some women from communities around Lago San Pablo.

Many Otavalos still insist on the significance, value, and preservation of their cultural traditions including their dress. Breenan Conterón of Ilumán wrote in 1989:

I wear this dress every day and when I leave my community and visit other cities in my country, Ecuador, I always wear this dress because in this way I valorize and respect my ancestors, who fought to main-tain their culture, tradition, and customs. And I am proud because through inheritance and in my blood I carry this culture. (Earthwatch Team Notes, July–August 1989; my translation)

Note the connection of costume to tradition and the ancestors, the opposite of Euro-American concepts of fashion, which imply constant change. Dress as a bridge to the past now competes with dress as a statement of intense involvement in the present, especially among young men with a desire to be hip. Not surprisingly, Lema wrote about traditional dress as embodying tradition and culture: "The indígenas of Otavalo wear with pride and elegance handmade attire with colors, embroidery, and natural designs that symbolize the art, thought, and work of the Otavalos. Through these beautiful costumes cultural riches are exalted, which we still conserve in our communities" (1995: 111; my translation). More than just wearing traditional dress is important; it should be neat, clean (if not spotless on public occasions), and of the best materials the wearer can afford. Presentation is almost as important as the garments themselves.

At any given time, a particular form of dress has distinguished the Otavalos as an ethnic or cultural group; but this costume has undergone continual change (Meisch 1996 [1991]: 165). One pattern of change I have observed throughout Ecuador is that of survivals, the continuity of an older trait into a new era (Tylor 1920: vol. 1, 71). There are a number of survivals in Otavalo costume, including a survival I call an archaic residue, which is daily dress from an earlier era that is used only for special occasions. Dress whites and the poncho are becoming archaic in Otavalo, worn by some young men only on such special occasions as their confirmation or wedding.

The survivals and archaic residues in Otavalo dress suggest that there is not an inevitable progression leading to the loss of traditional dress. Instead there has been gradual change until the 1990s, with the new eventually becoming the traditional and, in some instances, the traditional becoming archaic and then disappearing (Meisch 1996 [1991]). In the 1990s, there was rapid change in the men's dress as well as reactions to this. As old styles disappear, something new always becomes defined as *churajuna* (Q. indigenous clothing), even if it is only long hair for males.

According to Carlos Conterón, the Otavalos are "encountering the disappearance of their traditional customs," meaning dress and language change among young people. These "different fashions of the young" include "no headcloths; hair worn in braids with barrettes or loose; no shoulder fachalina, but a foreign sweater; shoes and even hose; a hand-carried leather purse instead of a rebozo; anacos wrapped with a black band; and although they are speaking better Spanish they are forgetting their own language, Quichua" (n.d. [1994]: 26; my translation). Nonetheless, female costume in Otavalo is highly conservative, with many pre-Hispanic elements (belt, headcloth, body wrap). The blouse-and-slip combination is the main modern element; with its use the full-body anaku became a half anaku. The changes in female dress are generational, with young women more experimental than their older relatives. Nonetheless, young and old still wear a costume that is recognizably Otavaleña (see Meisch 1998a).

For indígenas, long, thick hair "is a sign of health and strength, and signifies feminine fertility and masculine virility" (Rivero 1988: 178; my translation). Otavaleños traditionally have worn their hair long; cutting indígenas' hair was one of the punishments for the 1777 revolt. Long hair is so important to the males of these ethnic groups that young indígenas who serve in the Ecuadorian army are allowed to keep their braid. On rare occasions Otavaleños cut their hair short, sometimes as a requirement for obtaining work on sugar plantations on the coast, but most indígenas regrow their braids when they return to Otavalo.

Because it is such an important boundary marker between indigenous and white-mestizo males, there is a vocabulary of insults about hair length. Indígenas call whites-mestizos or indigenous males who have cut their hair *mocho* (Sp. cropped, shorn, mutilated). The term *mocha* is used less frequently to refer to females who have cut their hair. Whites-mestizos call indígena males *wangudos* from the Quichua *wangu*, meaning a long, straight stick. Although I have never heard the term *wanguda* applied to indígena females, Barbara Rivero reported its use (ibid.: 179). When the indígena father of one of my godsons moved to Quito to work as a watchman, he cut off the braids of his young sons because he felt they would have a better life in Quito as whites-mestizos, but he carefully wrapped their braids in cloth and kept them. More than ten years later, his oldest son, a teenager living with relatives in Ilumán and dating an Otavaleña (whom he married), regrew his hair. In 1987, Charijayac started the fad for long hair pulled back in a ponytail. Some young men and women are now cutting several inches to a foot off their hair as "the latest fashion" but still wear it in a ponytail or braid or wrapped with a tape in the case of females.

The pullover white cotton shirt with narrow tucks across the chest (Sp. *tiu camisa*), which was worn in the 1940s, is no longer worn daily by younger men, although some older men still wear it. In the 1970s, the tiu camisa evolved into a tourist item that is sold as the "Otavalo wedding shirt" and through the J. Peterman catalog as the "Otavalo Mountain Shirt." By 1992, members of traditional music groups had revived the style for performances. Some younger Otavaleños, as an expression of

Poster for a Charijayac reunion concert using the cover photo from their 1987 recording *Cielo Rosa*, which started the fad for unbraided hair among young men. Otavalo, June 2000.

cultural pride, wear the tiu camisa at such public events as a photo exhibition opening and the projection of the video *Mashicuna* during Yamor in 1994.

Male costume in Otavalo is changing far faster than female costume. Today it is possible to see three main variations being worn daily by different generations. The wasipungu generation, the *taitas* (Q. fathers, an honorific for elderly men in their fifties and older), tend to wear the oldest style, dress whites: white shirt, alpargatas, and baggy, midcalf-length white pants that tie at the waist. The *tius* (from the Spanish *tío*, meaning uncle), the married men through their forties, usually wear white alpargatas and white pants, but in the form of tailored trousers with a zipper fly and a leather belt. Some tius wear ponchos daily, but more wear jackets or sweaters and shirts of varying colors.

The *wambras* (Q.) or *solteros* (Sp.), the unmarried boys and young men, particularly those from Quito, Otavalo, and the communities closest to Otavalo, are in the vanguard of change. Some of them are wearing clothing bought in Europe and the United States during their travels: baggy jeans, high-top athletic shoes (sometimes worn with the laces untied), bandannas around their forehead, baseball caps worn backward, dark glasses, T-shirts or sweatshirts, down vests, and denim, Gore-Tex™, or leather jackets. My Peguche godson, who lived with me in 1999, gave me a detailed analysis of the clothing styles worn by the ethnic groups in his American high school and favored Tommy Hilfiger and FUBU brands. Some young men are sporting one earring. These changes are relatively recent. In the summer of 1989 or 1990, I was surprised to see a young Peguche compadre wearing tan cargo pants. His nephew, my godson mentioned above, who is now the picture of hip, was still wearing dress whites in 1990.

One Otavaleño from Peguche cited *envidia* (Sp. envy), peer pressure, as a reason for costume change, mentioning envy of whites-mestizos as well as of indígenas. Although he began wearing the latest Euro-American fashions several years ago, he said it was "foolishness, stupidity" to abandon traditional dress. In the 1970s, adult males working in the fields and young boys around the house sometimes wore dark-colored pants, but this dress was considered improper in public or at formal events in the community. By 1988, I noticed a few young Otavaleños wearing jogging suits or sweatpants in Otavalo; this was so unusual that I made notes of it.

Another young Peguche indígena said to me that the changes in dress "began when indígenas traveled abroad." When they come back to Otavalo the other indígenas in the market see them wearing "a sweater, blue jeans, and shoes and they want these clothes, too." He added, "We are losing our culture."

One godson (whose mother concurred) said that white pants got dirty too fast, especially during the rainy season. There is some truth to this in that the old-style pants were much shorter, coming to mid-calf or just below the knee. But my godson also admitted that he wanted to wear "the fashion of the youth."

The changes in male costume are not examples of classic acculturation to the clothing styles of the local dominant group. In fact, young Otavaleños completely leapfrog local dress styles. Witness the male fad of wearing one (or more) earring in the left earlobe, which they picked up in Amsterdam; or the young Otavaleño wearing a blue chambray shirt, blue denim jeans, socks, and Birkenstock sandals; or the young indígena back from New Mexico and Arizona wearing a bolo tie. Most Otavalo whites-mestizos are baffled by these fashions, particularly by the earrings, which to them imply homosexuality.

In wearing clothes bought abroad, young Otavaleños are no different from their Euro-American counterparts who bring home and wear ponchos, Otavalo wedding shirts, and handknit sweaters as trophies from their trips to Ecuador. Other young Otavaleños are buying the latest Euro-American garments in Ecuador in the form of imports or copies. One of my teenage godsons got his left earlobe pierced and wore a silver stud after his cousin returned from Holland sporting this style. There is a generation gap with these trends reminiscent of the 1960s in the United States: sometimes it is fun to confound the elders. My godson's mother looked pained and told me earrings were *wambrakunapak costumbre* (Q., Sp. young men's custom). My godson's earring generated digs from his older relatives, "So now you're a girl?" His father also disliked his unbraided hair. My guess is that some fashions, such as earrings, are fads and will disappear within several years.

Although the long braid, dress whites, blue poncho, and felt hat with a medium-wide brim are still the identifying features of Otavalo ethnicity, the recent change is qualitatively different in that there is no uniform that marks the younger generation. So many young men are wearing other kinds of dress that long hair worn in a braid or ponytail is now the sine qua non of Otavaleño identity.

Although community styles are disappearing in general, there are still variations in costume within the valley, especially in the Cotacachi area and in Natabuela. Although the people of Natabuela (near Ibarra) represent a tiny portion of the population, their dress is so striking that CETUR, the government's national tourist organization, advertises Imbabura province with a large color poster of a couple from Natabuela wearing the old-style hand-felted hats.

Children are still dressed like tiny adults, although this tradition, too, is changing, a trend which began in the early 1970s. Many small boys and girls wear sweatsuits or other kinds of Euro-American clothes around the house but wear traditional dress for school, trips to Otavalo, and important occasions. I am seeing more indigenous children in Otavalo in nontraditional dress, especially little boys whose mothers despair of keeping their white pants clean. Clothes are still laboriously washed by hand in concrete washtubs or on rocks in the lakes or streams. I know of no indígenas who own mechanical washers and dryers—yet.

Children and young people are wearing traditional dress (however

that is defined at the time) as they get older and have a choice, an indi-
cation of the Otavalos' cultural vitality. Even the hip young men keep
their long hair and sometimes wear a fedora. Traditional dress is accept-
able as a school uniform for indígena children (since it is a uniform of
sorts), while white children must buy a special uniform. Many schools
require indigenous students to wear a school sweater or vest or for girls
a pinafore over their regular clothes, so that all the pupils at a school are
identifiable. But school insignia are worn over, not in place of, Otavalo
costume. Attendance at school including high school and the university
is thus compatible with indigenous identity. The schools are functioning as conservative forces in this regard, because the use of white shirts,
pants, and alpargatas as a school uniform or for special school events is
almost the only time some boys now wear dress whites.

There is considerable intra-Otavalo controversy about costume
change. In 1991, a Peguche indígena, Benjamín Terán, wrote an article
called "Los indios plásticos" (Sp. The Plastic Indians). He insisted:

It is not admirable to see a group of young indígenas dressed in NIKE
shoes, blue jeans, a Walkman in their ears and an empty Kangaroo
pack [i.e., fanny pack] covering the front part of their belt, asking for
the location of dances and discotheques in search of "Rap" music, and
dragging out words like a hippie, saying "Okey!" These youth want to
eat hamburgers, hot dogs with French fries and Coca-Cola instead of
our traditional midday meal. (1991: 20; my translation)

The article is accompanied by a drawing by Rodrigo Pichamba of
Peguche, showing an indígena wearing dress whites, a poncho, a hat, and
braided hair saying in Quichua, "How are you, son?" to a young man
wearing a bandanna on his head, a ponytail, dark glasses, one dangling
earring, a shirt, backpack, fanny pack, jeans, and shoes, who answers in
English, "How are you father . . ." He is still wearing long hair, however,
and that marks him as Otavaleño. To his credit, Benjamín Terán practices what he preaches and wears Otavalo dress whites daily, including
alpargatas.

Some older Otavalos see costume change as a loss of cultural capital
in Bourdieu's sense, although they do not use this terminology. By "cultural capital" Bourdieu meant the nonfinancial aspects of culture that
can be converted into economic wealth (1984). During San Juan 1995,
two Peguche compadres aged thirty-five and forty talked about their
concerns that "we are losing our culture" and said: "We discuss this a

lot among ourselves." They observed that the girls do not want to wear the headcloth anymore. José María Cotacachi, the older of the two, was wearing white pants and alpargatas as he usually does because he was "accustomed" to these. Segundo Santillán was wearing jeans and running shoes; he said he liked these clothes and that "fashions change." José thought that at least men should wear their ponchos and dress whites to the Saturday fair "for the tourists." He was "proud of the women's dress" and that, no matter what the cost, his wife and two daughters wore the best. When José said Otavalos should wear traditional dress to the fair for the tourists, he was referring to dress as cultural capital, part of the package that attracts tourists to the valley.

A Crisis in Values

The "entrepreneurial ethic" emphasizes self-reliance, hard work, innovation, and astute business decisions (Chavez 1982, 1985). There is no doubt that many Otavalos are experiencing a conflict between the values of entrepreneurship and those of harmony and reciprocity, with the balance tipping toward entrepreneurship and individualism. Otavalos themselves comment that more indígenas are *egoístas* (Sp. selfish, egotistical). Nonetheless, harmony and reciprocity (in theory if not in practice) are still core values. The minga is based on these values. Absences from public mingas to repair roads, paths, or water systems are punished by fines unless people hire a substitute. In June 1996, the fine for missing a minga for the Araque-Ilumán potable water project was S/30,000 ($10). Some wealthier Otavalos now hire replacements. The work gets done, but the face-to-face interaction and bonding among community members is lost. Private mingas to build or roof houses—of which there are fewer as people prefer to pay workers (Colloredo-Mansfeld 1994)—sanction absences with social disapproval and the threat of nonparticipation when the absent person needs help, but again commodified relationships are replacing personal ones.

Walter Anderson calls the postmodern era "the age of over-exposure to otherness—because, in traveling you put yourself into a different reality; because, as a result of immigration, a different reality comes to you; because, with no physical movement at all, only the relentless and ever-increasing flow of information, cultures interpenetrate" (1995: 6). Otavalos, like the rest of us, have been catapulted into postmodernity. Indígenas are asking what constitutes Otavalo culture, what is changing, what these changes mean, and what they should keep or revive.

Because the first book written by an Otavalo indígena was published in 1985 (Males), album liner notes written by indígenas constitute a main source for discussions of "nuestra cultura" in the 1970s. For example, the back cover notes for "Folklore de mi tierra" by Conjunto Indígena "Peguche" (1977) said: "[we] offer this partial example of our cultural values. . . . For more than four centuries, Mother Earth, symbolized by waterfalls, rivers, and springs, who transmits her vigor to our people, attenuated her song. Now she returns to life, resounding with a profound echo to encourage a people who were silenced, humiliated, dispossessed" (1977: my translation).

The inside cover includes the following: "The Quichua indigenous people slowly advance, carrying on our backs the breath of a remote time. Father Sun knows when the world that we dreamed was painful, but we did not grow weak. We accompanied the mountain, the water, the rock in our presentiments of revindication" (ibid.). This is a narrative of suffering and redemption, but indígenas are now constructing narratives with more confidence and less mention of being "humiliated" and "dispossessed."

In "Los indios plásticos" Terán wrote: "It is perverse to adopt indiscriminately foreign models or patterns of behavior. We cannot oppose technological and scientific innovations and advances, but they must be for the enrichment of our own indígena culture. We should only allow those that do not destroy our own values and we should be on the alert, with a critical conscience derived from wisdom" (1991: 21; my translation). Miguel Carlosama, president of FICI in 1994, said:

Many young indígenas don't think like their ancestors. Therefore, now more than ever we have to organize to recover our traditional values, to jointly export our products and not compete unequally, and to recover the agricultural technology of our ancestors because the land is now tired of chemicals. We also have to go in accord with technological advances and to proceed little by little, establishing a communal condition. (Ortiz de Rozas 1994: D10; my translation)

The theme of recovering traditional values and halting runaway competition while accepting technological advances is common to Carlosama and Terán. Terán also insists: "It is possible that we need fewer 'Lambada' rhythms and more discipline and work, to know more of our own language, Quichua, and fewer American words, to value our own foods based on corn, quinoa, and chochos [lupine] more than a hot dog made of putrefied meat, and more dedication to the investigation and study of our roots than to the designs of North American fashions" (1991: 22; my translation).

Terán advocates a revalorization of those Otavalo practices he sees as threatened by an overexposure to otherness. The foreign influences are not just Euro-American—he mentions the Brazilian lambada. Terán also wrote that some youth "[d]isparage vernacular music and only listen to it when they are drinking in groups, less for the value and message it has than because they want to be like the 'beautiful ones' of 'Los Kjarkas' [the Bolivian group]" (ibid.: 21).

Although Liisa Malkki has critiqued the "rooting of peoples" by scholars and refugees (1992), Otavalos themselves commonly use the word "roots" (Sp. raices, Q. sapikuna) to refer to their traditions and history—they see themselves as rooted. In 1986, the Conjunto Indígena "Peguche," anticipating the movie Back to the Future, wrote on their record album: "The History of the Future. Indígena culture is not simply a temporary accident but an urgent historical reality. To recognize this is to re-encounter yourself . . . it is to recuperate your true identity. Those who do not recognize their historical origin and cultures are like trees without roots" (1986; my translation).

Olga Otavalo, who worked at the Hotel Ali Shungu, told me in 1994 that "economically you see improvements, but we are losing the culture. Before, indigenous people did not celebrate such fiestas as birthdays and Christmas eve; now we do."

Themes emerge in the examples from the 1980s and 1990s: the necessity for a recovery of traditional values and customs with specific mention of agriculture, textile production, traditional dress, Quichua, and community; an acceptance of modern technology; and a wise, rather than blind, adoption of foreign food and music.

Lema (1995) titled his book Los Otavalos: Cultura y tradición milenarias (Sp. The Otavalos: Millennial Culture and Tradition). Note the emphasis on the antiquity of the culture and tradition. Lema says of his book: "It is the living testimony of a man who has striven for the advancement of his people, who fights to maintain his traditional culture" (ibid.: 11; my translation). Ordinary Otavalos, not just intellectuals, value custom and tradition, as my many conversations with Otavalos indicate.

Part 4 of Lema's book is titled "Otavaleños Abroad with Music, Crafts, and Political Thought" (ibid.: 191; my translation). I started writing this work in 1993 in Ecuador and, unaware of Lema's book in progress, chose an outline similar to his, with chapters emphasizing history and customs followed by chapters on transnational contacts. This coincidence reflects the effect of the Otavalo diaspora on those who are concerned about the direction "cultura indígena" is taking.

The laments for "the good old days" or aspects of them must be viewed with caution because of people's tendency to long for "the mythical security of a childhood long relinquished" (Featherstone 1995: 107). This is a time of greater community coherence and harmony, which is displaced further into the past as one goes back in history, occurring in each generation's or its parents' childhood (Pearson 1985). At the moment, the mythical Otavalo Golden Age occurred a generation ago, around 1975–1980. This era saw the rise in indigenous prosperity and is distant enough to be invested with a hazy nostalgia. A generation from now, the early 1990s may be seen as the golden age.

The Fiesta Cycle

Several fiestas are traditional in the region, including certain patron saints' days, Coraza, Pendoneros, San Juan and San Pedro (Inti Raymi), and Yamor. As with other aspects of Otavalo life, the fiestas are changing. The fiesta of San Juan embodies the paradoxes of life in the valley today. Is the glass half empty or half full? Should we focus on the changes or the continuities? How has the Otavalo diaspora affected the celebration of San Juan? And how does this fiesta create a sense of community?

Some terms related to fiestas are disappearing. One such phrase is *pasar el cargo* (Sp.), meaning to sponsor a fiesta. In the 1940s, Buitrón and Buitrón noted that indígenas spent vast sums of money on fiestas, working and saving all year just to sponsor one celebration, with the sponsors putting themselves "in the street" from the expense: "There is much social pressure obliging Indians to pass the cargo sponsoring these fiestas, and, moreover, to pass the cargo confers so much prestige on an individual that Indians will even steal with the objective of meeting this social obligation" (1945: 200; my translation).

Several events have occurred since this was written. Because wasi-pungu severely limited opportunities for indígenas to gain prestige, this ambition was channeled into the cargo system. There are now other avenues to status and prestige: success as a weaver or merchant; ownership of a building in Otavalo, a motor vehicle, or a good house in the countryside; having one's children attend the university; and travel abroad. Protestant missionaries frowned on the stupefying consumption of alcohol at fiestas and perhaps on the "waste" of money, and the growth in com-

Musicians accompanying a Coraza and his entourage down Calle Bolívar in Otavalo. September 1995.

mercial weaving made indígenas reluctant to put themselves "in the street" just for a fiesta; indígenas have told me this since I began working in Otavalo.

In 1989, Carlos Coba Andrade published an article titled "Commentary on a Fiesta That Has Died: The Coraza" (1989; my translation). In fact, such fiestas as Pendoneros (Sp. Banners), celebrated on October 15 in communities on the south shore of Lago San Pablo, and Coraza were disappearing but have been resurrected as part of larger public events without ruinous individual expenditures. Although the wealthiest indígenas are no longer sponsoring these fiestas, especially Coraza and Pendoneros, the celebrations were revived by two groups at opposite ends of the social spectrum: agriculturists left out of the textile and tourist boom and the indigenous political and intellectual elite. I never saw a Coraza until 1989, although I was familiar with this fiesta from the literature (Ares Queija 1988; Banning 1992; Butler 1981; Coba Andrade 1989; Collier and Buitrón 1949: 124–139) and from indígenas' accounts of it.

The fiesta of San Juan Bautista (Saint John the Baptist) on June 24 is the major annual celebration in the valley. San Juan, also called Inti Raymi, overlaps the fiesta of San Pedro on June 29. Anciently, this may have been the indigenous new year. The name Inti Raymi, referring to the Inca's June solstice festival, was adopted in the 1990s as a result of Pan-Andean indigenous contacts. We do not know the aboriginal name for the celebration in Imbabura, but I find it ironic that Otavalos have substituted one conqueror's term (Inti Raymi) for another's (San Juan). Festivities now begin on the twenty-second (rather than twenty-third) and continue past the feast of San Pedro, a week to ten days of socializing, feasting, drinking, music, and dancing.

In Imbabura these fiestas celebrate the solstice and the corn harvest. Nina Pacari says that "Inti Raimy is the most important fiesta for indígenas; it's the summer solstice. People give thanks for the harvest, for abundance. The people prepare food, frames hung with food, bread, bananas, and such" (Bulnes 1990: 47; my translation). Narcizo Conejo of Peguche said, "San Juan is converted into a sacred time."

San Juan superficially resembles a combination of Halloween and Thanksgiving in the United States. It combines pre-Inca, Inca, and European elements (Coba Andrade 1994b: 13–14) and has features that many Otavalos consider holy or sacred, especially the ritual bathing, celebration of the harvest, and thanking the earth. Calling the fiesta "San Juan" was simply a nod to Catholic extirpators of idolatry in colonial times.

Hassaurek offers mid-nineteenth-century glimpses of San Juan and San Pedro in Otavalo, Cayambe, and San Pablo. When he rode through

San Juan/Inti Raymi dancers and onlookers at San Juan Capilla outside Otavalo. June 2000.

San Pablo during San Juan in 1863, he observed a group of costumed male dancers, some dressed as females, "gorgeously attired. . . . A very crude sort of violins and guitars constituted the orchestra which accompanied them. They went through a sort of contra dance, consisting of a variety of figures. They danced first in the streets and then in the plaza." Hassaurek described another feature of San Juan which has now disappeared: "The whole company held wooden arches in their hands, covered over with ribbons, and ornamented with flowers" (1967 [1867]: 149). On the outskirts of San Pablo he encountered more costumed dancers in small groups: "They danced continually, and only stopped to drink. Even those who played their poor flutes danced along, turning slowly around, bowing to one side, and stamping on the ground to keep time, without end. Others accompanied the performance with monotonous, pitiable songs" (ibid.: 150).

Later, at San Juan *capilla* (Sp. chapel) west of Otavalo, Hassaurek observed male indígenas "singing, with hoarse drunken voices, to the tune of the harp or guitar, or even without accompaniment . . ." (ibid.: 153–154). He described the "innumerable" musical instruments present, including the rondador ("few, and melancholy are the tunes it yields"), flutes, violins, guitars, several harps, and one or two horns. "I saw no drums, which, however, may have been accidental. With the Indians of Quito the drum is highly popular" (ibid.: 155). These same instruments, except for the harp and with a few additions, mainly harmonicas, are still played during San Juan.

Hassaurek described the customary San Juan circle dancing, wherein costumed males dance in a circle around the musicians, reversing direction from time to time, sometimes shouting, *Damos una vuelta!* (Sp. Let's turn around!). Also: "The members of the party cluster around one another, and then each man turns round, beating time with his feet in slow but continuous rotation. The musicians do the same, marking time with their heads and the upper part of their bodies." Hassaurek noted an essential feature of Otavalo musicianship: "The musicians are amateurs and enjoy the double pleasure of playing and dancing" (ibid.: 156).

The dancers formed a procession on the fairgrounds in front of the chapel of San Juan west of Otavalo and marched from one end to the other, occasionally going into the circle formation described above (ibid.: 156). Hassaurek wrote: "While marching, some of them will play their crude flutes or guitars. Even harps will be carried along in the procession with their bottoms resting on the back of a little boy, while the musician harps away at the strings, and one of his companions beats the time on the side of the instrument" (ibid.).

San Juan groups are composed of seven to twenty male musicians and dancers of all ages, and Hassaurek observed a salient feature of these groups: "The instruments just described were not united in an orchestra, but each of the many parties who marched up and down or around the grounds had at least two or three of them" (ibid.: 155). Each San Juan group is a separate entity; even when many groups assemble at San Juan Capilla, each group plays its own tunes, and musical anarchy prevails. On his way back to Peguche, Hassaurek observed more San Juan circle dancing at the chapel of Monserrat east of Otavalo.

As June commences, Otavalos begin talking about San Juan–Inti Raymi. A sense of anticipation and excitement is palpable by mid-month. Peggy Barlett observed that during San Juan Otavalos "from all parts of Ecuador" reunited with their families (1980: 116), and indígenas still return to Otavalo from throughout South America. Each fall when I leave Otavalo, my indígena friends, compadres, and godchildren insist that I return for San Juan.

A few days before San Juan, the females begin preparing "chicha de San Juan," fermented corn beer. Anyone present joins in the making of the *castillo* (Sp. castle), a bamboo framework about three feet square that hangs from the ceiling and is covered with bread, tangerines, oranges, and bananas. When I asked indígenas what this symbolized, people just said, "It's a sign of San Juan," although it appears to represent the bounty of the harvest (but without corn). People who take food from the castillo must return double the amount in the coming year; the same goes for borrowed money.

After sunset on the twenty-third, indígenas traditionally bathe (Q. *armay chishi*) in the streams and springs (which now occurs on the twenty-second as well). This has several possible meanings, not necessarily mutually exclusive. One is that bathing before the feast of Saint John the Baptist repeats the ritual of baptism, of spiritual cleansing. Several places are especially popular, including Peguche Falls and San Juan Pugyu (Q. springs) located below Ilumán, which are imbued with potent spiritual forces. According to Carlos Conterón, indígenas bathe to absorb the forces of the water, and they leave their musical instruments near the waterfalls or springs so that their instruments will also absorb this power.

On June 23, the vespers, an extra-large market is held in Otavalo because it is customary for Otavalos to buy new clothes. In 1999, this market lined the full four blocks of Calle Jaramillo between the Poncho Plaza and the food market. Males in masquerade are an essential part of San Juan, so costumes, masks, and musical instruments are also sold in town. Some Otavalos dress as whites-mestizos as a way of mocking and parodying the dominant group. In 1863, when Hassaurek visited, through the 1940s, costumes representing soldiers, overseers on haciendas, and town whites, black-face, and goatskin or sheepskin chaps were popular (Hassaurek 1967 [1867]: 154–155; Collier and Buitrón 1949: 104–105, 111–113; Parsons 1945: 108–111). Since at least the 1860s, males have also crossed-dressed as indígena women (Collier and Buitrón 1949: 105; Hassaurek 1967 [1867]; Parsons 1945: 110) and as *aya umas* (Q. spirit heads), who carry a whip and wear a double-faced mask with a projecting nose and horns (Parsons 1945: Plate 24). Aya umas are often inaccurately called "devils" by whites-mestizos. Indígenas gloss *aya* as energy or the forces of nature which can affect humans positively or negatively and *uma* as head, so the aya uma dancer represents the leader, guide, or head who possesses these natural forces (Cachiguango 1993: 16).

Ritual drinking has long prevailed, and large groups of drunken and assertive indígenas have caused consternation. Parsons wrote that "the White townspeople are said to be somewhat fearful of the Indians at this time because their usually submissive neighbors tend to be self-assertive and overbearing. For one thing the dancers dress like blancos and carry whips" (1945: 108–109). Scott (1990) has analyzed such situations as rites of reversal, one of the "arts of resistance" practiced by subordinate groups.

Anything goes as masquerade, including motley, and costumes change with the times. The mayordomo costume disappeared when the overseers did, after the abolition of wasipungu. The dance of the lances, depicted in an old photograph of Otavalos from Cerotal (Rubio Orbe 1956: 162), is no longer performed.

Since my first San Juan in 1978, I have seen indígenas dressed as Mexican mariachis, cowboys, Native North Americans, Bolivian indígenas, a Prussian soldier wearing an ulan helmet, Arabs, nuns, monks, brides, Afro-Ecuadorians (in black-face), soldiers, police, King Kong, Kalimán (a South American super-hero), monks, hippies, Davy Crockett, Chinese coolies, the pope, Star Wars characters, clowns, aya umas, penitents, Otavaleñas (a favorite), Otavaleños in archaic dress, Cayambe indígena women, and Sanjuanes in ponchos and goatskin chaps, and wearing indescribable get-ups. In 1990, a group of young Peguche Otavaleños dressed as foreign tourists, complete with blonde wigs, daypacks or baby carriers with blonde dolls, sunglasses, cameras, down jackets, running shoes, and blue jeans or denim skirts. In 1995 and 1996, another large contingent of "foreigners" wore blonde wigs made from Agave cactus fiber.

The practice of parodying whites perseveres—only now the whites are tourists.

On the evening of the twenty-third, females prepare food and drink to offer visiting dancers, while the males dress in their costumes and take to the streets. Most groups consist of relatives, neighbors, or close friends. The dancers move from house to house, performing the stomping circle dance. If the dancers come inside, it is customary to offer them chicha, trago, or corn meal soup, boiled corn kernels, or boiled potatoes. The dancers eat, drink, and dance for a while, stomping hard on the dirt or wood floor. Then they dance into the chilly Andean night and on to the next house or community. Dancing is primarily a male activity, but sometimes females dance inside the house or are invited to join a group in the street. Young Otavaleñas sometimes accompany younger male relatives to keep an eye on them or dance during the day, especially in front of San Juan chapel, and Otavalos sometimes invite foreign women to join their groups.

The Otavalo values of participation and inclusion are expressed in attendance at social and ritual events, which always include people of all ages. Babies and toddlers tied to their mother's or another relative's back attend weddings, wakes, burials, church services, mingas, and fiestas including San Juan. Older children come along, as do teenagers, adults, and grandparents. The wawas tumble and play; and if they cry they are picked up, kissed, and soothed by the nearest larger person, male or female. When children get tired, they are wrapped in a poncho or rebozo and put on the bed or on an estera on the floor to sleep. There are no "adults only" social events. Some years ago, I invited an Otavaleña friend to accompany me to an adult friend's birthday party in San Francisco. After the party I asked her what the biggest difference was between our fiestas and theirs. She answered immediately, "You don't have any children or grandparents." During San Juan, men and boys of all ages dance together. The amateur, participatory nature of Otavalo musicianship means that anyone with an instrument is welcome to play whether or not he is a particularly accomplished musician.

The dancing continues until dawn, when the dancers-singers-musicians stagger home and sleep most of the day, waking up with a hangover (Q. *chuchaki*) and sore feet. Because of the stamina involved in San Juan dancing, which occurs during part of the day and all night for a week, the core participants are young males between the ages of eight and thirty.

On San Juan day, while the dancers are asleep, the women of the household cook guinea pigs and prepare food for the inevitable guests.

Relatives from distant parts may be staying at the house or stopping by, and neighbors and compadres drop in. Even though San Juan has always appeared to be a male fiesta, everyone seems to enjoy it. Most commercial and productive activity shuts down completely for a week, and people socialize: "It is clear that the San Juan fiesta has important psychological functions as recreation and a time out, and for the release of aggression. It functions for the Indians as a group to reaffirm their ethnicity through partaking in a traditional ritual, and to cement ties of loyalty, friendship, etc." (Barlett 1980: 120). The reciprocal nature of San Juan drinking is also important for reaffirming links among families, compadres, and political leaders and followers (ibid.: 122–123).

Changes in Otavalo have resulted in changes in San Juan, starting with the name. "Inti Raymi" is now heard with increasing frequency. Beginning around 1991, people commented on the absence of young male dancer-musicians, who were playing music in Europe and the United States. In 1994 and 1999, my godchildren complained to me about the lack of San Juan groups, "because all the young men are abroad." Although it is important to be in Otavalo for San Juan, the fiesta falls in the middle of the most lucrative time for street music and artesanías sales in the northern hemisphere, so thousands of Otavalos are absent.

In the summer of 1993, the Otavalos in Amsterdam rented a huge hall ("in a poor neighborhood") and more than 300 Otavalos assembled with instruments to dance San Juan in the traditional fashion with about fifteen groups, each dancing in a circle and playing its own music (Adi Willnauer, personal communication, 1994). Otavalos, including my godsons who have traveled abroad, told me that they also dance San Juan in Germany and Spain. In the summer of 1998, a caravan of cars drove from Chicago to New York, where a group of Otavalos numbering at least 300 danced San Juan (Narcizo Conejo, personal communication, 1999).

By the summer of 2000, the Chicago fiesta made headlines in the Ibarra newspaper: "¡Inty Raimi en Chicago!" According to the article, for more than three years "indígenas imbabureños" in the United States have congregated to celebrate an Imbaburan tradition, San Juan. In Chicago, Nivo Paredes and "other valuable young indígenas" including Elvis Lema, William Pineda, Humberto Males, Vicente Cruz, and other members of the "Colonia de Otavaleños" (Sp. Otavalo Colony) in that city organized sports, artistic, music, and dance events in Lincoln Park, culminating in the traditional San Juan circle dancing. More than 200 expatriates attended, "indios y mestizos," including Otavalan, Imbaburan, and "Ecuadorian residents of the city who had lived there many years" and Otavalos from other U.S. cities. The organizers planned to maintain their organization as a self-help group for their *paisanos* (Sp. fellow countrymen and women) in the expatriate community (Proaño 2000: 2; my translation).

Note the variation in ethnic terms in the short piece, including *indio, indígena,* and *mestizo,* as well as the city, provincial, and national identifiers of the participants. The story is ambiguous but implies that Cayambe indígenas and whites-mestizos from Imbabura, as well as Ecuadorians of all ethnicities from outside the province, are celebrating San Juan as a national event for Ecuadorian expatriates. Abroad, among strangers, Ecuadorian-ness becomes the unifying factor. The story illustrates the way identities overlap and subsume one another. For example, Otavalo indígenas are members of all three "colonies," and, of course, non-indígenas from Otavalo can also claim the city identifier. Inti Raymi in Chicago is an excellent example of diasporic interculture, the subcultures' linkages across national borders.

In 1998, UNAIMCO, the indigenous market vendors of the Poncho Plaza, sponsored a new Inti Raymi event in Otavalo for the evening of June 23. They invited interested groups to assemble at the traffic circle at the north end of Calle Bolívar and dance to the Poncho Plaza, where UNAIMCO had erected a stand with a castillo and sound system. There was a blessing of the harvest by a local yachac, indicative of the increasingly public presence of traditional healers. At least twenty groups participated. Some of the music and singing was excellent, played by former street musicians. One group, composed of twenty-five middle-aged tíos and taitas from Otavalo town and Ciudadela Imbaya, was especially impressive. Instead of masquerading, they wore their finest dress whites, hats, and blue ponchos, and each man played a guitar or gaita. One compadre said that wearing traditional dress was a demonstration of ethnic pride. When the parade was repeated in 1999, 2000, and 2001, about forty groups from the region, including Ibarra and Rinconada, participated. The parade is becoming an annual event.

A change in the past five years is the increasingly self-conscious nature of the fiesta at home and abroad and attempts to promote it as a tourist event in Imbabura. San Juan used to be just San Juan, celebrated without commentary or publicity. Now it is Inti Raymi, and indigenous intellectuals are organizing programs and conferences such as the UNAIMCO parade. Beginning in 1998, Cotacachi began publishing glossy color brochures announcing "Inti Raymi" at the *"destino turístico* [Sp. tourist destination] Cotacachi-Cuicocha." In 2000, the brochure invited participants to the ritual bathing at Cuicocha with cleansings and curings by *shamanes* and listed events from June 22 through June 30, including the traditional "taking of the plaza" in Cotacachi by competing dance groups.

In 1999, CEPCU (Sp. Center for Pluricultural Studies) and the United Nations Volunteers held a two-day seminar in the Otavalo town hall on "The Andean Wisdom of Inti Raymi." An eclectic coalition including the Universidad Técnica del Norte in Ibarra, ASHIM (Sp. Association of Shamans of Imbabura), Monsignor Antonio Arregui of the Catholic church, and CERCCI (Sp. Ecuadorian Corporation for the Recovery of Indigenous Ceremonial Centers) sponsored an "Inti Raymi Cultural Week" that included lectures by local healers and doctors, a ceremony at the pyramids of Cochasquí, a march to the lechero tree for ritual offerings, a blessing of the harvest by Monsignor Arregui, purification ceremonies and ritual bathing at Peguche Falls, and more. The events were announced in a widely distributed flyer drawing on sources from the Incas to New Age "bioenergetic-magnetic forces" (my translation).

Attempts to commercialize the fiesta are mixed. The all-night dancing in the communities is organized ad hoc, and there are no night buses to and from the outlying towns. Because most dancing takes place in public, there is no way to charge admission. Also, since Otavalos are busy socializing, drinking, and dancing, and the fiesta is a break from normal activities, they are not overly interested in selling artesanías at this time. The Saturday market is often smaller than usual, and many stores close for a few days around June 24.

Another change concerns sponsorship. As early as the 1940s, San Juan groups in Peguche were not sponsored by a particular person (Sp. *prioste*); the fiesta had become free form (Parsons 1945: 108). This had the advantage of relieving a household of high costs. By the late 1970s, the fiesta was celebrated this way, as far as I know, in most Otavalo communities.

Since 1994, I have been invited to the Coraza at San Juan Pugyu near Ilumán. The Coraza or sponsor of the fiesta wears a spectacular costume: shiny white pants and a shirt decorated with sequins, appliqués, buttons, gilt trim, fake pearl necklaces, and a plumed cocked hat hung with costume jewelry chains, beads, and pendants that hide the Coraza's face and head. He rides a horse, wears shoes, and carries an umbrella, all status symbols associated with whites in an earlier era. Indígenas have described him as a "symbol of authority." The Coraza is accompanied by two or three mounted men called Yumbos, in white-face and wearing glitzy costumes, and by a young boy, the Loa, also in white-face, who recites poetry and praises the Coraza. Structuralists (for example, Ares Queija 1988) have a field day with this event because of the many binary oppositions it evokes.

First, it is important to note that Coraza was revived in communities to the north of Otavalo that had not celebrated it recently. The first Coraza I witnessed was for the inauguration of a new community center in Angelpamba above Ilumán in 1989. The Corazas for San Juan in 1994 and 1995 were from San Luis de Agualongo. A relative of the 1994 Coraza said his family spent approximately $350 on the fiesta, which is chicken-feed by contemporary Otavalo standards, although it may have represented quite an outlay for this particular family. (Coraza is also being resurrected in the communities around Lago San Pablo, where it was celebrated formerly.)

Second, the annual celebration at San Juan Pugyu was a unique combination of public and private. The fiesta is held in a meadow where the creek flows through a canyon about 100 feet below the Pan-American highway. The Coraza and his family set up the traditional fiesta food hut (Q. *buda wasi*), where the Coraza's family served food to his compadres, neighbors, and relatives. There was a brass band, and the priest said mass. But in addition to these participants, at any given time there were about a thousand indígena, white-mestizo, and foreign onlookers who arrived on foot or in buses, cars, and pickups which lined the highway. The onlookers brought their own food and drink or bought refreshments from the ambulatory vendors or those with stands. People came and went all day, and perhaps four thousand persons attended. The Coraza was the center of attention and gained prestige for sponsoring the event, but he and his family paid the expenses of only a fraction of the participants.

Meanwhile, there were changes in the celebration in front of San Juan chapel. As in Hassaurek's time, the edge of the large plaza in front of the chapel is lined with booths selling hot food, taffy, and alcohol. Other booths have paddle-board tables and other games, and there is a Ferris wheel and little train. Accounts from 1863 through 1949 (Hassaurek 1967 [1867]; Parsons 1945; Collier and Buitrón 1949) noted the large number of white and mestizo townspeople who came to eat, drink, and watch the dancers from the nearby communities of Santiaguillo, San Juan, and Monserrat.

These accounts mention ritual fights. Descriptions of a pitched battle between indigenous groups with the intent of spilling blood to pay the earth are common in the literature, especially for the southern Andes (Harris 1986; McIntyre 1975; Rasnake 1988), where such a battle is called

San Juan/Inti Raymi dancers in Cotacachi. June 1997.

a *tinku* (Q. an encounter or coming together). In Imbabura these ritual battles are called *peleas* (Sp. fights) or *tingrina* (Q. coming together, from the same root as tinku) and are contests among local communities whose dancers try to take possession of the plaza. Deaths and serious injuries often ensue. According to Narcizo Conejo (personal communication, 1996), "You can say we are paying the earth because the earth is our mother and we can offer our blood." He emphasized that if there are deaths during the fights, "there are no protests."

By the 1940s, town officials decided the custom was barbaric and attempted to stop the fights, with local police reinforced by soldiers from Ibarra (Collier and Buitrón 1949: 101; Parsons 1945: 111). There was more operating than paternalistic interest in the indígenas' welfare, and that was a fear of the lower orders getting out of hand. The possibility of violence and danger, however, is one of the attractions of the event, especially since the males fight with one another and do not turn on bystanders, although there is always the possibility of being brained by a stray rock. Thousands of people, including women with babies on their backs and children at their sides, assemble each year on the hill above the fairgrounds, patiently waiting for the fighting to start. In recent years, the Otavalo police have moved in with tear gas before more than a few rocks are thrown; but June 29, San Pedro in Cotacachi, is renowned for the ferocity of its fights, with dancers "bathed in blood," as one comadre put it. In 1999, an indígena was killed.

As more indígenas have moved to Otavalo, and with better public transportation and the burgeoning indígena ownership of private vehicles, more groups and bystanders now attend the dancing at San Juan chapel, especially on the last two days, June 26 and 27. In 1995, town officials decided to try to channel the aggression into a dance contest with cash prizes. Each group carried a number and was judged on its instrumental music, singing of Quichua Sanjuanitos, and costumes. To no one's surprise, the usual fighting erupted (as it has every year since): the police lobbed tear gas, the crowd scattered screaming in all directions, a merry time was had by all, and San Juan came to a satisfactory close.

San Juan socializing has now expanded from interhousehold to intercommunity. On Sunday, June 25, 1995, after feasting and drinking at their house, Peguche compadres loaded their families and me (about twenty-five persons) into two Nissan pickup trucks and drove first to San Juan Pugyu to watch the Coraza then through Quinchuquí, where people were hauling brush to the plaza for a huge bonfire later that night. We encountered dance groups on the road and visited with them as a pickup loaded with dancers drove into Quinchuquí from Agato. From Quinchuquí we drove around Lago San Pablo to Chilcapamba, where there was a large gathering in the schoolyard behind the church. We observed these festivities for a while then drove on to San Pablo, where hundreds of cars and pickups created a monumental traffic jam on the town's steep, narrow cobbled streets. The town was hosting "The first intercultural event, Inti Raymi" (my translation). The San Pablo area has Otavalo communities interdigited with those of Cayambes. Dancers, singers, and musicians from both indigenous groups, white-mestizo musicians and dancers masquerading as indígenas, and thousands of onlookers filled a huge, open field on the side of Imbabura. The usual food and drink vendors enticed the crowd; after making a thorough inspection of all the groups, which took us several hours, we piled into the pickups and drove home.

In line with Connerton's argument (1989), the Otavalos collectively remember the past through such commemorative ceremonies as baptisms, weddings, funerals, and fiestas and in such bodily practices as costume and performance, which is one reason why these customs are so important. San Juan–Inti Raymi is a classic example of a physically embodied commemorative ceremony or ritual (as opposed, for example, to a passive audience watching television). Masquerade costumes change

Three generations in the de la Torre family dancing San Juan at home in San Luis de Agualongo. June 1997.

with the times, Corazas surface in new places, Otavalos drive from town to town for the festivities, and dispersed Otavalos dance San Juan in distant countries; but San Juan–Inti Raymi remains the most important fiesta of the year, an expression of "nuestra cultura indígena" that reaffirms family, community, ethnic group, and even national ties.

Summary

The term "summary" better represents my stance—and the current state of affairs in Otavalo—than the word "conclusion," which implies that something is over. Although certain aspects of new wealth, increasing transnational linkages, and the Otavalo diaspora are unsettling to both Otavalos and researchers, a century from now—if I may hazard a prediction—there will still be a culture that is recognizably Otavalo, with Quichua spoken; females wearing a costume with obvious links to that worn today; males in long hair, with ponchos worn on special occasions; household-based textile production; compadrazgo; a Saturday fair; the sounds of Sanjuanitos; and the celebration of such fiestas as Inti Raymi, among other features of contemporary Otavalo life. What may not exist is an agriculture-based lifeway that has economic significance.

As many Otavalos have insisted, adopting technology does not mean adopting the values and lifeways of the societies that produced the technology; nor do increasing transnational contacts equal homogenization. I am not Japanese even though I own many Japanese-made electronic goods. What technology seems to be doing, in line with Wilk's argument (1995) summarized in the introduction, is channeling the expression of local differences in specific ways across greater distances. There are two main reasons for this. One relates to the nature of the technologies themselves, the limitations imposed, and the different kinds of information conveyed by print, radio, telephone, digital sound recording, video, television, film, and the Internet.

The second reason is that the conventions for conveying messages in these media—and they are socially constructed conventions (the three-minute musical selection, the clichés of tourism publicity, formats for e-mail)—originated in the more industrialized nations and have been adopted along with the technology. But it is important to understand the extent to which small groups such as the Otavalos have used technology to make a mark in the global cultural arena, particularly in music, that is totally out of proportion to their size. Technology for small groups can be a great equalizer. If the Otavalos are suffering to some extent from a

Otavalos recharging emotional batteries and reaffirming community ties at a wedding fiesta in Ilumán. May 1993.

The Otavalo crafts market. July 2001.

postmodern "overexposure to otherness," their ubiquity on the streets of Europe and the United States has led to others suffering from an overexposure to them.

Globalization—the increasingly rapid flow of images, capital, people, information, and goods across nation-state boundaries—does not supersede the local, and the two are not dichotomous. In fact, international tourism and global cultural circulation depend on the local, on culturally specific sites of production and on local differences. The reproduction of human populations and cultures also takes place on the local level, initially in households and families, with all their specificities and peculiarities of language, belief, custom, and adaptation to the local environment. The local *is* the world to a child, the reality (or doxa) against which other realities are judged.

The global and the local and homogenizing and heterogenizing trends exist concurrently and are "mutually implicative" (Robertson 1995: 27). Globalization is not the same as homogenization or the construction of a world culture on a Euro-American model. The Otavalos are coping with globalization by revaluing and emphasizing what is unique (and often marketable) about their culture, including their identity as indigenous people, their cultural capital. Globalization of the textile and music industries and transnational migration are ways for Otavalos to cope with population growth, land shortages, and increased competition for textile sales, enabling them to be simultaneously indigenous and citizens of a nation-state (or several) as well as traditional, modern, and postmodern—with all the paradoxes, problems, and possibilities these terms imply.

References

Alchon, Suzanne Austin
    1991 *Native Society and Disease in Colonial Ecuador.* Cambridge, New York, and Melbourne: Cambridge University Press.
Allen, Catherine J.
    1988 *The Hold Life Has: Coca and Cultural Identity in an Andean Community.* Washington, D.C.: Smithsonian Institution Press.
Alvarez, Robert R., and George A. Collier
    1994 The Long Haul in Mexican Trucking: Traversing the Borderlands of the North and the South. *American Ethnologist* 21, no. 3: 607–627.
American Express
    1991 *American Express Vacations: Latin America 1992.* N.p.
Anderson, Benedict
    1983 *Imagined Communities: Reflections on the Origin and Spread of Nationalism.* London: Verso.
Anderson, Walter Truett
    1990 *Reality Isn't What It Used To Be: Theatrical Politics, Ready-to-Wear Religion, Global Myths, Primitive Chic, and Other Wonders of the Postmodern World.* San Francisco: Harper San Francisco.
Anderson, Walter Truett, ed.
    1995 *The Truth about the Truth: De-confusing and Re-constructing the Postmodern World.* New York: G. P. Putnam's Sons.
Appadurai, Arjun
    1986 Theory of Anthropology: Center and Periphery. *Comparative Studies in Society and History* 28: 356–361.
    1990 Disjuncture and Difference in the Global Cultural Economy. In Mike Featherstone, ed., *Global Culture: Nationalism, Globalization and Modernity,* pp. 295–310. Newbury Park, Calif.: Sage Publications.
    1991 Global Ethnoscapes: Notes and Queries for a Transnational Anthropology. In Richard G. Fox, ed., *Recapturing Anthropology: Working in the Present,* pp. 191–210. Santa Fe, N. Mex.: School of American Research Press.
Ares Queija, Berta
    1988 *Los Corazas: Ritual andino en Otavalo.* Otavalo: Instituto Otavaleño de Antropología; Quito: Ediciones Abya-Yala.

Arriaga, Father Pablo Joseph de
   1968 [1621] *The Extirpation of Idolatry in Peru.* Ed. and trans. L. Clark
        Keating. Lexington: University of Kentucky Press.
Banning, Peter
   1992 El sanjuanito o sanjuan en Otavalo: Análisis de caso. *Sarance (Re-
        vista del Instituto Otavaleño de Antropología–Centro Regional de
        Investigaciones)* 16 (August): 131–150.
Barlett, Peggy F.
   1980 Reciprocity and the San Juan Fiesta. *Journal of Anthropological Re-
        search* 36, no. 1 (Spring): 116–130.
Barth, Fredrik
   1969 Introduction. In Fredrik Barth, ed., *Ethnic Groups and Boundaries:
        The Social Organization of Cultural Difference,* pp. 9–38. Boston:
        Little, Brown and Co.
Basch, Linda, Nina Glick Schiller, and Christina Szanton Blanc
   1994 *Nations Unbound: Transnational Projects, Postcolonial Predica-
        ments and Deterritorialized Nation-States.* Langhorne, Penn.: Gor-
        don and Breach Science Publishers.
Baudrillard, Jean
   1983 *Simulations.* New York: Semiotext(e).
Baumann, Max Peter, ed.
   1992 *World Music, Musics of the World: Aspects of Documentation,
        Mass Media and Acculturation.* Wilhelmshaven, Germany: Florian
        Noetzel Verlag.
Bedoya, Jimmy
   1993 La identidad binacional. *El Comercio,* Thursday, April 29, 1993,
        p. A-2.
Belote, Jim, and Linda Belote
   1977 The Limitation of Obligation in Saraguro Kinship. In Ralph Bolton
        and Enrique Mayer, eds., *Andean Kinship and Marriage,* pp. 106–
        116. Special Publication No. 7. Washington, D.C.: American Anthro-
        pological Association.
Belote, Linda Smith, and Jim Belote
   1981 Development in Spite of Itself: The Saraguro Model. In Norman E.
        Whitten, Jr., ed., *Cultural Transformations and Ethnicity in Modern
        Ecuador,* pp. 450–476. Urbana, Chicago, and London: University of
        Illinois Press.
   1984 Drain from the Bottom: Individual Ethnic Identity Change in South-
        ern Ecuador. *Social Forces* 63, no. 1 (September): 24–50.
Berkhofer, Robert F., Jr.
   1979 *The White Man's Indian: Images of the American Indian from
        Columbus to the Present.* New York: Vintage Books.
Birnbaum, Stephen
   1984 *Birnbaum's South America 1985.* Boston: Houghton Mifflin Com-
        pany.
Bourdieu, Pierre
   1977 *Outline of a Theory of Practice.* Trans. Richard Nice. Cambridge:
        Cambridge University Press.

1984 *Distinction: A Social Critique of the Judgment of Taste*. Trans. Richard Nice. London: Routledge and Kegan Paul.

Brooks, John
1986–1994 *The 1987–1993 South American Handbook*. 63d through 69th annual eds. Bath, England: Trade and Travel Publications Ltd.

Broughton, Simon, Mark Ellingham, David Muddyman, and Richard Trillo
1994 *World Music: The Rough Guide*. London and New York: Penguin Books.

Browman, David L.
1994 Cultural Process, Cultural Context, and Revisionism: Recent Works on Andean Civilization and Cosmology. *Latin American Research Review* 29, no. 2: 235–248.

Brysk, Alison
2000 *From Tribal Village to Global Village: Indian Rights and International Relations in Latin America*. Stanford: Stanford University Press.

Buitrón, Aníbal
1947 Situación económica y social del Indio Otavaleño. *América Indígena* 7, no. 1 (January): 45–62.
1951 Notas bibliográficas: Misión cultural indígena a los Estados Unidos. *América Indígena* 11, no. 3 (July): 271–272.

Buitrón, Aníbal, and Barbara Salisbury Buitrón
1945 Indios, blancos y mestizos en Otavalo, Ecuador. *Acta Americana* 3: 190–216.

Bulnes, Martha
1990 *Hatarishpa ninimi, Me levanto y digo: Testimonio de tres mujeres quichuas*. Quito: Editorial El Conejo.

Butler, Barbara Y. (see also Rivero, Bárbara B.)
1981 Indígena Ethnic Identity Change in the Ecuadorian Sierra. Ph.D. dissertation, Department of Anthropology, University of Rochester.

Büttner, Thomas
1993 *Uso del quichua y del castellano en la sierra ecuatoriano*. Quito: P. EBI (MEC-GTZ) y Ediciones Abya-Yala.

Cabildo de Quito
1992 [1577] Relación de la Ciudad de Quito. In *Relaciones histórico-geográficas de la Audiencia de Quito (Siglo XVI–XIX)* (hereafter referred to as *RHG*), introductory study and transcription by Pilar Ponce Leiva, vol. 1, pp. 251–265. 2 vols. Quito: MARKA y Ediciones Abya-Yala.

Cachiguango C., Luis Enrique
1993 Aya-Uma: Símbolo de la cultura indígena. *Shimishitachi: Información y Reflexión sobre Temas Indígenas* (Peguche, Ecuador: Centro de Desarrollo Comunitario Ingapirca) 16 (June): 16–20.

Caillavet, Chantal
1981 Etnohistoria ecuatoriana: Nuevos datos sobre el Otavalo prehispánico. *Cultura* (Quito: Banco Central del Ecuador) 11: 109–127.
1982 Caciques de Otavalo en el siglo XVI: Don Alonso Maldonado y su

esposa. *Miscelánea Antropológica Ecuatoriana* (Quito: Museos del Banco Central del Ecuador) 2: 38–55.

Campbell, Leon G.
  1987 Ideology and Factionalism during the Great Rebellion, 1780–1782. In Steve J. Stern, ed., *Resistance, Rebellion, and Consciousness in the Andean Peasant World, Eighteenth to Twentieth Centuries*, pp. 110–139. Madison: University of Wisconsin Press.

Carpenter, Lawrence K.
  1981 "Making the Baby Fall": Ethnomedicine and Birth in Northern Ecuador (1). *Florida Journal of Anthropology* (Gainesville) 6, no. 2: 47–57.
  1983 Social Stratification and Implications for Bilingual Education: An Ecuadorian Example. In Andrew W. Miracle, Jr., ed., *Bilingualism: Social Issues and Policy Implications*, pp. 96–106. Athens: University of Georgia Press.

Carrera, Adriana
  1999 Nueva York: Ecuatorianos, un mordisco de la Gran Manzana. *El Universo*, Sunday, August 15, 1999, p. 7.

Casagrande, Joseph B.
  1981 Strategies for Survival: The Indians of Highland Ecuador. In Norman E. Whitten, Jr., ed., *Cultural Transformations and Ethnicity in Modern Ecuador*, pp. 260–277. Urbana, Chicago, and London: University of Illinois Press.

[Castillo, Juan Piñán?]
  1994 [1605] Descripción de la Villa de Villar Don Pardo. In *RHG*, vol. 2, pp. 1–10.

Cerrón Palomino, Rodolfo
  1987 *Lingüística quechua.* Cuzco: Centro de Estudios Rurales Andinos Bartolomé de las Casas.

CETUR (Corporación Ecuatoriana de Turismo)
  1992 *Boletín de estadísticas turísticas 1992.* Quito: CETUR.

Chavez, Leo Ralph
  1982 Commercial Weaving and the Entrepreneurial Ethic: Otavalo Indian Views of the Self and the World. Ph.D. dissertation, Department of Anthropology, Stanford University.
  1985 "To Get Ahead": The Entrepreneurial Ethic and Political Behavior among Commercial Weavers in Otavalo. In Jeffrey Ehrenreich, ed., *Political Anthropology in Ecuador: Perspectives from Indigenous Cultures*, pp. 159–189. Albany: Society for Latin American Anthropology and Center for the Caribbean and Latin America, State University of New York at Albany.

Che-Flechas
  1994 Defraudó Charijayac. *Diario del Norte*, Monday, March 21.

Chiriboga, Jaime, ed.
  1990 *Ecuador: Guía nacional de turismo 1990/91.* 7th ed. Quito: Teibe Asociados C. A.

Chiriboga, Lucía, and Silvana Caparrini
1994 *Identidades desnudas: Ecuador 1860-1920—La temprana fotografía del indio de los Andes.* Quito: ILDIS–Abya–Yala–Taller Visual.
Cieza de León, Pedro de
1959 [1553] *The Incas of Pedro de Cieza de León.* Ed. Victor Wolfgang von Hagen. Trans. Harriet de Onis. Norman: University of Oklahoma Press.
Cifuentes, Fabricio
1994 Otavaleños en la capital del mundo. *Hoy,* Saturday, January 15, 1994, p. 7-A.
Claus, Luc
1993 Ali Shungu, Ecuadoriaanse indianenmuziek in de Westhoek. Belgian newspaper (exact name unknown), July or August.
Clifford, James
1988 *The Predicament of Culture: Twentieth-Century Ethnography, Literature, and Art.* Cambridge: Harvard University Press.
Coba Andrade, Carlos Alberto G.
1981 *Instrumentos musicales populares registrados in el Ecuador: Tomo I.* Colección Pendoneros no. 46. Otavalo, Ecuador: Instituto Otavaleño de Antropología.
1989 Comentario a una fiesta que ha muerto: El Coraza. *Sarance (Revista del Instituto Otavaleño de Antropología–Centro Regional de Investigaciones)* 13 (August): 99–104.
1992 *Instrumentos musicales populares registrados in el Ecuador: Tomo II.* Colección Pendoneros No. 47. Otavalo, Ecuador: Instituto Otavaleño de Antropología.
1994a *Danzas y bailes en el Ecuador.* 2d ed. Quito: Ediciones Abya-Yala.
1994b Persistencias etnoculturales en la fiesta de San Juan en Otavalo. *Sarance (Revista del Instituto Otavaleño de Antropología–Centro Regional de Investigaciones)* 20 (October): 13–36.
Cobo, Father Bernabe
1979 [1653] *History of the Inca Empire.* Trans. and ed. Roland Hamilton. Austin: University of Texas Press.
1990 [1653] *Inca Religion and Customs.* Trans. Roland Hamilton. Austin: University of Texas Press.
Collier, Jane Fishburne
1974 Women in Politics. In Michelle Zimbalist Rosaldo and Louise Lamphere, eds., *Women, Culture and Society,* pp. 89–96. Stanford: Stanford University Press.
Collier, John, Jr., and Aníbal Buitrón
1949 *The Awakening Valley.* Chicago: University of Chicago Press.
Colloredo-Mansfeld, Rudolf
1994 Architectural Conspicuous Consumption and Economic Change in the Andes. *American Anthropologist* 96, no. 4: 845–865.
1998a "Dirty Indians," Radical *Indígenas,* and the Political Economy of Social Difference in Modern Ecuador. *Bulletin of Latin American Research* 17, no. 2: 185–205.

1998b The Handicraft Archipelago: Consumption, Migration, and the Social Organization of a Transnational Andean Ethnic Group. *Research in Economic Anthropology* (ed. Barry L. Isaac) 19: 31–67.

1999 *The Native Leisure Class: Consumption and Cultural Creativity in the Andes.* Chicago and London: University of Chicago Press.

CONAIE (Confederación de Nacionalidades Indígenas del Ecuador)

1988 *Derechos humanos y solidaridad de los pueblos indígenas.* Quito: CONAIE.

1989 *Las nacionalidades indígenas en el Ecuador: Nuestro proceso organizativo.* 2d ed. Quito: TINCUI-CONAIE.

Conejo, Mario

1995 Los mindalas que migraron. *Azul: Revista Quincenal* (Otavalo) 8 (August 26): 9.

1997 Los migrantes modelan una Nueva Ciudad: El caso de Otavalo. Interview by L. F. Tocagón. In *Identidad indígena en las ciudades*, pp. 121–151. Quito: Fundación Hanns Seidel.

Conejo Maldonado, Mario

1995 El indígena Otavaleño urbana. In José Almeida Vinueza, ed., *Identidades indias en el Ecuador contemporáneo*, pp. 157–185. Serie Pueblos del Ecuador 4. Quito: Ediciones Abya-Yala.

Connerton, Paul

1989 *How Societies Remember.* Cambridge: Cambridge University Press.

Conrad, Peter

1993 Arcadia: Last of the Head Trips. *New York Times Book Review*, June 6, p. 11.

Conterón, Laura

n.d. [1985] Comercialización de tejidos en Ilumán. Thesis, Sexto Curso Comercial, Año Lectivo 1984–1985. Colegio Nacional de Señoritas "República del Ecuador," Otavalo.

Conterón Córdova, Carlos

n.d. [1994] El tejido de la faja, una indumentaria indispensable de la mujer otavaleña. Thesis, Ciencias Sociales, Año Lectivo 1993–1994. Colegio a Distancia "31 de Octubre," Otavalo.

Cooper, Jed Arthur

1965 *The School in Otavalo Society.* Tucson, Ariz.: Panguitch Publications.

Coronel C., Willy

1995 En comité del Yamor se discrimina a indígenas. *Presencia* (Año XIV, Otavalo), 253 (August 19): 1.

Crabb, Mary Katherine

n.d. [1994] Otavalo: A Case Study of "Successful" Ethnic Tourism. Unpublished MS.

Crain, Mary

1990 The Social Construction of National Identity in Highland Ecuador. *Anthropological Quarterly* 63, no. 1 (January): 43–59.

Craps, Marc

1992 Personajes indígenas: Entrevista con Mario Conejo. *Shimishitachi:*

Información y Reflexión sobre Temas Indígenas (Peguche, Ecuador: Centro de Desarrollo Comunitario Ingapirca) 10 (February): 8–15.

Crespi, Muriel

1973 When *Indios* Become *Cholos:* Some Consequences of the Changing Ecuadorian Hacienda. In John W. Bennett, ed., *The New Ethnicity, Perspectives from Ethnology*, pp. 146–166. American Ethnological Society Proceedings. St. Paul, Minn.: West Publishing.

Crick, Malcolm

1989 Representations of International Tourism in the Social Sciences: Sun, Sex, Sights, Savings and Servility. *Annual Review of Anthropology* 18: 307–344.

de Kadt, Emmanuel

1992 Making the Alternative Sustainable: Lessons from Development for Tourism. In Valene L. Smith and William R. Eadington, eds., *Tourism Alternatives: Potentials and Problems in the Development of Tourism*, pp. 47–75. Philadelphia: University of Pennsylvania Press.

de San Pedro, Fray Juan

1992 [1560] *La persecución del demonio: Crónica de los primeros agustinos en el norte de Perú (1560)*. Manuscrito del Archivo de Indias transcrito por Eric E. Deeds. Introducción Teresa Van Ronzelen. Estudios preliminares Luis Millones, John R. Topic, and José L. González. Málaga-México: Algarza-CAMEI.

de Sarte, Estela

1993 Sacos "Made in Ecuador." *El Comercio* (Quito), Saturday, August 21, p. B-4.

de Saussure, Ferdinand

1960 [1949] *Course of General Linguistics*. Trans. W. Baskin. New York: Philosophical Library.

Descola, Philippe

1996 *The Spears of Twilight: Life and Death in the Amazon Jungle*. Trans. Janet Lloyd. New York: New Press/Harper Collins.

Descripción de los pueblos de la jurisdicción del corregimiento de Villar Don Pardo en la provincia de los puruhaes.

1994 [1605] *RHG*, vol. 2, pp. 48–70.

de Vaca, Nuria

1995 Artesanía o comercio? *Azul: Revista Quincenal* (Otavalo) 8 (August 26): 3.

Diario del Norte

n.d. Daily newspaper published in Ibarra, Imbabura, Ecuador.

di Leonardo, Micaela

1991 Introduction: Gender, Culture and Political Economy: Feminist Anthropology in Historical Perspective. In Micaela di Leonardo, ed., *Gender at the Crossroads of Knowledge: Feminist Anthropology in the Postmodern Era*, pp. 1–48. Berkeley, Los Angeles, and Oxford: University of California Press.

Dogar, Rana

1998 Why Can't We Get Away? *Newsweek*, August 3, pp. 40–44.

Eadington, William R., and Valene L. Smith
  1992 Introduction: The Emergence of Alternative Forms of Tourism. In
        Valene L. Smith and William R. Eadington, eds., *Tourism Alterna-
        tives: Potentials and Problems in the Development of Tourism*, pp.
        1–12. Philadelphia: University of Pennsylvania Press.
El Comercio
  n.d.   Daily newspaper published in Quito, Ecuador.
El Universo
  n.d.   Daily newspaper published in Guayaquil, Ecuador.
Enda, Jodi
  1993 Under the Spell of Otavalo. *Philadelphia Inquirer*, Sunday, Octo-
        ber 24, Section R.
Enloe, Cynthia
  1981 Foreword. In John F. Stack, ed., *Ethnic Identities in a Transnational
        World*, pp. xi–xii. Westport, Conn.: Greenwood Press.
  1989 *Bananas, Beaches and Bases: Making Feminist Sense of Interna-
        tional Politics*. Berkeley and Los Angeles: University of California
        Press.
Erisman, H. M.
  1983 Tourism and Cultural Dependency in the West Indies. *Annals of
        Tourism Research* 10, no. 3: 337–361.
Espinosa Fernández de Córdoba, Carlos R.
  1989 La mascarada del Inca: Una investigación acerca del teatro político
        de la colonia. *Miscelánea Histórica Ecuatoriana* (Quito: Museos del
        Banco Central del Ecuador) 2, no. 2: 6–39.
Espinosa [*sic:* correct spelling is Espinoza] Soriano, Waldemar
  1988 *Los Cayambes y Carangues: Siglos XV–XVI, El testimonio de la
        etnohistoria*. 3 vols. Otavalo: Instituto Otavaleño de Antropología.
Espinoza Soriano, Waldemar
  1999 *Ethnohistoria ecuatoriana: Estudios y documentos*. Quito: Edi-
        ciones Abya-Yala.
Fairley, Jan
  1991 "The Blind Leading the Blind": Changing Perceptions of Traditional
        Music, the Case of the Peruvian Ayllu Sulca. In Max Peter Bau-
        mann, ed., *Music in the Dialogue of Cultures: Traditional Music
        and Cultural Policy*, pp. 272–316. Wilhelmshaven, Germany: Flo-
        rian Noetzel Verlag.
Featherstone, Mike
  1990 Global Culture: An Introduction. In Mike Featherstone, ed., *Global
        Culture: Nationalism, Globalization and Modernity*, pp. 1–14.
        Newbury Park, Calif.: Sage Publications.
  1995 *Undoing Culture: Globalization, Postmodernism and Identity*.
        London, Thousand Oaks, Calif., and New Delhi: Sage Publications.
Febres Cordero, Francisco
  1993 Otavalo ¿Como es la cosa? *Hoy*, Tuesday, May 25, p. 1-C.
Feld, Steven
  1995 From Schizophonia to Schismogenesis: The Discourses and Prac-

tices of World Music and World Beat. In George E. Marcus and Fred R. Myers, eds., *The Traffic in Culture: Reconfiguring Art and Anthropology*, pp. 96–126. Berkeley, Los Angeles, and London: University of California Press.

Femenias, Blenda, with Mary Ann Medlin, Lynn A. Meisch, and Elayne Zorn
    1987 *Andean Aesthetics: Textiles of Peru and Bolivia*. Madison: Elvehjem Museum of Art, University of Wisconsin–Madison.

Fisch, Olga
    1985 *El folclor que yo viví: The Folklore through My Eyes*. Bilingual Spanish-English edition. Cuenca, Ecuador: CIDAP.

Frank, Florian
    1995 Otavalo: entre el telar el dólar. *El Comercio*, Wednesday, January 4, p. B-7.

Freedman, Dan
    1996 Data Challenge Image of Illegal Aliens. *San Francisco Examiner*, Friday, January 26, 1996, A-14.

Frith, Simon, ed.
    1989 *World Music, Politics and Social Change*. Manchester and New York: Manchester University Press.

Garzón Guamán, Raúl
    1994 Acercamiento a la chirimía. *Sarance (Revista del Instituto Otavaleño de Antropología Centro Regional de Investigaciones)* 20 (October): 103–120.

Gladhart, Peter Michael, and Emily Winter Gladhart
    1981 *Northern Ecuador's Sweater Industry: Rural Women's Contribution to Economic Development*. Women in International Development Working Paper no. 81/01 (June). East Lansing: Michigan State University, Office of Women in Development.

Glick Schiller, Nina, Linda Basch, and Cristina Blanc-Szanton
    1992 Transnationalism: A New Analytic Framework for Understanding Migration. In Nina Glick Schiller, Linda Basch, and Cristina Blanc-Szanton, eds., *Towards a Transnational Perspective on Migration: Race, Class, Ethnicity and Nationalism Reconsidered*, pp. 1–24. Annals of the New York Academy of Sciences, vol. 645. New York: New York Academy of Sciences.
    1995 From Immigrant to Transmigrant: Theorizing Transnational Migration. *Anthropological Quarterly* 68, no. 1 (January): 48–63.

Goffman, Erving
    1959 *The Presentation of Self in Everyday Life*. Garden City, N.Y.: Doubleday.

Goldman, Laura C.
    1979 Perspectives of Balance: A Study of Health Traditions in Ilumán, Ecuador. M.A. thesis, Department of Anthropology, Goddard College.

Graburn, Nelson, ed.
    1976 *Ethnic and Tourist Arts: Cultural Expressions from the Fourth World*. Berkeley: University of California Press.

Gray, Patrick M., Bernie Krause, Jelle Atema, Roger Payne, Carol Krumhansl, and Luis Baptista
2001 The Music of Nature and the Nature of Music. *Science* 291 (January 5): 52–54.
Greenberg, Arnold, and Harriet Greenberg
1987 *Frommer's South America on $30 a Day. 1987–1988* ed. New York: Prentice-Hall Press.
Guaman Poma de Ayala, Felipe
1980 [1615] *El primer corónica y buen gobierno.* Trans. Jaime L. Urioste; ed. John Murra and Rolena Adorno. Mexico City: Siglo Veintiuno.
Guaña, César
1994 The Province of Imbabura—Otavalo—Her People and Her Age-Old (Millennial) Riches in Handcraft. In César Guaña, ed., *Ecoturismo Otavalo—94'2. 2000,* p. 13. Otavalo: Jatun Pacha Productions.
1996 Y retornan las garzas. *Pueblos Indios* (Otavalo, Ecuador; multilingual ed.) 1, no. 3 (May–June): 7.
Guerrero Gutiérrez, Pablo
1993 Los fandangos. *Sarance (Revista del Instituto Otavaleño de Antropología-Centro Regional de Investigaciones)* 17 (May): 131–142.
Gupta, Akhil, and James Ferguson
1992 Beyond "Culture": Space, Identity, and the Politics of Difference. *Cultural Anthropology* 7, no. 1 (February): 6–23.
Hall, Stuart
1990 Cultural Identity and Diaspora. In Jonathan Rutherford, ed., *Identity: Community, Culture, Difference,* pp. 222–237. London: Lawrence and Wishart.
Hallo, Wilson
1981 *Imágenes del Ecuador del siglo XIX: Juan Agustín Guerrero 1818–1880.* Quito, Ecuador, and Madrid, Spain: Ediciones del Sol y Espasa-Calpe, S.A.
Hannerz, Ulf
1990 Cosmopolitans and Locals in World Culture. In Mike Featherstone, ed., *Global Culture: Nationalism, Globalization and Modernity,* pp. 237–252. Newbury Park, Calif.: Sage Publications.
Hanratty, Dennis M., ed.
1991 *Ecuador: A Country Study.* 3d ed. Area Handbook Series. Washington, D.C.: U.S. Government Printing Office.
Hardin, Garrett, and John Baden
1977 *Managing the Commons.* San Francisco: W. H. Freeman.
Harris, Olivia
1978 Complementarity and Conflict: An Andean View of Women and Men. In J. S. la Fontaine, ed., *Sex and Age as Principles of Social Differentiation,* pp. 21–40. New York: Academic Press.
1986 From Asymmetry to Triangle: Symbolic Transformations in Northern Potosí. In John V. Murra, Nathan Wachtel, and Jacques Revel, eds., *Anthropological History of Andean Polities,* pp. 260–279. Cambridge: Cambridge University Press and Maison des Sciences de l'Homme.

Harrison, Regina
  1989 *Signs, Songs, and Memory in the Andes: Translating Quechua Language and Culture.* Austin: University of Texas Press.
Harvey, David
  1989 *The Condition of Postmodernity: An Enquiry into the Origins of Cultural Change.* Oxford, England, and Cambridge, Mass.: Basil Blackwell.
Hassaurek, Friedrich
  1967 [1867] *Four Years among the Ecuadorians.* Ed. and intro. C. Harvey Gardiner. Carbondale: Southern Illinois University Press.
Healy, Kevin, and Elayne Zorn
  1983 Lake Titicaca's Campesino-Controlled Tourism. *Grassroots Development, Journal of the Inter-American Foundation* 6, no. 2/7: 3–10.
Hobsbawm, Eric
  1983 Introduction: Inventing Tradition. In Eric Hobsbawm and Terence Ranger, eds., *The Invention of Tradition,* pp. 1–15. Cambridge: Cambridge University Press.
Horse Capture, Joseph D.
  1992 Eagle-Feather Headdress. Catalog Entry No. 214. In Evan M. Maurer, *Visions of the People: A Pictorial History of Plains Indian Life,* p. 232. Minneapolis: Minneapolis Institute of Arts.
Hoy
  n.d. Daily newspaper published simultaneously in Quito and Guayaquil, Ecuador.
Indian Textiles from Ecuador
  1958–1959 *Handweaver and Craftsman* 10, no. 1 (Winter): 19–21, 56.
Johnston, Barbara R.
  1990 *Cultural Survival Quarterly: Breaking Out of the Tourist Trap* (Parts One and Two), 14, nos. 1 and 2.
J. Peterman Company
  1994 *The J. Peterman Company Owner's Manual No. 32a* (Fall). Lexington, Ky.: n.p.
Juan, Jorge, and Antonio de Ulloa
  1982 [1826] *Noticias secretas de América.* Parts 1 and 2. Facsimile edition of the publication by David Barry, London, 1826. Madrid: Ediciones Turner; Quito: Librimundi.
Kandell, Jonathan
  1993 Shuttle Capitalism. *Los Angeles Times Magazine,* Sunday, November 14, 1993, pp. 30–34, 46–48.
Kantrowitz, Barbara, and Joshua Cooper Ramo
  1993 A Woodstock for Hackers and "Phreaks." *Newsweek,* August 16, pp. 33–34.
Kinzer, Stephen
  1996 Röderau Journal: Germans in Their Teepees? Naturally. *New York Times,* Tuesday, April 2, p. A-4.
Kipu, el mundo indígena en la prensa ecuatoriana
  n.d. (Biannual reproduction of articles on indigenous affairs published in Ecuadorian newspapers.) Quito: Ediciones Abya-Yala.

Kleymeyer, Charles D.
  1992 Cultural Energy and Grassroots Development. *Grassroots Development: Journal of the Inter-American Foundation* 16, no. 1: 22–31.
Kline, Stephen
  1995 The Play of the Market: On the Internationalization of Children's Culture. *Theory, Culture and Society* 12: 103–129.
Klumpp, Kathleen M.
  1974 El retorno del inga: Una expresión ecuatoriana de la ideología mesiánica andina. In *Cuaderno de historia y arqueología*, pp. 99–135. Guayaquil: La Casa de la Cultura Ecuatoriana, Núcleo de Guayas.
Korovkin, Tanya
  1997 Taming Capitalism: The Evolution of the Indigenous Peasant Economy in Northern Ecuador. *Latin American Research Review* 32, no. 3: 89–110.
Korovkin, Tanya, Vidal Sánchez, and José Isama, comps.
  1994 *Nuestras comunidades ayer y hoy: Historia de las comunidades indígenas de Otavalo. Ñucanchic aillu llactacuna ñaupa, cunan pachapash.* Trans. Luz María del la Torre from Spanish to Quichua. Quito: Abya-Yala.
Kowii, Ariruma
  1992 El derecho internacional y el derecho de los pueblos indios. In E. Ayala et al., *Pueblos indios, estado y derecho*, pp. 213–227. Biblioteca de Ciencias Sociales, vol. 36. Quito: Corporación Editora Nacional–Abya-Yala–CORPEA–Taller Cultural Causanacunchic–ILDIS.
  1998 *Diccionario de nombres Kichwas: Kichwa shutikunamanta shimiyuk panka.* Biblioteca General de Cultura, vol. 9. Quito: Corporación Editora Nacional.
Kyle, David Jané
  n.d. [1993] Peguche: Resultados de encuesta 1993. Unpublished MS.
  1995 The Transnational Peasant: The Social Construction of International Economic Migration from the Ecuadoran Andes. Ph.D. dissertation, Department of Sociology, Johns Hopkins University.
  2000 *Transnational Peasants: Migrations, Networks, and Ethnicity in Andean Ecuador.* Baltimore and London: Johns Hopkins University Press.
La Hora
  n.d. Daily newspaper published in Quito, Ecuador.
Lanfant, Marie-Françoise, John B. Allcock, and Edward M. Bruner, eds.
  1995 *International Tourism: Identity and Change.* London, Thousand Oaks, Calif., and New Delhi: Sage Publications.
Larraín Barros, Horacio
  1980 Demografía y asentamientos indígenas en la sierra norte del Ecuador en el siglo xvi: Estudios etnohistóricos de las fuentes tempranas (1525–1600). *Sarance (Revista del Instituto Otavaleño de Antropología)* 12 (August).

Latham, Aaron
  1994 Walking the Walk in L.A. *New York Times*, Sunday, September 11, 1994, pp. 12, 27.
Lathrap, Donald W., Donald Collier, and Helen Chandra
  1975 *Ancient Ecuador: Culture, Clay and Creativity 3000–300 B.C.* Chicago: Field Museum of Natural History.
Lavenda, Robert H., Emily A. Schultz, et al.
  n.d. [1978] Otavalo 1978: University of Minnesota, Morris, Summer Research Program Reports. Unpublished MS on file at the Instituto Otavaleño de Antropología and the University of Minnesota, Morris.
Leheny, David
  1995 A Political Economy of Asian Sex Tourism. *Annals of Tourism Research* 22, no. 2: 367–384.
Lema A., Germán Patricio
  1995 *Los Otavalos: Cultura y tradición milenarias.* Quito: Ediciones Abya-Yala.
León Mera, Juan
  1983 [1892] *Cantares del pueblo ecuatoriano.* Illus. Joaquín Pinto. Quito: Museo del Banco Central del Ecuador.
Lyotard, Jean-François
  1984 *The Postmodern Condition.* Minneapolis: University of Minnesota Press.
MacCannell, Dean
  1976 *The Tourist: A New Theory of the Leisure Class.* New York: Schoken Books.
  1992 *Empty Meeting Grounds: The Tourist Papers.* London and New York: Routledge.
MacGlobe
  1991 Computer program (version 1.0). Copyright 1991 P.C. Globe, Inc., Tempe, Arizona.
Males, Antonio
  1985 *Villamanta ayllucunapac punta causai: Historia oral de los Imbaya de Quinchuquí–Otavalo 1900–1960.* Quito: Ediciones Abya-Yala.
Malkki, Liisa
  1992 National Geographic: The Rooting of Peoples and the Territorialization of National Identity among Scholars and Refugees. *Cultural Anthropology* 7, no. 1 (February): 24–44.
Manuel, Peter
  1988 *Popular Musics of the Non-Western World: An Introductory Survey.* New York and Oxford, England: Oxford University Press.
Marin, Rick, with Adam Rogers and T. Trent Gegax
  1996 Alien Invasion! *Newsweek*, July 8, pp. 40–46.
Mattelart, Armand
  1993 *Transnationals and the Third World: The Struggle for Culture.* South Hadley, Mass.: Bergin and Garvey.
Mauldin, Chelsea S., ed.
  1995 *Fodor's South America.* New York: Fodor's Travel Publications, Inc.

Maurer, Evan M.
　　1992　*Visions of the People: A Pictorial History of Plains Indian Life.* Minneapolis: Minneapolis Institute of Arts.
McIntyre, Loren
　　1975　*The Incredible Incas and Their Timeless Land.* Washington, D.C.: National Geographic Society.
Meier, Peter C.
　　1981　Peasant Crafts in Otavalo: A Study in Economic Development and Social Change in Rural Ecuador. Ph.D. dissertation, University of Toronto.
Meisch, Lynn A.
　　1980　The Weavers of Otavalo. *Pacific Discovery* (California Academy of Sciences) 33, no. 6 (November–December): 21–29.
　　1987　*Otavalo: Weaving, Costume and the Market.* Quito, Ecuador: Ediciones Libri Mundi.
　　1992　"We Will Not Dance on the Tomb of Our Grandparents": "500 Years of Resistance" in Ecuador. *Latin American Anthropology Review* 4, no. 2: 55–74.
　　1995　Gringas and Otavaleños: Changing Tourist Relations. *Annals of Tourism Research* 22, no. 2: 441–462. Special issue on Gender in Tourism, ed. Margaret Byrne Swain.
　　1996 [1991]　We Are Sons of Atahualpa and We Will Win: Traditional Dress in Otavalo and Saraguro, Ecuador. In Margot Blum Schevill, Janet Catherine Berlo, and Edward B. Dwyer, eds., *Textile Traditions of Mesoamerica and the Andes: An Anthology,* pp. 145–172. Austin: University of Texas Press.
　　1997　Traditional Communities, Transnational Lives: Coping with Globalization in Otavalo, Ecuador. Ph.D. dissertation, Department of Anthropology, Stanford University.
　　1998a　Otavalo, Imbabura Province. In Ann Pollard Rowe, ed., *Costume and Identity in Highland Ecuador,* pp. 50–78. Seattle and London: University of Washington Press; Washington, D.C.: Textile Museum.
　　1998b　The Reconquest of Otavalo, Ecuador: Indigenous Economic Gains and New Power Relations. *Research in Economic Anthropology* (ed. Barry L. Isaac) 19: 11–30.
Meisch, Lynn A., and Laura M. Miller
　　1988　The Case of Rudy Masaquiza and the Salasacas. *Latin American Anthropology Review* 1, no. 1 (Fall).
Miles, Ann
　　1997　The High Cost of Leaving: Illegal Emigration from Cuenca, Ecuador and Family Separation. In Ann Miles and Hans Buechler, eds., *Women and Economic Change: Andean Perspectives,* pp. 55–74. Washington, D.C.: Society for Latin American Anthropology and American Anthropological Association.
Milner, Andrew
　　1991　*Contemporary Cultural Theory: An Introduction.* North Sydney, Australia: Allen and Unwin.

Miranda, María Alejandra
1994 "Tejer es una parte de mí." *Hoy*, p. 8-B.
Mirzoeff, Nicholas
1999 *An Introduction to Visual Culture.* London and New York: Routledge.
Moreno Yánez, Segundo E.
1985 *Sublevaciones indígenas en la Audiencia de Quito, desde comienzos del siglo XVIII hasta finales de la colonia.* Quito: EDIPUCE.
Morgan, Judith
1996 Otavalo's Colorful Indian Market: Legendary Social and Economic Crossroads in Ecuador. *San Francisco Examiner*, Sunday, February 4, 1996, p. T-11.
Morris, Walter F., Jr.
1991 The Marketing of Maya Textiles in Highland Chiapas, Mexico. In Margot Blum Schevill, Janet Catherine Berlo, and Edward B. Dwyer, eds., *Textile Traditions of Mesoamerica and the Andes: An Anthology*, pp. 403–433. New York and London: Garland Publishing.
Mother Jones
1992 (Advertisement.) 17, no. 1 (January–February).
Muratorio, Blanca
1981 Protestantism, Ethnicity and Class in Chimborazo. In Norman E. Whitten, Jr., ed., *Cultural Transformations and Ethnicity in Modern Ecuador*, pp. 506–534. Urbana, Chicago, and London: University of Illinois Press.
1993 Nationalism and Ethnicity: Images of Ecuadorian Indians and the Imagemakers at the Turn of the Nineteenth Century. In Judith D. Toland, ed., *Ethnicity and the State*, pp. 21–54. New Brunswick, N.J., and London: Transaction Publishers.
Murra, John
1989 [1962] Cloth and Its Function in the Inka State. In Annette B. Weiner and Jane Schneider, eds., *Cloth and Human Experience*, pp. 275–302. Washington, D.C., and London: Smithsonian Institution Press.
Muysken, Pieter
1985 Contactos entre quichua y castalleno en el Ecuador. In Segundo E. Moreno Yánez, comp., with Sophia Thyssen, *Memorias del Primer Simposio Europeo sobre Antropología del Ecuador*, pp. 377–452. Quito: Ediciones Abya-Yala.
Nettl, Bruno
1983 *The Study of Ethnomusicology: Twenty-nine Issues and Concepts.* Urbana and Chicago: University of Illinois Press.
1985 *The Western Impact on World Music: Change, Adaptation, and Survival.* New York: Collier Macmillan.
Newson, Linda A.
1995 *Life and Death in Early Colonial Ecuador.* Norman and London: University of Oklahoma Press.
Oberem, Udo
1981 Contribución a la historia del trabajador rural en América Latina: "Conciertos y Huasipungueros" en Ecuador. In S. Moreno Y. and

U. Oberem, *Contribución a la etnohistoria ecuatoriana,* pp. 299–342. Colección Pendoneros no. 20. Otavalo: Instituto Otavaleño de Antropología.

Ode, Kim
   1992 The Pipes of the Andes. *Minneapolis Star Tribune,* Wednesday, August 26, 1992, pp. 1-E, 10-E.

Ong, Walter
   1991 *Orality and Literacy: The Technologizing of the Word.* London: Routledge.

Organization of American States
   1973 *Tourism in the Americas: Road to a Better Life.* Washington, D.C.: OAS General Secretariat.

Orlove, Benjamin S.
   1977 *Alpacas, Sheep, and Men: The Wool Export Economy and Regional Society in Southern Peru.* New York: Academic Press, Inc.

Orlove, Benjamin S., and Henry J. Rutz
   1989 Thinking about Consumption: A Social Economy Approach. In Benjamin S. Orlove and Henry J. Rutz, eds., *The Social Economy of Consumption,* pp. 1–57. Lanham, Md.: University Press of America.

Ortiz de Rozas, Marilu
   1994 Otavalo, centro indígena y capitalista. *El Mercurio* (daily newspaper published in Santiago, Chile), p. D10.

Pandya, Mukul
   1995 Special Report, Travel: All Signs Point East. *Time* 23 (June 12): 42–43.

Parsons, Elsie Clews
   1945 *Peguche: A Study of Andean Indians.* Chicago: University of Chicago Press.

Pascual, Aixa
   1996 Traveler's Advisory. *Time* 148, no. 11 (September 2): 4.

Paz y Miño, Isabel
   1994 Two Tongues Are Better Than One. *Q. Ecuador's English Language Newspaper,* April 9, p. 13.

Pearse, Andrew
   1975 *The Latin American Peasant.* London: Frank Cass and Co., Ltd.

Pearson, Geoffrey
   1985 Lawlessness, Modernity and Social Change. *Theory, Culture and Society* 2, no. 3: 15–35.

Penley, Dennis
   1988 *Paños de Gualaceo.* Cuenca, Ecuador: Centro Interamericano de Artesanías y Artes Populares (CIDAP).

Perkins, John
   1994 The Dream Changers of Otavala. *Shaman's Drum* 35 (Summer): 54–60.

Phelan, John Leddy
   1967 *The Kingdom of Quito in the Seventeenth Century: Bureaucratic Politics in the Spanish Empire.* Madison, Milwaukee, and London: University of Wisconsin Press.

Ponce de León, Sancho Paz
  1992 [1582] Relación y descripción de los pueblos del Partido de Otavalo. *RHG*, vol. 1, pp. 359–371.
Portocarrero T., José Luis
  n.d. [1976] Informe final sobre las ferias de Otavalo y Pimampiro. Unpublished MS in the library of the Instituto Otavaleño de Antropología, Otavalo.
Pratt, Mary Louise
  1992 *Imperial Eyes: Travel Writing and Transculturation.* London and New York: Routledge.
Preston, David A.
  1963 Weavers and Butchers: A Note on the Otavalo Indians of Ecuador. *Man* 63, nos. 175–176 (September): 146–148.
Proaño, Eduardo
  1986 Ecuador: Small, Rich and Majestic. In Audrey Liounis, ed., *Fodor's South America 1986*, pp. 333–362. New York: Fodor's Travel Guides.
Proaño, Fausto Romero
  2000 ¡Inty Raimi en Chicago! *Diario del Norte,* July 30, p. 2.
Q. *Ecuador's English Language Newspaper*
  n.d. Quito.
Rachowiecki, Rob
  1992 *Ecuador and the Galápagos Islands.* Hawthorne, Australia: Lonely Planet Publications.
Rasnake, Roger Neil
  1988 *Domination and Cultural Resistance: Authority and Power among an Andean People.* Durham, N.C., and London: Duke University Press.
Reinhard, Johan
  1991 *Machu Picchu: The Sacred Center.* Lima, Peru: Nuevas Imágenes, S.A.
Requena y Herrera, Francisco
  1994 [1774] Descripción histórica y geográfica de la Provincia de Guayaquil, en el Virreinato de Santa Fe. *RHG*, vol. 2, pp. 502–651.
RHG
  1992, 1994 *Relaciones histórico-geográficas de la Audiencia de Quito.* 2 vols. Introduction and transcription by Pilar Ponce Leiva. Quito: MARKA y Ediciones Abya-Yala.
Riley, Pamela J.
  1988 Road Culture of International Long-Term Budget Travelers. *Annals of Tourism Research* 15, no. 3: 313–328.
Rivera Vélez, Fredy
  1988 *Guangudos: Identidad y sobrevivencia — Obreros indígenas en las fábricas de Otavalo.* Quito: Centro Andino de Acción Popular.
Rivero, Bárbara B.
  1988 Cabello y etnicidad en Cantón Otavalo. In *Ecuador indígena: Estudios arqueológicos y etnográficos de la Sierra Norte*, pp. 175–185. Otavalo: Instituto Otavaleño de Antropología; Quito: Abya-Yala.

Robertson, Roland
  1990 Mapping the Global Condition: Globalization as the Central Con-
        cept. In Mike Featherstone, ed., *Global Culture: Nationalism, Glob-
        alization and Modernity*, pp. 15–30. Newbury Park, Calif.: Sage Pub-
        lications.
  1995 Globalization: Time-Space and Homogeneity-Heterogeneity. In
        Mike Featherstone, Scott Lash, and Roland Robertson, eds., *Global
        Modernities*, pp. 25–44. London, Thousand Oaks, Calif., and New
        Delhi: Sage Publications.
Robinson, Deanna Campbell, Elizabeth B. Buck, Marlene Cuthbert, and the
International Communication and Youth Consortium
  1991 *Music at the Margins: Popular Music and Global Cultural Diver-
        sity.* Newbury Park, Calif., London, and New Delhi: Sage Publica-
        tions.
Rogers, Elizabeth Marberry
  1998 Ethnicity, Property and the State: Legal Rhetoric and the Politics
        of Community in Otavalo, Ecuador. *Research in Economic Anthro-
        pology* (ed. Barry L. Isaac) 19: 69–113.
Rogers, Mark S.
  1995 Images of Power and the Power of Images: Identity and Place in
        Ecuadorian Shamanism. Ph.D. dissertation, Department of Anthro-
        pology, University of Chicago.
  1998 Spectacular Bodies: Folklorization and the Politics of Identity in
        Ecuadorian Beauty Pageants. *Journal of Latin American Anthro-
        pology* 3, no. 2: 54–85.
Rosaldo, Renato
  1989 *Culture and Truth: The Remaking of Social Analysis.* Boston: Bea-
        con Press.
Rossel, Pierre
  1988 Tourism and Cultural Minorities: Double Marginalisation and Sur-
        vival Strategies. In Pierre Rossel, ed., *Tourism: Manufacturing the
        Exotic*, pp. 1–20. Document 61. Copenhagen, Denmark: Interna-
        tional Work Group for Indigenous Affairs.
Rowe, Ann Pollard
  1977 *Warp-Patterned Weaves of the Andes.* Washington, D.C.: Textile
        Museum.
Rowe, Ann Pollard, ed.
  1986 *The Junius B. Bird Conference on Andean Textiles, April 7th and
        8th, 1984.* Washington, D.C.: Textile Museum.
  1998 *Costume and Identity in Highland Ecuador.* Seattle and London:
        University of Washington Press; Washington, D.C.: Textile Mu-
        seum.
Rowe, John Howland
  1963 [1946] Inca Culture at the Time of the Spanish Conquest. In
        Julian H. Steward, ed., *Handbook of South American Indians, Vol. 2,
        The Andean Civilizations*, pp. 183–330. New York: Cooper Square
        Publishers, Inc.

Rubio Orbe, Gonzalo
1956 *Punyaro, estudio de antropología social y cultural de una comunidad indígena y mestiza.* Quito: Casa de la Cultura Ecuatoriana.

Rueda Novoa, Rocio
1988 *El obraje de San Joseph de Peguchi.* Quito: Ediciones Abya-Yala–TEHIS.

Rymland, Lizbeth
1994 Ecstasy in Ecuador: Experiences with Curanderos and Plant Teachers. *Shaman's Drum* 34 (Spring): 38–51.

Salinas, Raúl
1954 Manual Arts in Ecuador. *América Indígena* 14, no. 4: 315–326.

Salomon, Frank
1981 [1973] Weavers of Otavalo. In Norman E. Whitten, Jr., ed., *Cultural Transformations and Ethnicity in Modern Ecuador*, pp. 420–449. Urbana, Chicago, and London: University of Illinois Press.
1986 *Native Lords of Quito in the Age of the Incas: The Political Economy of North Andean Chiefdoms.* New York and Cambridge: Cambridge University Press.

Samaniego Salazar, Filoteo
1977 *Ecuador pintoresco: Acuarelas de Joaquín Pinto seleccionadas y comentadas por Filoteo Samaniego Salazar.* Quito: Salvat Editores Ecuatoriana, S.A.

Santiestevan, Gaspar
1994 [1808] Descripción del pueblo de Otavalo. *RHG*, vol. 2, pp. 739–744.

Schafer, Murray R.
1977 *The Tuning of the World.* New York: Alfred A. Knopf.

Schechter, John Mendell
1982 Music in a Northern Ecuadorian Highland Locus: Diatonic Harp Genres, Harpists and Their Ritual Junction in the Quechua Child's Wake. Ph.D. dissertation, University of Texas at Austin.
1992a *The Indispensable Harp: Historical Development, Modern Roles, Configurations, and Performance Practices in Ecuador and Latin America.* Kent, Ohio, and London: Kent State University Press.
1992b Latin America/Ecuador. In Jeff Todd Titon, general ed., *Worlds of Music: An Introduction to the Music of the World's Peoples*, pp. 376–428. 2d ed. New York, Toronto, Oxford, Singapore, and Sydney: Schirmer Books, a Division of Macmillan, Inc.

Scheper-Hughes, Nancy
1996 Theft of Life: The Globalization of Organ Stealing Rumors. *Anthropology Today* 12, no. 3 (June): 3–11.

Schevill, Margot Blum
1986 *Costume as Communication: Ethnographic Costumes and Textiles from Middle America and the Central Andes of South America.* Mount Hope Grant, Bristol, R.I.: Haffenreffer Museum of Anthropology, Brown University.

Schevill, Margot Blum, Janet Catherine Berlo, and Edward B. Dwyer, eds.
1996 [1991] *Textile Traditions of Mesoamerica and the Andes: An Anthology.* Austin: University of Texas Press.

Schiller, Herbert I.
   1976 *Communication and Cultural Domination.* White Plains: IASP.
Schneider, Jane
   1994 In and Out of Polyester: Desire, Disdain and Global Fibre Competitions. *Anthropology Today* 10, no. 4 (August): 2–10.
Schultz, Emily A., et al.
   n.d. [1978] Tourism in Otavalo. In Robert H. Lavenda and Emily A. Schultz, eds., Otavalo 1978: University of Minnesota, Morris, Summer Research Program Reports. Unpublished MS on file at the Instituto Otavaleño de Antropología, Otavalo, and the University of Minnesota, Morris.
Scott, James C.
   1990 *Domination and the Arts of Resistance: Hidden Transcripts.* New Haven: Yale University Press.
Seiler-Baldinger, Annemarie
   1988 Tourism in the Upper Amazon and Its Effects on the Indigenous Population. In Pierre Rossel, ed., *Tourism: Manufacturing the Exotic*, pp. 177–193. Document 61. Copenhagen, Denmark: International Work Group for Indigenous Affairs.
Silk, Steve
   1994 Market in Andes a Shopper's Paradise. *Arizona Republic*, Sunday, July 3, p. T2.
Silver, Ira
   1993 Marketing Authenticity in Third World Countries. *Annals of Tourism Research* 20: 302–318.
Silverblatt, Irene
   1987 *Moon, Sun and Witches: Gender Ideologies and Class in Inca and Colonial Peru.* Princeton, N.J.: Princeton University Press.
Slobin, Mark
   1993 *Subcultural Sounds: Micromusics of the West.* Hanover and London: Wesleyan University Press and University Press of New England.
   1994 Music in Diaspora: The View from Euro-America. *Diaspora* 3, no. 3 (Winter): 243–252.
Slobin, Mark, and Jeff Todd Titon
   1992 The Music-Culture as a World of Music. In Jeff Todd Titon, gen. ed., *Worlds of Music: An Introduction to the Music of the World's Peoples*, pp. 1–15. 2d ed. New York, Toronto, Oxford, Singapore, and Sydney: Schirmer Books, a Division of Macmillan, Inc.
Smith, Valene L.
   1989 Introduction. In Valene L. Smith, ed., *Hosts and Guests: The Anthropology of Tourism*, pp. 1–17. 2d ed. Philadelphia: University of Pennsylvania Press.
Smith, Valene L., and William R. Eadington, eds.
   1992 *Tourism Alternatives: Potentials and Problems in the Development of Tourism.* Philadelphia: University of Pennsylvania Press.
Snyder, Gary
   1990 *The Practice of the Wild.* San Francisco: North Point Press.

Sollors, Werner
1995 [1986] Who Is Ethnic? In Bill Ashcroft, Gareth Griffiths, and Helen Tiffin, eds., *The Post-Colonial Studies Reader*, pp. 219–222. London and New York: Routledge.

Sontag, Deborah
1993 Unlicensed Peddlers, Unfettered Dreams. *New York Times*, Monday, June 14, 1993, pp. A1–B2.

Stack, John F., Jr.
1981 Ethnicity and Transnational Relations: An Introduction. In John F. Stack, Jr., ed., *Ethnic Identities in a Transnational World*, pp. 3–15. Westport, Conn.: Greenwood Press.

Stark, Louisa R.
1981 Folk Models of Stratification and Ethnicity in the Highlands of Northern Ecuador. In Norman E. Whitten, Jr., ed., *Cultural Transformations and Ethnicity in Modern Ecuador*, pp. 387–401. Urbana, Chicago, and London: University of Illinois Press.
1985a Ecuadorian Highland Quechua: History and Current Status. In Harriet E. Manelis Klein and Louisa R. Stark, eds., *South American Indian Languages: Retrospect and Prospect*, pp. 443–480. Austin: University of Texas Press.
1985b The Role of Women in Peasant Uprisings in the Ecuadorian Highlands. In Jeffrey Ehrenreich, ed., *Political Anthropology in Ecuador: Perspectives from Indigenous Cultures*, pp. 3–20. Albany: Society for Latin American Anthropology and Center for the Caribbean and Latin America, State University of New York at Albany.

Starn, Orin
1992 Missing the Revolution: Anthropologists and the War in Peru. In George E. Marcus, ed., *Rereading Cultural Anthropology*, pp. 152–180. Durham, N.C., and London: Duke University Press.

Stephen, Lynn
1991a Export Markets and the Effects on Indigenous Craft Production: The Case of the Weavers of Teotitlán del Valle, Mexico. In Margot Blum Schevill, Janet Catherine Berlo, and Edward B. Dwyer, eds., *Textile Traditions in Mesoamerica and the Andes*, pp. 381–402. New York: Garland Publishing.
1991b *Zapotec Women*. Austin: University of Texas Press.
1993 Weaving in the Fast Lane: Class, Ethnicity, and Gender in Zapotec Craft Commercialization. In June Nash, ed., *Crafts in the World Market: The Impact of Global Exchange on Middle American Artisans*, pp. 25–58. Albany, N.Y.: SUNY.

Stern, Steve J.
1982 *Peru's Indian Peoples and the Challenge of Spanish Conquest: Huamanga to 1640*. Madison: University of Wisconsin Press.

Stevenson, William Bennett
1825 *A Historical and Descriptive Narrative of Twenty Years' Residence in South America*. Vol. 2. London: Hurst, Robinson, and Co.

Stocking, George W., Jr.
   1982 [1968] *Race, Culture and Evolution: Essays in the History of Anthropology.* Chicago: University of Chicago Press.
Stokes, Martin, ed.
   1994 *Ethnicity, Identity and Music: The Musical Construction of Place.* Oxford, England, and Providence, R.I.: Berg.
Stoll, David
   1990 *Is Latin America Turning Protestant? The Politics of Evangelical Growth.* Berkeley, Los Angeles, and Oxford: University of California Press.
Straub, Sydney Patricia
   1994 From Otavalo to the Student Union. *Metropolitan* (Metropolitan State College of Denver), January 28, pp. 12–13.
Stutzman, Ronald
   1981 El Mestizaje: An All-Inclusive Ideology of Exclusion. In Norman E. Whitten, Jr., ed., *Cultural Transformations and Ethnicity in Modern Ecuador,* pp. 45–94. Urbana, Chicago, and London: University of Illinois Press.
Swain, Margaret Byrne
   1993 Women Producers of Ethnic Art. *Annals of Tourism Research* 20, no. 1: 32–51.
Taussig, Michael
   1987 *Shamanism, Colonialism, and the Wild Man: A Study in Terror and Healing.* Chicago and London: University of Chicago Press.
Taylor, Timothy D.
   1997 *Global Pop: World Music, World Markets.* London and New York: Routledge.
Tello Espinosa, Rolando
   1996a EE. UU.: 93% pide amparo. *El Comercio,* Saturday, July 13, p. C-7.
   1996b Migrantes: Una confesión en Brooklyn. *El Comercio,* Friday, July 12, p. A-7.
Terán, Benjamín
   1991 Opinión: Los indios plásticos. *Shimishitachi: Información y Reflexión sobre Temas Indígenas* (Peguche, Ecuador: Centro de Desarrollo Comunitario Ingapirca) 9 (December): 20–22.
Tice, Karin E.
   1995 *Kuna Crafts, Gender, and the Global Economy.* Austin: University of Texas Press.
Titon, Jeff Todd, ed.
   1992 *Worlds of Music: An Introduction to the Music of the World's Peoples.* 2d ed. New York: Schirmer Books, a Division of Macmillan, Inc.
Torero Fernández de Córdova, Alfredo
   1974 *El quechua y la historia social andina.* Lima: Universidad Ricardo Palma.
Tramo, Mark Jude
   2001 Music of the Hemispheres. *Science* 291 (January 5): 54–56.

Trouillot, Michel-Rolph

1991 Anthropology and the Savage Slot: The Poetics and Politics of Otherness. In Richard G. Fox, ed., *Recapturing Anthropology: Working in the Present*, pp. 17–44. Santa Fe, N. Mex.: School of American Research Press.

Turino, Thomas

1991 The State and Andean Musical Production in Peru. In Greg Urban and Joel Sherzer, eds., *Nation-States and Indians in Latin America*, pp. 259–285. Austin: University of Texas Press.

1993 *Moving Away from Silence: Music of the Peruvian Altiplano and the Experience of Urban Migration*. Chicago and London: University of Chicago Press.

Tylor, Edward B.

1920 *Primitive Cultures: Researches in the Development of Mythology, Philosophy, Religion, Language, Art and Custom*. 2 vols. New York: G. P. Putnam's Sons.

Tyrer, Robson Brines

1976 The Demographic and Economic History of the Audiencia of Quito: Indian Population and the Textile Industry, 1600–1800. Ph.D. dissertation, Department of History, University of California, Berkeley.

Ulcuango, Neptali, Floresmilo Tamba, Mario Mullo, and Guillermo Churuchumbi

1993 *Historia de la organización indígena en Pichincha*. Cayambe: Abya-Yala.

Vallejo Pérez, Gustavo

1993 *This Is Ecuador: What, Where and When for the Tourist* (Quito) 26, no. 284 (August).

van den Berghe, Pierre L.

1974 Introduction; and The Use of Ethnic Terms in the Peruvian Social Science Literature. In Pierre L. Van den Berghe, ed., *Class and Ethnicity in Peru*, pp. 1–22. Leiden: E. J. Brill.

1992 Tourism and the Ethnic Division of Labor. *Annals of Tourism Research* 19, no. 2: 234–249.

1994 *The Quest for the Other: Ethnic Tourism in San Cristóbal, Mexico*. Seattle and London: University of Washington Press.

Van Der Spek, Jo

1993 Quichuas en un circo europeo. *Hoy*, Sunday, September 26, p. 6-C.

Varese, Stefano

1991 Think Locally, Act Globally. *Report on the Americas: The First Nations 1492–1992* 25, no. 3 (December): 13–17.

Villavicencio R., Gladys

1973 *Relaciones interétnicas en Otavalo—Ecuador: ¿una nacionalidad india en formación?* Mexico City: Instituto Indigenista Interamericana.

von Hornbostel, Erich M., and Curt Sachs

1992 [1961] Classification of Musical Instruments. In Helen Myers, ed.,

Ethnomusicology: An Introduction, pp. 444–461. New York and London: W. W. Norton and Co.

von Lindert, Paul, and Otto Verkoren
    1994 *Bolivia: A Guide to the People, Politics and Culture*. London: Latin American Bureau.

Waldo, Myra
    1976 *Myra Waldo's Travel Guide to South America*. Revised and updated. New York: Collier Books.

Wallerstein, Immanuel
    1974 *The Modern World System: Capitalist Agriculture and the Origins of the European World-Economy in the Sixteenth Century*. New York: Academic Press.

Wallis, Roger, and Krister Malm
    1984 *Big Sounds from Small Peoples: The Music Industry in Small Countries*. London: Constable and Co., Ltd.

Walter, Lynn
    1981 Otavaleño Development, Ethnicity and National Integration. *América Indígena* 41, no. 2 (April–June): 319–337.

Weber, Max
    1947 *The Theory of Social and Economic Organization*. Trans. A. M. Henderson and Talcott Parsons. New York: Free Press.

Weinstock, Steven
    1970 Ethnic Conceptions and Relations of Otavalo Indian Migrants in Quito, Ecuador. *Anuario Indigenista* 30 (December): 156–167.

Whitten, Norman E., Jr.
    1976 *Ecuadorian Ethnocide and Indigenous Ethnogenesis: Amazonian Resurgence amidst Andean Colonialism*. Document 23. Copenhagen, Denmark: International Work Group for Indigenous Affairs.
    1986 [1974] *Black Frontiersmen: Afro-Hispanic Culture of Ecuador and Colombia*. Prospect Heights, Ill.: Waveland Press.

Wilk, Richard
    1995 Learning to be Local in Belize: Global Systems of Common Difference. In Daniel Miller, ed., *Worlds Apart: Modernity through the Prism of the Local*, pp. 110–133. London and New York: Routledge.

Windmeyer, Jeroen
    1998 *Modern Traditions: The Otavaleños of Ecuador*. Amsterdam: CNWS/CEDLA.

Wolf, Eric R.
    1982 *Europe and the People without History*. Berkeley, Los Angeles, and London: University of California Press.

Worsley, Peter
    1990 Models of the Modern World-System. In Mike Featherstone, ed., *Global Culture: Nationalism, Globalization and Modernity*, pp. 83–95. Newbury Park, Calif.: Sage Publications.

Yanagisako, Sylvia, and Carol Delaney
    1995 Naturalizing Power. In Sylvia Yanagisako and Carol Delaney, eds., *Naturalizing Power: Essays in Feminist Cultural Analysis*, pp. 1–22. New York and London: Routledge.

Discography

Note: The group name is listed first, followed by the members' names (when available) in brackets. For Otavalo artists and groups I have given as much information as possible about their recordings. Spellings are given as they appear in the originals. The following audio sources contain addresses, phone numbers, e-mail and web addresses, and other contact information that has not been verified by the author. They may not be functional. In addition, the material below is presented as it appears on the covers of the works and has not been edited for consistency of format.

$33\frac{1}{3}$ RPM Long-Playing Records

Conjunto Indígena Folklórico Indoamérica [Enrique Atuntaquimba, Alfonso Cachiguango, Segundo Gramal, Lucita Pichamba, Alejandro Plaza, Gonzalo Vinueza]

    n.d. [1976] *Alegrías de Imbabura, Vol. 3.* Producciones COLOSAL, Ecuador.

Conjunto Indígena "Peguche"

    1977 *Folklore de mi tierra, Conjunto Indígena "Peguche."* Industria Fonográfica Ecuatoriana S.A. (IFESA), Guayaquil, Ecuador. 330-0063.

    1979 [Integrantes: Ema Lema, Antonio Lema C., Rafael Lema C., Roberto Lema, Francisco Lema, Alberto Perugachi, José Quimbo P. (Director Musical), Isabel Remache; plus 18 dancers] *Mushuc Huaira Huacamujun.* Industria Fonográfica Ecuatoriana S.A. (IFESA), Guayaquil, Ecuador. 339-0651.

    1986 [Integrantes: Antonio Lema (Arado), Rafael Lema (Cumba muchila), Marcelo Lema, Rolando Lema (Churi), Marco Lema Q., Martha Santacruz, Antonio Moreta (Huaichuro), Ernesto Amaguaña, Marcelo Lema Q., Carlos Perugachi (Papacho), José Quimbo (Taita cultura)] *Huiñai Causai.* Producción del Centro Cultural Peguche. Realización y Dirección: José Quimbo, Coordinador del Centro Cultural Peguche. Grabación y Mezclaje: Estudios SONOX Quito. IFESA, Guayaquil, Ecuador. 339-0652.

Grupo Típico de Luis Aníbal Granja

    1970 *Llacta-Pura: Exitos del Folklore Ecuatoriano.* IFESA, Guayaquil, Ecuador. Discos Granja. LP 12042.

Inca-Taki [Eduardo Gonzáles, Marco Campos, Patricio Campos, Miguel Salazar, Alfonso Gualsaquí]

    n.d. [1978] *Alegrías de Imbabura, Vol. 4.* Fábrica de Discos S.A. (FADISA), Quito, Ecuador.

La Banda de Andrade Marín

    1989 *Viva la fiesta con la Banda de Andrade Marín.* Producciones Zapata. Fabricación ordenada por Lda. Zapata Palma, Quito. Arr. y Dir.: José Beltrán. FEDISCOS, Quito, Ecuador. LP-13515.

Los Calchakis (performing music by Mikis Theodorakis)

    1973 *State of Siege, Original Soundtrack Recording.* A film by Costa-Gavras. Columbia Records/CBS, New York. S 32352.

Los Calchakis y Alfredo de Robertis
  1973 *Música indígena de América.* Discos CBS S.A. Colombia. S.A.
       144400.
Los Corazas [Sr. Mena e Hijos]
  n.d. [ca. 1969] *Raza de bronce.* IFESA, Guayaquil, Ecuador. Discos Granja.
       LP 12008.
  1982 *Aires de mi tierra: Música folklórica Ecuatoriana.* FEDISCOS,
       Guayaquil, Ecuador. LP 50081-A.
Los Pucara [Rubén Usiña, director; José Morales, César Maigua, Ernesto
Males]
  1977 *Canción y Huayno.* FEDISCOS, Guayaquil, Ecuador. LP 25063.
       Fabricación ordenada por Studio 2. Arr. y Dir.: Ney Moreira. One $33\frac{1}{3}$
       RPM LP record.
Los Ulpianinos [Clímaco Vaca, director; Edgar Hidrobo A., Luis H. Hidrobo,
Galo Guzmán, Juan Martínez]
  1981 *Añoranza: Alegrías del Imbabura.* Vol. 6. Producciones COLOSAL.
       IFESA, Guayaquil, Ecuador. Producción ordenada por Chiluiza Rhea
       Hnos. 376-0004.
Lucho Soto y su Conjunto Imbabureño
  n.d. [1979 or 1980] *Alegrías del Imbabura.* Vol. 5. Producciones COLO-
       SAL. Ecuador.
Ñanda Mañachi [Azucena Perugachi, Rosa Sandoval, Zoila Saravino, Alfonso
Cachiguango, Juan Cayambe, Alberto Chuquin, Luis Fichamba, Carlos Perugachi, Pedro Tubumbango]
  1979 [Azucena Perugachi, Alfonso Cachiguango, Carlos Perugachi,
       Guillermo Contreras, y Bolivia Manta, con la participación de
       Chopin Thermes] *Ñanda Mañachi 2 (Préstame el camino).* Grabado
       en Ibarra. Producción por Chopin Thermes. LLAQUILLA—Indus-
       tria Fonográfica Ecuatoriana S.A. (IFESA), Guayaquil, Ecuador. 339-
       0502.
  1983 *Bolivia Manta reencuentra: Churay, Churay!* Grabado en Colonia,
       Alemania, 1982. FEDISCOS, Guayaquil, Ecuador. LP—59003.
  1984 [1973–1977] *Ñanda Mañachi 1 (Préstame el camino).* Grabación
       por Chopin Thermes entre 1973–1977. Edición final por Chopin
       Thermes y Leonardo Lasso, 13 de julio de 1984. LLAQUILLA—
       Industria Fonográfica Ecuatoriana S.A. (IFESA), Guayaquil, Ecua-
       dor. 339-0504.
  1988 *Internacional.* Director: Alfonso Cachiguango. Grabado: Estudios
       Sysmo Records, Paris. Producción Musical: FUSA Recors. Fabricado
       y Distribuido por: INMUSA, Guayaquil y Quito. Edición: Estudios
       "FUSA" Quito. LP-02-001.
Orquesta Típica "Rumba Habana" de Cotacachi [Intérpretantes: Enrique
Montenegro, Guillermo Grijalva, Rodrigo Grijalva, Alberto Haro, Alfonso
Ale Castro, José Moreno, Arturo Toro, Diego Moreno, Tarquino Saavedra]
  1983 *Cotacachi Tierra Mia.* Vol. 3. Arreg. y Direc.: Guillermo Grijalva.
Quinchuquimanda Imbayacuna [Músicos Participantes: Segundo Terán,
Tixi; José Lechón, Jefe; Segundo Cotacachi, Berraco; José Saravino, Teniente;

Segundo Maigua, Carchi; Segundo Chiza, Chileno; Jorge Cotacachi, Mochila; Humberto Visarrea, Pajarito; Ernesto Males, Ocótero; Mariano Cachimuel, Chavo; Alfonso Cachiguango; Azucena Perugachi; Rafael Cotacachi; Enrique Males]

    1979 *Llaquiclla: Músicos populares de la provincia de Imbabura.* Arr. y Dir. Mus.: Enrique Males. Fabricación Ord. por Enrique Males y Rosana Anaya—Ibarra. Grabación: Chopin Thermes. Las grabaciones fueron realizadas en Ibarra durante las vísperas de los inicios de las cosechas del maíz, en el campo del Tambo, y en diferentes comunas de Imbabura, Ecuador, 1979. FEDISCOS, Guayaquil—Ecuador. LP 5330-A.

Runallacta [Enrique Flores, Humberto Lema, Alberto Perugachi, Humberto Sinchiko]

    1988 *Causay.* Grabación: Iglesia Saint Pancrace de la Batie Nueve (Haute Alpes) Gap France, por Acousti Studio, Paris, France. INMELSA, Quito, Ecuador. LP 01. 029.

Urubamba [Peruvian musicians, formerly Los Incas]

    1974 *Urubamba.* Columbia Records, New York KG 32896. Produced by Paul Simon.

Tape Cassettes

"Cantores del Rey" [Pedro, Francisco, Segundo, José, Alberto y Julián Guamán, de Pulucate, Chimborazo]

    n.d. *Grande es El Señor.* Vol. 7. Estudio "Salem," Guayaquil, Ecuador. [Bought in Otavalo in September 1994.]

Charijayac [Amahua Morales, Yuyay Tituaña, Rupay Cachiguango, Sayri Cotacachi, Quipus Cotacachi, Raymi Tituaña, Chasqui Tituaña]

    1985 *Ajcha Suni.* Fabricado por SONIDUPLEX, S.L. Barcelona. Editado por E.C.B. Records, Pasaje Garrofers, 4. 08026 Barcelona [Spain]. EC 1010. Dep. Legal B. 19604/85.

    1986 *Cita en el sol.* [Originally recorded in Barcelona, Spain. Ecuadorian copy.]

    1987 *Cielo Rosa: Inca-Quechua.* Fabricado por SONIDUPLEX, S.L. Barcelona. Editado por E.C.B. Records, Pasaje Garrofers, 4. 08026 Barcelona [Spain]. EC 1027. Dep. Legal B. 9602/87.

    1989 *Otavalo y . [punto].* Fabricado por SONIDUPLEX, S.A. Barcelona. Editado por E.C.B. Records, Pasaje Garrofers, 4. 08026 Barcelona EC 1043. Dep. Legal B. 24576/89.

Ecuador Inkas

    1993 *Llaqtaymanta: Traditional Music from the Andes.* A-31894. No locale or recording company given. Contact: Ecuador Inkas, P.O. Box 13093, Los Angeles, CA 90013. (818) 242-8210, (818) 249-8997. Contact in New York: Raúl Santillán, (718) 397-1304. 30-46-90 St. East Elmhurst, N.Y.

Fichamba [Jess]

    1991 *Lo nuestro.* FEDISCOS—Ecuador. Cass. 59. 027.

Karu Ñan [Director: Humberto Córdova; Integrantes: H. Córdova, O. Ruiz, H. Chico, S. Conejo, Y. Cruz, H. Sarabino, L. Cangos]

   n.d.   *Ecuador Tahuantinsuyo.* Vol. 3. Instrumentos: Guitarra, violín, charango, quenas, quenillas, antara, rondador, zampoñas, bombo, chagchas, mandolín. Contactos: España 98/500407 Oviedo—Francia 60130759 París—Bélgica 02/374618 Bruxelles—Portugal 76/341271 —Ecuador 593-2-922757 Otavalo. [Bought in Otavalo in August 1996.]

Los Kjarkas

   1989   *Los Kjarkas al Ecuador: El Picaflor.* FEDISCOS—Guayaquil, Ecuador. Fabricación ordenada por José Johnny Echeverría. Cass. 5717.

Ñucanchi Ñan

   1995   *Mejores éxitos: Vida por la vida.* No locale given. C.V. Records Estudios.

Otavalo Manta

   1991   *Sentimiento noble.* FEDISCOS—Guayaquil, Ecuador. Cass. 41. 707.

Quichua Marka

   1991   *Runa Tushuri.* FEDISCOS—Ecuador. Cass. 41. 706.

Sajama [Rubén Ortiz (Chile), José Arciniegas (Ecuador), Mario Cajas (Ecuador), William Sepúlveda (Bolivia), Chjochjo West (Canada)]

   1992   *Dreams.* Vol. 2. Recorded in December 1992. Los Angeles area contact: telephone (213) 934-9456. [Bought in Los Angeles at Citywalk, January 1994.]

Winiaypa [Humberto Gramal, Segundo Gramal, Héctor Maigua, César Santillán; Colaboración: J. Alexis Maigua]

   n.d.   *"Sueños": Music from the Andes.* Contactos: Obere Königstr. 50, 8600 Bamberg [Germany], Tel. 0951—22047. [Bought in Otavalo in July 1995.]

Winiaypa [Humberto Gramal, Segundo Gramal, Richard Maldonado]

   n.d.   *Quichua Mashis, Music from the Andes.* Made in Germany by Record Partner Hamburg. Arp. 24611. Contact: 10013 Holman Rd. N.W., Seattle, WA 98177, (206) 440-1316. [Bought in Otavalo in August 1995.]

Yahuar Wauky [José Cachimuel, Manuel Cachimuel, Alberto Cachimuel, Roberto Cachimuel, Anita Cachimuel, Rosita Cachimuel, Carlos Cachimuel, Pedro Vásquez, Carlos Burga]

   n.d.   *Yarihuangui Yarina: Native Music from Ecuador.* YW 1002. Contactos: Alberto Cachimuel, Calle Bolívar—Quiroga—Telf. 920410, Otavalo, Ecuador. [Bought in Otavalo in July 1995.]

Compact Discs

Americamanta [Gustavo Sandoval, Milton Sandoval, Wilman Maygua]

   1994   *Mundo Nuevo: The Music of the Andes "Diferente."* Fábrica: Ibermemory, S.A. Grupo Iberofon. Edita: Edivox, S.L. Sant Agustí, 3– 5 08012 Barcelona. Tel: (93) 237 30 56 / 415 36 00. Fax: (93) 415 45 54. Contactos: Americamanta en: Ecuador—P.O. Box No. 22, Otavalo, Tel: 02-920 686. Italia—Pizza Mascani, No. 67 Firenze, Tel: 055-4361280. España—Crta del Prat 32 No. 4a., Barcelona. Tel: 908-591536. USA—Rankin Skinner 606-7448376. Suiza—David Estrella, 021-206221. Japon—Chieko Sakurai, 775-797 573. Depósito Legal: B-2. 258-1. 994. CD/EDIVOX-509.

American Inkas [Actual musicians are members of Ñanda Mañachi and Ñu-canchi Ñan]
    1992 *Los Andes: Original Version aus Bolivien • Perú • Ecuador • Chile.* Record Partner, Hamburg, Deutschland. RP 12462. Produced by Ecuador Inkas (Segundo Amaguaña, Sergio Narea).

Chacras
    n.d. *Volume 4. Tierra Nuestra: Otavalo.* CDLC-4. Canada. [Bought in Otavalo in July 1996.]
    1996a *New Generation from the Andes.* Manufactured and printed by Disc Makers, Pennsauken, N.J., USA. Phone/Fax: 718/617-1843, N.Y. EE. UU. Bolivar 1303, Otavalo, Ecuador. DIDX 041225 100019.
    1996b [Integrantes: Segundo Muenala L. (Jr.), Roberto Muenala L., Henry Muenala L., Hernan Lema C.] *Traditional Music from the Andes (Vol. VI).* Manufactured and printed by Disc Makers, Pennsauken, N.J., USA. Phone/Fax: 718/617-1843, N.Y. EE. UU. Bolivar 1303 8, Otavalo, Ecuador. Phone/Fax: 0115936 920-410. DIDX 041229 100121.
    1998 *Amiga Mujer: Authentic Folklore Music of the Andes.* Recording Studio: Chacras Native Indian Sound. For Booking: 3810 N. Whipple St. Chicago, IL 60618, Tel. 773/279-8036. Manufactured and printed by Disc Makers, Pennsauken, N.J., USA.

Charijayac [Amahua Morales, Yuyay Tituaña, Rupay Cachiguango, Sayri Co-tacachi, Quipus Cotacachi, Raymi Tituaña, Chasqui Tituaña]
    1992 *Quemando las nubes.* E.C.B. Records C.B., Barcelona, España. C.D. 1002. Contactos: Grupo Charijayac; Incas Artesanía: c/Boquería, 21. 08002 Barcelona. Tel. (93) 301 97 34. Fax: (93) 301 97 34.
    1995 *Charijayac, Made in Ecuador: Sus mejores éxitos.* E.C.B. Records C.B. [Barcelona]. DL. B-27-629-95. Made in E.U.

Charijayac—Winiaypa—Dave West
    n.d. *Jailli.* Produced by Sayri Cotacachi and Jailli. Recorded in Bar Studio, Sabadell Barcelona. For information & booking: Lea Boi-cel Management Canada (514) 425-1404. CWDW-0197-2. Made in Canada. [Bought in the Otavalo market in 1997.]

Chayag [Jaime Parades, Pedro Parades, Patricio Parades, Luis Palacios]
    1996 *The Best of South American Folk Today: Ecuador.* Arreglos y di-rección musical Chayag. Vintage Recording Studio, Czech Republic. Contact fono: 0042/0/601 235 844, Czech Republic. PAR 004-2.

Chayana'k' [Integrantes: Suny Cáceres, Rumy Perugachy, Chayak Perugachy, César—Cáceres, Yuyary—Cáceres]
    1995 *Quichua Imaginación.* Grabado en Estudio Sonocentro, c/. Ignacio de Ros, 7. Barcelona (Spain). Tel. (93) 352 85 94. Fab. por: ATD, S.A., Sant Marti de l'Erm, 10. 08970 Sant Joan Despi. Editado por E.C.B.

Records, Pasaje Garrofers, 4-6. Barcelona (Spain). Tel. 456 57 65—
Fax. 450 37 84. Contactos: Ecuador, 5936/921805—921728. España,
Movil: 908 786023. Movil: 908 533679. Tel. (93) 4070920. Portugal
352 9720384. Noruega 47 22606242. Dirección: España: Pasaje Lugo,
17 Enlo. 1º08032 Barcelona. Portugal: Urbanización Maos A Obra,
Hab. 47, 4435 Rio Tinto (Porto). EC-2030. Dep. Legal B. 46166/95.

Cocha Marka [José Julian Anrango, Germanico Anrango, Fernando Anrango,
José Cruz Perugachi, Alberto Jimbo, Rafael Arias]

1997 *Solo por ti.* Contactos: José Julian Anrango, Morales y Ricuarte 8-
05 Otavalo, Ecuador. Tel.: 02-921273. Gail Martin, 2368 Ridgecrest
Place, Ottawa, Ontario, Canada.

Cochasqui

n.d.a *Tawantinsuyo . . . Libertad: Music from the Andes. Musique Tra-
ditionelle des Andes.* Cochasqui Textiles y Music from the Andes.
Morales y Ricuarte 8-05, Otavalo—Ecuador. Telf.: 011-593-6 921-
273. c/o Pylaar and Luis Arias, 2610 Onix, Eugene, Oregon 97403.
Phone and Fax # (503) 344-0824 USA. Made in USA. [Bought in the
Otavalo market in 1996.]

n.d.b *Traditionelle des Andes.* Cochasqui Textiles y Music from the
Andes. Morales y Ricuarte 8-05, Otavalo—Ecuador. Telf.: 011-593-
6 921-273. c/o Pylaar and Luis Arias, 2610 Onix, Eugene, Oregon
97403. Phone and Fax: # (503) 344-0824. Made in USA. [Bought in
the Otavalo market in 1996.]

Ecuador Inkas [José Luis Pichamba, Alonso Pichamba, Humberto Pichamba,
Antonio Maldonado, William Albancando]

1990 *Traditionelle Musik aus de Anden, Original Version aus Bolivien ·
Peru · Ecuador.* Hamburg, Germany, is mentioned in the German-
language album notes. CD RP 12280. Produced by Segundo A. Amaguaña.

1993 [Segundo Amaguaña, musical director; and six unidentified Otava-
leños] *American Inkas, Traditionelle Musik aus den Anden.* Original Version aus Bolivien · Perú · Ecuador · Chile. Record Partner,
Hamburg, Deutschland. RP 1446. Contact: Ecuador Inkas, P.O. Box
13093, Los Angeles, CA 90013, c/o Segundo Farinango, (818) 242-
8210 Phone / (818) 249-8997 Fax.

Enrique Males

1994 *Ñaupamanta Cainamanta Cunancaman.* Autor de todas los temas:
Enrique Males; Ejecución de instrumentos: Enrique Males. Can-
ción #14 RUNA CAI—SE HOMBRE Música: Enrique Males, Letra:
A. Kowii. Producido por Industrias Famoso C. A. Quito, Ecuador.
C 060401636. Made in Canada.

Jailli [Sayri Cotacachi, David West, H. Gramal, S. Gramal Colaboradores:
Panco (Bajo), Igor (Bateria), Malik (Percusión), Mayu Quiñones, Cesar Cotacachi (rico trago), Segundo Caceres)]

1996 *Cuatro direcciones.* Tecnicos y Midi: Carles Santiesteban, Jordi
Busch. Producido por: J. L. Cotacachi, Incas Arte-sano, Boqueria, 21.
Tel/Fax 301/97-34-08002 Barcelona (España). E.C.B. Records, C.B.,

D.L. 8-44. 681-96. Made in E. U. [Note: this is the same album as Charijayac—Winiaypa—Dave West n.d.]

Jumandy [Ligia Becerra, Rocio López, Andrea Untuña, Yoly Flores, Mayrene Imbaquingo. Amigos Invitados: Cristian Erazo, Diego Bolaños, Rodolfo López, Javier Untuña, Diego López, Blanca Vega, Azucena Armas]

    1998 *Eclipse de amor.* Etudio de Grabación Imbaya. Mallku Producciones. Contactos: Mallku producciones, 593-6 922-619, e-mail: pegtio@uio.satnet.net. Peña Amauta, Tel.: 922-435, Cel. 09780347, Otavalo, Ecuador.

Kanatan Aski "Clean Land" [Marcos Arcentales, Quito Ecuador, Antonio Maldonado, Otavalo Ecuador, Luis Abanto, Cajamarca Peru, Amado Maigua, Otavalo Ecuador, Fernando Hinojosa, Otavalo Ecuador]

    1993 *Andean Colours.* X-IT Music Productions, Toronto, Canada. Produced and arranged by Kanatan Aski.

Kapary-Walka [Kapary: Nelson Tuntaquimba, Alfonso Tuntaquimba, William Albacando, Cesar Albancando, Pedro Daza. Walka: Marco Farinango, Alex Farinango, Carlos Heredia, Wilson Quinche]

    1992 *"Alpamanda": Traditional Music from the Andes, Ecuador • Perú • Bolivia.* Recorded and Mixed at Constain Studios, Bogotá, Colombia. CD manufactured by Record Partner, Hamburg, Deutschland. RP 12477. Contact: 119 Rue de Courcelles, 75017, Paris. Telefon: 1-40 54 87 50. Schrammsweg 27 B, 2000 Hamburg 20. Telefon: 040/480 22 13.

Karullacta [Amauta, Rupay, Rumi, Aspic, Sisa, Pakarina, Inti]

    1993 *Quinchuquimanda: Music of the Andes.* Disc Makers, Philadelphia, PA, USA. QMO2CD.

Karu Ñan Ecuador [Humberto Córdova]

    1997 *Causangapag: Music from the Andes.* Vol. 4. Contacto: Humberto Córdova. Fono: 06 922-869 Agato. Carretera San Pablo, Otavalo, Ecuador. 0K0S4<[325>]CDGRUPOKARUNA ADFL.

Kausay [Kausay: Rául Córdova, Rolando Córdova, Antonio Córdova, Jose M. Córdova. Collaborators: Alberto Segovia, Enrique Ascanta, Segundo Cañamar]

    1999 *Vuelve: Music from the Andes.* Contacts: Antonio Córdova, Kralenbeek 528, 1104 KH Amsterdam, Netherlands, Tel.: (020) 690-98-85. Luis Córdova, 38 Upper Road Plaiston, London E-13 ODH, England, Tel.: 0831435651. Enrique Ascanta, Ecuador, Tel.: 09475927. C7223.

Llaqtamasi [Manuel Ipeales, José Cacuango (Sara Urcu), Alberto Quilachamín (San Roque)]

    1994 *Llaqtamasi, Musik aus den Anden, Peru, Bolivien, Equador.* München, Deutschland. June.

Llaqtaymanta [Jaime Rodriguez, Marco Quenallata, Enrique de la Torre, José Castañeda, with Eduardo Mena, Joaquin Diaz, Rafael de la Torre, Augusto Agüero, Alberto de la Torre, Nilo B. Tito, Luis Otavalo]

    1992 *Llaqtaymanta, Traditionelle Musik der Inkas.* Vol. 2. Power Play, Hamburg, Germany. Qu 31894. Kontakt: Frankenstr. 51—5405 Ochtendung, Germany. Tel. 02625/5679.

Mashicuna

> 1996 *Music from the Andes: Ecuador • Peru • Bolivia.* © 1966 Mashicuna/Quichua Mashis. Contact: 10013 Holman Rd. NW, #101, Seattle, WA 98177.

Native's [Songs are credited to Causary Cotacachi, Humberto Cotacachi, Ernesto Cotacachi, Osvaldo Cotacachi]

> 1995 *Continuidad.* Colaboración: Denis "Kuki." Técnico de Sonido: Arnold Ivan. Gemecs. EI—196 CD. Depósito Legal B-41965-95. Contactos: c/o Boqueria, 21, 08002 Barcelona. Tel. y Fax: (93)301-97-34.

Ñanda Mañachi/Shikan [Integrantes: Alfonso Cachiguango—director, Dave West—Compositor—Arreglista, Enrique Condolo (Saraguro, Loja), Ernesto Tituaña, Efraín Enríquez (ex integrante de grupo Altiplano de Chile), Jaime Guerrero]

> 1998 *Ñanda Mañachi/Shikan Peguche.* Texto y Producción: Edwin Shuguli. Recorded at Walk on Waters Studios Hollywood, CA. Printed in the USA. Distribución: Saucisa. Av. Amazonas 1125 y Pinto. / Juan León Mera 639 y Veintimilla. Tel.: 543-487 Cel. 09-783-669. DDD SUACISA 01.

Ñuca Llacta

> 1996 *"Ñuca Llacta" Ecuador: Music from South America.* Vol. 5. Producer: E. R. Luna Y. Recorded at Utopia Studio. Engineered by Bendo Gergo, Szolosi Vígó János. [Locale probably Hungary.] Ñuca's production ÑLCD 002.

Ñucanchi Ñan [Miguel Cabascango T., Segundo Cabascango T., Alfonso Cabascango T., Jaime Vásquez C., Olger Vásquez C., Armando Pinsag C., José Ramírez C., Edison Moreto M., Yolanda Chicaiza, Segundo Amaguaña A.]

> n.d. [ca. 1984] *Ñucanchi Causay, Original-Version aus den Anden.* West Germany. RP 12 213.

> 1985 [Jaime Vásquez C., Olger Vásquez C., Miguel Cabascango T., Segundo Cabascango T., Alfonso Cabascango T., José Ramírez C., con la participación de Enrique Flores y Lola Flores] *Kangunapag. Original-Version from the Anden.* ODT, Berlin, Germany. CD 1985.

> n.d. [Integrantes: Miguel Cabascango, Segundo Cabascango, Alfonso Cabascango, Jaime Vásquez, Olguer Vásquez, Gustavo Vásquez, Armando Pinsag, Ernesto Cachimuel. Participación: Sarwed Pineda, Efrain Enriquez, Roberto Proaño, Vladimir González] *Fenomenal: Music from the Andes.* Ecuador: Contactos: Comunidad San Juan Alto, Tel.: 922 624, Otavalo—Imbabura. Italia: Dante Alighieri 47, 28041 Arona, Telf. 0322/249032 Italia—No. Made in USA. Nan 1014. [Bought in Otavalo in the summer of 1997.]

Otavalomanta

> n.d. [ca. 1993] *Vol. 3, Karu Ñan: Musik from the Andes.* Luis Burga: 3932 Sepulveda Blvd. #2, Culver City, CA 90230. (310) 204-1813. Irma Longworth: Public Relations Director. 421 Milton Drive, San Gabriel, CA. (818) 308-9657. Fax: (818) 485-3360. CDD-003.

> 1994 *Vol. 4, "Ñucallacta" aus Ecuador: Music from South America.* Kontaki: Alberto De La Torre, Liszt Ferenc u., 11. Bp., 1172 Hungria.

Ramiro Maigua: 3932 Sepulveda Blvd. #2, Culver City, CA 90230. (310) 204-1813. Irma Longworth: Public Relations Director. 421 Milton Dr., San Gabriel, CA. (818) 308-9657. Fax: (818) 485-3360. CDD-004.

1995 *Vol. 5, Cullqui Illac: Music from the Andes*. L.A. CA USA. Luis E. Burga, 3932 Sepulveda Blvd. #2, Culver City, CA 90230. (310) 204-1813. CDD-005.

Pachamama [Músicos Investigadores: José Quimbo (Taita Cultura), Antonio Lema (Arado), Carlos Perugachi (Papacho), Marcelo Lema. Músicos Arreglistas: José Quimbo (Taita Cultura), Antonio Lema (Arado), Alfonso Perugachi. Músicos Participantes: Ernesto Amaquaña, José Quimbo (Taita Cultura), Marco Lema, Rolando Lema, Antonio Moreta, Carlos Perugachi, Antonio Lema (Arado), Rafael Lema (Cumba), Marcelo Lema, Francisco Lema, Alfonso Perugachi, Alberto Perugachi. Cantantes: Enma Lema, Isabel Remachi, Martha Santacruz, Carlos Perugachi]

1997 *Antología de la música indígena: Anthology of Native Andean Music*. Centro Cultural "Peguche." Producción: Runa Mausay, José Quimbo Pichamba, Director General del Centro Cultural "Peguche." Grabación: Estudios Sonox, Quito 1988. Estudios Llaquilla, Ibarra 1997. Mezcla Digital: Estudios Llaquilla, Ibarra 1997. Disc Makers, Pennsauken, NJ, USA. Contactos: Centro Cultural "Peguche." Telefax: 593-6-922864. DIDX 051568.

Paul Simon

1986 *Graceland*. Produced by Paul Simon. Warner Brothers, New York.

Peguchemanta [CD made from master tape sold to Peguchemanta by Quichua Marka; musicians listed on CD cover are Amado Lema, César Lema, Mario Zambrano, Humberto Muenala, Humberto Zivinta, Alonso Fichamba, Armando Ipiales; actual musicians are members of Quichua Marka, aka Inca Marka: Hector Lema, Humberto Lema, Luis Cabascango, Humberto Quinatoa, Fabián Morales]

n.d. (before 1995) *Tushay Cumari, Music of the Andes*. Duplicase, Boskoop, Holland. DPCD 1276. Produced by Quichua Marka.

Pucará [Band members (1994): Victor Ushiña—director, Ernesto Males, Iván Tapia, Alonso Muenala, Jorge Egas, Gilberto Reyes. Special thanks to Mario Arroyo, Marcelo Enriques, Carlos Chavez, Jorge Muenala, Alfonso Cachiguango, and all the other musicians who have performed with Pucara over the past twenty years]

1993 *"Cainamanda Cunangaman": Music of the Andes*. Vol. 6. Contacts: 300 Ozier Dr., Batavia, IL 60510, USA 1 708 879 5932. Canada 1 416 269 1811. Machala 2284, Quito, Ecuador 538079. Sucre 744, Ibarra, Ecuador 06959685. Recorded 1993 in "Octavo Arte, Studio 2." Manufactured in Canada by Accudub, Inc.

Quichua Marka

n.d. (before 1995) *Tandanajushpa*. Duplicase, Boskoop, Holland. DPCD 1282.

Quichua Mashis [MUSICOS: Jaime Perugachi, Luis Gramal, Raul Lema, Joaquin Quinche, Ruben Terán]

1996 *Catishun: Music from the Andes*. World Rhythms Recording Studio.

Text L. Gramal/Quichua Mashis. Contact: 10013 Holman Rd. N.W., #101, Seattle, WA 98117. (206) 440-1316.

1997 [Musicians: Marcelino De la Torre, Alberto Visarrea, Luis Gramal, Enrique Jimbo, Alberto De la Torre, Segundo Lema] *El Caminante: Music from the Andes.* Recorded at WRPS, Redmond, WA. Mastering: Max Rossat Martin Audio, Seattle, WA. Made in Canada. Contact: Quichua Mashis at P.O. Box 77474, Seattle, WA 98177. Tel: (206) 440-1316.

Quichua Mashis/Pablo Cachiguango/Imbaya Kuna

n.d. *Imbaya Kuna: Music from the Andes.* Classic #2. Contact: Quichua Mashis, P.O. Box 77474, Seattle, WA 98177. [Bought in Otavalo in June 1998.]

Quillas [Integrantes: Ernesto Cordova (Potente), Fernando Conejo (Molleja), Alonso Fichamba (Luiqui), Segundo Muenala (Siqui), Luis H. Muenala (Huacaba), Rubén Terán (Rutino), Eduardo Cordova (Washington)]

1993 *Ecuador: Traditional Music from the Andes.* Colaboración: Segundo Condor, Estudio: Octavo Arte-Quito, Técnico: Silvio Moran. Producción: Quillas Marzo/93. Made in Belgium by I.S.P. Contacto: Pascale Engelen, Graaf Van Loonstraat 17 Bus 3, 3580 Beringen, Belgica. Tlf: 011/42/07/05. Rita Vandevenne, Keiveldstraat 10, 3583 Paal, Belgica. Tlf: 013/66. 83. 68.

n.d. [Ernesto "Senor Direc" Córdova, Eduardo "Potentico" Córdova, Richar "Cuerpo" Maldonado, Oscar "Metalico" Rojas, Róben "Rofos" Terán, Alonso "Luiqui" Pichamba. Artistas Invitados: Rolando "Warinson" Tolentino, Homberto "Lizandro" Morales, Eduardo "llu-llu-do 2" Megia, Jaime "Pillínae Perugachi, Homberto "Maldi" Gramal, Manuel Aleman, Jaime Morales] *Siempre.* Grabado en G.C.T. Producciones, Atuntaqui, Ecuador. Mastered by Mx Rose at Martin Audio Duplication, Seattle, Washington. Contact in USA: PO Box 77474, Seattle, WA 98133. Website: www.incasite.com. Contact in Ecuador: 593/6-921-604. [Bought in the Otavalo market in January 1999. An inside photo is dated 1998.]

1999 *The Best of the Quillas: Inca Kichua Sound.* Kichua Vision (212) 289-5531 NY, USA. Traditional Kichua Crafts (718) 617-1843. Producción Ramiro Muenala V. Contactos: Hostería Peguche Tío. Telefax: 593/6-922619. e-mail: pegtio@uio.uio.satnet.net.

Richard & Louis [Integrantes: "Charijayac": Sayri Cotacachi, Quipus Cotacachi, Louis Cotacachi, Richard Cotacachi, Mayu Quiñones, Chasqui Tituaña, Raymi Tituaña, Yuyay Tituaña, Rupay Cachiguango]

1996 *"Charijayac": New Generation—Inka Quechua.* Music Richard's Company Records. Recording Studio: E.C.B. Records—Barcelona. Album mixed by: Richard S. Cotacachi C. Composed and Conducted by: Sayri R. Cotacachi C. Performed by: Tim Wright, Richard S. Cotacachi. Collaboration: Dorothy Kassel & Bill Garret, Mickey, Juan Stephen Gutierrez, Segundo Cotacachi Teran. Contact: Richard Cotacachi or Richard Arreozola, 430 W. Jefferson, Dallas, TX 75208. Phone: (214) 943-4780, Fax (214) 943-4780. Cellular Phone (210) 219-2701.

Runakuna

1991 *Music from the Andes, Ecuador.* The Basement Tapes, Amsterdam, Holland. BTS 79.

n.d. [Germán Sinchico A., José Manuel Anrango A., Ivan Maigua, Jorge Castañeda C., José Raul Bautizta] *Runakuna Ecuador, Traditional Music from Latin America.* The Basement Tapes, Amsterdam, Holland. BTS 200. [Bought in Otavalo in 1994.]

1994 [Germán Sinchico A., José Jimbo M., Rafael Jimbo M., Enrique Jimbo M., Alberto Mendoza P.] *Sumaj Punlla, Music from Ecuador, Peru & Bolivia.* Vol. 4. The Basement Tapes, Amsterdam, Holland. BTS 639. Produced by Germán Sinchico Arias. Contact: RUNAKUNA 020-6336165.

1996 [Germán Sinchico, Oswaldo Sinchico, Humberto Sinchico, Alfonso Sinchico, Ernesto Sinchico] *Shamuni: Native Music from the Andes.* Produced by Germán Sinchico Arias. Contact: Humberto Sinchico, "Runakuna," 84-88 Homelawn Street, Jamaica, NY 11432. (718) 523-5204. Disc Makers, Pennsauken, NJ, USA. BTS340CD.

Runallacta

1994 *Lo mejor de Runallacta Otavalomanta: Music of the Andes—Ecuador, Bolivia, Peru.* Made in Canada by Canatron Corporation.

1998 [Enrique Flores, Alberto Visarrea, Héctor Flores, Enrique Jimbo. Con la participacíon de Marco Aldana, Fabian Cabascango, Eddy Fuentes & César Fuentes] *Sumakta Churay: Traditional Music of the Andes Vol. 6.* Grabacíon realizada entre Marzo y Abril de 1998. C.V. Records, Quito-Ecuador. Manufacturado e impreso por Disc Makers, Pennsauken, NJ, USA. Contactos: Peña Amauta, Enrique Flores, Morales 5-11 Tel.: 011-593-6-922-435, Cel: 011-593-9-780-347, Otavalo, Ecuador. Hostería Peguche Tío, Panamericana norte KM. 2, Otavalo, Ecuador. Tel.: 593-6-922619. E-mail: pegtio@UIO. Telconet.net. Sumakta, Enrique Flores, Cesar Fuentes, 7590 Slate Hill Court, Worthington, OH 43085, (614) 858-5818. DDIX 062223.

R.Y.CH. [Rymi Tituaña, Yuyay Tituaña, Chasqui Tituaña]

1996 *Runa Song.* c. R. Y. CH. Grabado en Ecuador: Studio: Arbol Records. Masterizado en Italy e USA. Contactos: Luis Tituaña, Corso Piomonte # 28, 12037 Saluzzo (CN), Tel. Celular: 0368-619367, Italy—E.U. Chasqui Tituaña, Calle Bolivar # 13-03, Fax. 06-920410, Otavalo, Ecuador, SUD AM. RS400, Made in USA.

Sisai [Byron Vaca, Jose Muenala, Milton Perugachi, Patricio Perugachi]

1995 *Music of the Andes.* Recorded and Mixed at Island Recorders, Chicago, Illinois. To contact SISAI please write to: Suzanne Reed, 1725 Forest, Wilmette, IL 60091.

Sisa Pacari [Alonso Farinango, director; Fausto Jimbo, coordinator; Jacinto Anguaya, Rodrigo Anrango, Oswaldo Farinango, Domingo Maldonado, Alberto Mendoza, Jorge Perugachi, Susana Farinango]

1994 *Sisa Pacari, Traditional Music from the Andes.* Canatron, Canada. C940508. Contacts: 306 Beechgrove Ave., Ottawa, Ontario, Canada K1Z 6R3, Tel.: 613/729-5337. Fax: 613/729-4765. Philip Schubert,

613/592-4190 or, Tel.: 819/997-0841, Fax: 819/953-4676. Calle Sucre #5-16, Barrio La Joya, Tel: (5936) 921844, Otavalo, Ecuador.

Taki Sumaj [Pedro F. Daza/Pactara, Carlos E. Heredia/Charli, Javier Maigua/Casco]

1994 *Taki Sumaj: The Music of the Andes, Ecuador • Peru • Bolivia • Colombia.* Recorded and mixed at Constain Studios, Bogotá, Colombia. CD manufactured by Custom Cassette, Minneapolis, Minnesota, USA. TS1994-1. Produced by Pedro F. Daza. Contacto: Pedro Daza o Maria Digitano at (612) 823-1749 o (612) 537-1888 in Minneapolis, Minnesota, USA.

Trencito de los Andes [Felice M. Clemente, Raffaele M. Clemente, Claude Ferrier, Paola Frondini, Laura Grasso. Italian guest participants: Massimo Pirone, Francesco Clemente. Otavalo and Salasaca guest participants: Juanita Reascos, Hector Maigua, Marina Maigua, Elvia Cajas, Enrique "Tio" Maigua, Osvaldo Morales, Luis Quinche, José Farinango, Remigio Reascos, Luis Alfonso "Molde" Terán, Segundo "Casero" Cáceres, Jaime Amaguaña, Rafael Masaquiza]

1992–1993a *Zig Zag, Parte Primera.* "Digital Inca's Studio," Roma, Italia. 136 C. D. Produced by Luis "Sayri" Cotacachi and Umberto "Canguro" Burga. Incas Artesanía, c/. Boquería 21—TL—Fax: 301 97 34. Bxda. de la Librería, 9—TL—Fax: 268 34 73, 08002 Barcelona—España.

1992–1993b [Felice M. Clemente, Raffaele M. Clemente, Claude Ferrier, Paola Frondini, Laura Grasso. Felice M. Clemente, Raffaele M. Clemente, Claude Ferrier, Paola Frondini, Laura Grasso. Part Two: Italian guest participants: Claudio Montuori, Mauro Argiolas, Michele Macarovich, Massimo Pirone, Beatrice Clemente. Otavalo participants: Segundo "Casero" Cáceres, Rosa Elena Maldonado Amaguaña, Jaime Amaguaña, "Chasco" and Luis "Sayri" Cotacachi] *Zig Zag, Segunda Parte.* "Digital Inca's Studio," Roma, Italia. 137 C. D. Produced by Luis "Sayri" Cotacachi and Umberto "Canguro" Burga. [Same contact as above.]

Tucuy Yahuar [Integrantes: Luis Muenala, Marcelo Simbaña, Walter Villa, Mauricio Vinueza]

1995 *(Vol. II) "Katishun."* Gemecs. E. I. 161 CD. Depósito Legal B—15184 —95. Fabricado en España por Techno CD. Participación Especial: Alberto Cabascango: Instrumentos de Viento; Fausto Cahuasqui: Mandolina; Manu Jopeca: Teclados.

Wayanay

1993 *The Magic Music of the Andes.* Tee Pee Encounters Catacoma. AVL93049. Made in USA. Produced by Wayanay. Contact: 1331 Franklin, #F, Denver, CO. 80218. [Sold by Ecuadorian-Peruvian group "Alma Andina" during performance in White Plaza, Stanford, June 9, 1995.]

Winiaypa [Musicians: Segundo Gramal, Richard Maldonado, Eduardo Prado, Ernesto Altamirano, Jaime Perugachi. Guest artists: Orquesta Sabor a Mango, Cecil Vidal]

n.d.   *Quichua Mashis.* Contact: 10013 Holman Rd. N. W, #101, Seattle,
   WA 98177. (206) 440-1316. [Bought in Otavalo in July 1996.]
Winiaypa [Músicos: Humberto Gramal, Segundo Gramal, Dave West, Carlos
Carpio, "Dimitri"]
   n.d.   *Gotitas de amor.* Estudio: Ref Recording Deurne. © Incas Trading
   Co. Made in Canada. MAG-WIN-4.
Yahuar Wauky [Manuel Cachimuel, founder/coordinator; Luis R. Cachi-
muel, musical director/composer; Alberto Cachimuel, José M. Cachimuel,
Carlos Cachimuel, Pedro Vasquéz. Special guest: Chris Caouette, keyboards.
Dance members: Ana Lucia, Rosa Elena (Kayita), Rumiñahui, Curi Inti, Anti
Amaru, Tupac Amaru, Sumac Raymi Cachimuel]
   1993   *Yarina 500 Years: Traditional Music of the Andes, Vol. 3.* Recorded
      1993 at Sound Station Studio, Union, CT. Contact: Luis R. Cachi-
      muel, Yarina, 16 Gorman Str., Somerville, MA 02144 USA, (617) 776-
      0946.
Yawar Inca
   1992   *Sturm in den Anden, Vol. VI.* Khantaro Music Studios, Lima, Peru,
      and Living Music Studio, Hamburg, Germany. Produced by Condor
      for Amaru Records. Inka 11. Contact: Dario Argumendo, Türkenstr.
      33, 8000 München, Germany. Tel. (089) 2-80-99-17.
Yuyari [Francisco Tixicuro, José M. Conejo, Luis E. Cáceres, Alejandro
Cáceres, Pedro J. Cáceres, Bolívar Cáceres, Jaime Tixicuro]
   1995   *"Volveré."* Fabricado en España por MPO Ibérica. E.I. 181 CD. Depó-
      sito Legal B—29087/95. Colaboración: Luis Cabascango, Segundo
      Cáceres. Contactos: Francia, Tel.: 45-40-44-00. España, Tel.: (971)
      26-04-88, (971) 49-03-81.

Films

Dances with Wolves
   1990   35 mm, 180 min. Kevin Costner, director. United States: Guild/Tig
      Productions.
If Only I Were an Indian
   1995   16 mm, 80 min. John Paskievich, director. Canada: Zemma Pic-
      tures/National Film Board of Canada.
Young Guns II
   1990   35 mm, 103 min. Geoff Murphy, director. United States: Fox/
      Morgan Creek.

Index